The March of Empire

Frontier Defense in the Southwest
1848-1860

by

Averam B. Bender
*Professor of History, Harris
Teachers College, St. Louis*

GREENWOOD PRESS, PUBLISHERS
NEW YORK

To
RALPH P. BIEBER

Preface

Between 1845 and 1848 the United States came into possession of a princely domain. During that short period of time it acquired Texas, the Oregon country, and the Mexican Cession—more than a million square miles of territory—and thereby virtually established its present western and southern boundaries. Then came the discovery of gold in California and the mighty emigrant waves to the El Dorado. The problem of frontier defense, ever present from the beginning of the nation's history, was truly formidable now. The frontier was much longer and more remote, and the pioneers, though more numerous, were often dangerously scattered. The Indian was too close to the white man. The national government had acquired an added responsibility—defense of the new frontier.

The period 1848-60 witnessed the evolution of the trans-Mississippi policy of defense. United States armies and engineers, supplementing the activities of the unofficial explorers, traders and trappers, blazed the trail for the march of empire. By gradually pacifying the wild tribes, establishing chains of military posts, building roads, and surveying western streams, the federal government paved the way for greater peace and safety, trade and settlement. Moreover, the frontier army created an era full of color and romance which left a deep impression on our literature, our drama, and our arts. Some of our most distinguished military leaders of the Civil War—McClellan, Sherman, Grant, and Lee—served their apprenticeship on the western frontier. It is the purpose of this study to examine important phases of frontier defense in our Far Southwest—Texas, the Territories of New Mexico and Utah, and California—in the twelve years preceding the Civil War. Neighboring areas, such as present-day Kansas, Colorado, and Oklahoma, necessarily formed an integral part of the Southwest of the period.

This study has been made possible through the advice, aid, and encouragement of many persons and institutions. The officials in charge of the formerly scattered archives of the War Department and Department of the Interior in Washington were courteous and obliging. Staff members of the Library of Congress, as well as Drs. P. M. Hamer and Elizabeth B. Drewry, and Miss Elizabeth Bethel of the National Archives, were especially helpful. The librarians and assistants of the University of Texas, the Texas State Library, the New Mexico Historical Society, as well as those of the California State, the Bancroft, and Huntington libraries, rendered valuable assistance. Thanks are also due to the staffs of the St. Louis Public Library, the St. Louis Mercantile Library, the Missouri Historical Society, and the Washington University Library. The writer is grateful to the *New Mexico Historical Review* and the *Pacific Historical Review* for permission to reprint his articles in those magazines, "Military Posts in the Southwest, 1848-1860" (April, 1941) and "The Soldier in the Far West, 1848-1860" (June, 1939), as chapters III and VII of this volume.

The author is particularly indebted to Professor Ralph P. Bieber, Chairman of the Department of History at Washington University, whose scholarly criticism and kindly interest have been most helpful in the preparation of this entire work. Gratitude is due Mrs. Ida Parker Bieber, who has carefully examined the manuscript and made valuable suggestions. Dr. Kate L. Gregg, formerly of Lindenwood College, has been very helpful in the final revision of this study. The author is also indebted to Professor George L. Anderson, Chairman of the Department of History at the University of Kansas, for his critical reading and constructive criticism of the manuscript. For constant encouragement and valuable assistance in preparing the manuscript for publication, the author is grateful to his wife, Fannie L. Bender.

A. B. BENDER

HARRIS TEACHERS COLLEGE

ST. LOUIS, MISSOURI

Contents

		PAGE
PREFACE		vii

CHAPTER

I.	The Land and the People	3
II.	Evolution of a Defense Policy	17
III.	Fortifying the New Frontier	32
IV.	Opening New Trails to the Far West	51
V.	Western River Surveys	73
VI.	Explorations for Defense	88
VII.	Life of the Soldier on the Frontier	108
VIII.	Texas Indians Hurl a Challenge	130
IX.	New Mexico Tribesmen Go on the Warpath	149
X.	Friction with the Mormons and Indians in the Great Basin	171
XI.	California Indian Wars	191
XII.	The Texas Reservation Experiment	206
XIII.	California Indian Reservations	218
XIV.	On the Eve of the Civil War	229

REFERENCES	237
ABBREVIATIONS	237
PRINCIPAL MILITARY POSTS IN THE SOUTHWEST, 1848-1860	285
BIBLIOGRAPHY	286
INDEX	303

Illustrations

FACING
PAGE

Map: Military Posts and Some Principal Trails 3

Cavalry and Dragoons, 1855-58 86

The "Explorer" 87

Don Fernando de Taos, 1853 87

Engineer, Footrifles, Dragoon, Light Artillery,
    Infantry, 1851-54 102

Fort Yuma, California 103

The Presidio of San Francisco 103

The
March of
Empire

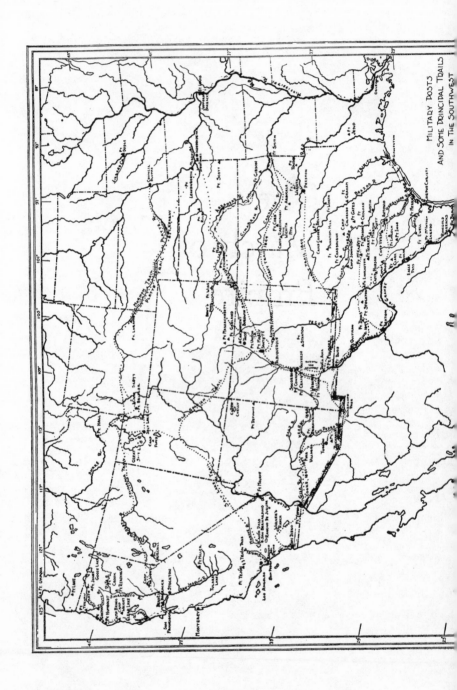

MILITARY POSTS
AND SOME PRINCIPAL TRAILS
IN THE SOUTHWEST

CHAPTER I

The Land and the People

WHEN the Mexican War ended and the United States extended its southwestern frontier to the Pacific Ocean, many persons—statesmen and army officers, as well as ordinary citizens—criticized the government for annexing barren and unproductive lands. Senator Roger S. Baldwin of Connecticut, in a speech before the Senate on March 15, 1848, vigorously opposed the annexation of New Mexico and California because the new lands were of "comparatively little value." New Mexico he described as "a country fit only for the residence of a Mexican and Indian population," while California, with the exception of San Francisco Bay and Sacramento Valley, he deemed worthless. Its interior he considered no better than a desert. Baldwin prophesied that the federal government would not realize $50,000 in fifty years from the sale of land in the Mexican Cession.[1]

Senator Baldwin was unduly pessimistic. In the mid-nineteenth century the entire Southwest certainly did not fit the description which he gave. Texas, for example, in spite of its mountains, cañons, and desert plains, was unusually rich in agricultural resources. Along the gulf coast and inland to a line drawn from Nachitoches to Eagle Pass on the Rio Grande was a vast area of nearly 90,000 square miles, primarily adapted to sugar growing. Merging with the sugar country and extending northward for about a hundred miles lay the famous "Black Waxy," a vast treeless plain of fine farm land, especially suitable for cotton culture. Still farther to the north, in the high tablelands, stretched wheat and grazing lands, which comprised almost one-half of the total area of Texas. Throughout the state an abundance of corn could be produced, as well as many varieties of fruit. Tobacco could be grown in many sections, and stock raising was an exceedingly

profitable business.[2] East Texas possessed immense forests of pine
and other valuable timber.[3] All these productive regions, with their
diversified geographic features, varied and healthful climate,[4]
attracted emigrants from the older states as well as from abroad.
In 1855, for example, some 100,000 pioneers established homes in
the wheat country along the upper Brazos, Trinity, and Colorado
rivers.[5]

But the western and northernmost portions of the state caused
the government grave concern. A large section of country south
of the Red River, with its many ravines and eroded lands, was so
wild and desolate in appearance as to offer but slight inducement
to settlers. But this rough and broken country made an admirable
rendezvous for hostile Indians. Here they planned their depredations, and here they took refuge when their marauding expeditions were completed.[6] Portions of the Rio Grande Valley, the
Llano Estacado or staked plains, and the Panhandle, one contemporary described as a "dreary and desolate region where nothing
lived but Indians, snakes, and other venomous reptiles."[7] A traveler
in 1860 found south and west Texas a land of "exquisite pests of
fleas, . . . snakes, centipedes, and tarantulas."[8]

To counteract the wild tales about the dangers in west Texas
and to attract emigrants, contemporary newspapers painted rosy
pictures of that area: the San Antonio *Western Texan* flatly denied
that west Texas was a dry, sterile country;[9] the Corpus Christi
Nueces Valley felt confident that the "fertile soil, perennial pro-
ductions, and unsurpassed climate of the Rio Grande Valley . . .
would constitute a home and a happy one for a million freemen."[10]
"It is a fact," asserted an enthusiastic Texas correspondent, "on
this western border of the 'Lone Star' State, we have the brightest
waters, the broadest ranges, the tallest grass, the fattest cattle, the
fastest men, the prettiest women to be found within the realm of
'Uncle Sam.' "[11] Not unlike some patriotic, native sons of today,
the Houston *Democratic Telegraph and Texas Register* clinched
the argument by declaring: "We [the Texans] are indeed a won-
derful people."[12]

Other contemporaries pictured Texas as a veritable sportsman's paradise. In the southwest roamed vast herds of wild horses and cattle; the streams teemed with fish.[13] The strongest appeal to settlers, perhaps, was made by the Washington *Texas Ranger,* which stated: "She [Texas] has no paupers. . . . The fertility of the soil is such that even the sluggish and indolent are kept from want."[14]

Such favorable advertising could not fail to attract settlers. The steady advance of the frontier during the fifties averaged about ten miles a year, but the settlements remained scattered, and exposed. In west Texas, subject to depredations of Comanches and Kiowas, the federal government had to evolve a program of defense.[15]

A similar problem confronted the government in New Mexico. That vast, unexplored territory attracted but few emigrants, and these, because of the geography of the region, the location of its natural resources, and the presence of hostile Indians, concentrated in a few areas.

New Mexico contains extensive and arid plains, lofty mountains, sandy deserts, and occasional fertile valleys.[16] West of the Rio Grande and for nearly 500 miles beyond the Sierra Madre lies the mesa country. Here a succession of mesas, or tablelands, rise abruptly above great tracts of barren country. Covered with rich grass in the rainy season, the mesas contained some of the finest grazing lands in the world.[17] With the rapid settlement of California, a brisk trade in sheep sprang up with that new El Dorado. Large flocks driven across the desert from New Mexico commanded high prices in the San Francisco market. Besides, eastern manufacturers bought New Mexican wool, their purchases amounting to nearly one-half million pounds in 1859 alone.[18]

The fertile areas, of course, were in the principal river valleys. The San Pedro and the Sonoita valleys possessed fine agricultural lands. The valley of the Rio Grande produced rich fields of grain and famous fruits and wines. The fertile lands along the Gila and the Colorado were suitable for the production of tobacco, cereals,

fruits, and many varieties of vegetables. The Colorado bottom was
especially adapted for the cultivation of rice, sugar, and cotton.[19]

Rich and diversified mineral deposits, whose whereabouts had
been known for centuries, were scattered widely over the territory. With the exception of mercury, practically every important
mineral was represented. In 1855 at least a hundred silver mines
were said to be located within sight of Las Cruces. Veins of gold
and silver were also reported near Santa Fe and Taos. Virgin copper was found along the sources of the Mimbres, gold on all the
tributaries of the Gila, and coal in the Raton Mountains. Inexhaustible quantities of building material were scattered in many
places. Only lack of capital and fear of the wild tribes postponed
development of the mineral resources.[20]

New Mexico's climate was no mean asset. At the opening of
the Mexican War the territory had already become famous as a
health resort. Several years later a correspondent of the Austin
Texas Sentinel, writing from Las Cruces, appraised it thus: "The
climate of the southern portion of New Mexico is unsurpassed in
beauty and salubrity. The sky is seldom clouded; our mountains
are gilded by eternal sunshine. There are no diseases peculiar to
the climate."[21]

Despite New Mexico's agricultural, grazing, and mineral pos-
sibilities and its healthful climate, a considerable portion of the
territory was, in the mid-nineteenth century, practically a *terra
incognita,* "a thousand miles from nowhere." With the exception
of hunters, traders, and trappers, and some scholars who had
delved into the Spanish records, very few people in the United
States knew the real character of the country. The impression prevailed that the land was a hopeless and inaccessible desert, entirely worthless, and utterly incapable of sustaining civilized beings.[22]

A small, scattered, and extremely backward people occupied
this comparatively unknown region. The United States census of
1850 reported a total population of some 61,000, exclusive of Indians, distributed among seven counties.[23] In the late fifties more

than 60 per cent of the inhabitants lived in towns along the Rio Grande and in the neighboring ranches; the Americans were concentrated mostly in the center of the territory, in and near the Santa Cruz Valley, and at the gold mines on the lower Gila.[24] The standard of living, especially among the Mexican populace, was woefully low; and law, order, and morals sat very lightly on the conscience of the inhabitants. Gambling, drunkenness, and vice prevailed everywhere. W. W. H. Davis, Judge and Secretary of the territory, found vice more prevalent among the New Mexicans than among any other civilized people. Prostitution was common, beggars were numerous, and belief in witchcraft and sorcery was widespread. But with all their shortcomings, the New Mexicans were a devoutly religious and affectionate people, suave in manners; an air of refinement and courtesy pervaded all classes.[25]

Utah, too, was a vast and varied land. Emigrants from the "old country" characterized the territory as a "mean land," hard, dry, and suitable only for steady, sober, and hard-working Mormons. According to one contemporary, scarcely one-fiftieth part of the land was fit for cultivation. Except where alkali abounded, the earth was generally fertile, and industrious Mormons under shrewd and able leaders converted what appeared to be a desert country into a "land of smiling valleys." They cultivated grain in the valleys of the Jordan, the Provo, the Weber, and the Ogden.[26]

On the mountains were forests of timber. In the valleys and foothills were rich pasture lands for sheep and cattle. Quantities of game browsed in the meadows, swarmed the lakes and streams. Gold, silver, coal, and iron awaited the miner. An abundant supply of water and water-power awaited the home-seeker.[27]

To Spanish adventurers and missionaries, as well as to American traders and trappers, California was a land of extreme contrasts. Prior to the American occupation, adventurous Jedediah Smith, James Pattie, and Ewing Young could not but marvel at California's strange and magnificent scenic wonders.[28] Walter Murray, a volunteer of a New York regiment landing in Califor-

nia in the spring of 1847, gave vent to his feelings thus: "Our
country is green but it can not surpass this. Our skies are serene
and beautiful, but what can compare with California skies and
California atmosphere? We have gardens, it is true . . . but in the
beauty and variety of its wild flowers, what country can compare
with California? It is dry and arid enough in its long lapse of
summer time, but what country can outnumber its myriad out-
gushing fountains in spring?"[29]

Keen observers, such as Baron Alexander von Humboldt and
Richard H. Dana, Jr., noted that the varied climate and rich soil
made California one of the best-adapted countries in the world
for the production of grains, fruits, and vegetables. But up to the
time of the American conquest comparatively little agriculture
was carried on, except at the missions; and as late as 1860, of the
forty million acres of tillable land, only one-fortieth was being
cultivated.[30] California's other valuable natural resources—the
great subterranean reservoirs of petroleum, the large areas of magnificent timber, and the vast quantities of gold, silver, and other
minerals awaited the coming of the Americans.[31]

Despite its many advantages, California, prior to the American
conquest, had attracted a population of only 5,000.[32] By the close
of the Mexican War, however, the number of whites had increased
to about 20,000, most of whom lived in small towns and villages.
San Diego, the largest settlement, could boast of some 1,300 inhabitants, while Monterey had 1,000, and Yerba Buena (San
Francisco) and Santa Barbara 800 each; the rest of the white inhabitants were scattered among the various missions, ranchos, and
presidios.[33] The gold discovery, of course, caused a sudden spurt
in the growth of the population; by 1850 the number had increased
to more than 92,000, and ten years later to almost 380,000.[34] With
the rapid influx, a new type soon dominated the scene. A young,
healthy, vigorous, intelligent, and enterprising lot, interspersed
with a few outcasts, scoundrels, and fugitives from justice, sup-
planted the kindly, hospitable, but indolent and thriftless Californians.[35]

In control of the Far Southwest during the period under discussion was a large array of native tribes, differing in numbers, strength, and hostility to the white man. In Texas were two types of red men, the semicivilized and the wild. The former, comprising three important groups, the Southern Wichitas, the Creeks, and the Algonquins—had settled down and cultivated the soil.[36] In general, these natives, who lived in villages along the rivers in the eastern half of the state, proved industrious, reliable, friendly, and comparatively peaceful; they gave the state and federal government but little concern.[37]

The wild tribes, on the other hand, having no fixed habitation, depending on the chase for their food supply, and frequently engaging in plundering expeditions against whites as well as other Indians, roamed freely in the western part of the state. In this group the Northern Wichitas, Comanches, Kiowas, and Apaches played a leading role. The Northern Wichitas, occupying the country primarily north of the Red River, made frequent excursions into Texas and became a scourge of the northern part of the state. Captain (later Brigadier General) Randolph B. Marcy, who saw service on the frontier for nearly half a century and knew Indians, declared that the Wichitas had given more trouble to the people of the northern border than any other tribe. They had no regard for truth; they would steal and rob consistently; fear alone kept their vicious practices in check.[38]

The Comanches, a Shoshonean tribe of nomad buffalo hunters, forced southward by Sioux and other tribes from their original homes in Wyoming, had entered Texas in the eighteenth century. During the summer months Comanche warriors roamed as far north as the waters of the upper Arkansas, but in winter the war parties moved southward and westward across the Rio Grande and invaded the northern provinces of Mexico. A fine-looking people and superb horsemen, the Comanches had an unsavory reputation. Wild Cat, a crafty Seminole Chieftain, called them treacherous and "double-tongued"; Kennedy referred to them as a nation of robbers. Being almost constantly on the move and hence seen in so many places, they gained the reputation of being a numerous people. Of all the Texas tribes, they constituted the largest band.[39] In 1849, Major Robert S. Neighbors, special agent for the Texas Indians, estimated their number at 20,000, of whom 4,000 were warriors.[40] Their constant depredations kept west Texas sparsely settled until after the Civil War.[41]

Kiowa warriors—perhaps the most predatory and bloodthirsty of all prairie tribes—frequently joined with the Comanches in raiding frontier settlements. Resembling their northern kinsmen in the love of war and thirst for plunder, their forays took them across the present states of Colorado, New Mexico, Oklahoma, and Texas.[42] Though few in number they proved, when combined with the Comanches, a veritable terror on the Texas-Mexican border.[43]

In southern and western Texas, in the mountainous regions between the Pecos and the Rio Grande, roamed the dreaded Apaches, "the Ishmael of the Plains." Like the Comanches, this tribe lived chiefly by depredation and looked upon cultivators of the soil with contempt. The man who had not stolen a horse or scalped an enemy was not worthy of association with these lords of the woods and forests. Only theft and prowess in battle were honorable.[44] In the late eighteen-forties the Texas Apaches numbered only 3,500 people, or about 700 warriors,[45] but their reputation for bloodthirstiness kept the frontier settlers in constant dread. Military men referred to them as "the greatest fighting men who ever lived of any race in any period of history." Their remarkable strength, endurance, and stamina, together with their duplicity, diplomacy, and knowledge of woodcraft, made control over them by white men extremely difficult.[46]

At the close of the Mexican War the wild Indians of Texas far outnumbered the peaceful tribes. Out of a total native population of nearly 30,000, the agricultural tribes numbered only about 4,000. Determined to remain masters of the Far Southwest, the wild Indians prepared to resist the ever-increasing tide of migration; the inevitable clash was on.[47]

The Indians in the Territory of New Mexico presented a problem no less serious. Various tribes, representing different stages of civilization—agricultural, semi-agricultural, and wild, nomadic tribes—held possession of the country. In the first group were the Pueblos, the Zuñis, and Moquis. One group of Pueblo Indians occupied about a dozen scattered villages along the Rio Grande. The Zuñis had their home between the Rio Grande and the present state of Arizona; the Moquis lived in permanent homes north of the San Francisco Mountains and along the Little and Great Colorado rivers. Life among the Pueblo villagers was somewhat communal. Each village was a distinct community, having a *gubernador,* or chief, and a council; each village tried its own criminals; each community owned the land and, like the eighteenth century French villagers in the Missouri country, the natives worked together. The governor would go out on the housetop, as his predecessors had done for a thousand years, and the criers would call out: "Now is the time to water the fields!" or "Now is the time to bring in wood!" And the work was done together. Numbering between 7,000 and 10,000 souls, these peaceful, intelligent people led a quiet, industrious life, cultivating the soil. Many had rich flocks and herds; they had no paupers.[48] Against Indians such as these the government never had to provide any frontier defense. In fact, the Pueblo tribes had need of government protection, for not infrequently the Navahos and Apaches, as well as white emigrants, swooped down upon their villages to steal stock and grain.[49]

Along the Gila and Colorado rivers lived other kindred bands —the Papagos, Pimas, Maricopas, Yumas, and Mohaves—whose mode of life and attitude toward the white man usually resembled the Pueblos'. The Navahos in the north also belonged to the semi-agricultural tribes. The Papagos, who lived in villages in the southwestern part of the present state of Arizona, had been among the first Indians of the Southwest to come under the influence of the Spanish missionaries. For several centuries they had cultivated the lowlands by a system of irrigation; some possessed large herds of horses, sheep, and cattle; others were expert in the manufacture of pottery and willow ware. Peaceable and friendly, these natives in the past had assisted the Spaniards, Mexicans, and Americans in warding off attacks of the Apaches.[50] North of the Papagos, occupying eight or nine villages along the Gila River, lived the Pimas, an industrious, cheerful, and innocent people. Judge Benjamin Hayes, who made an overland journey from Socorro to Warner's Ranch in 1849-50, found these natives "a pleasant, social, lively people ... very polite ... the children fat as pigs." Like their neighbors to the south, the Pimas cultivated the soil and wove excellent blankets and baskets. The Maricopas, less honest and less amiable, occupied several villages along the banks of the Gila and the Colorado. These Gila tribes, estimated at between five and ten thousand, proved a boon to white men, for not only did they serve as a defense barrier for the Mexicans against the wild tribes north of the Gila, but they also assisted thousands of emigrants on their way to the California gold fields.[51]

The Yumas, described by a contemporary as a "sprightly, sociable, but excitable people," lived in villages along both sides of the lower Colorado. Unlike their peaceful neighbors, this tribe had a reputation for treachery and thievery. The Mohaves, who claimed undisputed sway east of the Colorado River, between Needles and the Black Cañon, proved more hostile and treacherous than the Yumas.[52] Occupying some 15,000 square miles of territory, in the northwestern part of the present state of New Mexico, lived the Navahos, the most populous of all New Mexican Indians. A virile race, industrious, intelligent, independent in spirit, and warlike, they caused more trouble and expense both to the government and people than any other tribe in the territory.[53]

The Utes (Utahs) and Apaches comprised the principal nomadic tribes in the territory. Proud and fearless, Ute warriors roamed over a large section of country. Some wandered over the central and western parts of present Colorado and eastern Utah, including portions of the Great Salt Lake and Utah valleys; others entered northern New Mexico and occupied much of the drainage area of the San Juan River country. They proved an elusive foe. During the summer months it was impossible to wage war against them, since they found a safe retreat in their mountain fastnesses. Only during the winter season, when driven into the plains by the snows, could they be readily overtaken.[54]

Numerous bands of New Mexican Apaches[55] occupied the *Apacheria,* an extensive region reaching from the Rio Grande to the Great Colorado and from the San Francisco Mountains to the heart of Mexican Chihuahua. Here these "Bedouins of the American desert" lived principally by the chase and plunder. They made depredations upon stock, robbed ranches, killed rancheros, and harassed emigrant parties. Of all the Southwest Indians they were the most powerful tribe in New Mexico Territory, and the terror of the Mexican border.[56]

The wild bands of New Mexico, like those in Texas, far outnumbered the peaceable tribes. Out of an Indian population estimated at between 40,000 and 58,000, only about 7,000 were friendly. The others, the semi-agricultural and wild tribes, occupied or roamed over 80 per cent of the territory.[57] This large and hostile Indian population in a wild, desert, mountainous country—ideal terrain for Indian attacks against scattered, heterogeneous, and sometimes lawless white inhabitants—complicated the problem of frontier defense.

In comparison with the Texas and New Mexico tribes, the natives in the Utah country, numbering some 18,000, gave the government and the white man little or no trouble.[58] The principal divisions of Shoshones (or Snakes), Bannocks, and Utes, separated into more than a hundred small, independent bands, ranged over a vast territory. The eastern Snakes, who traversed the country from South Pass to Bear and Wind River, and their western kinsmen, who made their homes on Camas Prairie, in the Goose Creek Mountains, and along the Humboldt, were reputed a warlike but honest and sober people, decidedly friendly toward the white man.[59] Various bands of Bannocks, inhabiting the southern border of Oregon, along the Humboldt River and the emigrant road were considered thievish and treacherous. The Utes, to whom reference has already been made, comprised many divisions. The bands occupying the country east of the Wasatch Mountains and containing the best warriors were less influenced by the Mormons and were most friendly to the whites. Their western and southern kinsmen, living in the desert portions of the territory, were miserable and degraded creatures.[60]

Contemporary accounts of these natives certainly were not flattering. The Diggers, for example, were described as the "most repulsive looking wretches, . . . little less degraded and uncivilizable than the blacks of New South Wales."[61] Of arts and crafts, the western bands were extremely ignorant, although some exhibited unusual skill in basket-weaving. The desert tribes wore little or no clothing. Generally, they were "naked as a worm." In western Utah, where food was scarce, they ate everything—creeping, flying, or running—usually raw.[62] When Mormon settlers and emigrants bound for California depleted the game, the plight of the natives became desperate. The meager and irregular relief of the government proved far from adequate.[63]

The California Indians were among the least-known natives of North America. Unlike the Texas, New Mexico, and Utah tribes, they were not nomadic and always lived within limited areas. Culturally, they were among the most backward of the North American Indians. With the exception of basket-making, they had developed no arts. They had no system of writing, knew nothing of metals, and had only the simplest knowledge of social organization, government, and military methods. Miserable huts of grass, tule, or brush, sometimes covered with earth, served as homes, and rude rafts of tule constituted the only means of navigation. Prior to the coming of the white man, they practiced no agriculture. Although they hunted deer and small game and did considerable fishing, the bulk of their food was vegetable.[64] But with all his primitiveness, the California Indian had one cardinal virtue—he stored food for the future and seldom went hungry.[65]

At the time of the American occupation three groups of Indians lived in California. A mild, patient, and tractable people, who had come under the influence of the Spanish and Mexican mission-aries,[66] occupied the valleys. The peaceable nature of these inhabitants is attested by the fact that as late as 1850 they possessed no clubs, scalping knives, or tomahawks. The mountain tribes, on the other hand, seem to have been a brave, independent, and intractable lot, often characterized as idle, thriftless, and debased. Physically and mentally they towered above the valley Indians. The third group, occupying homes between the plains and immediately within the foothills, possessed intermediate characteristics of their stronger and weaker brethren.[67] The number of Indians in California before the coming of the white man has been variously estimated at between 50,000 and 260,000. When the United States took possession of the country the native population was still quite large—probably between 100,000 and 125,000. A dozen years later the California tribesmen had dwindled to less than 18,000[68]—a decline more sudden and rapid than on any other part of the American continent.[69]

When the many peaceable and warlike tribes in Texas and in the Mexican Cession came under the jurisdiction of the federal government, the question of an Indian country for these people naturally arose. The problem of a permanent home for the natives, to be sure, was not new. A quarter of a century earlier Secretary of War Calhoun, recognizing the plight of the Indians, recommended a permanent home for the tribesmen in the great plains country.[70] The Indian Intercourse Act of June 30, 1834, had created the "Indian Country"—the region west of the Arkansas Territory, Missouri, and the Missouri River—where Indians were to be given permanent homes for themselves and their posterity and be free from intrusion of the white man.[71] But the law which had established one country for white men and another for Indians soon had to be modified.[72]

Revision or modification of this law, however, was no simple matter and the acquisition of the southwestern tribes only added to the difficulties of the government Indian policy. In Texas, for example, the authority of the federal government over Indians and Indian lands was limited, since that state entered the Union without surrendering any of her public lands. In the Mexican Cession the validity of the Intercourse Act was also challenged. Since the law had been passed long before the Treaty of Guadalupe Hidalgo, it was contended that it did not apply to any portion of the new territory. The New Mexico courts forthwith ruled that there was no Indian country within the territory. Such interpretation, of course, played right into the hands of unscrupulous traders. Restraint of traffic between Indians and whites became nil. On the other hand, as late as March, 1855, the Santa Fe *Weekly Gazette* complained that the whole territory was apparently Indian country, that Indians had not been confined within any particular boundary but had been allowed to roam at will. Such confusion added to the complexity of frontier defense.[73]

Meanwhile, the California gold discovery had ushered in a new, get-rich-quick era, a dream of easy wealth. The gold fever attacked every class of society.[74] To the new El Dorado now streamed thousands of men, women, and children with their household goods and cattle, on foot, on horseback, or in covered wagons.[75] Farmer, shopkeeper, mechanic, teacher, preacher, lawyer, gambler, and adventurer—all turned their faces to the land of gold. Whether they followed the northern route via the Platte River, South Pass, and the Humboldt, used the Southwestern trails through Texas, or traveled the Arkansas, Cherokee, or Missouri trails[76] to Santa Fe and thence westward to the Pacific, they were encroaching upon the newly acquired and vaguely defined "Indian Country." Before the Mexican War and the gold rush the Indian had maintained an almost unbroken, if irregular, line against the advance of the white settlers; but henceforth he was being surrounded by settlements—his country was steadily but ruthlessly being wrested from him.[77] The inevitable clash was on.

CHAPTER II

Evolution of a Defense Policy

ROM the time the English established their first settlement on the Atlantic seaboard to the late nineteenth century, frontier defense formed a major task of our statesmen and military leaders. Successive governments, in dealing with this problem, had no uniform, definite policy, but rather "a series of experimentations on successive frontiers."[1] When the white man began his westward march and the Indian slowly retreated, the governments of England, of the colonies, and of the United States, each in turn attempted to protect the frontier by making peace with the red man. Treaties of friendship, cession of Indian lands, annuities and presents, and the creation of an Indian country secured only periods of temporary truce.[2] The Factory System, established primarily for the protection of the Indian against the unscrupulous trader, only lessened the Indian's respect for the Great Father as he saw him in the guise of a trader.[3] When pioneers and prospectors settled on unceded Indian lands, massacres, retaliation, and organized military campaigns invariably followed.

During the long period of conflict administrative machinery for handling Indian affairs was gradually being evolved. In the colonial era a miscellaneous group of individuals served as intermediaries between white men and the natives. Explorers, missionaries, traders, settlers, military officers, and official agents and commissioners were not clearly defined. At the time of the American Revolution the term "agent" [Indian] was still applied indiscriminately to any representative of the government among the Indians, whether he was a man of influence or a half-breed trader who lived among the natives by preference and served the government only occasionally.[4]

In the first year of Washington's presidency, Indian affairs fell

under the jurisdiction of the newly created Department of War.[5]
Under the secretary of the new department was the regional Superintendent, who was often the governor of a territory, one of whose
duties was the administration of Indian affairs. Below the Superintendent was the agent, who was usually assisted by a subagent.[6]
For a quarter of a century the difference between agents and subagents seems to have been very slight—merely a matter of rank
and salary. Whereas the Superintendent was in charge of a vast
region with numerous tribes, the agent or subagent lived with a
certain tribe or in a center where he could have easy access to two
or more tribes. Usually frontiersmen themselves, such as fur
traders, trappers, missionaries, or discharged army men, these
agents and subagents were the most important figures in the Indian service.[7]

In order to define more clearly the authority of the agents and
to provide more adequately for the administration of Indian affairs, Congress in 1832 created the office of Commissioner of Indian Affairs.[8] Two years later the Department of Indian Affairs
was established. The newly created Indian country was divided
into superintendencies, agencies, and subagencies, where whites
without licenses were prohibited. As the tribes were to be colonized, agents, teachers, mechanics, and farm implements were to
be furnished; annuities in the form of goods were to be paid to
chiefs of tribes.[9] To give the Indians additional protection, still
more national laws provided fines and imprisonment for the introduction, sale, "barter, or exchange of any spirituous liquor or
wine . . . into the Indian country."[10]

Meanwhile, the national government, in its anxiety to deal
fairly with the Indians, proceeded to make treaties.[11] But written
agreements decided nothing permanently either for the Indian or
the white man. In the first place, the Indian, with very few exceptions, had no clear conception either of individual or tribal owner-
ship of land. To the native, land was a gift of nature like air and
water—something he needed and enjoyed but not something to
be bought and sold. That a few marks on a sheet of paper could

mean the permanent cession of land was never clearly understood
nor taken very seriously by the Indian. In June, 1856, Mrs. Helen
M. Carpenter, a member of a California emigrant party, wrote in
her diary: "As for the treaty of peace with the Sioux, it is not
worth the paper it is written on, when once the Indian begins to
feel ugly, and is aching for a scrap."[12] Then again, chieftains and
leaders possessed neither the power nor the authority to bind their
fellow-tribesmen to agreements; to hold entire tribes responsible
for the misdeeds of a few was neither fair nor feasible. Moreover,
the matter was further complicated by the fact that numerous
tribes frequently hunted over the same territory and a treaty made
with one tribe could, therefore, not be binding with equal validity
on other tribes claiming title in the same region.[13]

The Indian, of course, was not alone in his disregard of treaties;
the white man was no less to blame. By a decision of the Supreme
Court in 1823 the United States government formally recognized
the Indian's title to the soil by virtue of his occupancy,[14] but deci-
sions of courts, treaties, and acts of Congress meant little or nothing to the land-hungry frontiersman. To enforce the Indian's right
to the soil proved a herculean and well-nigh impossible task.

Then there were the unscrupulous Indian traders. This gentry
not infrequently helped to bring about situations leading to treaties
in order that they might claim annuities in payment for debt contracted by Indians for goods and whiskey at greatly inflated prices.
As late as November, 1861, Secretary of the Interior Caleb B.
Smith reported that annuities usually found their way into the
hands of traders, while the Indians received from them goods
which netted the traders a profit of 300 to 400 per cent.[15]

Government officials, too, in administering the peace program,
frequently committed blunders. Particularly was this true in the
selection of Indian gifts. Instead of beef and corn, the gifts were
usually showy ornaments, trinkets, gay calicoes, and other articles
of a trivial nature. For example, Indian goods costing some $25,000
delivered to California in 1852, consisted mainly of beads, scarlet

prints, shawls, and coarse blue cloth. The California natives rarely used beads, and what the Indians would do with blue cloth the *Daily Alta California* was at a loss to imagine. Of course, facetiously observed this paper, the Indians might wear blue clothing if the government would send tailors to make it. "Why not satisfy their only irresistible natural craving—something to eat?" queried the *Alta*. But much more serious was the distribution of arms and ammunition, which the Indians used only for war.[16] Thus, carelessness or shortsightedness of officials often frustrated the very purpose they aimed to achieve. Periodically the government had to resort to force.

Other events, in the meantime, had been moving rapidly. The Santa Fe trade materially hastened the white man's advance into the Southwest. The ever lengthening frontier with the inevitable rush of emigrants to the newly acquired lands, completely destroyed the former notion of an "Indian country." It is quite apparent that by the mid-nineteenth century the policy of the federal government toward its Indian wards had been benevolent and sincere, but somewhat shortsighted. The gravest error, perhaps, had been its inability to anticipate the constant, restless, and unforeseen movements of population to the new Indian frontier. For decades the red man had been driven from pillar to post in a desultory fashion. Now came a time when he was pressed on all sides by the white man. There was no place to which he might be moved. The once proud owners of a continent became a people without a home.[17]

When the Mexican War extended our southwestern frontier to the Pacific, many persons felt that the former methods of dealing with the Indians would no longer prove adequate. In February, 1849, Commissioner of Indian Affairs William Medill wrote to Major Neighbors that the policy of the federal government toward the Texas tribes was indefinite and unsatisfactory, and that unless Congress adopted a more definite system of management of Indian relations, there would be no peace on our frontiers.[18] Since it was believed that the civil administration would be more effective in civilizing and educating the Indian than military supervision had been, the Indian Office, early in March, 1849, was transferred to the newly established Department of the Interior.[19] But the results were disappointing. The other experiment tried at this time—the policy of consolidation and segregation in place of simple removal practiced in earlier years—also proved no solution.[20]

With the transfer of control of Indian affairs to the Department of the Interior, officers of that department at once attempted to bring about much-needed reforms. In 1849 the new Commissioner of Indian Affairs Orlando Brown and two years later Commissioner Luke Lea characterized the existing organization for handling Indian affairs as defective and inefficient. These officials pointed out that although the department had been well adapted to the conditions in earlier years, it no longer was able to discharge the enlarged and complicated duties which devolved upon it. Some 124,000 new Indian wards came under our jurisdiction in Texas, New Mexico Territory, and California. But the personnel of the Indian service was not materially changed. The handful of officials had a most difficult task. The number of agents was limited by law; subagents performed duties of their superiors but received only half as much salary; the offices of territorial governor, Superintendent of Indian affairs, and agent were often lodged in the hands of the same person.

To secure greater efficiency Commissioner Brown recommended the establishment of seven full and independent superintendencies: four for the tribes east of the Rocky Mountains and one for each of the Territories of Oregon, California, and New Mexico. Brown also recommended that subagencies generally be dispensed with and that minor agencies—involving fewer Indians and lesser duties—should be established with a lower grade of salary. Such a rearrangement, with a proportionate revision in salaries, the commissioner believed, would attract more competent and efficient men to the Indian service and provide more safety for the frontier.[21]

Brown's and Lea's suggestions, in the main, soon were put into operation. An act approved on February 27, 1851, abolished the old superintendencies east of the Rocky Mountains and established three new ones. In place of the twenty-three agents and subagents east of the Rocky Mountains and north of Texas and New Mexico, the President might appoint eleven agents at an annual salary of $1,500 each and six at $1,000. Four agents were assigned to New Mexico and one to Utah at an annual salary of $1,550. The pay of interpreters in the Far West was increased to $500 per year.[22]

Despite these changes, criticism continued throughout the period. Alexander Ramsey, Governor and Superintendent of Indian Affairs of Minnesota Territory, in his annual report of 1851 declared: "Our Indian policy has been vacillating, full of inconsistencies and incongruities, of experiments and failures."[23] Two years later the Tahlequah (Oklahoma) *Cherokee Advocate* expressed the opinion that our Indian affairs demanded a thorough overhauling. In Congress the idea prevailed that Indian appropriations were charities instead of meager payment for our vast public domain.[24]

Meanwhile, the phenomenal westward migration was accompanied by a corresponding increase in the number of Indian officials and in the amount of money and goods which they handled. Between 1853 and 1856 fifty-two treaties were made with the various tribes, and the jurisdiction of Indian agents was extended over an additional area of from 4,000 to 6,000 square miles. By 1860 eleven additional treaties were negotiated and more than 30,000,000 acres became part of the public domain. This increase was necessarily accompanied by the creation of new agencies and subagencies, chiefly in the Far West. Expenditures for Indian service rose constantly. For 1860 the various tribes, in compliance with treaty obligations, received nearly $3,000,000 in money, goods, and provisions.[25] The annual cost of maintaining the frontier army was many times that amount.[26]

The constant increase in the operations of the Indian Department, requiring the expenditure of vast sums of money, naturally brought forth investigation and criticism. Senator John J. Crittenden of Kentucky pointed with pride to "the benevolence of Congress toward this race of beings [the Indians]," but at the same time he considered it high time to call a halt to enormous expenditures. Appropriations for the Indian Department for 1857-58, Crittenden showed, were equal to the amount required for all expenses of government during Washington's administration.[27] When Crittenden advocated reduction, Senator Sam Houston at once marshaled the opposition forces. Rarely, declared the Texas Senator, had the Indian received a "square deal," financial or otherwise, at the hands of the white man. Out of $115,000,000 appropriated for the Indians since 1789, Houston pointed out, the beneficiaries of that huge amount had "never realized $20,000,000 of advantages."[28]

Houston's contention was not idle oratory. "Fat plums" and downright graft were frequent in the Indian service. Many administrative positions in the fifties were desirable, both on account of the salaries paid and the opportunities for graft. When the office of Superintendent of Indian Affairs for California was created in March, 1852, the salary was not to exceed $4,000, while the clerk might receive as much as $2,500. Three years later Congress appropriated $12,000 for three Indian agents there, $28,850 for incidental expenses, $54,300 for payment of such employees as physicians, smiths, and carpenters, and $125,000 for the removal of the California tribes to three military reservations and for their subsistence.[29]

Supplying food and clothing to the Indians—particularly those on reservations—furnished golden opportunities to dishonest officials. Although laws existed for the punishment of fraudulent practices involving Indian contracts, conviction was difficult.[30] In 1854 Congress appropriated more than $242,000 to cover drafts made by California agents for beef and flour which the Indians did not receive.[31] In 1858, after an examination of the California reservations, Godard Bailey, special agent of the Department of the Interior, and J. Ross Browne, special investigating agent for the Treasury Department, declared them to be mere almshouses, where large numbers of Indians were "lying on bare ground without a rag of clothing, dying of starvation."[32] The pay and rations of the employees, however, totaled about $100,000, a sum sufficient to sustain more than all the Indians on the California reservations.[33]

In an attempt to keep the Indians contented and peaceful, the government from time to time tried the old policy of bringing prominent chieftains to Washington. The effectiveness of such visits to the capital, however, met with considerable difference of opinion. The advocates of the policy felt confident that it impressed the red man with the white man's power; the opponents dubbed it pure humbug. The only benefit resulting from such visits, declared the *Daily Missouri Republican,* was the rich harvest reaped by the white man. As for the Indians, since the expense of these excursions came out of their annuities, they suffered a reduction in their pay. Consequently, far from being impressed, they questioned the good faith of the white man and brooded revenge.[34]

A more severe criticism launched against the government was the inconsistent policy of furnishing the red man with arms and ammunition. As late as 1858 some of the warlike tribes on the western frontier—Kiowas, Cheyennes, and others—received presents totaling some $20,000 annually, of which a portion was in arms and ammunition. Despite protests of Indian officials, who pointed to the danger of such a practice, the arms were forwarded on the grounds that it was in accordance with treaty stipulations. This practice, to be sure, originated in a humanitarian motive. Arms, it was believed, were necessary for the natives to procure food as well as to defend themselves against other tribes. The Austin *State Gazette* has thus aptly stated the peculiar position in which the government found itself: "To deny arms . . . is virtually to condemn them to starvation; whilst to furnish them is to incur the certainty of having them turned against us."[35] The government truly found itself in a dilemma. What the Indian thought of such procedure is not known; possibly, he laughed at the stupidity of the white man.[36]

The Fort Smith (Arkansas) *Times* was even more severe in its criticism. Councils, talks, and presents, this paper contended, were only temporary palliatives. "Give them a few more presents —blankets, clothing, beef and a few guns to murder our people with"—continued the *Times,* "and they will remain peaceable until they want more presents; and then they will be found at the old trade of murder and robbery." Peace was a complete failure; force, this paper insisted, was the only language the Indian understood.[37] Judge Davis, of New Mexico Territory, agreed with the *Times* that the only suasion the Indian understood was the "moral suasion of powder and lead." Dr. Jacob Forney, Superintendent of Indian Affairs in Utah, also believed "a military thrashing . . . more effective than so many gifts and treaties." On the Pacific coast the *Daily Alta California* pleaded for more adequate protection. For, added the *Alta,* Indian affairs were very little understood in Washington; the administration was imposed upon and misled by designing speculators, whose sole aim was to make money regardless of the effect upon our Indian relations.[38]

In carrying out the federal policy of frontier defense, the Indian agent exerted a tremendous influence upon his charges. Living among the tribes and serving as the "eyes and ears of the government," he had an unusual opportunity for promoting good will. His duties were numerous. Sometimes he made long journeys through the wilderness, visiting tribes or Indian bands and holding talks with the chiefs. At home his duties were myriad. He punished Indians who committed depredations on whites; he protected the Indian from white encroachment; he licensed traders, issued permits to whites to travel in the Indian country, tried to prevent liquor from being smuggled among the Indians, prosecuted whites for crimes committed against natives, and served claims for damages due the red man.

One of the most difficult of all the duties of the Indian service, perhaps, was to prevent the importation and sale of liquor to the Indians. Try to stop it as the agents might, the traders always managed to find a way. Despite acts of Congress, orders of military officers, and energetic efforts of agents, the illicit liquor was being brought into the Indian country in great quantities. When agents diligently searched all the boats on the Mississippi and Missouri rivers for the forbidden firewater, pack trains took it by the keg to the mountains.

Moreover, it was the duty of the Indian agent to enforce treaty stipulations, superintend the payment of annuities, take the census, compile lists of Indians to whom payments were made, and supervise schools, farming instruction, and blacksmith service. Not infrequently the agent was called upon to settle tribal and intertribal disputes. The latter were especially difficult, since young braves, anxious to prove their mettle, "broke over" and attacked parties of the tribe with whom peace had been concluded. Finally, the Indian agent gave aid and hospitality to white people in need in the Indian country. In short, as one historian expressed it, the agent was to the United States government "what fingers are to a blind man."[39]

Indeed, the qualifications of the ideal agent were those of a superman. As one authority has quite aptly described it: "He needed the wisdom of the serpent and the guilelessness of the dove, the patience of a Job and the energy of a Hercules." He could well use the special equipment of a half dozen professions if he were to do anything like justice to his multifarious task.[40] But the ideal agent —the man who was honest, who had frontier training, and who was friendly to the Indians—was not easily found. And when one could be found there was a likelihood that some political favorite, often a failure in the East, would receive the appointment. The Spoils System was no stranger to the Indian service.[41] In 1862, Bishop Henry Benjamin Whipple of Minnesota wrote to President Lincoln about the character of the Indian administration as he had known it: "The Indian agent, . . . generally selected without any reference to fitness . . . appoints his subordinates on the same basis . . . often no better than whiskey-sellers, barroom loungers, debauchers."[42]

All Indian officials, to be sure, did not belong to this class. Such men as Robert S. Neighbors and Shapley P. Ross in Texas, James S. Calhoun and Kit Carson in New Mexico Territory, and Adam Johnston, B. D. Wilson, and E. F. Beale in California established an enviable record in their efforts to give the Indian, as well as the white man, a square deal.[43] But whether honest or unscrupulous, the Indian agent had no sinecure, and his job, at best, was a difficult one. Some of the agency districts were large. Frequent conflict of authority and difference of opinion between military officers and agents did not make the latter's task any easier. Unscrupulous traders often marred the good work of agents who had the best interests of the Indians at heart.[44] On more than one occasion Indian agents paid with their lives for devotion to duty.[45]

The government's peace policy, it seems, was never entirely adequate and had to be supplemented constantly by the use of force. But whereas in earlier years the army had been called upon only occasionally to chastise hostile bands, in the mid-nineteenth century the frontier soldier was to play a more prominent role than ever before. The virgin lands of the Far Southwest, which at the opening of the century had an interest only for traders, trappers, and merchants, now beckoned miners, speculators, adventurous land-hunters, and home-seekers from the more populated districts of the East. When the Indian resented the new encroachments of the white man and attempted to stem the rising tide of migration, the soldier again came to the defense of the frontiersman.

But frontiersmen, as well as others, were not satisfied. The number of men in the regular army was too small, and most of them were infantry. The western outposts were too thinly garrisoned and the foot soldier was greatly handicapped when pitted against the well-mounted Indian warrior. Mounted volunteers were considered the ideal fighters to pursue and chastise the Indians.[46] The

Texans, in particular, took special pains to point to the superiority of Rangers over regulars. T. C. Alexander, a citizen of Bosque County, wrote to President Buchanan that the regular troops had shown themselves totally unqualified for defense of the Texas frontier. The Indians could steal horses from under the soldiers' very guns and escape without injury. One Texas Ranger, Alexander considered, was worth two regular dragoons, while infantry was of no earthly use except to guard military stores.[47] The Dallas *Herald* declared that one company of Rangers under Captain Ford and a like number of friendly Indians under Captain Ross had done more actual good in a brief campaign than the "3,000 regulars who live in comfortable quarters and are only serviceable in keeping up 'the pomp and circumstance of glorious war.' "[48] Senator Sam Houston in fiery speeches before the Senate in January and February, 1858, bitterly denounced the regular army, condemning it as incompetent to give protection and as a reproach to our country. "You may withdraw every regular soldier . . . from the border of Texas," he declared, "if you will give her but a single regiment, 1,000 or even 800 men of Texas Rangers."[49] Similarly, on the Pacific coast, the San Francisco *Evening Picayune* considered the miners better suited for Indian warfare "than any other species of troops in the world."[50]

Despite the glowing reputation of frontiersmen as superb Indian fighters, some, however, considered them a bad lot, unworthy of having defense placed in their hands. Father Domenech, a contemporary Catholic missionary, described the Texas Rangers as the "very dregs of society, and most degraded of human beings."[51] P. D. Turner, an army beef contractor, found the Texas volunteers "dooing [*sic*] nothing only hunting Buffalo and drinking whiskey."[52] Disagreements between civil and military authorities about the relative merits of regulars and volunteers certainly were not wanting. Governors Pease and Houston of Texas, Rencher of New Mexico, and McDougal and Bigler of California periodically enrolled volunteers while regular army officers attempted to discourage such action.[53] Some army men maintained that punitive expeditions undertaken by state and territorial troops were carried on primarily for personal gain. Others, such as Colonel Sumner and General Persifor F. Smith, doubted the wisdom of permitting frontiersmen to restore order.[54]

Friction between civil and military authorities resulted from other causes. In the course of the Mexican war, when federal military officers at Santa Fe issued orders regulating the conduct of the civilian population as well as soldiers, they came into direct collision with civil officers. Likewise, when Colonel Edward W. B. Newby, commandant at Fort Marcy, issued orders suppressing gaming and the sale of "spirituous liquors" (the latter extending only to soldiers), he was charged with "trampling upon civil government." And a storm of protest arose over Brigadier General Sterling Price's Orders Number 10, which attempted to regulate gambling and the sale of intoxicants, and levied a duty on merchandise entering the territory. Citizens and merchants of Santa Fe drew up and signed memorials and resolutions denouncing the proposed import duty as illegal, unjust, and unconstitutional.[55] Colonel Sumner attempted reforms which succeeded only in bringing down a storm of abuse on his head and in causing his ultimate removal.[56] In Utah, General A. S. Johnston and Governor Cumming failed to agree,[57] and in California General Wool clashed with Governor Johnson.[58]

Administration of justice in the Indian country was neither swift nor sure. There was too much division of authority. Depredations, for example, first had to be investigated by the Indian agent, then reported to the Superintendent of Indian Affairs, who in turn usually referred the matter to the military department. Such regulations, together with a lack of understanding and the presence of two independent authorities not always working in harmony, caused considerable delay and gave the wild tribes greater courage. When civilian authorities complained that the military refused to furnish aid and even accused commanders of a lack of energy, the latter countered—and with considerable truth—that the civil officers curried favor with the settlers and often tried to bring on unnecessary Indian wars. Divided Indian control certainly was not conducive to efficiency.[59]

Throughout this period conflicting opinions prevailed concerning the proper attitude towards the western tribes. Some condemned the government policy entirely, characterizing it as full of promises, blunders, and crimes; others thought the government apathetic and negligent in all problems relating to the West, especially towards the Indian. The federal land policy and system of annuities were roundly condemned. Some criticized the military policy as lacking in firmness, while others considered it too harsh. The system of Indian reservations was characterized both as good and an evil. Partisan appointments, clashes between civil and military authorities, and the distribution of arms to the Indians were additional grave weaknesses and inconsistencies in the Indian policy. The federal government seemed bewildered. The Far West was so distant, the communications were so poor, that government policy could not keep up with events.[60] However, had greater foresight been exercised, considerable loss of life and huge expenditures of money undoubtedly would have been avoided. The story of Indian relations might have been more creditable. As recently as 1891, Commissioner of Indian Affairs T. J. Morgan blamed the white man for the complexity of the Indian problem.[61]

Despite the many blunders, it should be noted, however, that the federal Indian policy had a brighter side. Throughout its history, the United States government, with few exceptions, had high ideals in regard to its relations with the Indians and although it did not realize these worthy aspirations, it kept them more or less constantly in mind. The government was ever eager to give the Indian the civilization of the white man. Constantly, the government attempted to convert the Indian from a hunter to a farmer. It passed intercourse laws to prohibit the traffic in whiskey and "high wines." It established trading houses primarily for the

Indians' benefit. The government sent agents, teachers, and other employees to live among them and look after their welfare. It furnished food and clothing to the needy, and provided medical attention, especially vaccination against the ravages of smallpox. At times, it stationed soldiers among the Indians to protect them against hostile tribes and dangerous white men.

The federal Indian policy was worthy of praise as well as condemnation. The American government did as well under the circumstances as could be expected. It tried various methods. An Indian policy gradually evolved, although at times it was indefinite, inconsistent, and vacillating. But our government, like a partially blind man, felt its way, and after two more decades of experimentation finally found the proper solution.[62]

CHAPTER III

Fortifying the New Frontier

THE white man's government, in its search for the ideal method of dealing with the Indian, constantly held out an olive branch in one hand and a sword in the other. While it transferred the red man to new homes and gave him gifts or annuities, it also established a chain of forts at the edge of the frontier settlements or in the heart of the Indian country. Prior to the Mexican War some fifty military posts guarded the nation.[1] It soon became apparent, however, that the extreme western outposts, extending from the Gulf of Mexico to the Canadian border,[2] would have to be strengthened. To furnish protection to emigrant trains, to protect the Overland Mail and the new settlements, as well as to defend the peaceful tribes from unscrupulous white men, required a new line of military stations. Since the war called for the presence of troops in the Indian country and since civil and military officers emphasized the urgent need for a new line of defense, such recommendations could not go long unheeded.[3] Thus, from the western outposts along the Mississippi River a cordon of forts was gradually extended westward along the Arkansas River to the Rio Grande, the Gila, the Great Colorado, and the Pacific Ocean. Many people, however, including military officers on the frontier, questioned both the wisdom and the effectiveness of this policy. To what extent the new line of military posts solved the problem of frontier defense in the Far Southwest in the period preceding the Civil War remained a moot question for many a year.

Troops moved westward; new posts began to appear. Fort Mann, situated on the north bank of the Arkansas River, about five miles west of the present Dodge City, Kansas, was built in 1847.[4] Opposite Grand Island, on the south bank of the Platte,

Fort Kearny[5] was established, and some 350 miles beyond, the famous Fort Laramie was purchased by the government from the American Fur Company.[6] Both of these posts were intended as protection for emigrants bound for California and Oregon. Three military posts were constructed on the lower Rio Grande: Fort Polk, situated at Point Isabel,[7] and Fort Brown, opposite Matamoros, were established in the spring of 1846.[8] In the fall of 1848 troops occupied Ringgold Barracks, about one-half mile below Rio Grande City.[9] General Kearny ordered construction of Fort Marcy, named in honor of the Secretary of War, shortly after he entered Santa Fe, in August, 1846. About a hundred troops and thirty Mexican masons soon set to work but did not complete the post until the following year.[10] In California, army officers made military inspections and strengthened several positions. Captain Kimball Hale Dimmick, of the New York volunteers, directed a working party in repairing the presidio of San Francisco. Troops also mounted guns at San Pedro and Los Angeles, and built a redoubt on a hill overlooking Monterey and mounted it with 24-pounders and 8-inch mortars.[11]

At the end of the Mexican War the defense program in the Far West naturally received greater attention. In December, 1848, orders issued from the Adjutant General's office directed officers of the Corps of Engineers and Topographical Engineers to make a careful examination of Texas, New Mexico, Oregon, and California, for the purpose of locating permanent military stations within those areas.[12] The system of defense, however, was not developed according to any definite or scientific plan; military officers were directed to establish forts when and where the need was greatest. Not infrequently, special interests greatly influenced the selection and maintenance of such positions. Merchants, unlicensed traders, speculators, and whiskey dealers played a decisive part in the defense policy in the Far Southwest.[13]

In Texas—the Eighth Military Department—[14]where a frontier of between 1,300 and 2,500 miles had to be protected against some

25,000 Comanches, Kiowas, and Apaches,[15] the government evolved a system of an inner and outer chain of defenses. The inner chain, established in 1848 and 1849 in advance of the frontier, began above San Antonio and ran parallel with the settlements in a northeasterly direction to the Red River. As the emigrants moved westward, the outer chain was created as far as the Rio Grande. An intermediate group of defenses connected the inner and outer lines. Posts were also established to the south and in the "Big Bend" sector.

The original inner chain, erected as a protection for the settlements between the Guadalupe and Trinity rivers, consisted of Forts Mason,[16] Croghan, Gates,[17] Graham, and Worth. Of this line, Fort Graham, established early in February, 1849, in Hill County, was the best planned. It enjoyed an ample water supply, fertile lands, abundance of timber and other building materials, and was connected with Fort Gates and the city of Austin by good wagon roads.[18] Fort Worth, the most northerly of the original inner chain of defense, was built in the same year about thirty-five miles west of the village of Dallas. The post was abandoned in the fall of 1853, but its location became a thriving town, in large part supplying the needs of the border settlements.[19] These military positions, however, failed to impress the Indians. Within the next five years many Texas tribes harried the region along the inner line of defense. The Apaches robbed and killed emigrant parties; the Comanches paid flying visits to the Arkansas country; the Wacos conducted raids from the Wichita Mountains to the southern border; the Kickapoos were even bold enough to murder Indian agent Jesse Stem within a few miles of Fort Belknap.[20]

The government had to decide upon a more vigorous policy. In 1851 Secretary of War Conrad ordered the movement of more troops into Texas. A regiment of infantry was directed to march from Jefferson Barracks,[21] Missouri, to the Indian country west of Arkansas, while the Fifth Infantry, stationed in the latter country, was to advance farther into the interior and establish a chain of forts across northern Texas from the Red River to the Rio Grande in the Comanche country. A regiment of Mounted Riflemen was ordered from Oregon to Texas and remounted for active service. Two more companies were to proceed to Corpus Christi.[22]

In accordance with this policy seven new posts soon supplemented the inner line. To overawe the hostile tribes along the Red River, Colonel G. Loomis, in June, 1851, established Camp Belknap (later known as Fort Belknap) on the Red Fork of the Brazos River,[23] and in November of the same year troops from this garrison built Fort Phantom Hill on the Clear Fork of the Brazos.[24] To the southwest three additional posts, Forts Chadbourne, McKavett,[25] and Clark, were built in 1852 to guard the zone of Indian depredations. The last post, in particular, occupied a position of primary importance, since it faced both the Rio Grande and the Indian frontiers.[26] Camp Cooper, in Throckmorton County, was established to protect the reservation Indians stationed there. Camp Colorado was built in the present Coleman County.[27] The northern line of defense extended from Eagle Pass on the Rio Grande to Preston on the Red River. Leaving Texas at this point the line proceeded northward via Forts Washita, Arbuckle, and Cobb[28] in the present state of Oklahoma.

Meanwhile, the valley of the Rio Grande—probably the largest and most exposed of any part of the Union—as well as the settlements along the Gulf and the northern frontier, was kept in a constant state of alarm and excitement. "The whole lower country is swarming with Indians and is one continual scene of outrage and murder," declared the *Democratic Telegraph and Texas Register*.[29] To escape from the Indian danger, entire families were moving to the Mexican side of the Rio Grande. In defiance of military escorts, bands of Indians armed with guns attacked army wagon trains and killed the teamsters.[30] Of course, frontiersmen and special interests deluged Congress, the Secretary of War, and the President with petitions and memorials, pleading for greater protection.[31]

The War Department, in the meantime, had not been idle: it had established an outer chain of defense. Along the lower Rio Grande, Forts Polk, Brown, Ringgold Barracks,[32] McIntosh,[33] and Duncan[34] served as key positions to the upper provinces of Mexico. These outposts not only formed a bulwark against the wild tribes but also served as a salutary influence along the boundary line, especially in the enforcement of the revenue laws.[35] Three forts—Merrill, Ewell, and Inge—strengthened the rear of this line,[36] while to the northward and eastward nine additional posts served as connecting links between the outer and inner chains. From the subsidiary defenses, occupying a central position and garrisoned principally with cavalry, mounted troops could easily be dispatched to any threatened point—eastward toward the settlements or westward toward the Rio Grande.[37] Among these defenses, Fort Martin Scott, established in 1848, Fort Lancaster in 1855, and Camp Wood in 1857 occupied strategic positions,[38] since they commanded numerous Indian trails leading into southern Texas and across the Rio Grande into Mexico.[39] The "Big Bend" sector, favorite resort for Indians attacking California-bound emigrant and cattle trains,[40] was guarded by four additional outposts —Forts Stockton, Davis, and Quitman,[41] which protected the stage line and emigrant road between San Antonio and El Paso; and Fort Bliss,[42] which guarded against Mexican raids.[43] The marauding activities of the picturesque Mexican bandit, Cortinas,[44] in the summer of 1859 and spring of 1860 led to the strengthening of the defenses in the lower Rio Grande. Fort Brown, which had been abandoned, was again reoccupied; a detachment of artillery was ordered to take station between Forts Clark and Duncan, and a company of cavalry was on its way from Camp Hudson. Four new camps were established along the lower Rio Grande. Meanwhile, many military positions established on earlier frontiers were abandoned.[45]

Theoretically the double system of defense—the series of posts erected at strategic positions from thirty to 300 miles beyond the frontier settlements—was quite effective, but actually it proved inadequate. In the "Big Bend" sector and in the region between the Nueces and the Rio Grande (where the country was sparsely settled and infested with thieves, robbers, and murderers from Mexico and Texas) its effectiveness was questionable. The military posts furnished only partial security.[46]

In the Territory of New Mexico or Ninth Military Department, there was no definite line of defense as in Texas, since most of the land was more or less under control of the Indians and a few bold traders and cattlemen.[47] The comparatively small and scattered white population and the peaceful Pueblos, surrounded by a host of wild and hostile Indians, did not create a situation conducive to peace. The contemporary press pictured the Indian danger as very grave. Reports of periodic attacks on emigrants and scattered settlements, paralyzing industry and endangering life, brought forth memorials and petitions declaring: "We must have more troops . . . or we are lost."[48] To cap the climax, the Mexican government filed huge claims against the United States for depredations committed by Indians from across our border.[49]

To remedy this state of affairs, the War Department strengthened the original fortified positions along the upper Rio Grande, such as Fort Marcy, Taos, Albuquerque, and El Paso, by building additional forts. By 1852, upon recommendations of civil and military officers in the territory,[50] seven new posts were established. Of this number, three bordered the Rio Grande and the others guarded the Navaho and copper mine country. Fort Conrad, situated near Valverde, and Fort Fillmore, on the east side of the Rio Grande about ten miles south of Las Cruces, were established in 1851.[51]

About 100 miles northeast of Santa Fe in the present Mora County, the celebrated Fort Union was built during the summer of the same year as a check upon the northern tribes of Apaches and Utahs. The site was selected by Colonel Sumner, and buildings were erected by troops from Las Vegas and Santa Fe under

the command of Colonel E. B. Alexander of the Third Infantry.
The absence of stockades or breastworks and the widely scattered
buildings gave Fort Union more the appearance of a quiet frontier
village than that of a military outpost. It was, however, one of the
most important military establishments in the Southwest, serving
as a supply center for forty or fifty lesser forts within a radius of
500 miles. During the Civil War the Confederates attempted to
capture the post, but did not succeed. In 1867 Fort Union was
described as "a vast collection of workshops, storehouses, barracks,
officers' quarters, and offices of all kinds belonging to different
departments." More than a thousand workmen were employed
here.[52]

Fort Defiance and Cantonment Burgwin were built in the
Navaho Country and Fort Webster in the Santa Rita Copper Mine
district. Fort Defiance, some 190 miles west of Albuquerque, was
very strategically located at the mouth of Cañon Bonito, a favorite
resort of the Navahos. In the summer of 1855, when Judge Davis
visited the post, it was garrisoned by three companies of troops,
one of light artillery and two of infantry. The quarters of the
officers and men were built around a large parade ground covered
with fine grass. Some of the buildings were of adobe and others of
pine logs. A battery of six-pounders and six mountain howitzers
served as armament. Cantonment Burgwin, named in honor of
Captain J. H. K. Burgwin, was about nine miles north of Taos, in
a beautiful but rough and mountainous country. Fort Webster
was in the northeastern part of the present Grant County.[53] Fort
Massachusetts, the most northerly post in the territory, situated in
a sheltered valley on Utah Creek in the present southern Colorado,
was designed as a defense against the Utahs and Apaches.[54]

The new military positions, like those in Texas, did not intimidate the wild tribes, who continued to keep the settlers along our
Southwestern border in a constant state of fear and who extended
their depredations into Mexican territory. The Mesilla Valley the
treacherous Apaches had converted into a "land of widows," in

which agricultural and mining activity had virtually stopped; even pastoral life could be carried on only under the protection of artillery. The distribution of gifts in the form of meat, flour, "red cloths and calico shirts," served only as temporary palliatives.[55]

The acquisition of the Gadsden Purchase made the problem of defense more acute in New Mexico. A prevalent belief in the existence of rich mineral deposits in the territory brought a great influx of emigrants into the region between the Santa Rita Mountains and the Colorado River.[56] To protect the new arrivals from the attacks of some 5,000 newly acquired Indian wards and also from the depredations of the older tribes required additional defenses. Consequently, between 1853 and the beginning of the Civil War new posts were built on both sides of the Rio Grande, in the southwestern part of the territory, in the northern part, and along the upper Colorado; several of the older positions were abandoned. The repeated and insistent demands of the Mexican government that we restrain the wild tribes, as well as the clamor of the frontier settlers for greater protection, led to the establishment of Forts Thorn and Craig. The former was situated at Santa Barbara and garrisoned with troops from Fort Webster. The latter, at the entrance of the *Jornada del Muerto,* was about nine miles to the south of Fort Conrad.[57] But there was no peace in the territory. When the Mescalero and Jicarilla Apaches took to the warpath, Fort Stanton was established on the Bonita River some twenty miles east of the White Mountains.[58] To protect the Santa Cruz Valley and to restrain the tribes north of the Gila, Fort Buchanan was built on the Sonoita.

Fort Buchanan, it should be noted, was conducive neither to health and comfort nor safety. In the late fifties an army surgeon described the fort as a series of temporary *jacal* buildings constructed of upright posts of decaying timber and covered with mud. In the rainy season the earthen floors were covered with water. The troops suffered continually from malaria and other diseases. Since there was no stockade, "Apaches would prowl about the doors of the various houses so that officers had to travel at night within the fort with cocked pistols."[59]

When the Mormon War broke out and some of the troops were transferred from the Southwest to quell that disorder, the warlike bands cast all caution to the winds. Some crafty warriors levied tribute on commercial and emigrant trains entering the Territory of New Mexico. Bolder spirits defied the government by murdering Indian Agent Henry L. Dodge.[60] Colonel Bonneville's Gila expedition against the Apaches and that of Lieutenant Colonel Miles against the Navahos into Cañon de Chelly brought only temporary relief;[61] demands for greater protection became more insistent than ever. But petitions of New Mexican citizens and recommendations of military officers and Indian agents for additional cavalry posts had little effect. Only one new military position—Fort Garland—was established in 1858.[62] In the following year Colonel Bonneville attempted to inject greater vigor into the defense program of New Mexico by reorganizing the existing military posts and by shifting the troops to more strategic positions. Fort Thorn was abandoned and its property moved to Fort Fillmore. A detachment of Mounted Rifles was stationed at the Copper Mines on the site of Fort Webster. A company of Third Infantry was stationed at Hatch's Ranch on the Gallinas River. Fort Breckinridge was erected on the San Pedro River.[63] Bonneville's achievements, however, failed to impress the territorial legislature, who, influenced, no doubt, by the frontiersmen, petitioned Congress for no less than seven more permanent military posts.[64]

Meanwhile, Colonel Thomas T. Fauntleroy, Bonneville's successor, worked out an elaborate program for military reorganization, which was intended both to strengthen the defenses within the department and to protect the emigrant and mail route from Missouri. Fauntleroy's proposals provided for the abandonment of some of the existing military positions, the creation of new forts, the strengthening of the garrisons, and the more efficient and economical supplying of the mounted troops.[65] His recommendations produced drastic changes, but before his new plan could be effective, the Civil War broke out. Some of the military positions in New Mexico were temporarily discontinued and the troops removed.[66]

In the Utah country, until the outbreak of the "Mormon War" in 1857, defense was largely in the hands of the Mormons; but with the movement of Johnston's army against the Saints,[67] the government established several temporary camps and permanent posts. The famous Fort Bridger, situated on Black's Fork of Green River in the southwest corner of the present state of Wyoming, had been burned by the Mormons upon the approach of the United States troops. In November of the same year, Jim Bridger, who had served as guide for the Army of Utah, leased the ruins of his establishment to the United States government. Johnston's men soon rebuilt and improved it. They surrounded it by a moat and further strengthened it by a rampart of earthworks and palisades and lunettes mounted with cannon.[68] Some two miles to the north of Fort Bridger the bulk of Johnston's army went into winter quarters at Camp Scott. In the summer of 1858 the troops built and occupied Camp Floyd, about forty miles to the southwest of Great Salt Lake City.[69] Two years later, when the tribes of Carson Valley took to the warpath, the federal troops built Fort Churchill on Carson River.[70]

The establishment of a line of military posts in California completed the system of frontier defense in the Southwest. Whereas in Texas and New Mexico the chief problem was the protection of emigrants and settlers from Indian attacks, on the Pacific coast it involved the additional task of defending the peaceful tribes from the mad rush of prospectors and home-seekers, who seemed content with nothing less than possession of the entire country. In wrestling with this problem, military officers fortified the coast settlements, built forts in the mining districts, as well as near the mouth of the Gila and along the upper Colorado.

During 1849 and 1850 clashes between whites and Indians in the Russian River country and in the upper San Joaquin and Sacramento valleys led to the stationing of troops at Benicia Barracks[71]

on Suisan Bay, at Camp Far West on Bear Creek some thirty miles
from Sutter's Fort, and at Cajón Pass. The post on Bear Creek
occupied a strategic position, since the Truckee emigrant route
and the wagon roads to the Yuba mines and Feather River dry
diggings all intersected at this point. Cajón Pass guarded the Indian approach from the east into San Bernardino.[72] The murder
of Captain William H. Warner of the Topographical Engineers
in the fall of 1849 near Goose Lake[73] was followed by an order for
the establishment of a post in the Sierra Nevada near the forty-
second parallel.[74] In the following year troops were stationed at
Camp Yuma, at Warner's Ranch,[75] and on the San Gabriel.[76]

Of all the military positions in southern California, Fort Yuma
was by far the most colorful and important. The hostile conduct of
the Yumas toward the westbound emigrants using the southern
trails to the California mines, caused a great clamor for the location of a fort at the mouth of the Gila. On July 4, 1850, Major
Samuel P. Heintzelman was ordered to establish a military post
at the junction of the Colorado and Gila rivers. Late in November
of that year Heintzelman, in command of three companies of infantry, established the post on the right bank of the Colorado
River, within the present Imperial County, California. At first it
was situated in the bottoms, about half a mile below the mouth of
the Gila; but in March, 1851, it was moved to a higher elevation,
the site of a former Spanish Mission, the Mission Concepción. In
the fall of the same year, because of Indian hostilities, the post was
temporarily abandoned, the government stores cached or destroyed. In February of the following year the fort was again reoccupied, and six months later garrisoned by more than 500 men.
Fort Yuma rendered invaluable service. It protected the southern
emigrant route, controlled the numerous warlike bands, and
commanded the land passage into Mexico. From 1857 it flourished
as a station on the early stagecoach lines. Today the Fort Yuma
Indian School and the Mission of St. Thomas are situated on the
former site of the historic military post.[77]

The disturbances of 1849 and 1850 showed the need of winning the Indians' good will. The President therefore appointed three special agents for California, who were to go into the Indian country, study the Indian needs, select sites for agencies, and negotiate treaties. In the spring and summer of 1851 the newly arrived officials succeeded in carrying out the President's orders, but when the prospectors and miners nullified the work of the peacemakers, the natives rose up to defend their rights.[78] The Indian war scare naturally brought forth numerous petitions for protection. To appease such clamors, the California legislature instructed its representatives in Congress to secure additional troops and to have a line of military posts established along the California borders.[79]

More troops soon arrived. Along the northern frontier the government established Forts Umpqua, Lane, Jones, Humboldt, and Reading; in the south Forts Miller and Tejón.[80] Troops also took station at Rancho del Chino and Rancho de Jurupa,[81] at Stockton, on the Sacramento, and on the Trinity. Of the northern posts, Fort Humboldt was the most important. Captain U. S. Grant of the Tenth Infantry was stationed there for a time. In the south Fort Tejón occupied a strategic position. Built at the *Cañada de las Uvas* ("cañon of currents"), it was intended to quiet the reserve Indians at the mouth of the Tejón Cañon, to command Tejón Pass, as well as to control the tribes along the Mohave and Colorado rivers. In 1858 Fort Tejón became a station of the Butterfield Overland Mail route, the soldiers from the fort serving as military escort through the pass.[82] But these military positions did not satisfy the Californians. Some went so far as to declare it "a disgrace to our government" that a line of posts from the Humboldt to Independence, Missouri, had not been erected.[83]

Although Washington did not take such criticism too seriously, military officers in California attempted to placate the frontiersmen. Early in May, 1857, when General N. S. Clarke assumed command of the Department of the Pacific, he introduced a more

vigorous defense policy. Within a few months Camp Bragg and
Fort Crook were built in the Pit River country.[84] Indian alarms
in the Humboldt and Klamath regions led to the erection of Fort
Terwaw on the Klamath reservation.[85] In the following year,
when the northern tribes attacked a mail stage, massacred an
emigrant company, and were reported planning a mass uprising, Fort Gaston in Hoopa Valley and Camp Wright in Mendocino County were established.[86] When the Mohave and Paiute
tribes in the vicinity of the thirty-fifth parallel became troublesome, Lieutenant Colonel William Hoffman, in the spring of the
same year, led more than 700 men from Fort Yuma to Beale's
Crossing on the Colorado River and established Fort Mojave.[87]
Hoffman's display of force humbled the neighboring tribes only
for the time being.

Meanwhile, in the spring of the same year, Inspector J. K. F.
Mansfield arrived in San Diego from Fort Yuma to examine the
military positions on the Pacific coast. His inspection of posts,
troops, depots, and arsenals, which lasted several months and extended from San Diego in the south to Fort Umpqua in the north,
disclosed many weaknesses. The post at the old mission of San
Diego, Mansfield found abandoned and in a very dilapidated condition, while at the important supply depot of new San Diego,
about three miles south of the old position, water had to be hauled
three miles and wood twenty miles; grazing facilities were entirely lacking. Fort Tejón he considered badly situated, since the
surrounding country was exposed to earthquakes. A sandy plain
and sandy bluffs to the west and northwest of Fort Umpqua en-
circled the post and rendered its location unsuitable.[88] In January,
1861, when the departments of California and Oregon were
merged into the Department of the Pacific and more than 1,700
troops occupied the dozen posts and stations in California,[89] the
defense problem still remained unsolved.

The question of the effectiveness of the long line of military
posts did not fail to bring forth animated discussion and considerable difference of opinion. Secretary of War Conrad maintained

that safety could best be secured only by a constant display of
military force in the Indians' immediate neighborhood.[90] Territorial and state governors, importuned by settlers and special interests, invariably championed the establishment of new posts.
Governor Bigler of California in a message to the legislature declared that the erection and maintenance of military stations at
intervals of seventy-five or a hundred miles, garrisoned with fifty
men each, would afford needed security for the entire trans-
Mississippi country.[91]

A unique proposal for defending the Far West was made by
Henry O'Reilly, pioneer builder of telegraph lines. O'Reilly's
plan, which involved the establishment of postal and telegraph
facilities, the erection of stockades twenty to thirty miles apart,
also provided for mounted troops to patrol the routes, to transmit
the mail, and to protect emigrants and settlers. Legislatures and
governors of western states and territories favored the "stockade-
patrol" plan, but since General Scott pronounced it "impracticable,
uneconomical, and ineffectual," it was not tried.[92]

On the whole, officials in Washington as well as officers in the
field condemned the policy of numerous small posts. Quartermaster General Jesup and Secretary of War Davis contended that
a more effective plan was to mass a few large bodies of troops at
strategic positions and from these to dispatch large detachments
annually into the Indian country.[93] General Worth, commander
of the Eighth Military Department, and other officers held similar
views.[94] More critical of the government's defense policy was B. E.
Tarver, member of a surveying and exploring expedition across
northern Texas. Writing to Governor Pease in June, 1857, Tarver
declared: "The system of frontier defence as applied to Texas is a
signal failure . . . [it] has yielded neither laurels to our army nor
protection to our citizens. It should be changed."[95]

The most severe critic was Captain (later General) John Pope
of the Topographical Engineers. In a fifty-nine page "Military
Memoir of the Country between the Mississippi River and the

Pacific Ocean . . ." addressed to Secretary of War Floyd, Pope analyzed the existing system of defense in great detail, pointed out its weaknesses, and proposed changes. Pope agreed that prior to the Mexican War the employment of numerous small posts had proved effective, since they were situated in fertile lands and formed nuclei for rapidly growing settlements. But with the acquisition of the Mexican Cession the former method was no longer adequate. Despite the new conditions, however, special interests in the distant territories proved so powerful that the government was virtually compelled to establish a multitude of posts along the whole line of frontier settlement.[96]

In Texas, for example, where the first line of defense was within the cultivable region, successful results could be noted. But with the movement of troops into barren areas, cries for protection immediately arose, the loudest clamors coming from merchants, traders, and profiteers. "So soon as the small posts were fairly established in this desert region, a number of people at once flocked around them," Pope declared, "not . . . to make permanent settlements . . . but simply to sell forbidden articles to soldiers and employees of the garrison. . . . Some (and they were only few) cultivated small fields of grain to be sold as forage to the Government,"[97] while others sold whiskey and guns to the Indians. An exceedingly profitable trade thus readily converted quasi-settlers into champions of frontier defense, who no sooner heard of the government's intention to remove a military post than they immediately raised a cry of "defense."[98]

Pope was not alone in the belief that reports of Indian atrocities were greatly magnified and that selfish motives greatly outweighed the actual need for the establishment and maintenance of new military positions. A French traveler, passing through northern Texas in the fifties, declared that, except on the very distant frontiers, the Indian danger was reduced to a minimum. This observer, in fact, made the startling statement that a degree of security prevailed in the Indian country which was superior to that found in the streets of New York, London, or Paris.[99] Similarly,

Captain (later General) George B. McClellan and Secretary of War Conrad did not hesitate to explode the highly exaggerated Indian danger. "It is well known to this Department," wrote Conrad to Governor Bell of Texas, "that the inhabitants in the neighborhood of military posts, have other reasons for wishing them to be kept up, besides the protection they afford. The Department, therefore, is frequently urged to establish posts where there is no real necessity for them."[100] The settlers strenuously denied such charges; and the *Texas State Gazette,* championing the cause of the frontiersmen, berated the federal government for its inaction and indifference. "Texas has all along been treated as a discarded child," bitterly complained the *Gazette.*[101] The States Rights faction even went so far as to declare that since the national government failed or refused to render adequate protection the citizens were justified in severing their relations with the Union.[102]

The clamor for protection in New Mexico was on an augmented scale, not because the Indian danger was greater but because the New Mexicans had no other market for their surplus products than the government. Eighty per cent of the money in circulation in the territory, it was estimated, had been contributed by the civil and military departments of the United States government.[103] Naturally, when attempts were made to remove troops from the towns into the interior or to abandon a military post, the business interests became panicky. The Santa Fe *Weekly Gazette* declared the removal of troops would ruin the country, for it would deprive the people of thousands of dollars in trade.[104] Much of the profit was legitimate; but some of it was derived from trade in whiskey and arms, plied by unlicensed traders in defiance of the law. It often resulted in violence and in subsequent pleas for more adequate defense.[105] Too often demand for protection was only a plea for the continuance of a lucrative trade.

The one-sidedness of Indian treaties added much to the New Mexican Indian's discontent and often resulted in clashes with the white man. The natives of New Mexico had little faith in agreements which stipulated that Indians give up stolen stock and captives, when the white man's government did little towards the recovery of thousands of Indian women and children held in bondage by New Mexicans—a condition "worse than southern slavery." As late as 1866 the whites held no less than 2,000 Indians as slaves and peons.[106]

Friction which was ever present between the two races frequently played into the hands of the "champions of frontier defense." During the so-called periods of peace when the New Mexican Indian visited the towns he was usually fleeced by the white man. Since the Indian rarely received justice in the courts he sought redress in the only way he knew. A cry of Indian danger at once arose.[107] The common herding of flocks, with each herd under the charge of a single man or boy many miles away from the settlements, frequently created trouble. If in the course of a quarrel between herders, a New Mexican killed an Indian and took away part or all of the flock, little was known of the matter; but if the Indian committed the violent act, the settlers at once pleaded for greater military protection.[108] Since many of the western newspapers magnified the Indian danger and the press in other sections of the country reproduced such reports, the special interests won out. The numerous posts remained.[109]

In California, where the white man encountered the least war-like tribes of the North American continent, the outcry against the Indian danger was no less constant and no less exaggerated. The rougher elements in the mining districts, acknowledging the red man's right neither of property nor of life, often ruthlessly and wantonly attacked his settlements because of imaginary offenses. Miners took great pleasure in their inhumane treatment of the natives. "Christian maxims and precepts are naught with the frontiersmen," wrote Dr. James L. Tyson, a California physician in his diary in 1849. When an Indian refused to work for a white miner he was liable to be murdered. To show off their marksmanship, some of the rougher class of whites considered it excellent sport to shoot down an Indian.[110] Then the Indian, feeling himself greatly outraged, proceeded according to the principle of "an eye for an eye, a tooth for a tooth."[111] When ambitious politicians and greedy war speculators "manufactured" Indian atrocities, and Mexican greasers kidnapped Indian children and wantonly killed the parents, the war was on.[112] The cry for greater protection was followed by the establishment of new posts.

Because of the vast area of the trans-Mississippi country, and the character of the roving Indian population, many critics considered the numerous small frontier posts, garrisoned largely with infantry, a highly useless and expensive luxury. Pope recommended drastic changes. First of all, he proposed that the trader, the emigrant, the traveler, and the business man should confine their travel to the summer months. Moreover, he suggested that the small posts beyond the reach of the settlements should be broken up and the troops concentrated at three or four large forts within the settlements themselves. From these large, well-equipped and strongly manned outposts some mounted troops were to patrol the Indian country during the summer months, while others were to serve as escorts on the great overland trails. Like Jesup, Davis, and Johnston, Pope believed that constant pressure of troops in the immediate neighborhood of the Indians and their families would create a deeper impression upon them than a thousand ineffective engagements directed from numerous small outposts.[113] Whether the system of numerous small posts was entirely wrong or whether the recommendations of Captain Pope and his supporters would have solved the problem of defense any better is not at all certain. Probably neither method would have proved a complete solution. Since this was a transition period, the successful method of defense had to be evolved gradually.

In the twelve years preceding the Civil War the federal government had erected more than sixty military posts and stations in the Far Southwest, but Indian outrages and depredations continued daring and numerous. Discounting the exaggerated reports of settlers, speculators, and the frontier press, the fact remains that marauding bands murdered settlers, drove off stock, and even dared to attack the military posts. During this period of unrest some two hundred whites were killed, in New Mexico Territory alone, and a million dollars' worth of property was destroyed. Women and children captured by the Indians were frequently sold as slaves to distant tribes.[114] The bloody campaigns waged on both sides of the Pacific coast range, while proving disastrous for the Indian, failed to establish a permanent peace. The frontier defense policy had been but partially successful.

Despite harsh criticism the military stations in the Far West performed a real service. They served as pioneers of civilization; they furnished much-needed supplies to destitute travelers; they served as nuclei for important punitive and exploring expeditions.[115] As officers and men scoured the plains and penetrated the mountain fastnesses in search of plunderers, they learned about portions of Indian country hitherto almost entirely unknown. Along the Rio Grande frontier the military posts played an important part in the development of an extensive trade with Mexico.[116] The distant military stations materially aided in binding together the older settlements with the newer ones. They paved the way for the disappearance of the "Last American Frontier."

CHAPTER IV

Opening New Trails to the Far West

LONG before the discovery of gold in California the Pacific coast had attracted American traders, adventurers, and home-seekers. The first quarter of the nineteenth century witnessed hardy, adventurous spirits such as Jedediah S. Smith, Sylvester and James Pattie, and Ewing Young leading bands of traders and trappers to and through portions of California; Nathaniel J. Wyeth, Hall Jackson Kelley, and other pioneers stimulated interest in the Oregon country. In the eighteen-forties thousands migrated westward in search of homes. On the eve of the gold discovery the movement to the Pacific coast had already reached large proportions.[1] Heavier emigration in the gold rush necessitated the discovery of shorter and better routes to the Pacific. Opening new trails to the Far West for travel as well as for the movement of troops and supplies became a definite phase of the frontier defense policy of the federal government.

In the late forties and early fifties many overland trails[2] could be used to reach California and Oregon, but most of them were accompanied by grave hardships. Shorter and less hazardous routes had to be found. Expansionists, at an early date, had manifested an interest in land routes that would make travel to our distant settlements safe and easy; it was not, however, until the Mexican War and the gold discovery that a definite program of exploration and road building on an appreciable scale was actually attempted. Colonel Stephen W. Kearny, who had been ordered to capture New Mexico and California, conducted the first official expedition to the Pacific across the Southwest.[3]

Kearny was eminently fitted for the task; he certainly was no newcomer on the western frontier. Beginning his military career in the War of 1812 under Captain (later General) John E. Wool, the young lieutenant soon became identified with frontier defense and for more than thirty years—until his death in 1848—was instrumental in blazing many a western trail. In this long period of service Kearny led his troops across thousands of miles of unknown western wilderness—to the upper Missouri, the Red River country, and South Pass. By display of force and by councils with the Indians he succeeded in bringing peace among various tribes and giving protection to emigrants, Santa Fe traders, and settlers. Soldier, settler, and Indian held him in high esteem for his bravery and firmness, his sense of fairness and justice.[4] Such was the man, who, in accordance with orders from the War Department,[5] organized the "Army of the West"[6]—some 1,700 men—for the Santa Fe expedition.

In the last part of June, 1846, Kearny and the major portion of his force left Fort Leavenworth,[7] marching rapidly westward along the Santa Fe trail. After traveling some 900 miles of uninhabited plains, he entered Santa Fe on August 18. This feat Kearny accomplished without firing a shot. An extensive province containing perhaps 100,000 people—whites and Indians—passed into possession of the United States. To establish good will Kearny gave a ball for the officers and government officials and their families. It was a shrewd political move. The officers in their dress uniform and military bearing and the New Mexican women dressed in their native finery must have presented a colorful spectacle as they executed the cotillion and the waltz.[8]

Late in September, leaving Colonel Alexander W. Doniphan in charge of affairs and ordering Lieutenant Colonel Cooke to open a new wagon road to the Pacific, Kearny set out on the final stage of the journey with "300 wilderness-worn dragoons in shabby and patched clothing." With this small force mounted on mules, Kearny moved down the Rio Grande Valley some 230 miles. At Fray Cristobal the command, reduced to but 100 men and separated from Cooke's wagon train, which took a more southerly route, crossed the dividing ridge near the thirty-third parallel, struck the Gila and followed it to its junction with the Colorado of the West. In their journey the men and animals suffered great hardships. The march along the Gila proved extremely difficult; the mules stumbled repeatedly because of steep ascents and descents; deep gullies cut the river banks; the troops moved dizzily through cañons, over mountains, and under overhanging cliffs; huge boulders, deep sands, and sharp pebbles obstructed the trail; mirages distorted the landscape into many fantastic shapes; ruins of dwellings of an ancient race added to the barrenness of the scene; game was scarce, but lizards, scorpions, and tarantulas were plentiful. The tired men and animals crossed the Great Colorado about ten miles below the mouth of the Gila and struck out northwestward, where they encountered a region even more barren and desolate. Men, horses, and mules plodded through a ninety-mile stretch of drifting sand. Famished and jaded animals, dropping behind, became a prey to wolves or starved. Failing rations drove the soldiers to the necessity of eating their own horses. By December 2 the weary caravan came to Warner's Ranch. Ten days later they arrived at San Diego, the end of the trail.[9]

Though Kearny's expedition had been primarily military, an important aspect was exploration. The reconnaissance division accompanying the troops, headed by Lieutenant William H. Emory of the Topographical Engineers, had been directed to collect data which would furnish the government with a correct idea of the character of the region. Emory's journal, with its accurate description of the country, its inhabitants, its plant and animal life, accompanied by an excellent map and numerous sketches and drawings, proved highly valuable to military men and pioneers. The relics of the ancient inhabitants—the ruins of dwellings, pottery, and rock inscriptions including drawings of mastodons, horses, dogs, and men—which Emory was the first to examine, attracted considerable attention. The astronomical observations, table of distances, and location of mountains, plains, cañons, and streams served as valuable guideposts to those who were to follow.

Kearny's expedition was the first in a series of scientific transcontinental surveys of the Far Southwest.[10]

Lieutenant Colonel Philip St. George Cooke, one of Kearny's
officers, conducted the second expedition to California. Cooke,
like Kearny, had already seen extensive service in the Far West.
In 1829 and again in 1843 he had commanded military escorts
protecting Santa Fe traders. He also had served in the Black Hawk
War. In the thirties he had made visits to the villages of the Oto,
Omaha, and Pawnee Pict tribes and in 1845 had accompanied
Colonel Kearny on his famous expedition to the South Pass. Between expeditions, he had been stationed at Jefferson Barracks,
Forts Crawford, Snelling, Leavenworth, Gibson, and Wayne (In-
dian Territory).[11]

In October, 1846, Kearny made him head of the Mormon Battalion[12] with orders to return to Santa Fe, lead the battalion to
California and open a wagon road to the Pacific. When Cooke
inspected his new command, he felt discouraged. He had inherited
a "much worn," shabby-looking, and "undisciplined" lot, "enlisted too much by families, some too old, some feeble, some too
young, and embarrassed by many women."[13]

On October 19 this motley crowd—it was called five companies of infantry—left Santa Fe and moved slowly down the
valley of the Rio Grande. A long train of ox and mule wagons
carried rations. A herd of beeves, later supplemented by a large
flock of sheep, lazily brought up the rear. Pauline Weaver, a famous frontiersman, served as guide and later additional pathfinders from Kearny's detachment joined the battalion. Leaving
the Rio Grande near the site of the present town of Rincon, New
Mexico, Cooke proceeded southwest to the Ojo de Vaca, or Cow
Spring, and from there struck out southwestward over the mountains near the Guadalupe Pass to the San Pedro River. By this time
his problems had become quite serious. Sickness had been increasing; the men were not sufficiently clothed; food was becoming
scarce. Henry Standage, a member of the battalion, noted in his
journal: "I eat guts today for the first time, though many have

eat them before." At the Guadalupe Pass the men were obliged to
hew a passage with axes through solid rock. But upon arriving at
the Pima Indian villages on the Gila the drooping spirits of the
men quickly revived as the natives entered into a brisk trade with
the soldiers. "Our camp is full of Indians . . . and resembles a
crowded New Orleans market," wrote the much relieved commander. Picking up Kearny's trail, the train continued westward
to San Diego, where it arrived on January 29, 1847.[14]

Cooke had accomplished his object. He brought his command
to California with "arms . . . bright . . . in excellent discipline and
without any loss." The hardy commander and his men were proud
of their achievement—they had opened the first wagon road
through the Southwest to California. The new trail became popular with emigrants almost immediately. Practicable as a railroad
route, it was one of the principal reasons for the Gadsden Purchase. Today the Atchison, Topeka and Santa Fe and the Southern
Pacific lines follow a portion of the trail from New Mexico to
southern California.[15]

Upon conclusion of the Mexican War the exploration policy
of the government assumed a more definite character. The location of shorter and better routes, the selection of sites for military
posts and Indian reservations, the construction of roads, the sink-
ing of artesian wells, and the dispatch of punitive expeditions
served as occasions for numerous explorations across the entire
Far West. In 1849 Captain (later General) Randolph B. Marcy of
the Fifth Infantry opened a new trail from western Arkansas to
Santa Fe. This young officer, who already had a dozen years of
frontier service to his credit and who was to devote many years
more to the same cause, rightfully belongs to that brilliant group
of official pathfinders who made possible the settlement of our
great West.[16]

Early in the spring of 1849, Marcy received elaborate instructions from the headquarters of the Seventh Military Department,
directing him to ascertain and establish the best route from Fort
Smith to Santa Fe and California, to explore and survey a wagon

road, to conciliate the Indian tribes, and to serve as an escort to California-bound emigrants.[17] On April 5, Marcy's expedition left Fort Smith, Arkansas, with an exploring party of more than seventy officers and men and a train of eighteen wagons. Lieutenant James H. Simpson of the Topographical Engineers was chief reconnaissance officer. Two famous frontiersmen, Black Beaver[18] and Jesse Chisholm,[19] served as guides. Following a general westerly course along the south bank of the Canadian, the large caravan arrived near the Upper Cross Timbers about the middle of May. From that point it accompanied the Fort Smith Company of emigrants to California. While encamped on Antelope Buttes near present Crawford, Oklahoma, the expedition had its first experience with Indians. Four Kiowa braves dressed in war costume and armed with rifles, bows, lances, and shields came into camp, boasting that they were on their way to Chihuahua on a horse- and mule-stealing expedition. Given presents and told that the "Great Father" was desirous of peace with all his "red children," the braves departed, promising to deliver this friendly message to their kinsmen on the north fork of the Canadian River. Near present Tucumcari, New Mexico, the Comanche chieftain Is-sa-ki-ep (Wolf Shoulder), with a band of about fifty followers, including women and children, paid the explorers a visit. Marcy's "talk" emphasized the white man's need to move westward and expressed the hope that the Indians would create no obstacle in the white man's path. Is-sa-ki-ep considered the "talk" good and pledged friendship. On June 23, when Marcy entered Anton Chico, the people were celebrating St. John's Day. Dressed in gala attire, the several hundred inhabitants had turned out en masse to attend the horse races, chicken fights, and dances. Even Marcy was persuaded to attend a fandango. Five days later the command entered Santa Fe.[20]

On the return trip, six weeks later, Marcy established a new trail across northern Texas. From Santa Fe he moved down the Rio Grande as far as Doña Ana and, after separating from the emigrant party, traveled southeastward until he struck the Pecos at the thirty-second parallel. The remainder of the journey he pursued in a northeast course along the headwaters of the Colorado and Brazos rivers. He crossed the Red River at Preston and continued northward to Fort Smith, where he arrived on November 20. Except for the murder of an officer by Kiowa Indians and the loss of mules in a severe snowstorm, the expedition was highly successful.[21]

Both of Marcy's routes between Fort Smith and Santa Fe were reported on favorably. The northern (outbound) trail Marcy considered "as good as any in the known world"; Simpson described it as one of the best he had ever seen. That the scenery for some 170 miles west of Fort Smith made a profound impression on the poetic and nature-loving Simpson is evident from the following entries in his journal: "The graceful undulations of the mountain heights beyond, the sweetly swelling surface of the prairies below, presenting curves of beauty which Hogarth might envy . . . delicately shaded tints of the green velvety sward. . . numerous rivulets coursing in various directions . . . sweetly embosomed prairie retreats or glades, giving you the idea of peace and contentment."[22]

The southern route, if not painted in equally brilliant colors, was also believed to be highly practicable. Because of the abundance of water, timber, and rich, fertile soil many considered it the best overland wagon route to California.[23] Since the frontier press gave the new trail much favorable publicity—Marcy's report was published in installments in the Fort Smith *Herald*—it soon became popular with overland travelers and partially superseded the Independence road. The Butterfield Stage Route—the first Overland Mail to the Pacific—followed Marcy's southern trail across Texas.[24]

The establishment of military posts along Marcy's route, many people felt, would go a long way toward solving the problem of frontier defense. The Fort Smith *Herald* and the *Democratic Telegraph and Texas Register* believed that a line of such forts erected at intervals of thirty or forty miles would not only protect California-bound emigrants and check incursion of prairie tribes into

Texas but would also reduce materially the expense of maintaining frontier protection. "Around every post," declared the *Herald,* "would soon be clustered traders, mechanics, and farmers. . . . Emigrants can then travel to and from California without fear or molestation."[25] The federal government acted upon these recommendations. In April, 1851, Marcy established Fort Arbuckle to protect emigrants against depredations of Comanches, Kiowas, and other prairie tribes.[26] In June of the same year Fort Belknap was established on the Red Fork of the Brazos River; and later Forts Conrad, Craig, Thorn, and Fillmore along the Rio Grande, and Fort Cobb near the Wichita Mountains.[27]

One of the most able and exhaustive surveys of a central route to the Far West was that carried on in 1849-50 by Captain Howard Stansbury of the Topographical Engineers, assisted by Lieutenant John W. Gunnison of the same corps. The center of operations was the Great Salt Lake of Utah. In the spring of 1849, when Colonel William Loring conducted the Regiment of Mounted Riflemen from Fort Leavenworth to Oregon, Stansbury was ordered to accompany Loring's command as far as Fort Hall and from there to conduct an independent reconnaissance. Elaborate instructions from the Chief of Topographical Engineers, Colonel John J. Abert,[28] directed Stansbury to make careful surveys of the Great Salt Lake and Utah Lake, to study the Mormon character, to observe carefully the nature of the region, the labor supply, the Indians, and feasible sites for military posts. He was to keep a journal and make a map.[29]

Stansbury's party of eighteen men, wagons, and draft animals set out for Fort Leavenworth on the last day of May and, following the Platte trail, reached Fort Bridger ten weeks later. Desirous of discovering a more direct trail to the Humboldt than the one used by the emigrants, Stansbury dispatched his wagon train under Lieutenant Gunnison to Salt Lake City via the Mormon route; then Stansbury, with a small party, accompanied by Jim Bridger, set out to find a shorter route to the Humboldt by the north end

of the Great Salt Lake. From Fort Bridger his tortuous trail led
along the Mormon road to the crossing of Bear River, up that
stream to the Medicine Buttes, then westward and northwestward
into the foothills and mountains to the headwaters of Pumbar's
Creek, a tributary of Weber River. Stansbury's attempt to follow
this stream brought him to impassable cañons with precipitous
walls. He therefore turned northwestward to Ogden's River,
which he descended by a difficult path. Diverging northward
through Ogden's Hole, he crossed the mountains and followed
the wagon road southward to Salt Lake City.[30]

Upon arriving at the Mormon capital, Stansbury learned that
an attaché of General John Wilson, newly appointed Indian agent
in California,[31] had passed through Salt Lake City shortly before
and had spread rumors that a United States army was on its way
to expel the Mormons from Utah. Stansbury forthwith held an
interview with Brigham Young and succeeded in winning him
over to active aid for the survey. Not only the leaders but the mass
of the Mormon population seemed eager to treat the army engineers with kindness and consideration. "Every facility has been
studiously afforded us for the prosecution of our duties," wrote
Stansbury. He was very favorably impressed.[32]

In September, Stansbury with only two companions—a sutler
of the regiment and a St. Louis merchant—explored a new route
from the head of the Great Salt Lake to Fort Hall. The reconnaissance from Salt Lake City northward, via the headwaters of the
Malade and Bannock rivers, convinced the explorer that an excellent wagon road could be built from the Mormon settlements to
Fort Hall. On the return he reconnoitered Cache Valley for a
suitable location for a permanent military post and government
grazing ground, and for a shorter route between Salt Lake and
Fort Bridger.[33]

Stansbury next embarked on the most important part of his
mission—the exploration of the Great Salt Lake. This undertaking
experienced mountain men and Indians considered extremely

hazardous, especially in the late season of the year. Many of them had tried but none had succeeded. Late in October, accompanied by Albert Carrington, a prominent Mormon, and three other companions, he left Bear River. Traveling west and southwest over an artemisia and sandy plain, the small band struck out for Pilot Peak, and after laboriously plodding southeastward across a seventy-mile stretch of salt desert, returned to Salt Lake City on November 7.[34] Meanwhile, Lieutenant Gunnison, who had been engaged in surveying Utah Lake, was halted in his operations by cold weather.[35]

The explorers had suffered severe hardships. To find fresh water while crossing the mud flats and salt marshes presented the greatest difficulty. On one portion of the barren route Stansbury, twice a day, had to give each of his jaded animals a pint of water from the indiarubber bags of his pack train. Frequent mirages interfered with accurate gauging of distances. One field of pure white salt covering an area of seventy square miles had a crust strong enough to bear the weight of the entire train. High, rocky "islands" occurred at short intervals over the alkaline plain. The entire journey was most desolate—"silent as the grave"—with no other evidence of life than an occasional Indian regarding them furtively from a distant hill, a solitary wild duck floating motionless on the bosom of the lake, a crow, or a grasshopper.[36]

After spending the winter months in writing reports, the engineers completed their reconnaissance in the following spring and summer. With one party of men in boats and another following the shore line, Stansbury and Gunnison made a careful survey of the lake to determine its extent and shape, the position of its islands and jutting promontories. The engineers followed the Jordan Valley to the lake, then moved along the south shore toward the west, and up the west shore line to the north; from Bear River, they returned to the east shore. The desert to the south and west of the lake with its salt plains, mud flats, and myriads of gnats and mosquitoes made their task almost unbearable. In the latter part of June, despite terrible hardships, they completed the survey. The return march eastward from Fort Bridger to Fort Laramie was essentially the route later followed by the Overland Stage line, the Pony Express, and the Union Pacific railway.[37]

Stansbury and his assistants had observed some 5,000 square miles of territory and traversed the hitherto unknown deserts to the west of the lake; they were the first white men to succeed in making the entire circuit of the lake by land. Where hardy trappers in early times had failed, Stansbury succeeded. His surveys made possible the shortening of emigrant roads and proved valuable in the subsequent location of the Pacific railroads.[38]

The government, meanwhile, had become interested in finding an easier and more practicable overland route to California. Particularly desirous of obtaining more accurate knowledge of the "caravan route" by Cañada, Abiquiu, and San Joseph's Spring, leading to Los Angeles, the War Department in 1849 proposed a reconnaissance across the northern part of the present state of Arizona.[39] It was not until two years later, however, that Captain Lorenzo Sitgreaves of the Topographical Engineers carried out this plan.

Sitgreaves assembled his men and equipment at Santa Fe and moved on to Zuñi, the starting point of the survey, where he was joined by a military escort. The exploring party also included a physician and naturalist, a photographer and draftsman, a guide, and fifteen packers and *arrieros*. Some thirty pack-mules carried the equipment and a flock of sheep furnished the main food supply.[40] On September 24, 1851, the command left Zuñi and struck out westward across the present state of Arizona. Marching along the thirty-fifth parallel, Sitgreaves passed north of the San Francisco Mountains and through the Yavapai Indian country. Early in November he reached the Colorado River about 240 miles above Camp Yuma. From this point he had intended to explore the river upward to the Grand Cañon and determine accurately the mouth of the Virgin River, but the exhausted condition of the animals and the scanty food supply caused him to abandon this plan. He therefore turned southward and traveled along the east bank of the Colorado until he arrived at his destination—Camp Yuma.[41]

Sitgreaves painted a graphic picture of the journey. Between the San Francisco Mountains and the Colorado River he found a succession of mountain ranges and desert plains. In the neighborhood of the Little Colorado fallen trunks of giant petrified trees impeded the march. Below the point where the explorers reached the Colorado, rugged mountains skirted the river bank so closely that there was scarcely room for a roadway. The passage of these defiles proved the most difficult part of the journey, requiring long detours over extremely high, naked cliffs. To cross safely, the men were obliged to cut steps in the rock and help the animals along by ropes. Terrain such as this was extremely hard on the animals. To lessen their suffering, the men reshod the mules and filled the cracks in the hoofs of the sheep with resin and pine-tree gum.

Food and water were exceedingly scarce. Though antelopes, bears, deer, and wild turkeys were seen from time to time, rarely was a guide, soldier, or packer able to get within range of them. Sometimes, for days at a stretch they could find no water and little or no forage. As the weary, famished, and thirsty caravan approached Yuma its sufferings increased. Day by day the mules dropped by the wayside until it became necessary to discard almost everything that was not absolutely essential to life. In this deplorable and almost starved condition the explorers, on the last day of November, reached Camp Yuma and relief.[42]

The laborious march was not entirely without incident. In the San Francisco Mountain region the silence of the night was occasionally broken by the cry of a panther or some other wild animal. The explorers came across encampments of Yavapai and Yuma Indians, but upon approach of the white men the natives fled, leaving their belongings behind. To secure their friendship, Sitgreaves ordered his men not to disturb the abandoned lodges, and he himself left "small presents of tobacco, handkerchiefs and knives." The Mohaves seemed more bold than the Yavapais. A band of some two hundred Mohave men, women, and children who overtook the expedition as it moved down the Colorado, proved a nuisance by their constant demands for trading and by their inveterate thieving. The Yumas were openly hostile. Some fifty braves, after dispatching a straggler, made a general attack. In the sharp engagement which followed, the Indians were beaten with a loss of several warriors; the white men suffered no casualties.[43]

The journey, at best, was a dreary one, beset with many hardships and dangers. The men suffered from intense heat and lack of food and water; they were compelled to give battle to hostile natives. But Sitgreaves succeeded in his mission. He completed the first official exploration across the northern part of the present state of Arizona; he contributed an interesting itinerary, a valuable map, and various scientific reports on the new region.[44]

To find a shorter route to California as well as to select lands suitable for Indian reservations, Lieutenant Edward F. Beale of the United States navy, newly appointed Superintendent of Indian Affairs for California, led an expedition from Westport, Missouri, to Los Angeles in the spring of 1853. Beale was well qualified for this undertaking, though, unlike Kearny, Cooke, and Marcy, he had been identified largely with the United States navy. In fact, both his father and grandfather had been naval officers and had received medals of honor from Congress. After graduating from Georgetown College, Washington, D.C., young Beale received an appointment to Annapolis, from which he graduated with high honors in 1842. During the Mexican War he distinguished himself as a bearer of dispatches through the enemy lines. For this gallantry he was presented with a sword by fellow officers from the army and navy and was complimented by Commodore Stockton. At the close of the war, he carried the message of the gold discovery to Washington. In the fall of 1848 and in the winter of

1849, Midshipman Beale again carried important dispatches, this time from Secretary of War Marcy to military officers in New Mexico and California. On this heroic overland trip Beale encountered severe snow storms, some of his animals froze to death, and some of his men deserted. In 1852 Lieutenant Beale resigned from the navy. In the spring of the following year he led another expedition to California.[45]

On May 15, 1853, this "smart, active, energetic . . . pioneer of pioneers of California, friend of Argonauts, military men, and statesmen,"[46] assembled a dozen men and pack-trains at Westport and began the westward march along the Santa Fe trail. Vast herds of buffalo and long emigrant trains from Texas and Arkansas dotted the line of march. From Fort Atkinson the trail followed the Arkansas to Bent's Fort.[47] Reaching the Huerfano River, Beale continued up this stream to the Sangre de Cristo Mountains and through them to Fort Massachusetts. Gwinn Harris Heap, a member of the expedition, was not overimpressed with this frontier outpost, since it was too far removed from the "general track of Indians to be of much service in protecting the settlements in the San Luis Valley."[48] After a ten days' rest the command moved up that valley, made its way through Cochatope Pass in southwestern Colorado, and there crossed the Grand River. Upon reaching the Mormon settlements of Parowan and Cedar City in the Green River country, the pathfinders landed in the midst of an excited Mormon populace, who were preparing to defend themselves against Utah chief Walker, then on the warpath.[49] Continuing southwestward along the Los Angeles-Salt Lake trail, across the desert to the Mohave River and through Cajón Pass, the explorers reached their destination—Los Angeles—on August 22. Beale and his small band had been more than three months on the march, had covered more than 1,850 miles, and had opened a new route from the mouth of the Huerfano River to the Little Salt Lake.[50]

Four years later Beale led a second exploring expedition to the Far West. His survey, extending from Fort Defiance to eastern

California, was a phase of the elaborate Pacific Wagon Road program for which Congress appropriated more than one-half million dollars.[51] Beale was superintendent of construction of the wagon road from Fort Defiance to the Colorado River.[52]

Beale assembled his outfit at Zuñi. Composed of mules, twenty-five camels,[53] a drove of 350 sheep, Turk, Greek, and Armenian camel drivers, a military escort, heavy wagons and ambulances laden with supplies,[54] the huge caravan presented a colorful spectacle. Starting on the last day of August, 1857, the long train moved along the thirty-fifth parallel, following in the main the route of Sitgreaves' and Whipple's surveys.[55] After a week's travel over a comparatively level tableland the caravan forded the Little Colorado. The trail blazers now found themselves in an unexplored but rich game country; they saw elk, antelopes, and deer, besides beavers and coyotes, in large numbers. Shifting his course some thirty miles to the north, Beale advanced to the base of the San Francisco Mountains and then continued westward to the Great Colorado. He made the crossing on October 18 in an india-rubber boat near the present Mohave City, some 200 miles above Fort Yuma. He spent four trying days in transporting supplies to the west bank. Although a dozen horses and mules drowned, the camels, to Beale's great relief, swam boldly and without mishap across the swiftly flowing stream. Following the United States surveyor's trail from the Colorado River to Los Angeles, the train moved on to Fort Tejón to secure provisions.[56]

On New Year's Day, 1858, Beale started homeward and three weeks later reached the Colorado about twelve miles above Whipple's crossing. Upon recrossing this stream, he found that his wagons had clearly defined the road he had explored the previous summer. Indians had already commenced to follow the broad, well-beaten trail; horse, mule, moccasin, and barefoot tracks were plainly evident. Making the return trip over essentially the same route he had taken in the outward-bound journey, Beale was back in Fort Defiance in the latter part of February, 1858.

During this expedition he had traveled about 4,000 miles through a wilderness of forest, plain, and desert, had tested the value of camels, and had marked a new route to the Pacific.[57]

The practicability of this route in the winter season Beale definitely established in the ensuing winter, for in the fall of the same year he started out upon an elaborate nine-month expedition from western Arkansas to the Colorado River. With a huge caravan, including Indian guides, hunters, engineers, a military escort of 130 men, camels, and two pieces of artillery, he set out from Fort Smith late in October. Following Marcy's trail, he reached Anton Chico two months later and went into winter quarters. In the latter part of February, 1859, he resumed his march westward. Before reaching the Colorado, he had an encounter with Indians who were bold enough to attack the caravan in midday. The warriors, however, succeeded only in killing a mule. In retaliation Beale's men secured four Indian scalps and many bows and arrows.[58]

Meanwhile, Samuel A. Bishop, who had been a member of Beale's road expedition the previous year and had conducted a party of emigrants to California, was moving eastward with some forty men and supplies for Beale. When he arrived at the Colorado River, Bishop found about a thousand Paiute, Mohave, and Yuma warriors assembled in battle array to bar the crossing until every brave was given a shirt. Since this strange demand was impossible to meet, a fight took place. Despite overwhelming odds, the white men not only held their ground but succeeded in completely routing the Indians. Bishop crossed the river and after sending back twenty men and posting a small detachment on the river, again defeated a band of 200 "choice warriors." Bishop, meanwhile, had sent to Fort Yuma for help. When Beale arrived at the Colorado early in May he was met by a detachment of federal troops under Brevet Major L. A. Armistead.[59]

Beale's survey of 1858-59 again proved the practicability of a wagon route along the thirty-fifth parallel and showed that the winter season was no obstacle. Many spoke of this route in very laudatory terms. J. R. Crump, a civil engineer and member of the expedition, characterized it as possessing in the "highest degree all the requisites of a first class emigrant and stage route." Beale declared it "the best, shortest, and most easily travelled of any thoroughfare leading from the eastern states to the Pacific."[60] Champions of the competitive Southern Overland Mail route, of course, were not so optimistic. In fact, they denounced Beale's line as "worse than a swindle—a humbug." His route, nevertheless, was being used daily by many emigrants.[61] The *Daily Missouri Republican* even went so far as to declare that Beale had done more to develop and open up overland travel than had any man who preceded him. His surveys, supplemented by road improvements between Fort Smith and Albuquerque and the construction of a road between Albuquerque and the Colorado River, laid the basis for a through route from the Arkansas frontier to California. Before the completion of the Pacific railroads this direct artery of travel and communication was no small factor in the program of frontier defense in the Far Southwest.[62]

While Beale was exploring along the thirty-fifth parallel, Captain Simpson, who had been Marcy's chief reconnaissance officer on the march to Santa Fe, led reconnoitering expeditions north of Beale's line for the purpose of opening more direct and better roads to California and establishing military posts. Ever since the days of Fathers Escalante and Domínguez[63] in the eighteenth century the Great Basin of Utah had been an object of mystery as well as interest. In the first half of the nineteenth century American fur traders, trappers, and government officers had traversed portions of this region but none had ventured to blaze a direct trail from Great Salt Lake to San Francisco. In every instance fear of desert hardships had deterred them.[64] The route to California across the Great Basin, used for the first ten years after the gold discovery, was long, circuitous, and full of hardships. Emigrants traveling by Salt Lake City or Camp Floyd had to go far to the north and around the lake, thence across the Humboldt and down that river to its sink, and then far southward to Carson Valley at the eastern foot of the Sierra Nevada.[65] A more direct, practicable route across the unknown desert country was needed.

In the fall of 1858, therefore, Simpson with a large escort examined some 150 miles of country between Camp Floyd and Fort Bridger and about eighty miles westward from Camp Floyd to Short Cut Pass in Carson Valley. The lateness of the season and a severe snowstorm caused the explorers to return to their base of operations at Camp Floyd. But the new routes Simpson had discovered were found practicable and soon government explorers, soldiers, emigrants, and traders were using them. The Chorpenning Mail Company used the route via Short Cut Pass to carry mail to California in the winter season.[66]

In the following spring Simpson completed his explorations. Early in May, 1859, the exploring party, comprising topographical officers, scientists, photographers, artists, quartermaster's employees, and a military escort—sixty-four men in all—followed by fourteen wagons, set out from Camp Floyd to complete the hitherto untried and dangerous venture. The westward march towards Short Cut Pass, Simpson wrote, extended across a "somber, dreary waste where neither man nor beast can live for want of the necessary food and water and over which a bird is scarcely seen to fly." But the country beyond was less forbidding. A pass in the Goshoot Mountains brought the explorers to Pleasant Valley, where the men saw the first cultivable land since leaving Camp Floyd. Here, too, many miserable Goshoot and Digger Indians, "the most wretched-looking creatures—the meanest of the animal creation—" came into camp. After passing through several pleasant valleys and cañons, the command reached Carson River. On June 12 the tired men arrived at Genoa. There the citizens greeted them with a salute of thirteen guns and the hoisting of the American flag. Simpson and his band had been forty days on the march and had traveled some 560 miles.

Upon returning to Camp Floyd in the early part of August, Simpson completed his exploration program by ascertaining the practicability of a wagon road to Green River through the Uinta

River Valley. Within a period of three months Simpson had opened two new wagon routes across the Great Basin of Utah from Camp Floyd to Carson Valley and had shortened the distance from Camp Floyd to San Francisco by more than 250 miles. Simpson advertised his routes in the western newspapers. Soon California emigrants and others with large herds of stock were using them. The Overland Mail and Pony Express used the northern route along which the Placerville and St. Joseph Telegraph Company extended its wires.[67]

Simpson's comprehensive report, supplemented by detailed, scientific accounts of his corps of able assistants, proved a veritable mine of information.[68] The hitherto vague ideas about the mysterious portions of the Great Basin now gave way to accurate knowledge of the region. Another partially blank space in the map of the Great West had been filled in and an important link added to the chain of frontier defense.[69]

Construction of wagon roads followed the transcontinental surveys. Though the Mexican Cession, the California gold rush and necessity of supply for the additional military posts made government aid in construction of wagon roads imperative,[70] Congress delayed action until it became convinced of the necessity of such a program. Between 1850 and 1856 the citizens of Missouri, Iowa, and California held giant mass meetings in behalf of western roads and through their legislatures, representatives, and senators periodically petitioned Congress for construction of military and post roads across the plains and deserts.[71] The climax came in 1856 when 70,000 Californians petitioned Congress to construct a military road from some point in Missouri to Carson Valley in eastern California.[72]

Congress yielded. In 1856 and 1857 it appropriated more than one-half million dollars[73] with which in less than two years the Department of the Interior constructed three Pacific wagon roads. One road, leading from Fort Ridgely, Minnesota Territory, through Fort Kearny and South Pass, extended to Honey Lake on the eastern border of California; a second, supplementing

Marcy's trail from Fort Smith to Santa Fe, ran from Fort Defiance to the Colorado River near the mouth of the Mohave River; the third road, running between the thirty-second and thirty-third parallels, connected El Paso and Fort Yuma.[74]

During the same period the federal government spent nearly a million dollars additional for construction and improvements of roads in other portions of the West.[75] Five new roads built by army engineers traversed the Territory of New Mexico. One from Taos to Santa Fe connected the upper posts of the Rio Grande Valley with the capital. Another, continuing from Santa Fe to Doña Ana, served as the most important artery of travel and communication north and south, connecting Santa Fe with the military posts along the Rio Grande and with those east and west of the river. A third road extended from Fort Union about 100 miles southwestward to Santa Fe. A road was also built from Cañada to Abiquiu, and another from Albuquerque to Tecalote. The Fort Union-Santa Fe road was perhaps the most important, for it was the principal entrance to the heart of the territory; it afforded communication between that post and the headquarters of the military department, and it served as a portion of the great mail route between the eastern states and the largest settlement in the territory.[76] Because of her peculiar public-land system, Texas did not share in the federal road-building program;[77] and California, despite constant appeals for federal aid, was obliged to build her own roads.[78] In the Far Northwest, however, the government played a prominent part in the construction of highways. Many roads, laid out by army engineers and built in part by soldiers, connected important points in the trans-Mississippi country. Practically every fort was on or near a well-constructed road.[79]

The significance of this road program was recognized almost immediately. In the spring of 1857 the Santa Fe *Weekly Gazette* jubilantly declared that the opening of western roads would not only have a most salutary effect upon our Indian neighbors but would be followed by the formation of new settlements, the opening of farms, and the establishment of stage routes. "Thus, in a short time," continued this champion of western roads, "civilization will spread across the continent from the Atlantic to the Pacific Ocean."[80] The prophecy of the *Gazette* was soon fulfilled. The Pacific mail stages and thousands of emigrants traveling with heavy trains and large herds of cattle used these highways. The new network of roads not only facilitated the movement of troops and supplies but also aided in the protection and growth of the frontier settlements. The western roads played a vital part in opening up the new country.

But an adequate transportation system presupposed another prime essential—water. In fact, one of the great obstacles in the way of the emigrant and the soldier was its scarcity. For military purposes, especially, artesian wells were an urgent necessity, both in the camps and on the roads, since the lack of water in the desert country made the passage of a considerable force extremely difficult.[81] As early as 1850, Colonel Joseph E. Johnston recommended the establishment of artesian wells along the northern frontier of Texas. Four years later, in the *Jornada del Muerto*,[82] the territorial legislature of New Mexico memorialized Congress for such wells. But it was the agitation for Pacific railroads that brought this idea to the fore. Such wells, the New Orleans *Daily Picayune* pointed out, would make practicable the building of long lines of wagon roads and railroads through regions where the lack of water was the chief obstacle. Well-watered stations at intervals of a few miles, it was believed, would soon form the nuclei of a continuous line of settlements across the continent, and would be followed by common roads, telegraph lines, and railroads, binding the East and the West by the new and rapid intercommunication. Moreover, success in the digging of artesian wells might bring millions of acres of arid lands under cultivation.[83]

Congress finally gave heed. In 1857 it appropriated $100,000[84] for the digging of artesian wells on a grand scale. Between 1855 and 1859, Captain John Pope of the Topographical Engineers, and a large corps of assistants, at one time numbering more than 200 men, were busily engaged in sinking wells in west Texas and a portion of New Mexico. But the boring operations, mainly along the thirty-second parallel in the Llano Estacado, at several points east of the Pecos, and at various points to the northwestward between the Pecos and the Rio Grande, were not successful. Though shafts were sunk to a depth of some 1,300 feet no water rose to the surface.[85] The high hopes held out for the artesian wells were at this time unfulfilled.[86] But these surveys, definitely related to defense of the frontier, were not entirely without value. Pope's reports, illustrated by maps and drawings, brought to light considerable information valuable to the emigrant, the prospector, the scientist, and the government.[87]

CHAPTER V

Western River Surveys

THE improvement of western rivers was a service of prime importance to the westward moving population as well as to the frontier army. Many pioneers depended upon the steamboats of the Mississippi and its branches to reach their new homes. Without the steamboat the West would have "remained a vast wilderness."[1] But the great Mississippi and other western streams needed constant improvement to make them safe and navigable. At the end of the first quarter of the nineteenth century, therefore, the federal government inaugurated a western river-improvement program which it has continued to the present day.

In the twenties the Corps of Engineers removed obstructions —tree trunks, sand bars, and rock strata—from the western waters. From 1828 such work on the Mississippi added to the safety of river travel. Captain Robert E. Lee of the Corps of Engineers did yeoman service for St. Louis harbor and the upper Mississippi and Missouri rivers. His engineering work served as a pattern throughout the Mississippi Valley. Nevertheless, heavy losses both in boats and cargoes continued for some time. In 1839 alone, losses from snags on the Mississippi totaled nearly one-half million dollars.[2]

The removal of the raft of the Red River of Louisiana was another important achievement of government engineers during this period. This accumulation of debris blocked the channel of that stream for a distance of nearly two hundred miles above Coushatta Bayou. In the spring of 1833, Captain Henry Miller Shreve, Superintendent of Western River Improvements, with a force of more than 150 men, embarked on the destruction of this "treacherous monster." Shreve employed specially constructed and equipped government steamboats, known as "Uncle Sam's tooth pullers," but it was not until five years later that the great mass of entangled timber was finally penetrated, and a half century more before it was permanently obliterated. As the raft disappeared, the area of settlement and of cotton production moved steadily westward. The removal of the Red River raft was one of the most important internal improvement projects undertaken by the federal government in the Southwest prior to the Civil War.

In the late thirties troops from Fort Jesup, Louisiana, improved the navigation of the Sabine. Government snag boats also labored on the Arkansas and on the Missouri. The army, in improving the western rivers, not only made safer and faster voyages possible but also protected the frontier and encouraged settlement.[3]

The acquisition of territory beyond the Rocky Mountains emphasized the need for the extension of the western river-improvement program on a grander scale. In November, 1849, Quartermaster General Thomas S. Jesup, in his annual report to the Secretary of War, recommended not only the construction of a good system of western roads but also the improvement of western rivers with all their navigable tributaries flowing through the Indian country. Such improvements Jesup considered "military works of greater importance in defense of the country against the Indian than the best system of fortifications that could be adopted." The frontier settlers, of course, heartily approved such a policy and pointed to the benefits that would accrue to commerce and to military transportation, as well as to frontier defense.[4] Congress, recognizing the logic in such arguments, made the necessary appropriations, and within the next dozen years army engineers surveyed the principal western streams. Among these, the Rio Grande, the Red River, and the Colorado of the West received the greatest attention.

To the Texans, in particular, the improvements of waterways was a matter of prime importance. Their rivers, though long, were not navigable except for short distances in the lowlands near the coast and then only for boats of light draft. Sand bars and mud flats obstructed the entrances to most of the streams; rafts, snags, and stumps impeded steam navigation in some of the most populous and commercially important parts of the state. Though some outlets of Texas flowed through fertile lands, the navigable ones flowed only through thinly inhabited swamps.[5]

In the late forties and early fifties, therefore, the Texans raised loud clamors for better transportation facilities than were being supplied by the ox wagon and stagecoach. Resolutions and memorials presented to the national and state governments urged that Texas streams be made permanently navigable.[6] The Texas legislature acted promptly in 1853 in appropriating $265,000 for work on nineteen different river projects. But when the appropriation bill was submitted to the voters for approval, it was defeated by an overwhelming majority. Politics had intervened. A more vital factor, perhaps, was the "railroad fever," which at this time had struck Texas. The river-improvement program was temporarily thrown overboard in the interests of the "Iron Horse."[7]

But the national government was not diverted from its course. Army engineers examined many Texas streams. Surveys extending from the Sabine to the Rio Grande and from the Gulf to the Red River resulted in improvements. Examination of the Sabine revealed that its chief impediments to steam navigation could easily be removed.[8] Surveys of the lower reaches of the Trinity, the Colorado, and the San Antonio augured successful navigation. An immense quantity of cotton was expected to come from the Trinity region. Some 2,000 bales awaited shipment at its mouth and large consignments were ready at the many landings.[9] The Neches and the Sabine seemed in navigable order, and navigation on the Colorado was improving. In 1853 Lieutenants Walter H. Stevens and William H. C. Whiting of the Engineers, by shunting the waters of the Colorado through a cutoff, and so avoiding an impenetrable raft that had accumulated, opened that stream to navigation. By the summer of the following year a number of heavily laden vessels made trips safely. The "Water Moccasin," loaded with cargoes, made regular trips; many flatboats passed through, delivering thousands of bales of cotton; a newly built steamer, the "Colorado," moved downstream to get her machinery at Matagorda.[10]

But of all the Texas streams, the settlers considered the Rio Grande of the greatest importance. Its navigability by steamers for only 500 miles was believed entirely inadequate for the commercial needs and settlement of the western part of the state. Army officers, merchants, and planters thought that removal of obstructions in its channel would not only facilitate the sending of supplies to the upper military posts and reduce transportation costs but also open the upper Rio Grande country to further settlement and keep the Indians in check.[11] Improved navigation, it was pointed out, would create new markets in the adjoining Mexican states as well as in our newly acquired possessions. Moreover, the long and arduous overland route which merchants and settlers from St. Louis had had to travel would be dispensed with when trade and transportation could be carried on by steamboats on the Rio Grande.[12]

The federal government, therefore, proceeded promptly to test the feasibility of steamboat navigation on this stream. In the fall of 1846, Lieutenant Bryant P. Tilden, Jr., of the Second Infantry, and a crew of some twenty men ascended the river successfully in the United States steamer "Major Brown." For nearly 100 miles above Mier the "Major Brown" experienced few difficulties, but beyond this point a series of shoals, rocks, and rapids caused the boat to ground repeatedly. She managed, however, to reach Laredo, some 600 miles above the mouth of the river.[13] Three years later Lieutenant Whiting, who was making surveys for a military depot on the lower Rio Grande, reported the river practicable for flatboats as far as Laredo. Lieutenant Charles C. Gilbert of the First Infantry traveled upstream in the "Major Brown" to about seventy-five miles above Camargo.[14]

Soon afterwards army officials made additional reconnaissances along the Rio Grande. Between March and August of 1850, Captain John Love of the First Dragoons, an experienced frontier soldier,[15] examined this river for about 1,000 miles north of Ringgold Barracks. With a crew of twelve men he ascended the Rio Grande in the keel boat "Major Babbitt" to Brooke's Falls, a distance of 967 miles. Love paddled upstream in a skiff forty-seven miles beyond, to Babbitt's Falls, where the reconnaissance terminated. As far as the mouth of Devils' River the explorers had traveled along a well-wooded country with "fruitful soil." Above Fort Duncan they entered a region "beautiful and rich beyond description," inhabited by herds of black-tail deer, as well as bear, jaguar, ocelot, puma, and many varieties of smaller game. But this hunter's paradise was wholly unprotected and entirely devoid of settlements. Love's survey showed that the Rio Grande could probably be made navigable at all seasons by steamboats for about 800 miles above its mouth.[16]

While Love was pushing his way up the Rio Grande, other officers also surveyed the river and adjacent country. One party examined the Rio Grande from El Paso to Presidio del Norte; another group examined the frontier from Eagle Pass to Presidio del Norte; a third party ascended the river from Ringgold Barracks for about 470 miles. The reconnaissance divisions operating from El Paso and the lower Rio Grande encountered numerous rapids, but despite these dangers the officers believed that navigation on the river could be extended to about 600 miles from the Gulf.[17] Improvements on the Rio Grande were made after the Civil War, but as late as the nineteen-thirties the stream continued a menace to what men built and planted in its valley. Except for a short distance from the Gulf, it is not navigable. "Its quicksands have swallowed horses, wagons, cattle, sheep, and men." Even today successful navigation has not been achieved.[18]

In the early eighteen-fifties interest in the Red River of the South or Louisiana was being revived. Settlers and merchants urged the removal of the raft for commercial reasons; congressmen and military officers were desirous of finding the true sources of the stream in the interest of more adequate frontier defense. Memorialists frequently complained to Congress that overflows of the Red River caused by the raft were responsible for tremendous losses, thousands of acres of excellent farm lands being rendered valueless. Improved navigation on this stream, these champions of the West confidently maintained, not only would stimulate commerce and encourage settlement, but also would prove of incalculable value in defending the frontier; the Indians would be favorably impressed.[19]

Early in July, 1848, Senator Henry Johnson of Louisiana introduced a bill for a survey of the Red River from its mouth to the head of navigation, and four years later Congress appropriated $100,000 for the removal of the raft.[20] But progress was slow. The government had difficulty in securing a reputable contractor. In the fall of 1854, C. A. Fuller, who had been employed as supervisor on government projects on the Ohio River and Cumberland Dam, was appointed "agent and engineer for the Red River improvement." Fuller entered upon his duties seriously but a yellow fever epidemic delayed his work; dredge and snag-boats were slow in arriving; slave labor added to the difficulties. During the cotton-picking season the laborers were withdrawn by their masters, and Fuller was left without a crew. Desertions were frequent. By December, 1856, the real work of removing the raft had just begun. Two years later, when the money was exhausted and no new appropriations were made, operations were halted.[21]

Then, a private venture with capital from Texas, Arkansas, and Louisiana made elaborate plans for the raft "to disappear like frost before the sun." The coming of the Civil War, however, interfered with execution of the ingenious scheme. For almost a quarter of a century longer the raft continued to be a barrier to navigation, shutting out a large portion of rich and productive country from access to any market and greatly hindering the settlement of northern Texas, northern Louisiana, and southwestern Arkansas.[22]

In tracing the Red River to its source, government officers accomplished more definite results. Ever since the days of Jefferson's presidency, explorers had sought this elusive object. But for nearly fifty years, despite the expeditions of Freeman, Pike, and Long, the upper Red River Valley remained practically a *terra incognita* to the white man. With the acquisition of Texas and the Mexican Cession this waterway became vitally important as a link in the chain of frontier defense. Correct knowledge of its upper waters and source, it was believed, would enable the government to establish a series of military posts upon that stream and to transport supplies upon it into the very heart of the Comanche country. Construction of a good military road from its headwaters to the Rio Grande would greatly strengthen defense of that frontier. It would make the predatory tribes along its shores feel the power of the United States. Besides, it would protect emigrants to California and others passing to the West.[23] When in 1852 the government became convinced of the military importance of that stream it sent Captain Marcy to trace the river to its true source.

Marcy's successful experience on the western frontier for nearly a quarter of a century easily qualified him for this important undertaking. Senators Solon Borland and William K. Sebastian of Arkansas recommended him as the "one of all others . . . suitable . . . to conduct such a survey."[24] On March 5 official orders from the Adjutant General's office assigned Marcy to the command and Captain George B. McClellan of the Corps of Engineers as one of his principal aides. Marcy's instructions directed him to proceed with his company of fifty-five men as escort "to make an examination of the Red River and the country bordering upon it, from the mouth of Cache Creek to its sources." Supplemental instructions also required him to report on the military features of the country, the number, character, and habits of the Indians, and to collect and report everything useful or interesting in relation to the resources, soil, climate, natural history, and geography. The commander was particularly instructed to treat the natives with kindness but at the same time to impress upon them the military power of the government.[25]

Marcy organized the expedition at Fort Belknap, on the Brazos River, and on May 2 the command, including Company D of the Fifth Infantry and a long train of ox-teams, left for Cache Creek, some 200 miles above the last white settlement along the Red River.[26] It was an eleven days' march. Thus far the country appeared well suited for farming. The land along the stream was well timbered with oak, pecan, and other fine trees, and game was abundant. The men had excellent sport killing bears, panthers, antelopes, and buffaloes. Beyond Cache Creek the explorers traveled through new and unexplored territory, through a country enveloped in mystery, fable, and tradition. After journeying westward through a beautiful, wild, and dreary region, they struck the north fork of the Red River at the western extremity of the Wichita Mountains. Near Otter Creek, they met a hunting party of about 150 Wichita Indians under Canaje-Hexie. The old warrior warned Marcy that the country beyond was dry and barren. But the command pushed on. About the middle of June, after an arduous march across the Llano Estacado, the vanguard reached the sources of the north branch of Red River. In commemoration of the discovery Marcy placed a memorandum in a bottle and buried it under one of the largest cottonwood trees standing near the river. The memorandum read: "On the 16th day of June, 1852, an exploring expedition, composed of Captain R. B. Marcy, Captain G. B. McClellan, Lieutenant J. Updegraff, and Dr. G. G. Shumard, with fifty-five men of Company D fifth infantry, encamped here, having this day traced the north branch of the Red River to its sources. Accompanying the expedition were Captain J. H. Strain, of Fort Washita and Mr. J. R. Suydam, of New York city." Marcy then blazed the tree on the north and east sides, and marked upon the north side with a pencil: "Exploring Expedition, June 16, 1852."[27]

Marcy was not yet entirely satisfied. Desirous of testing and checking the accuracy of his own observations with those of previous surveys along the stream, he made a twenty-five mile excursion northward to the valley of the Canadian at Sand Creek. The side reconnaissance completed, the command pushed on to Hind Creek, where Marcy again left the main body and with Captain McClellan and a small escort ascended the Red River to the spring from which it originates. The source of the Red River had at last been found. The small band of intrepid explorers were "the first white men" to accomplish this feat. On July 4, its objective achieved, the expedition started on its homeward march and twenty-four days later entered Fort Arbuckle, the end of the trail.[28]

Before the explorers arrived at the post, a rumor had spread that a band of some 2,000 Comanches had attacked the command at Cache Creek and had completely annihilated it. The remoteness of the upper Red River country at this time is revealed by the fact that for several months the rumor about the "massacre" was generally accepted as true. Even the War Department confirmed it. Upon reaching home, Marcy learned that members of his family had given him up for dead, had put on mourning attire, and had held a memorial service for him. He had the novel experience of reading complimentary obituaries in the newspapers upon his own death. As a matter of fact, Marcy and his men had encountered no hostility whatever; they did not lose even a horse or a mule on the entire journey.[29]

The Red River expedition had proved highly successful. Not only had it accurately traced the sources of the river but it had brought to light considerable knowledge about a region hitherto practically unknown to the white man. Marcy's accurate and lucid descriptions of the geography, geology, and physical features of the country he traversed and of the Indians he met constitute one of the most valuable and interesting accounts in the literature of the western frontier. The importance of the report so impressed Congress that it had the document published. As produced in 1853, Marcy's journal of more than 100 pages, together with the vast amount of scientific data prepared either by members of his own staff or by scientists from a subsequent study of the material he

assembled, formed an invaluable source of information for other
explorers, emigrants, and soldiers, as well as for historians.[30] And
withal, the expedition marked another milestone in the defense of
the frontier.

The Colorado of the West, like the Red River, served as a link
in the chain of frontier defense. White men had visited its upper
valleys as early as the sixteenth century, when Coronado and his
fellow adventurers, in their search for the land of gold, ascended
the river some 240 miles above its mouth. But for more than three
centuries thereafter the region through which it flowed remained
as unknown "as if it were the center of Africa." In the nineteenth
century trappers and fur traders penetrating that region reported
that the stream was cañoned between high mountains and preci-
pices for a large portion of its course and that the country generally was arid, sandy, and barren.[31] After the Mexican War the
Great Colorado, like the Red River, at once became important as
a possible medium of transportation to the newly established military posts. Provisioning Fort Yuma by pack train from California,
for example, proved extremely difficult and expensive. Government officers soon embarked on extensive surveys of the Great
Colorado.[32]

The establishment of Camp Yuma at the mouth of the Gila
served as the occasion for the initial survey. Lieutenant George H.
Derby of the Topographical Engineers conducted the expedition.
Early in November, 1850, Derby sailed from San Francisco on the
United States transport "Invincible" with a crew of fourteen men
and provisions for Fort Yuma. An old twelve-pounder carronade
and six flintlock muskets comprised the armament. Rounding
Cape San Lucas and sailing northward, the vessel entered Guaymas, "a dirty place with a dirty population" of some 1,500 inhabi-
tants. Derby found cholera raging in Guaymas, but fortunately
he and his crew escaped the deadly scourge. By December 24 the
"Invincible" reached the mouth of the Colorado and on Christmas
Day the survey commenced. Derby discovered and named Gull

and Pelican Islands from the numerous flocks of birds which inhabited them. Early in January he reached Howard's Point, where he met the first group of Cocopa Indians. He won over the shy natives by bread and molasses and sent one of their chieftains with a letter to Major Heintzelman[33] at Fort Yuma. Ten days later, while ascending the river in a long boat, Derby met Heintzelman and considered his mission ended. In the latter part of January, Lieutenant Edward Murray with a small detachment of men and a wagon arrived at Howard's Point from Heintzelman's camp on the Gila and safely landed the provisions. Early in March, Derby was back in San Francisco.[34]

Derby had accomplished his object. In the "Invincible" he had ascended the river about twenty-five miles and in a long boat had paddled upstream sixty miles farther. The new route was at once put into operation. Within three years steamboat navigation on the lower Colorado was assured. Between December, 1852, and the autumn of 1854 the steamers "Uncle Sam," "General Jesup," and "Colorado" carried cargoes of freight between the mouth of the Colorado and Fort Yuma. This military post now obtained its supplies by a more economical and certain method than before, when the slow and laborious wagon and pack mule brought them across the desert from San Diego.[35]

Steam navigation on only the lower part of the Colorado was, of course, insufficient. The constant flow of emigration to the Southwest and the establishment of new military posts in California and in New Mexico and Utah Territories created a demand for river freighting above Fort Yuma. Major Heintzelman in command of the post at the mouth of the Gila was a champion of steam navigation on the upper reaches of the Colorado. In the autumn of 1852, when he led a punitive expedition against some troublesome tribes and ascended the river to almost a hundred miles below the Grand Cañon, he found navigation above its junction with the Gila not only practicable but "far superior to the Ohio." The Colorado, he felt confident, would ultimately afford the best route to the

Great Salt Lake country.[36] Four years later the California legislature memorialized Congress for a "complete and thorough exploration of the Colorado River of the West from Fort Yuma to
its source."[37] In the spring of the following year Lieutenant Joseph
C. Ives of the Topographical Engineers was directed to make the
survey.

On May 15, 1857, Ives received elaborate instructions directly
from the Secretary of War. Although steamboat navigation on the
river was the principal object of the survey, scientific research and
the collection of data on the geology, ethnology, and botany of
the region formed an integral part of Ives's assignment. The commanding officer was particularly well fitted both technically and
temperamentally for the difficult task. Coupled with a sense for
the humorous and picturesque was his unusual gift for description. The narrative portions of his voluminous report make de-
lightful reading.[38]

About the middle of October Ives assembled his corps of assistants at San Francisco. Distinguished members of the expedition
included Dr. J. S. Newberry in charge of obtaining data on the
natural history of the region, F. W. Egloffstein, topographer, who
had been with Frémont, and H. B. Mollhausen, artist, who had
been a member of the exploring party of Prince Paul of Würten-
berg.[39] Ives divided his men into three detachments. Two groups
proceeded by steamer to San Diego and San Pedro, respectively,
and thence across the desert to Fort Yuma; Ives led the third division, which went entirely by water. On November 1, with a small
escort and with A. J. Carroll of Philadelphia as steamboat engineer,
Ives embarked on the government transport "Monterey" and a
month later arrived at the mouth of the Colorado.[40]

There Ives and his party boarded the "Explorer," an iron
steamer some fifty feet in length which had been built in Philadelphia. This vessel, after a trial on the Delaware, had been shipped
in sections to San Francisco and then conveyed to the head of the
Gulf of Lower California on the "Monterey."[41] At midnight on

New Year's Eve the "Explorer" began to ascend the Colorado for Fort Yuma, about 150 miles from the head of the Gulf. For nine days the newly assembled steamer battled with sand bars, snags, shoals, shifting sands, and earthquakes but she arrived safely.[42]

Within two days after the steamer's arrival the three detachments of the expedition united, and Ives, with a command of twenty-four men, set out on the "Explorer" upon the unknown waters of the Colorado. Above the mouth of the Gila the course of the stream was crooked and the channel obstructed by numerous sand bars. For a considerable distance the river flowed through a desert of light sand which filled the air, penetrating everything —eyes, provisions, and even watches. A few miles above Fort Yuma the explorers came to the first range of mountains that closed in on the water, and suddenly they entered a narrow pass several hundred feet deep. This they named "Explorer's Pass." Emerging, the steamer glided through a small cañon which penetrated another range. The explorers now passed through the Chocolate Mountains. By February 1 they reached the mouth of Bill Williams' Fork in latitude 35°30'.[43]

At different points along the route they met bands of Cocopa, Yuma, Mohave, and Chemehuevi Indians, but none gave any trouble. Most of the natives seemed friendly and intent only upon begging and pilfering. In the Mohave Valley the natives visited Ives's camp, where a brisk trade and exchange of gifts took place. Ives spoke to the Indians but strangely enough his "talk" contained nothing about the "Great Father" at Washington. He told them only about the peaceful object of the expedition.[44]

Engaging Ireteba, an intelligent Mohave, as guide, Ives and his men continued up the river. After battling with treacherous rapids and encountering a fierce gale, the "Explorer" reached the mouth, or head, of Black Cañon just below the thirty-sixth parallel, the practical head of steam navigation.[45] At this point the vessel almost met with disaster when its bow jammed against a sunken rock. Although the crash threw several men overboard and caused some damage, the rock had not punctured the hull of the boat. The men were able to tow her to a sand bank for repairs.[46]

Ives next decided to explore the cañon. Accompanied by two companions in a skiff, he steadily worked his way upward over many rapids for about twenty-five miles to the great bend at Fortification Rock. Two miles farther brought him to Vegas Wash, the terminus of the survey. Ives considered the mouth of Black Cañon, some 500 miles above the mouth of the Colorado, the practical head of steamboat navigation.[47]

The whole expedition returned downstream to Beale's Crossing. From there Ives sent the "Explorer" with about half of his men to Fort Yuma while he and the remainder explored the Colorado Plateau. Moving northeastward across a region practically unknown, Ives and his assistants reached the mouth of the Grand Cañon early in April. Reconnoitering parties found their advance blocked by impassable obstacles, the plateau being "cut into shreds by gigantic chasms resembling a vast ruin." So desolate and barren was the region that even birds and reptiles deserted it. The explorers proceeded southeastward to the Little Colorado, passing through a beautiful country abounding in game; water and grass were plentiful. They then crossed the Painted Desert and arrived at the rich agricultural lands of the Moquis. On May 22 they reached Fort Defiance.[48]

But while the "Explorer" was battling her way upward from Fort Yuma, Captain George A. Johnson beat Ives to the mark. Owner and pilot of several steamers, Johnson had already had half a dozen years of experience in steamboat navigation on the Colorado, freighting government supplies from the mouth of the river to Fort Yuma. Early in January, 1858, anticipating Ives's northern journey, Johnson piloted his "General Jesup" all the way through Black Cañon. Thus Ives was deprived of the distinction of being the first to ascend the Colorado to this point; yet to him belongs the credit of being the first to make a careful, scientific survey, and the first to make a map of the river.[49] The scientific observations

Cavalry and Dragoons, 1855-58 (St. Louis Mercantile Library)

The "Explorer" (Engineers' Office, Washington)

Don Fernando de Taos, 1853 (Office of the Chief Signal Officer, Washington)

incident to his surveys made a definite contribution to the knowledge of a region heretofore unexplored, and his report set a new style for descriptive writing in the field of scientific exploration.[50]

The Ives expedition had definitely established the practicability of steamboat navigation on the upper Colorado and opened a new medium of transportation in the Southwest. In the sixties the new artery saved thousands of dollars in the cost of freighting military stores and gave fresh impetus to the development of the resources of Arizona. And in the valley of the upper Colorado many flourishing Mormon settlements came into being.[51] The surveys of the western rivers, supplementing the land explorations, served not only as a medium of frontier defense but also as an aid in the settlement and growth of the Far Southwest.[52]

CHAPTER VI

Explorations for Defense

EXPLORATIONS formed an integral and major part of the government's policy of frontier defense. Ever since the days of Pike's expedition to the Southwest, American commercial interests in Mexico had been steadily growing. By the twenties and thirties the Southwest Overland trade had already assumed considerable proportions. Commercial caravans, composed of between seventy and 350 men and hundreds of wagons loaded with dry goods, hardware, and wet goods (whiskey), annually plied a lucrative trade between Franklin (later Independence), Missouri, and Santa Fe.[1] Adventurous American traders penetrated to Chihuahua while others established commercial relations between Santa Fe and the Pacific.[2] In the forties the Chihuahua and Santa Fe trade amounted to several million dollars annually. But since the cost of transportation by the old trails was extremely high, the opening of new commercial routes became very desirable. "To divert this trade and to control it," declared Dr. John S. Ford, a prominent Texan, "was an inducement of no ordinary character." When to the exigencies of trade were added those of defense, a program of exploration became imperative.[3]

Texas was an urgent and fruitful field. A considerable portion of Texas, to be sure, had already been explored. Spaniards, scouts, rangers, Indian agents, and other frontiersmen had penetrated most of it. But the information they obtained was neither exact enough nor well organized enough to be of great value. Hence, much of Texas was generally unknown at the close of the war with Mexico. An exploration program carried on by citizens of the state and contingents of the United States army was soon under way.

Six months after the treaty of Guadalupe Hidalgo some enterprising citizens of San Antonio, desiring to establish direct commercial communication with northern Mexico, sent Colonel John C. Hays of the Texas Rangers to find a practicable wagon road from San Antonio to Chihuahua via El Paso. The expense of the expedition, about $800, was raised by subscription in Bexar County. A practicable route across west Texas, it was believed, would prove of incalculable value, since a considerable portion of the Missouri-Santa Fe-Chihuahua trade would be diverted to Texas and troops could be moved to and from the Rio Grande frontier with greater ease. The Missouri-Santa Fe-Chihuahua traders and the military men awaited the report of the Hays expedition with great interest.[4]

John Coffee Hays, the leader of the expedition, was a true frontiersman and typical Indian fighter. Born in Tennessee of fighting stock, he left his native state at the age of about fifteen and came to Mississippi, where he surveyed its many swamp lands. Shortly after the Texas Revolution broke out, he came to Texas and within the next few years divided his time between surveying and fighting Indians. When the legislature of the new republic created the famous Texas Rangers, Hays, then only twenty-three years of age, received the chief command above older and more experienced officers. The fame of his exploits soon extended from the Brazos to the Rio Grande and from the Gulf to the headwaters of the Red and Colorado rivers. During the War with Mexico Hays and his Rangers proved a terror to the Mexicans. When the gold fever struck Texas the adventurous Hays set out for California, where he was elected sheriff of San Francisco County. In 1853 he became surveyor general of California. Hays had his last Indian fight in 1860 when he defeated and scattered the Paiutes in the "Washoe War." This rather small, modest, and retiring frontiersman, who thought much and spoke little, had a most remarkable control over men; all types—hunters, trappers, soldiers, surveyors, and adventurers—"yielded passive resistance and complete obedience to him." To the frontier settlers, "Colonel Jack" was a "tower of strength."[5]

Towards the latter part of August, 1848, this celebrated Indian fighter and a small party of Texans started on the exploring mission, with Chihuahua as their objective. Marching northward from San Antonio to a military camp on the Llano River, they were soon joined by a military escort of Rangers under another famous frontiersman, Captain Samuel Highsmith.[6] Early in September the combined force, now numbering some seventy men, struck out westward till they reached the Rio Grande. Because of the ignorance of their Indian guide the explorers lost their way and suffered many hardships. Food giving out, they were compelled to eat their horses and mules, as well as panthers, polecats, and snakes. They suffered from lack of water. On October 15 the emaciated band crossed the Rio Grande from the southern part of the present Brewster County, Texas, and moved northward to the Mexican town of San Carlos, where they secured supplies. The explorers reached Presidio del Norte[7] on October 22, after an arduous march of more than fifty days. Again recrossing the Rio Grande into the United States, Hays and his band spent ten days near Fort Leaton,[8] recruiting supplies and animals. Too fatigued to continue the rest of the journey, the expedition started on the homeward march.

From Presidio del Norte the explorers pursued a northeasterly course along the Sierra Madre range to the Pecos and thence southeast to San Antonio, arriving at their destination on December 10. The expedition had been away more than a hundred days and had traveled about 700 miles. Three members did not return. A Dr. Wahm, who had become insane from starvation, was believed to have perished in the mountains but returned to the settlements in the following year.[9] Both Hays and Highsmith reported that a practicable wagon route existed from San Antonio to the San Sabá River and thence northwestward across the Pecos to El Paso. According to Hays, he and his men were the first Americans ever to traverse that route. Government explorers, merchants, and emigrants soon followed the new trail; military encampments, mail stations, and settlements sprang up along the line of travel.[10] Four days after Hays's return the citizens of San Antonio celebrated his achievement with a ball in his honor.[11]

The War Department, meanwhile, inaugurated a program of exploration in Texas that eclipsed anything that could be sponsored by private enterprise. On the same day that Hays returned to San Antonio, Secretary of War Marcy ordered Brevet Major General William J. Worth to the Texas frontier. Worth, who was to become commander of the Eighth and Ninth Military Departments, was directed to station troops on the line of the Rio Grande and to explore the country along the left bank of the river and between San Antonio and Santa Fe, to determine the existence of a practicable route for "troops, munitions of war, etc."[12]

Shortly after his arrival in Texas, Worth proceeded to carry out his instructions. On February 9, 1849, he ordered Lieutenant Whiting of the Engineers and Lieutenant William F. Smith of the Topographical Engineers to reconnoiter Hays's trail to Presidio del Norte and thence to El Paso for a practicable and convenient military and commercial route between El Paso and the Gulf via Austin or San Antonio. Failing to find a suitable wagon road, the explorers were to return by a more direct route along the Pecos and San Sabá rivers. Assistant Adjutant General George Deas favored the Hays trail, for, he believed, it would induce settlement and readily furnish supplies to the proposed military posts along that line.[13]

Whiting's party of fifteen men, including experienced woodsmen and hunters, left San Antonio on February 12, but heavy rains, blustering winds, and wild mules made the first week's travel extremely slow. From the German settlement of Fredericksburg, Whiting led his men northwestward across the Llano River to the San Sabá and thence southwestward across the Pecos to the Rio Grande. As far as the headwaters of the San Sabá the explorers found the country well timbered and watered and well adapted for a good wagon road, but between the San Sabá and the Pecos there was a great scarcity of water. In the gullies of Cibolo Creek in present Presidio County Jack Hunter, the Delaware guide, killed a "very old, very lean, and very tough panther," which, however, proved a veritable godsend to the famished pathfinders. West of the Pecos the men were surrounded by several hundred hostile Apaches. Although the Indians did not attack, the small band escaped a bloody fight if not a disastrous defeat only by a ruse—Whiting kept his night fires burning while his men rapidly and silently marched away. The explorers spent five days at Leaton's Fort and then resumed the journey, traveling up the east bank of the Rio Grande. After fourteen days of toil through the wild mountains of the Apaches the small, weary band arrived at Ponce's Ranch opposite El Paso del Norte on April 12. Here the tired eyes of the rugged travelers, who had seen nothing but wild and desolate scenery, again beheld "houses, pleasant vineyards, grain and wheat fields."

After a week's rest the expedition started homeward. The commanding officers had intended to return by the same trail, but the scarcity of water between the San Sabá and the Pecos led them to adopt a more southerly route. Leaving Ponce's Ranch, the explorers traveled down the east bank of the Rio Grande for about 120 miles and then turned to the Pecos, whose course they followed for about sixty miles. While plodding southeastward, they encountered a drove of wild hogs on whose roasted ribs the hungry men soon feasted. But the savory feast was rudely interrupted by a terrific hailstorm and then by a none too friendly Indian visit. Near Comanche Spring some thirty Lipan Apaches under their Chief Capote dashed toward Whiting's camp in anticipation of easy plunder, but seeing that the white men were quite prepared to "rub the Indians out," the warriors professed friendship and withdrew. The remainder of the journey was without incident. The trail blazers arrived in San Antonio on May 25. They had found a new route to the West.[14]

While Whiting and Smith led their exploring party to El Paso, the citizens of Austin co-operated with General Worth in sending a joint exploring expedition under the celebrated Major Neighbors and Dr. John S. Ford. Late in February, 1849, Neighbors received orders from General Worth to examine the country between the Pecos and El Paso. A month later nine men, composed largely of friendly Indians and citizens of Austin,[15] assembled at Barnards' (or Torrey's) Trading House near the site of Waco to set out on the adventure. Crossing the Brazos, the explorers struck out northward and westward, and after spending about a week at Shanco's Comanche camp on the Colorado, continued their march to Horsehead Crossing. The small band reached the Pecos about the middle of April. Two weeks later the explorers arrived at San Elizario and on May 2 entered El Paso.

On the return march the expedition proceeded eastward by way of the Waco Tanks[16] and the Guadalupe Mountains to the Pecos River. The remainder of the journey it traveled by way of Horsehead Crossing, the Concho, the San Sabá, and the Llano rivers, reaching San Antonio on June 2. In their expedition Neighbors and Ford had passed near the spots where Belton and Waco were later built. They had traveled farther north than Whiting and Smith, but near El Paso their routes had merged.[17]

The journey had not been without discomfort. In mid-April a terrific norther with heavy sleet and snow struck the travelers at the head of the Concho. Near the Rio Grande "huge swarms of the most voracious mosquitoes that ever drew blood from man" invaded the encampment, "crawling under blankets and thrusting their bills an inch or so into the bodies of sleepless wights." The "hissing of huge rattlers" in a gulch close by added little to the peace of mind of the weary band. But Neighbors and Ford accomplished their mission.[18]

The return routes of Neighbors and Ford and of Whiting and Smith soon became known as the Upper and Lower roads, respectively. A new avenue of trade and transportation between San Antonio and El Paso, especially via the Lower route, was soon in full operation.[19] A section of country hitherto deemed impassable was open to the emigrant, the merchant, and the soldier. Before the completion of the transcontinental railroad the Lower road was used regularly by troops, government and commercial trains, the Overland Mail and Stage, Texas cattle drovers, and settlers migrating to New Mexico, Arizona, and California.[20]

In the fall of 1849, Lieutenant Smith explored the Organ and Sacramento Mountains above El Paso and found them practicable for wagon trains.[21] To determine the strength of future military posts, Lieutenant Whiting reconnoitered the central portion of the state between Eagle Pass on the Rio Grande and Coffee's Bend near the mouth of the False Washita.[22] Lieutenant Nathaniel Michler of the Topographical Engineers made two important reconnaissances. In the southwest he opened a new route between Corpus Christi and Fort Inge; his track across northern Texas, extending from Fort Washita some 500 miles southwestward to the Pecos, connected the frontier settlements of Arkansas with El Paso.[23]

During the decade 1850-60 these and other army officers and engineers penetrated other unexplored portions of the state as they searched for shorter and better routes, led punitive expeditions against the wild tribes, selected sites for military posts and reservations, and experimented with camels as a medium of military transportation. In the early fifties Lieutenants M. L. Smith, Michler, and Francis T. Bryan examined large sections of country extending from Fort Merrill in the south to Forts Belknap and Graham in the north.[24] Lieutenant Duff Green, attached to the United States-Mexican Boundary Survey Commission, reconnoitered the Rio Grande country between San Elizario and Fort Duncan.[25] Brevet Lieutenant Colonel Joseph E. Johnston and General Persifor F. Smith, the latter commander of the Eighth Military Department, made tours of military inspection from the headwaters of the Nueces northeastward to Fort Belknap. In the fall of 1852, General Smith, accompanied by Captain George McClellan, also examined a considerable portion of the central and southwestern Texas frontier. Their six weeks' tour of hard and rapid riding, extending from Corpus Christi to Camp Johnston on the Concho, eastward to the head of the Colorado, and then westward and southwestward to Eagle Pass and Laredo on the Rio Grande, was through a "perfect wilderness." Except at the garrisons, the men did not see a house on the entire journey until they reached Laredo.[26]

In searching for feasible sites for Indian reservations, Captain Marcy, who had already become famous for opening a new trail to Santa Fe and for tracing the Red River to its source, explored a vast stretch of uninhabited country along the sources of the Brazos and Big Wichita rivers. Late in June, 1854, Marcy organized an elaborate command at Fort Washita. With a caravan consisting of the special Indian Agent Robert S. Neighbors, W. B. Parker, the geologist Dr. George G. Shumard, Indian guides, interpreters, hunters, and forty men of the Seventh Infantry, with nine wagons, he struck out southwestward toward Fort Belknap. The trail to the Little Wichita led through Preston, at that time a "collection of low groggeries and few stores," through the upper and lower Cross Timbers and across a beautiful, picturesque, and rolling country abounding in game.[27] On July 21, Marcy left his wagon train and with a small escort set out on an excursion to Red River. This twenty-five-mile reconnaissance trip was across a barren and uninviting country. Eight days later Marcy left his command a second time and with a small pack train headed for the waters of the Big Wichita and Brazos. Traveling westward over a sandy and barren valley and steep bluffs, he reached the source of the Big Wichita and then struck out southward across a mountainous country to the head of the Brazos. The weary explorers, suffering intensely from the lack of water, continued southeastward until they struck the Qua-qua-he-no, or Paint Creek. Shortly after Marcy returned to the Brazos, the entire command moved to the Clear Fork of that stream, where surveying parties actively engaged in running and marking the lines. Early in September the command was back in Fort Belknap.[28]

Marcy added another achievement to his list of military ac-

complishments. In addition to locating two Indian reservations
on the main stream and Clear Fork of the Brazos,[29] he showed
that the headwaters of the Brazos and Big Wichita rivers drained
a wild and barren country. He explored no less than sixteen of
the present counties of northwest Texas.[30]

Other army officers in the later fifties supplemented the work
of Marcy and his fellow explorers. Lieutenants Hartz, Wood,
Hazen, and Echols, operating mainly in the "Big Bend" sector,
penetrated sections of country then little known.[31] These pathfinders, both the officers of the government and the men of science
in their reports, journals, and maps vividly described the character
of the land they traversed, and added considerably to the knowledge of north and west Texas—findings which ultimately led to
the white man's mastery over the Indian.

In the Territory of New Mexico army officers carried on a
similar program in the interest of frontier defense. When Kearny
left Santa Fe for California, Lieutenants James W. Abert and
William G. Peck of the Topographical Engineers remained behind with instructions to explore the Rio Grande country. Starting from Santa Fe early in October, 1846, with a small escort and
supply train, these officers spent three months in the field, examining the region on both sides of the Rio Grande as far south as
the ruins of Valverde. On the west bank of the river they examined the Rio Jemez, the Puerco, and the Rio San Jose, and visited
the pueblos of Moquino, Laguna, and Acoma. Their explorations
on the east side of the Rio Grande embraced the region between
the river and the ruins of Abo and the towns of Quarai, Manzano,
Torreon, and Chilili.

Abert's report, describing in detail the topography, inhabitants,
and plant and animal life of the region, proved highly valuable.
East of the Rio Grande, it stated, travel was comparatively easy,
but west of the river the explorers had had to plow through deep
sands and rough wilds. The Mexican inhabitants in the small villages, Abert found unusually kind, ceremonious and polite, but
extremely ignorant and deceitful. He met no hostile Indians but

heard many rumors of Navaho depredations. Near Joya the country was in a great state of alarm. The engineers found "the road
lined with *voluntarios* hurrying to the rendezvous." At Sabino, to
the south, many New Mexicans had already assembled, armed
with muskets and escopettes (*escopetas*).[32]

Three years later when Brevet Lieutenant Colonel Washington
led his punitive expedition into the Navaho country,[33] Lieutenant
Simpson, who was Washington's chief reconnaissance officer, and
his assistant surveyors made careful observations along the line of
march. From Santa Fe their route extended westward to Jemez
and thence northwest "over and through a series of arroyos,
cañons, mesas, and mountain passes . . . to the mouth of the re-
nowned Cañon de Chelly." All along the route Simpson examined
many pueblo ruins. *Pueblo Pintado* he believed originally to have
had four stories and as many as 800 rooms, and the ruins of Chaco
Cañon may have been the remains of the Aztecs of the twelfth
century. Upon reaching Cañon de Chelly, Simpson explored the
interior for a distance of about nine miles above its mouth and
dispelled the current notion of its being an impregnable fortress.
Indian Agent James S. Calhoun, a member of the expedition, reported the cañon "rich in fields of grain, rich in vegetables and
peach orchards." The return route lay more to the south, by way
of the pueblos of Zuñi and Laguna and Albuquerque.

Simpson described the region between Santa Fe and the Tunicha Mountains as "one extended, naked, barren, waste," but he
believed that a practicable wagon road could be constructed between Santa Fe and Zuñi. Such a road, he thought, would make
an excellent route to Los Angeles, and would shorten the distance
about 300 miles. Simpson also recommended the establishment of
a military post at Cebolletita, a strategic position about midway between Zuñi and Santa Fe. From a military point of view Colonel
Washington's expedition had not proved successful, but it was
not without its value. Troops had penetrated the heart of the
Indian country, and Simpson's explorations, carefully recorded in
his journal and accompanied by an excellent map and colored

drawings, added accurate geographical knowledge valuable for future military maneuvers, as well as for the emigrant.[34]

In the spring of 1850 Captain Henry B. Judd of the Third Artillery, while reconnoitering for a site for a military post, explored the Pecos Valley for about 200 miles, from Las Vegas to the southern extremity of the *Bosque Grande.* The noted photographer R. H. Kern and young Pierre Melicourt Papin[35] accompanied the expedition. With the exception of two famous *bosques,* or forests, the country Judd traversed was destitute of timber, but the plains and tablelands on both banks of the Pecos were covered with the finest buffalo and grama grass. Wide and fertile bottom lands lay along the river, and game and fish were abundant. About 130 miles below Las Vegas the reconnoitering party entered the *Bosque Redondo,* or round forest. In this wooded area Indians and traders from the settlements carried on a brisk trade. Each year from May till August this neutral ground was covered with Indian lodges and horses. About sixty miles to the south lay *Bosque Grande,* "great forest."

Judd considered both *bosques* highly suitable for military positions, particularly for mounted troops. He also urged the establishment, in the *Bosque Redondo,* of a trading house where the Indians could secure necessary supplies; the illicit traffic in firewater, arms, and other forbidden articles, as then carried on, could thus be abolished.[36] Judd's recommendation for the establishment of a military post on the Pecos was not carried out until the time of the Civil War,[37] but his reconnaissance added materially to the knowledge of the upper Pecos Valley.

As already described in a previous chapter, in the fall of 1851 Captain Sitgreaves led an exploring party from Santa Fe to Fort Yuma via the Zuñi and Colorado rivers and opened a new trail across the northern part of the present state of Arizona.[38] Two years later Brevet Major James B. Carleton of the First Dragoons made a topographic and geographic reconnaissance of the upper Rio Grande Valley, to explore the country and to impress upon the roving, thieving Apaches the power of the white man's government. With an imposing force of a hundred men and one twelve-pounder mountain howitzer Carleton left Albuquerque on December 14, 1853, for the Gran Quivira country. His line of march almost coincided with Abert's route east of the Rio Grande seven years earlier. He moved southward to Casa Colorada and then turned east to the ruins of Abo and Gran Quivira. Striking out northwestward, he passed rapidly through the settlements of Manzano, Torreon, Tagique, and Chilili. He was back in Albuquerque on Christmas Eve.

Carleton's impressions of the New Mexican population were not very flattering. In the dirty little villages picturesque and grotesque inhabitants turned out en masse to get a glimpse of the soldiers. "Some blanketed, with sombreros and cigarritos: some with white washed and some with scarlet-dyed faces; some with *rebosos,* some nearly naked"—these were the natives whom Carleton met.[39] In not a single rancho or village along the Rio Grande did he find an indication of industry, cleanliness, or thrift. Indolence, squalid poverty, filth, and utter ignorance of everything beyond the cornfields and *acequias* were characteristic of the inhabitants along the east bank of the river. Of all the New Mexican settlements, Manzano had the least savory reputation. It harbored "more murderers, robbers, common thieves, scoundrels and vile, abandoned women," Carleton declared, "than any other town of its size in New Mexico"; it did not possess a single redeeming trait.[40]

Carleton was unable to impress or to intimidate the troublesome Indians, who, upon learning of his approach, had gone far to the south. He had, however, secured valuable information about the country and its people. The Mescalero Apaches, he learned, numbered only about 200 warriors, but they had many good rifles and were excellent shots. In peace times they lived in small groups or families, but in times of war they united.[41] Carleton's expedition also dispelled the notion that Gran Quivira had once been the seat of an ancient Indian civilization. The skill, taste, and opulence formerly attributed to the ancient Indian inhabitants he believed a figment of the imagination. He thought that probably Gran Quivira, as well as Abo and Quarai, had been built under the direction of Spanish conquerors and missionaries of the sixteenth century and represented Spanish rather than native Indian culture.[42]

For three years after Carleton's examination of the Rio Grande country there was a lull in official explorations in the Department of New Mexico; then the movement was revived with considerable vigor. During 1857-59, Beale conducted his two expeditions along the thirty-fifth parallel,[43] and in 1859 army officers reconnoitered almost every portion of the territory.

In the summer of 1859, Captain John N. Macomb, a member of the Topographical Engineers who had been active in surveys along the Great Lakes and in New Mexico for more than a dozen years,[44] led an expedition from Santa Fe to southern Utah to ascertain the practicability of opening a wagon road. Accompanied by a detachment of infantry and by several assistants, among them Dr. John S. Newberry, a famous scientist, Macomb crossed the Rio Grande at the old Indian pueblo of San Juan and struck out northwestward. While marching up the valley of the Rio Chama, Macomb was joined by Albert H. Pfeiffer, subagent for the Utah Indians, and his interpreter, Noponiocino Valdez, who escorted the explorers safely through the country of the Capotes and other Utah bands. To the north of Abiquiu opened a "picturesque valley bounded by cliffs of varied and brilliant colors," but when the explorers crossed the San Juan River (in about thirty-seven degrees north latitude), the scene changed. For nearly 200 miles Macomb and his men now laboriously trudged over a gloomy, barren country, intersected by rapid mountain streams, until they came to *Ojo Verde,* about 340 miles from Santa Fe. At this point the commander left the main body and with a small escort advanced to within about six miles of the junction of the Grand and Green rivers. Here he was compelled to turn back. On its return march the expedition took a course somewhat to the south, and arrived in Santa Fe early in October.

Macomb had explored the country between the Spanish Trail on the north and Beale's wagon route along the thirty-fifth parallel, but he had found no practicable route that could connect the New Mexican settlements with those of southern Utah.[45] His reconnaissance, however, like those of his fellow officers, added valuable geographical and scientific information. Macomb's map was the first to give a correct idea of the now celebrated San Juan country, and the report of Professor Newberry, who had accompanied him, was the first to present an accurate account of the geology of the region.[46]

Meanwhile, the energetic Colonel Bonneville, then in command of the Department of New Mexico, sent out a series of exploring parties to examine the condition of the roads, to note suitable sites for military posts, and to overawe the Indians. Lieutenant Alexander E. Steen of the Third Infantry led a detachment of forty men from Fort Garland eastward to Bent's Fort, and then westward from Fort Garland to the Rio Grande and up that stream to the San Juan Mountains. Steen reported practicable wagon roads.[47] In an attempt to find a pass through the Sierra Blanca Mountains, Captain Thomas Claiborne of the Mounted Rifles conducted 120 men eastward from Fort Stanton to the Pecos and northward to Hatch's Ranch.[48] Lieutenant W. H. Jackson, with a command of some fifty Mounted Rifles, explored the country from Anton Chico northeastward to Rabbit Ear Creek on the main road from Independence.[49] Lieutenant Henry M. Lazelle, commander of the escort to the Texas-New Mexico Boundary Commission, accompanied by a train of twenty-two wagons loaded with 57,000 pounds of freight, examined the region from Anton Chico to the Pecos and southward along that stream to Fort Lancaster, Texas.[50] In the meantime, Brevet Major W. H. Gordon with an organization of more than a hundred men, conducted an expedition westward from Fort Fillmore to the Burro Mountains to select a site for a military post and to overawe the

Apaches.[51] Scouting parties also examined the country to the east and west of Fort Defiance, in the direction of Cañon de Chelly and the Moqui villages.[52]

The defense program in California, like that in Texas and New Mexico, necessarily involved explorations. One group of army officers and Indian officials conducted reconnoitering expeditions to find shorter and better routes, as well as suitable sites for military posts and reservations; others toured the country to determine the condition of the Indian tribes and the mining districts. Colonel Richard B. Mason, commander of the Tenth Military Department, inaugurated the program when, in the summer of 1848, he made the first official tour through the northern mining district. Accompanied by Lieutenant William T. Sherman and an escort of cavalry, Mason left Monterey on June 17 and proceeded northward to Bodega and then eastward to Sutter's Fort. Traveling about twenty-five miles up the American Fork to the Mormon diggings, he completed his examination at Sutter's Mill on the South Fork of the American. A month later he was back in Monterey.[53]

Mason's report, accompanied by sketches of the mining country, threw considerable light on conditions in Upper California. He estimated that upwards of 4,000 men were working in the gold districts, of whom more than half were Indians, and that from $30,000 to $50,000 of the precious metal was mined daily. His opinion that the California gold supply was virtually inexhaustible and that the amount soon to be mined would pay for the Mexican War a hundredfold proved to be substantially correct.[54] But the gold discovery, Mason shrewdly observed, was not an unmixed evil; the gold fever had greatly changed the character of Upper California. An agricultural and pastoral people had rushed to the mines overnight; laborers and tradesmen had left their shops; soldiers and sailors had deserted their garrisons and ships. Wages and prices had soared skyward; mechanics spurned offers of less than $15 and $20 per day. But despite these chaotic conditions and

Engineer, Footrifles, Dragoon, Light Artillery, Infantry, 1851-54 (St. Louis Mercantile Library)

Fort Yuma, California (Office of the Chief Signal Officer, Washington)

The Presidio of San Francisco (1849?) (Office of the Chief Signal Officer, Washingt‹

the feverish state of mind of the inhabitants, Mason found comparative law and order at the mines. In the summer months of 1848 he reported crime infrequent and no thefts or robberies in the gold districts.[55] With the rapid influx of prospectors and miners, however, waves of lawlessness soon swept over the mining country, and the California Indian was to pay a heavy price.

In 1849, General Bennet Riley, the new commander of the department and ex-officio provincial governor of California, examined a portion of the San Joaquin and Sacramento valleys to study the character of the country and to select a site for a military post. Like other officers of the period, Riley had a long and distinguished military career. Born of obscure parents in 1787 in Virginia or Maryland, he at first served as foreman in a shoemaker's shop in Baltimore and then as a sailor aboard a privateer. In 1813 he entered the army as Ensign Rifleman from Maryland, saw active service at Sackett's Harbor, New York, and five years later attained a captaincy. During the next quarter century he saw service on many frontiers. In the early twenties he fought with Lieutenant Colonel Henry Leavenworth in the Arikara campaign. When the Santa Fe trade became prominent he commanded the first military escort across the plains to protect the traders. He participated in the Black Hawk and Seminole Wars and for his distinguished record in the Mexican War he was brevetted twice —brigadier general and then major general. As commander of the Tenth Military Department and provincial governor he called the convention which framed the first California constitution. In commemoration of "his many gallant acts . . . and of the long and arduous services . . . upon the frontier," the Missouri legislature presented him a sword.[56]

This stern but chivalrous and likable officer early in July, 1849, left Monterey for the mining country, accompanied by Lieutenant George H. Derby of the Topographical Engineers, three other officers, and a small escort with pack mules. Moving eastward through Pacheco's Pass, Riley and his party crossed the San Joaquin and struck out northward for the mineral region on the headwaters of the Tuolumne, the Stanislaus, and the Sacramento rivers. After examining the Sacramento Valley for some eighty miles above its confluence with the American, he advanced as far east as Colluma on the South Fork of the American, where the reconnaissance terminated. The examination showed that, except in a few localities, along the borders of the streams, the country between the Stanislaus and Sacramento was exceedingly hilly and dry, for the most part consisting of arid plains unfit for cultivation. In the Lake Tulare country Riley found many independent Indian bands who he believed would be difficult to control unless troops were stationed in their midst. Riley also reported three possible routes by which supplies could be sent into the interior.[57]

The Bureau of Topographical Engineers also had a number of its officers actively engaged in explorations. Captain William H. Warner, who had been attached to Major Emory's military reconnoitering party, operating from Fort Leavenworth to San Diego in 1846-47, made extensive examinations of routes along the Pacific and the coast range of mountains, from San Diego to San Francisco. Before he had completed his map of the Pacific coast range, he was directed to make an exploration in the Sierra Nevada to discover a northern and, if possible, a better route from Sacramento to Salt Lake and the Mormon settlements.

In July, 1849, Warner assembled the nucleus of his command at Benicia but it was not until a month later that he got under way. At Sacramento he engaged François Berçier, an intelligent half-breed, as guide and with about a dozen men, wagons, and pack mules, proceeded up the Sacramento Valley to Peter Lassen's Rancho on Deer Creek. Here Warner spent a few days jerking beef until a military escort of eighty men arrived. But finding it impracticable to conduct such a large force through the mountains, he took some thirty men and about eighty animals and struck out eastward across the mountains and then northward to the source of Pit River. While passing through the mountains, the expedition met an advance guard of some 10,000 to 20,000 emigrants who were hurrying to the California gold diggings. Embarrassed by sickness, lacking sturdy pack mules, and wishing to avoid the late season, Warner decided to leave part of his command in charge of Lieutenant R. S. Williamson in camp near Goose Lake while he and a small party of nine men with ten days' provisions pushed on about sixty miles northward. Arriving at Lake Abert, Warner followed the east branch of the Sierra Nevada, where he discovered a pass practicable for a wagon road and railway.

Though Warner's expedition had accomplished its object it had a tragic ending. On September 26, in about forty-two degrees latitude, as the small party was moving southward, with the commander and his guide in the lead, about forty Pit River Indians suddenly rose up and poured a shower of deadly arrows into the expedition. Pierced by nine arrows, Warner died almost instantly; two of his men received mortal wounds. The survivors abandoned the reconnaissance; Lieutenant Williamson with the remnant of the party returned to Benicia. Fortunately, Captain Warner's notebooks were saved, and from them a sketch of the route and a report were later made by Lieutenant Williamson. The Warner range of mountains in Modoc County, California, was named in honor of the martyred engineer-explorer.[58]

Only four days before Warner met his tragic death, Lieutenant Derby conducted a reconnoitering party into the Sacramento Valley to assist in establishing a military post on Bear Creek, and to survey and mark out an Indian reservation. Leaving Sacramento City, with a small group of men, Derby moved northward to Bear Creek and, after examining the country for some twenty-five miles and making a map of the reservation, he crossed the Yuba and proceeded northwestward until he struck Butte Creek. There the reconnaissance ended. On the return march Derby passed many emigrant wagons with "dirty and unhappy-looking women and unwholesome children." Along the various streams he had met about 1,000 Indians, who were "ugly, harmless, and inoffensive

. . . but [who] being barbarous . . . might commit at any moment some unexpected outrage." Derby was back in Sacramento City early in November. He had marked out an Indian reservation and located a site for a military post on Bear Creek on the thirty-ninth parallel.[59]

Between April and June of the following year Derby, with a small topographic party, a guide, and a military escort, explored about 285 miles of the Tulare Valley country. His operations were carried on to ascertain the practicability of opening a wagon road in the Tulare Valley and to determine the feasibility of a military post in the vicinity of Lake Tulare. Early in June he completed the reconnaissance.

Derby reported to Colonel Abert that a good road connected San Miguel and San Luis Obispo and that three passes were available through the coast range. In the Tulare Valley, however, a wagon road was impracticable, for the major part of that country was a barren waste. The Buena Vista Lake region he considered a decided misnomer, since that body of water, for miles, was nearly surrounded with tule, a flooded, forlorn, desolate country.[60] Early in May when the explorers encamped there, insects and reptiles of all sizes and descriptions made life virtually unbearable. Mosquitoes tormented the men by day and goaded them to madness by night. The Lake Taché region to the north was no better—a miserable, barren desert, with no inhabitants but rabbits and gophers. The only point suitable for a military post in the entire valley was a small portion of land contained by the five creeks of the Francis River.

With the Indians of the region, Derby was favorably impressed. Of the 4,000 natives occupying the valley, those of the lower country, who came in contact with the white men, were inclined to be friendly. In crossing the many sloughs surrounding the Ton Taché Lake and the treacherous creeks of the Francis River country, Derby was greatly assisted by the natives, whom he rewarded with provisions, "some dirty shirts, stockings, and worn out boots," which of course, the Indians prized very highly.

Even the less friendly bands, Derby believed, could easily be kept in subjection by a small military force and by kind treatment. To keep the hill tribes in check, he recommended the establishment of a military post on the Francis River.[61]

Official explorations in the Utah country have already been described in an earlier chapter. Captain Stansbury and his assistants explored the Great Salt Lake and Utah Lake and observed some 5,000 square miles of territory. Lieutenant Beale opened a new trail across southern Utah, leading from the Huerfano River to the Little Salt Lake. Captain Simpson opened new wagon routes across the Great Basin of Utah from Camp Floyd to Carson Valley.[62]

In the dozen years preceding the Civil War the federal government had completed the major part of its exploration program. Army officers and engineers, in the course of their tours of inspection and reconnaissance for shorter or better routes, and during their surveys for military posts and reservations, and visits to the Indian tribes, had explored and mapped the least-known portions of the Far Southwest and had contributed information about hitherto unknown sections of country. They had accurately charted mountain, cañon, desert, river, and waterhole, as well as practicable and impracticable routes. The gold-seeker, the pioneer, the merchant, or the soldier could now travel to his destination with greater ease and safety. The Far Southwest was no longer a *terra incognita*. Official explorations formed a major link in the chain of frontier defense.

CHAPTER VII

Life of the Soldier on the Frontier

AMONG the heroic figures who have helped to build our nation, few have exerted a greater influence than the American soldier. From the days of the American Revolution to the late nineteenth century, he played a major role in extending our western frontier. Always stationed on the extreme edge of the settlements, he has been ever on the move—ever gathering information of the country beyond. Shortly after the Louisiana Purchase, the army penetrated the Indian country, explored the new region, and attempted to pacify the tribes by peace treaties or by punitive expeditions. Towards the middle of the century, when the domain reached the Pacific, the army became scattered over a vast area, and its activities multiplied. The discovery of gold in California made additional demands on the frontier army. In answering calls for defense, the troops stationed in the West performed a unique service for the nation. Between the Mexican and the Civil Wars they protected the emigrant, the frontier settler, and the Overland Mail. They opened new trails, built roads, surveyed the principal western rivers as well as routes for transcontinental railroads, mapped international and territorial boundaries, and overawed the Mormons.[1]

Indeed, these seem to be herculean tasks, to be performed by a gigantic force. The tasks were tremendous, but the size of the force was far from adequate. Besides, the conditions under which the soldier on the frontier lived and worked—his quarters and food, his manifold duties, his recreation and his punishment—shed additional light on the problem of defense in the Far West and tell a story of great human interest.

Prior to the Mexican War the United States army did not exceed 6,500 men.[2] This small force, distributed along the Atlantic seaboard, the Great Lakes, and the western frontier, occupied more than a hundred scattered posts and stations.[3] The army was temporarily increased during the Mexican War, reaching a peak strength of more than 47,000 men by 1848.[4] But upon the restoration of peace it was again reduced to slightly more than 10,000.[5] Thus, while the acquisition of new territory greatly extended the exposed frontier and rendered its defense more difficult, the military organization was not materially different from that of the prewar period. The West, however, received the lion's share of the available military strength. Of the entire postwar establishment of 166 companies, distributed among the three military-geographical divisions—Eastern, Western, and Pacific[6]—only forty companies were allotted to the East; the bulk of the army was stationed west of the Mississippi River.[7]

Meanwhile, frontiersmen, military officers, government officials, and the press regularly emphasized the need for more adequate protection.[8] The Corpus Christi *Star* considered reduction of the army at the close of the Mexican War not only a disgrace but also a grave danger. Our southwestern frontier, declared the *Star,* was as destitute of military protection as if we had no army at all. "Our national flag," continued this champion of frontier defense, "is waving in mute mockery on our frontier without a sufficient force to prevent it being torn down and trampled in the dust. . . . The garrisons . . . are scarcely large enough to protect themselves."[9]

General Winfield Scott, commander-in-chief of the United States military forces, dubbed the "peace establishment" of the army a misnomer, since the major portion—80 per cent—of the troops were engaged in constant activity on our Indian borders. Scott recommended an effective force of at least 10,000 men.[10] To strengthen the army, Adjutant General Roger Jones advocated that standard companies should consist of no less than sixty-four privates, while those serving on the distant frontiers should have between eighty and a hundred men.[11]

The advocates of more adequate defense did not lack champions in Congress. Representative Hugh A. Haralson of Georgia declared that an increase of military strength was absolutely imperative. "We would break faith with our frontier citizens as well as the government of Mexico," asserted Haralson, "if we were to refuse to increase the military force."[12] To placate this group, Congress in June, 1850, authorized the President to increase the number of privates to seventy-four in each company serving on the western frontier, and provided for bounties[13] for those enlisting at distant military posts. Three months later another law doubled the pay of enlisted men serving in California and Oregon. This apparent liberality, however, proved inadequate. The hardships incident to service on the frontier, coupled with reports of new Indian outrages, were not conducive to enlistments. Desertions were frequent. Many military units remained greatly undersized.[14]

During the next three years the rank and file were increased by some 3,000 men, but the actual strength, by the end of 1853, barely exceeded 10,000.[15] In 1854 the New York *Daily Times* declared that "our 'Skeleton Army' is already very lean, even for a skeleton,"[16] and Representative Charles J. Faulkner of Virginia, a champion of frontier defense, maintained that 5,000 additional men would be needed to make the western settlements safe.[17] The *Texas State Gazette* believed that our little army of 10,000 men could do no more than "keep their weapons and their quarters clean."[18] John W. Whitfield, Indian agent of the upper Platte, wrote to the *Texas State Gazette* that the great majority of the Indians in his agency had no respect for the government and considered "Uncle Sam a *weak old fellow*" who could be easily overcome. "And," added Whitfield, "they have . . . good reasons for coming to that conclusion."[19]

At every session of Congress between 1852 and 1855 the warning was repeated that unless the army was materially increased, bloody Indian wars would follow. The army bill of 1855 occasioned stirring and fiery debates. On January 31, Senator Augustus C. Dodge of Iowa pointed out that a great discrepancy existed between the authorized and actual strength of the army. Sickness, expiration of enlistment, desertions, and death, he said, always reduced the available force one-fourth and frequently as much as one-third.[20] Senator James C. Jones of Tennessee, waxing patriotically eloquent, asserted he was ready to vote the last man in the United States and the last dollar in the national treasury, to vindicate our honor, or to preserve the lives and fortunes of our citizens. Jones declared: "I am here to legislate for white folks and negroes, and not for Indians."[21] The latter outburst was intended, no doubt, as a slap at Houston and other friends of the Indian. The Senators from Texas were divided in their opinions. Rusk favored enlarging the army, and Houston, a champion of the Indian's cause, vigorously opposed any increase.[22] The freesoilers and abolitionists in the Senate voted with Houston.[23] But the advocates of more adequate defense finally won out. The law of March 8, 1855, authorized four new regiments, two of infantry and two of cavalry, and enlarged the army to more than 15,000.[24]

When the "Mormon War" broke out, some believed that the number of troops ought to be doubled or trebled, since it was feared that the Mormons would instigate a great Indian war in which some 20,000 warriors might be led against the whites.[25] During the months of January and February, 1858, a bitter struggle took place in the Senate. Jefferson Davis and Sam Houston clashed over the relative merits of the regular army and of forces of volunteers. Houston maintained that a large standing army in time of peace created a privileged class, whose officers and friends wielded too much political influence. "Never again," declared Houston, "while I live will I vote in time of peace to increase the regular army one man." Army officers, he hinted, were interested in increasing the size of the regular army primarily for their own advantage. Houston, moreover, believed a volunteer force more efficient, more useful, and far cheaper than regular troops. His high regard for volunteers led him to make these statements: "There is but one army in the country and that is the army of volunteers. . . . Troops in a garrison never gave protection to a frontier."[26] Houston and his supporters won the day. In the spring of 1858 some 2,000 volunteers were added to the rank and file.[27] But on the eve of the Civil War the size of the regular army was again reduced.[28] Of the 198 companies into which the army was divided, 181 companies were in the seventy-nine posts of the western frontier; the remainder manned the arsenals along the Atlantic coast and the Canadian border. More than 90 per cent of the troops were engaged in frontier duty,[29] but the number satisfied neither the authorities in Washington nor the officers in the field, nor the western settlers.

The composition of the army, as well as its size, met with uniform criticism. Infantry, which made up the bulk of the troops,[30] was deemed wholly inadequate for Indian warfare. The use of footmen in the Indian country, many considered a "capital military blunder."[31] From various sections of the West came the constant demand for dragoons and mounted riflemen. The *Daily Missouri Republican* characterized infantry on the frontier as a "dead and useless expense."[32] Another critic believed a company of foot soldiers about as effective as "so many head of sheep."[33] J. W. B. Reynolds, a member of a California emigrant company, writing from San Jose, California, contended that it would be about as sensible to dispatch a company of boys with popguns to storm Sebastopol as to send infantry to fight Indians.[34] Drawing almost as vivid a picture, the Brownsville (Texas) *American Flag* stated: "The government had as well place its soldiery on crutches and to command them to capture the wild antelope, as to send them, on foot, in the warpath of the well-mounted warriors of the plains."[35] Representative Joseph P. Caldwell of North Carolina considered it worse than a mockery to send footmen in pursuit of the best horsemen in the world. Senator Houston declared: "If all the armies of the United States were sent there [Texas], dismounted as infantry, they would be a jest for the Indians, who would dance there in the face of your eighteen-pounders."[36] Despite the uniform agreement that in combats with the well-mounted warriors of the plains and mountains the infantry was at a great disadvantage, the burden of defense remained largely in the hands of the plodding foot soldier. The difficulty in securing horses and the exorbitant cost of maintaining mounted men in the Indian country, undoubtedly, was a deciding factor.[37]

The small but scattered army of infantry, together with the few auxiliary units of cavalry and artillery, occupied posts more or less badly equipped.[38] On the more remote frontiers, where the stations were temporary, the troops had to be content with Sibley tents. These shelters were made of canvas or of buffalo hides dressed in Indian style, conical in shape, and supported by many poles, which interlaced at the top. The size varied. Generally they accommodated about a dozen men, but occasionally as many as twenty men shared one tent.[39]

Troops who saw service near the older settlements lived in permanent, well-built forts. Fort Leavenworth, at the outbreak of the Mexican War, was typical of the latter kind. Occupying about twenty acres, it was arranged in the form of a square, a blockhouse in each corner, the center forming the parade ground. On the east, two-story brick buildings, with capacious "porticoes," served as a barracks, while on the north the buildings housed the principal officers and their families. Near the southwest corner of the post stood the brick arsenal and several frame buildings, used as quarters for officers and privates. A long line of stables occupied the entire south side. About a hundred yards south of the arsenal stood the hospital, a substantial brick building completely surrounded by porches. Several small frame structures along the northern and western suburbs of the post housed the families of the troops and civil employees of the government. The powder magazine, mostly underground and completely fire-proof and bomb-proof, was situated in the heart of the fort.[40]

But the typical frontier post was more like the rude fort of earlier days. As a rule, an irregular collection of rough adobe or log huts served as quarters for both officers and men. Sun, wind, and rain readily found entrance into small, poorly heated, and badly ventilated rooms, with canvas or dirt roofs and earthen floors. During the winter months the troops suffered from intense cold. The mammoth open fireplaces devoured vast quantities of wood but they generally left the outer margins of the quarters like an icebox. Colonel Kearny records in his journal that when he was stationed at Fort Leavenworth it was so cold that the ink froze in his pen and the thermometer in the dining room registered thirty-three degrees below zero. Congested sleeping quarters added little either to the comfort or health of the troops; several men frequently shared one bunk. S. M. Yost, Indian agent and editor of the Santa Fe *Weekly Gazette,* writing from Fort Defiance in the winter of 1858, reported that the garrison at that post, originally intended for 300 men, was "stretched" to accommodate no less than 1,100. With myriads of fleas and bedbugs parading in the wooden bunks and woolen blankets, and with mice, snakes, and other reptiles slipping through the walls and bivouacking on the beds, the soldier's sleep frequently turned into a nightmare.[41] At posts in treeless areas bunks and benches were a luxury; Fort Quitman, Texas, did not have "lumber enough for coffins."[42] In the Southwest heavy rainstorms sometimes washed away the adobe buildings.

Water for men and animals was a real problem. Since some of the posts had neither wells nor cisterns, it was necessary to purchase water in the neighboring settlements or to secure it from the nearby creeks and rivers. Fort Leavenworth's water bill for 1855 was more than $2,700. Quite often it was necessary to haul water in barrels up a steep slope. In winter the men were obliged to cut the ice and dip up the water with buckets in subzero weather. Troops along the Rio Grande had to be content with water that was "too thick to drink and too thin to cultivate."[43]

To supply the scattered frontier army with subsistence and other necessities presented no small task. Advertising in the principal cities, the Commissary and Quartermaster Departments usually awarded contracts to the lowest reputable bidders. Clothing, blankets, and other quartermaster's equipment were purchased on the Pacific coast or in the East, and were shipped to the nearest military posts and stations.[44] Fresh beef, grain, hay, lumber, and commissary supplies were bought from local markets[45] if they could be secured more economically, while arms, ammunition, and other ordnance stores were forwarded from various government armories, arsenals, and depots.[46] A variety of water-craft and land conveyances, including camels, transported millions of pounds of subsistence stores.[47] The supplies did not always reach their destination without serious loss or damage. Food shipped by water from Baltimore to San Antonio often arrived unfit for issue; meats transported overland to Fort Yuma invariably spoiled; commissary stores, occasionally, were stolen and sold to private traders at a fraction of their value.[48] It is quite evident that the government made honest efforts to provide adequately for the army in the Far West, but the wide distribution of the posts, their great distances from the source of supply, and the excessive cost of transportation[49] made the task well-nigh impossible.

These conditions readily help to explain the food problem at the distant posts. As a rule the soldier had plenty to eat, but he was greatly limited as to variety. The reports of the Commissary General of Subsistence show that contractors furnished some twelve articles of food, but beef, pork, soup, bread, and coffee formed an endless chain in the soldier's menu. In comparison with the forty-odd articles available at the close of the century, the daily ration seems quite meager.[50] The records of the period, however, do not disclose glaring abuses such as existed during the Civil War. In the fifties the soldier seldom complained about stale salt beef or salt horse, and rusty, unwholesome pork. Although the bread, at times, was badly baked, as a rule it was palatable—not "mouldy hard-tack, honeycombed with bugs and maggots."[51] When weevils damaged the flour and rice, and when other food-stuffs became sour, rotten, or dirty, the post commanders con-demned the spoiled food.[52] Troops stationed in Texas and in the prairie country enjoyed fresh meat in abundance and many varie-ties of fish,[53] while coffee and sugar, ever present on the soldier's table, did not form part of the ration of any other army in the world.[54] But one essential food—fresh vegetables—the soldier on the frontier lacked—a deficiency which undermined his health. To supply this need some posts experimented with kitchen gar-dens.[55]

The dress of the frontier soldier was not any more satisfactory than his food. According to army regulations the officers and men should have been well clothed. Pictures of the soldier in full uniform, with his single-breasted frock coat, long loose trousers with colored cords on the outer seams, fatigue jacket of sky-blue cloth, black leather cravat or stock, blue cloth shako or foraging cap, pompons, and ankle-length boots, portrayed him as a strik-ingly dashing figure.[56] The actuality, however, often fell short of the ideal. Captain Freeman, who inspected the Texas posts in 1853, reported that the uniforms were so badly made and fitted that the finest soldier looked ridiculous. The coats were much too short; the jackets, intended to fit the largest men, were cut larger around the collar and waist than at the chest. The trousers fitted so tightly below that a large foot had considerable difficulty to pass through them, while at the seat and waist there was width and depth enough for two ordinary men. Rotten leather and de-fective sewing of bootees did not enhance the appearance or durability of the soldier's footgear.[57]

But on the frontier the trooper was not much concerned about appearances. If his coat, trousers, and shoes were in serviceable condition, he was content. During the summer months on the prairies, he wore a broad-brimmed slouched sombrero, white trousers, an old "hickory shirt," and shoes. A brace of pistols, a six-shooter or rifle, a long hunting knife, a powder flask, and a canteen of water completed the outfit. During the winter on the northern frontier, a tanned wolfskin cap, a deerskin coat, trousers of buffalo-calf leather, and shoes or moccasins constituted the trooper's dress.[58] Army officers frequently pointed out deficiency in dress. Champions of the frontier soldier contended that the clothing was neither sufficient nor proper. The critics declared that troops on the lower Rio Grande or on the upper Mississippi, summer or winter, appeared in the same apparel, and that on long or arduous campaigns, their clothing was reduced to rags. During winter marches the men suffered severely, since overshoes, mittens, or other extra wraps were not provided by the government nor kept for sale at the sutlers' stores. To secure protection from the bitter cold, the men wrapped themselves in anything they could lay hands on, such as skins and cast-off clothing. Not infrequently the troops were obliged to plow through deep snows without shoes or march barefooted for miles over solid rock and terrain thick with cactus and abounding in rattlesnakes, scorpions, and tarantulas.[59]

The poorly clad soldier was not always armed properly. To his disappointment and often to his disadvantage, he profited little by the improvements in firearms. French army officers, as well as English and American gunmakers, established the superiority of the grooved or rifled barrel gun and elongated ball over the smooth-bore firearms using cylindrical shot. After various tests army officers uniformly agreed on the effectiveness of Sharps' carbine and Colt's revolver, but the government was slow and cautious in adopting them. It wanted greater assurance that the new weapons were really superior to the old and more practical. Moreover, it had accumulated more than half a million smooth-bore rifles and muskets in its arsenals, and to discard these at one stroke would have been tremendously expensive.[60]

As a result, the frontier army in the fifties was equipped with a variety of arms. The infantry and riflemen were supplied with smooth-bore rifles and the new Minié guns;[61] the cavalry and dragoons had sabers, horse pistols, six-barreled Colt revolvers,[62] carbines, and Sharps rifles;[63] and the artillery was equipped with iron and brass cannon and mountain howitzers.[64] Since most of the troops were supplied with muzzle-loading guns,[65] the antiquated and obsolete weapons caused the frontier soldier considerable embarrassment and often placed him in grave danger. From Fort Riley, Kansas Territory, Major Emory wrote: "To practice with these arms is quite injurious. Many of these arms do not go off more than three times in five and it is only a chance shot which hits the regulation target at one hundred yards."[66] For several years Captain Ewell's mounted company stationed at Fort Buchanan had been supplied with firearms no better than "old rattletraps"—out of date and utterly inefficient. To make matters worse, while these troops were armed with eleven different kinds of guns, they were provided with only one kind of ammunition. No wonder the Indian held the white soldier in contempt.[67]

In spite of these discouragements, a soldier's life had its attractions. Newly arrived emigrants, unable to find employment and lured by generous bounties, tried their fortune in the army. Some native Americans, who had suffered financial reverses or social disappointments, or who had become involved in difficulties with the law, sought refuge in the distant army posts; others enlisted "for the purpose of getting comfortably transported to California at the expense of the government."[68] To the young, restless, adventurous spirits "whose imagination inflamed them with the thoughts of scouring the far prairies on fine horses, amid buffalo and strange Indians," military service in the Far West held out a particularly glamorous appeal.[69]

But upon arriving at his station, the recruit soon realized that he had no sinecure, and the glamor began to fade. The numerous and hazardous duties assigned him demanded great physical strength and an iron constitution; a weakling did not "belong" on the western frontier. Drilling and mounting guard were a part of the daily routine,[70] and periodically he was called upon for escort duty, protecting surveying parties, government and emigrant trains. Erecting buildings and fighting Indians claimed a major part of his time. On the Pacific coast and along the Gulf of Mexico, where smugglers plied their trade and filibusterers attempted to lead expeditions to the Central American states and Cuba, the trooper was called upon to enforce the law.[71]

Though leading an active, outdoor life, the frontier soldier was a constant prey to disease. Of the numerous ailments, disorders of the digestive organs seem to have been the most frequent and troublesome. Army surgeons enumerated a long list of causes, but improper diet, impure water, and "villainous" liquor were the chief offenders.[72] Since medical officers were rarely consulted in the selection of sites for military posts, the men invariably suffered from colds, rheumatism, abscesses, and ulcers. During the summer and autumn months troops stationed in the Southwest suffered from bilious, malarial fevers caused by mosquitoes in marshy bottom lands. In 1854 malarial fever at Fort Merrill, Texas, was so severe that within a two months' period every officer, private, and laundress was on the sick list. Four years later, at Fort Thorn, New Mexico Territory, scarcely a man was fit for garrison duty. At Fort Reading, California, the troops suffered so severely from the poisonous atmosphere that the post had to be abandoned.[73] Extreme and rapid changes in temperature produced diseases of the respiratory organs. At Fort Dodge, Iowa, in the winter months "constant hurricane-like winds rushing from the north and sweeping over the prairie, chilled the innermost blood of both man and beast"; at Fort Yuma, "the hottest post in the United States," a torrid sun caused the temperature to rise to 124 degrees.[74] Frozen ears, hands, and feet were not uncommon in the Far North. Amputations tried the courage and stamina of the frontier soldier, since, in the absence of chloroform, surgeons could administer a no more effective anaesthetic than a local application of ice and salt.[75] Yellow fever and cholera periodically visited the frontier posts and exacted heavy toll.[76] Exposure to the sun on the open prairie produced disorders of the brain and the nervous system;[77] the social diseases claimed many victims.[78] Because of ill-suited transportation facilities, the sick and wounded were subjected to undue suffering. The ambulances, Assistant Surgeon Roberts Bartholow wrote, were "so lofty that it was a difficult matter to get a sick man inside and so rough and jolting that the sick certainly were not improved by the riding."[79]

Hospital facilities, with few exceptions, were either inadequate or entirely lacking. When a post was constructed, no hospital was provided; but as need arose, a makeshift was created either by converting laundresses' quarters or by adding crudely built sheds. Army surgeons reported that the sick and wounded were housed in small, cheerless rooms where rain, wind, and snow readily found access.[80] Many a post hospital was in danger of "falling down or being blown down";[81] others lacked the necessary privacy and were so situated as to prevent observance of the simplest hygienic regulations. The equipment and medical supplies harmonized with the surroundings. Swarms of rats played havoc with hospital equipment at Ringgold and Benicia Barracks; the broken-down hospital furniture and bedding at Fort Belknap were no better than an "accumulation of rubbish and junk."[82] It certainly was no simple matter to secure either adequate or ample medicines at the distant posts. Coming from the East, the much-needed supplies necessarily were slow in reaching their destination; some were lost or spoiled in transit. Fires and losses at sea destroyed thousands of dollars' worth of vital medical and hospital supplies.[83]

The small corps of medical officers during this period could not possibly give the soldiers adequate attention. Rarely did the medical staff of the entire United States army exceed a hundred trained physicians. Troops sent on exploring or punitive expeditions did not have the services of a doctor. No medical officer accompanied Colonel Loring when he conducted the regiment of Mounted Riflemen from Fort Leavenworth to Oregon in 1849.

Percival G. Lowe records that his company, during five years of service on the plains, with but two exceptions, "never had a doctor."[84] When a soldier became ill, the commanding officer administered opium, salts, or quinine, and treated snake bite with a copious application of urine, tobacco, and salt.[85] Periodically Surgeon General Thomas Lawson brought to the attention of Congress the urgent need for increasing and improving the medical and hospital service in the army. When Congress finally did act in August, 1856, it provided only four extra surgeons and eight assistants. The support of Congress was halfhearted. The army medical staff for many years remained greatly undermanned.[86]

Despite these shortcomings, the sick seem to have been fairly well tended by the small corps of army doctors and private physicians.[87] The death rate from disease was remarkably low. In the Surgeon General's reports from 1848 to 1860, the mortality at the western army posts compared very favorably with that in the East.[88] With the addition of army surgeons and assistants and of periodic inspection by boards of survey, the glaring deficiencies in the medical and hospital service gradually became less pronounced.[89]

The pay of the soldier, like the food, clothing, shelter, and medical service, materially affected frontier defense. In the niggardly salary and in the antiquated method of payment, both officers and men had a real grievance. For more than fifty years the officers' salaries remained practically unchanged.[90] The New York *Evening Post,* a leader in the fight for more adequate pay, deplored the almost "beggarly compensation," altogether disproportionate to that obtained in civil employment. Such a policy, the *Post* contended, would surely drive the best men from the service; none but "sticks" would remain. Because of the poor salaries the quality of applicants at West Point had greatly deteriorated.[91] Although such agitation had continued for many years, commissioned officers received no additional pay until 1857, when they received an increase of twenty dollars per month.[92]

The common soldier found himself at an even greater disadvantage than the officers. The great distances separating the military posts on the outlying frontiers made visits of the paymaster unavoidably irregular. If he was in the vicinity, the men received their money every second month, but often they had to wait four, six, or eight months. Such irregularity the soldier considered a pecuniary injury,[93] as it obliged him to run into debt to the sutler[94] and others, and to pay extortionate prices—a condition which did not fail to foster discontent and encourage desertion.

The paymaster could not be held responsible for the tardy arrival of the pay. His job certainly was not an enviable one. The arduous and dangerous character of his work is illustrated in the case of Major Albert S. Johnston, who served as paymaster in Texas from 1849 to 1855. The money, in the form of gold and silver coins, the paymaster had to obtain in New Orleans or Austin. By 1854 Johnston's itinerary, which included payments to troops every two months at no less than ten military posts in central Texas, covered some 4,200 miles. On these jaunts Johnston, accompanied by a clerk, a Negro driver, and a Negro cook, traveled in a covered ambulance drawn by four mules. Although from four to twelve dragoons served as escort, the paymaster's life and his precious cargo were frequently in danger from attacks by hostile Indians. The paymaster often performed additional errands such as buying a horse, a gun, a pair of boots, or a ribbon, or paying taxes or carrying watches for adjustment. People from other states even asked the paymaster's advice about land purchases.[95]

And when the frontier soldier received his tardy wage, it was ridiculously low. Between 1833 and 1854, enlisted men received from six to eight dollars per month—a sum less than that earned by the common laborer.[96] From time to time the cry arose that the soldier's earnings did not keep pace with the increased cost of living. " 'Seven dollars a month and found,' " the New York *Daily Times* declared, "can only tempt the very dullest dogs to enlist, and of these, nearly all can do better in other ways."[97] Such criticism called forth fiery debates in Congress. In the Senate, R. M. T. Hunter of Virginia led the opposition forces, while James Shields of Illinois championed the cause of the soldier. On March 21, 1854, Shields pleaded that "some increase of pay of the army is absolutely necessary . . . recruiting stations might as well be abandoned, for no man fit to carry a musket will serve for seven dollars a month."[98] The soldier's cause finally won. According to the law of August 4, 1854, troops in the various branches of the service were now to receive the sums of eleven and twelve dollars a month.[99] The four-dollar increase, together with bounties and occasional "extras" for fatigue duty,[100] materially supplemented an otherwise niggardly wage.

The soldier on the frontier not only wanted greater recompense for his services but also craved some form of social life. When he found time heavy on his hands, he created his own form of amusement. Where books and newspapers were available, some of the men spent their leisure time reading, while others enjoyed hunting and fishing. Singers and comic artists enlivened many a camp; expert storytellers regaled appreciative audiences with "tall" yarns.[101] Although his pay was small and he was forbidden to gamble, the soldier readily engaged in such pastimes, and parted with his money freely and recklessly. Games of monte and chuck-luck, horse- and mule-racing, cock-fighting, and fandangoes held out a special lure for the young blood stationed at the isolated camps. When the trooper visited the towns, he proved easy game for sharp, unscrupulous tradesmen, and gamblers. Independence, Missouri, like other border settlements, presented a lively scene of bustle and activity where sharpers and speculators busily engaged in fleecing the poor soldier of his hard-earned pay.[102] To protect the improvident recruit from spending his money too freely, army sutlers were forbidden to sell to enlisted men on credit to a sum exceeding one-third of the monthly pay. But neither sutler nor soldier took this injunction very seriously; the post store continued to be an ever-favorite resort.[103]

Balls, concerts, and theatricals helped to ease the monotony of garrison life. Some military posts had bands of professional standing. In 1855 the brass band of Fort Tejón not only entertained its own garrison but furnished music for the Fourth of July celebration at Los Angeles.[104] Thespian societies sprang up on the frontier throughout this period. In October, 1846, a portion of the Army of the West stationed at Santa Fe organized a dramatic association and gave its first performance to a "crowded house." Painting scenery especially for the occasion and dressing the men for the feminine roles, the Thespian Company scored a triumph with its stirring drama, *Pizarro in Peru; or, The Death of Rolla.* After the tragedy came a Negro-minstrel performance, violins, flutes, and cornets furnishing the music. Four years later a Thespian society was formed at Fort Leavenworth;[105] in the fall of 1858 troops at Camp Floyd, Utah Territory, engaged in theatricals. In an improvised theater filled to capacity with officers, officers' wives, and privates, a breezy comedy, *Used Up,* preceded a blood-curdling melodrama, *The Dead Shot.*[106]

Drinking was another favorite pastime of the frontier soldier. His overindulgence in the "villainous" or "lightning" whiskey, a concoction of alcohol, tobacco, and other narcotics, invariably undermined his health.[107] He naïvely defended his partaking of alcoholic beverages by attributing to them rare healing qualities. In summer, he maintained, they prevented nervous disorder of the bowels, in winter they warded off colds, while in the spring and autumn they kept away the chills. "Fortunately," observed Assistant Surgeon Rodney Glisan, at Fort Arbuckle, Indian Territory, "the price of intoxicating spirits is, . . . so high that even the most inveterate tiplers cannot afford the indulgence of a big spree very frequently."[108] While no whiskey was allowed in the soldiers' quarters, some of the posts permitted drinking under special conditions. At Fort Leavenworth, for example, no effort was made to conceal the extensive consumption of liquor. At "Budgen-Ken," a sort of company club improvised between two stables, each drinker "chipped in" to provide a ready supply. When the stock of liquor ran low, the men visited "Whiskey Point," about one mile above the post on the opposite side of the Missouri River, where anything could be sold or traded for whiskey. New arrivals who readily found their way to this favorite resort often parted with their overcoats or other articles of apparel.[109] In New Mexico the territorial legislature enacted a law forbidding "any person to sell or give intoxicating liquors . . . to any non-commissioned officer or soldier in the United States army." Violation of this act was punishable by a fine of $25 to $100.[110]

Unable to eliminate the sale of liquor, the government attempted to control the traffic in it by permitting certain favorite sutlers to sell it, but only in moderate quantities. At Taos Major Beall issued his order: "In no case will Spiritus [sic] Liquors be sold to any Regular or Volunteer Soldier in such quantity as to produce intoxication."[111] Quite obviously such orders could not be enforced. The government made another compromise in June, 1857, when the Adjutant General's office directed the commanding officers to issue whiskey to enlisted men, when unduly fatigued, but not to exceed a gill per man, per day. On special occasions, such as Christmas and the Fourth of July, whiskey was distributed among the troops in honor of the day.[112]

Some public-spirited citizens who felt concerned about the health of the frontier soldier organized temperance societies at several western military posts. When late in 1847 such an organization was formed at Fort Mann, within six weeks the *Daily Missouri Republican* was happy to announce that the "beneficial tendency was not unfelt." Two years later the temperance society at Fort Washita was described as "flourishing beyond conception," and the Fort Smith *Herald* prophesied that "in twelve months not a whiskey drinker will be seen in these parts." This editor, apparently, did not know the frontier soldier. To the trooper, who was ever ready to pay for his drink with his meager and hard-earned wage as well as to take punishment, preachment about the evil of intemperance was like asking him to surrender part of his daily bread. The temperance societies sank into oblivion almost as quickly as they arose; indulgence in alcoholic beverages at the military posts continued to relieve the monotony of life on the frontier.[113]

The operations of women camp followers also tried the patience of civil as well as military authorities. In the spring of 1853, when these undesirables were debauching the troops at Fort Union, Colonel Sumner of the Department of New Mexico established a reserve eight miles square and issued orders that no citizen should be permitted to settle on this area. The territorial legislature in turn enacted a law "punishing all lewd women, pursuing their profession, with thirty stripes, after having their guilt proclaimed by a town crier, and then to be bound to hard labor for three months, with a chain around their ankles." Several prostitutes were arrested, put off the reserve, and warned not to return. Repeating their offenses, the "fancy" women had their hair cropped and were drummed out of camp, after having been given ten light blows on their backs. The remedy proved effective.[114]

Keeping the ranks filled presented another serious problem. Throughout this period Secretaries of War reported that losses from desertion were greater than from any other single cause— no less than 3,000 men annually.[115] The gold fever played great havoc among the troops, particularly in the Far West. During 1849 fully 40 per cent left their posts in California to rush to the mines.[116] Two years later Governor McDougal of California wrote to President Fillmore that because of frequent desertions the military force had been "almost reduced to nothing."[117] In an attempt to refill the ranks on the Pacific coast, General Hitchcock issued a proclamation extending a full pardon to deserters on condition that they deliver themselves up and forfeit their pay.[118] When some sixteen riflemen at Fort Laramie overpowered the guard, seized horses, and made a dash for California, a command of twenty-five men gave chase. But whether they brought back the culprits or they themselves decided to "visit" the mines is not apparent.[119] Recruits at Fort Arbuckle and troops attached to the Utah Expedition, upon receiving their pay, deserted, taking with them mules and clothing.[120] Such a state of affairs was but the natural outcome of existing conditions. Besides the lure of gold, the frontier soldier had other reasons for deserting his post. In his annual report of December, 1856, Secretary of War Davis stated the case of the common soldier. Primarily, the enlisted man was dissatisfied with his meager and irregular pay; other grievances included frequent construction and abandonment of military posts, severe discipline, and the rigorous life on the frontier.[121] "Intolerable ennui," declared a famous traveler, caused most desertions.[122]

Because of his youth and because of his strenuous life, the frontier soldier frequently broke the military rules and suffered accordingly. For minor infractions of discipline or for trifling neglect of duty he was subjected to severe and ingenious punishments. Customary penalties meted out by courts-martial embraced reduction in pay and in rank, riding the "wooden horse" in the center of the parade ground, and solitary confinement on bread and water.[123] Teresa Vielé, who toured the West in the fifties, recorded that at the Texas posts habitual drinkers were compelled to wear a "barrel jacket" every day for a week. This mode of dress, an old flour barrel with a hole cut for the head and a pair of holes for arms, added neither to the comfort nor to the dignity of the wearer. Father Domenech, a contemporary Catholic missionary, saw soldiers suspended by the arms from branches of trees for drunkenness. "Sometimes," wrote Father Domenech, "they tie their arms and legs and fling them repeatedly into a river, and then drag them to the bank with a cord."[124] At Fort Brown thieves were drummed out of service. Mrs. Vielé, an eyewitness of such a ceremony, wrote that the culprit had his head shaved, was stripped to the waist, and at the evening parade was called in front of the ranks, where the officer of the day read aloud the offense and its penalty. The trooper was then obliged to walk three times around the parade ground, the corporal and the sergeant of the guard following closely with bayonets pointed downward, while a fifer and two drummers played the tune of "Poor Old Soldier, I hope the devil won't catch you."[125]

Some offenders were sentenced to the stocks or were bucked—their wrists tied together and pinioned over the bent knees. Gagging, which occasionally accompanied "bucking," sometimes resulted in the death of the victim.[126] Other luckless troopers, wearing an iron yoke, were compelled to parade in front of the guardhouse with a fifty-pound sack of stones or a knapsack loaded with sand. The most brutal and degrading punishments—flogging and branding—were meted out to deserters.[127] The customary procedure was to tie the guilty soldier to a post or a tree and administer fifty lashes with a cat-o'-nine tails on the bare back. Senseless, the victim was carried to the post hospital, where salt and water were roughly applied to his wounds. He was then indelibly branded on the left hip with the letter D, one and a half inches long, to signify desertion, had his head shaved, and was drummed out of service.[128]

Judged by modern standards, conditions at the frontier posts in the mid-nineteenth century were far from ideal; but for the shortcomings the government cannot be censured too severely. Considering the great distances between military stations, poor roads, and absence of transcontinental railroads, the War Department did remarkably well. The failures merely illustrate the unavoidable difficulties in frontier defense. Sensing the complexity of these problems, the small army, scattered over a vast area and in many instances sacrificing personal comforts, rendered inestimable service. The soldier in the trans-Mississippi country, in the face of numerous hardships and handicaps—suffering from intense heat and cold, hunger and thirst, receiving beggarly pay, and often waging an inglorious war against a relentless foe—extended his country's domain to the Pacific and made its occupancy and development possible. By supplementing the work of the explorer, the missionary, the Indian trader and the engineer, he helped to bind the Far West—"the Last American Frontier"—to the rest of the United States.

CHAPTER VIII

Texas Indians Hurl a Challenge

BETWEEN the Mexican War and the Civil War the Far Southwest was a battleground between the Indian and the white man. The conflict which began with the establishment of the first white settlements in the New World had deep-rooted causes. The Indian's lack of food, no doubt, was the basic cause for the almost constant state of war. As the white man relentlessly moved westward, the buffalo[1] and other game became more scarce and the Indian was driven from his hunting ground and his home. His condition became truly desperate. In the fifties the Texas, New Mexico, and California tribes were confronted with the choice of eating their horses, stealing, killing, or starving.[2] Some succumbed to starvation; the bolder spirits chose to steal and to kill.

The wild tribes of Texas challenged the onward march of the white man. In 1845 one Texas editor expressed the sanguine belief that "the giant arms of the United States would soon sweep the few bands of hostile Indians from our borders."[3] But this editor did not know his Texas warriors. As late as 1859 the Austin *Southern Intelligencer* declared: "The advance of the settlements has been everywhere marked with blood."[4]

When Texas entered the Union and began to dispose of large tracts of public land where Indians had long been accustomed to hunt, trouble arose at once. In June, 1847, Major Robert S. Neighbors wrote to the Commissioner of Indian Affairs that the Texas tribes were becoming angry and restless, since the white settlers were pushing them from their lands.[5] When Mexican spies tampered with the dispossessed natives and when surveyors penetrated their country and traders swindled them, Indian wars seemed imminent. It was only the tact, courage, and energy of

Neighbors, who succeeded in conciliating the Northern Comanches, that prevented a general Indian outbreak.[6] Disturbances had already occurred. Along the Gulf and lower Rio Grande, raiders were active. When Captain M. T. Johnson's company of Texas volunteers attacked a band of Wichitas and killed a Caddo boy, the natives retaliated by killing three members of a surveying party on the Llano River. The murderers showed rare fiendishness, cutting out the hearts of their victims and suspending them from the necks of the murdered men.[7]

Despite such unsavory incidents, the Texas tribes until 1848 remained comparatively quiet. Then they took to the warpath on a grand scale. From Port La Vaca came the report that near by some twenty persons had been killed by Indians. Only the timely arrival of federal troops quieted the fears of the townsmen. When a band of about 150 Comanches attacked a body of whites in a narrow defile west of San Antonio and succeeded in killing and wounding some half dozen men, the citizens of Gonzales dispatched couriers to the neighboring frontier settlements, warning the inhabitants of the danger.[8] Early in 1848 the *Democratic Telegraph and Texas Register* announced that a large body of emigrants, many from Alabama and Georgia, were on their way to the western counties of Texas. But in December of that year the same paper reported that depredations not only had retarded settlement but had converted beautiful and populous hamlets into a dreary wasteland. "Its once flourishing and populous towns," declared the *Register,* "are deserted and the few settlers that visit it are compelled to search amid the tangled thickets and grass covered paths of the mustang and wild cattle for the roads that once were the avenues of commercial wealth."[9]

The War Department, in the meantime, had inaugurated a vigorous policy of defense. In August, 1848, the Adjutant General's office directed the commanders of Texas and New Mexico to establish military posts and to station troops in such a manner as to secure the "best protection and defense of the frontiers."[10]

Late in October, General David E. Twiggs arrived in Galveston and soon afterward the United States steamer "Colonel Stanton" landed there with troops and horses for Twiggs's command. The troops occupied Forts Brown and Polk and eight other stations.[11] The presence of twenty-two companies (sixteen of infantry and six of dragoons), however, did not satisfy the Texans, who contended that a force of no less than 2,000 mounted men was needed to assure security to their settlements.[12]

During 1849 the entire Texas frontier seems to have been thrown into a panic by Indian raids. Hundreds of tribesmen from Mexico, New Mexico, and Indian Territory embarked on a series of attacks which lasted for several years. The task of restraining the intruding bands proved extremely difficult. The presence of Mexican sympathizers along the border and often within the limits of the United States, the operations of unprincipled traders and speculators, the conflict between federal and state, as well as civil and military, authority, and the lack of agreement between the United States and Mexico for reciprocal crossing of the border in pursuit of the raiders only emboldened the invading tribesmen.[13]

Comanche marauding expeditions kept regular and volunteer troops constantly on the alert. Forays of Comanche and kindred bands, prompted either by a desire for revenge or for profit, were almost continuous. To punish a foe for real or imaginary wrongs was a rather infrequent occurrence among the Indians, but the desire for plunder was an ever-present incentive for them to attack. And according to their standards, to work was ignoble; an ambitious warrior therefore must earn a living in some other way. In what better way than by raids on the settlements could he enrich himself with plunder and captives and satisfy his desire to become a great warrior? The tribesmen certainly had little difficulty in disposing of their legitimate or illegitimate wares. Comanche, Apache, Lipan, and other warlike bands engaged in a lively traffic with the settlers at Fredericksburg. A varied assortment of goods, including horses, skins of panthers, bears, deer, and buffaloes, the raiders exchanged for brandy, knives, blankets, venetian pearls, and cast-off gold lace. The *Comanchéros* (New Mexican traders) were a ready market, ever eager to buy stolen horses, mules, and other plunder. For profit unlicensed Anglo-American traders helped to foment Indian raids.[14]

Thus, hardy warriors, aided and abetted by unscrupulous white men, swooped down on frontier settlements, drove off stock, and killed inhabitants or carried them off into captivity.[15] The frontier press pictured the whole Rio Grande country, with the exception of the larger towns, as virtually deserted, the Indian roaming at will, killing man and beast. The Texas legislature reported during 1849 more than 200 persons killed, wounded, or made captive and a property loss of more than $103,000.[16] By the fall of the same year, after suffering several defeats, the Comanches through Buffalo Hump, their newly elected chief, sued for peace. But depredations continued.[17] Although more than 1,500 troops occupied Texas, its citizens considered the Rio Grande frontier inadequately protected and petitioned the President for a cavalry force. Each community wanted a military post in its own neighborhood.[18]

As the years passed, relations with the Indians became no better. In 1849 the massacre by Rangers of a "whole division of the Lipan tribe," while it was quietly encamped near Castorville,[19] created bitter resentment and a wave of Indian outbreaks. In the spring of 1850, Captain G. K. Lewis of Texas reported the Indians the most hostile in fifty years. Lewis painted a dire picture. Many of the white settlers, he said, were forced to flee into Mexico for protection. And persons who formerly had property valued at between $20,000 and $50,000 were compelled to live for months almost entirely upon goat's milk, "without meat, without bread, and without any vegetable food." They could not go into business, because they had no capital, all of their movable property having been swept away by the Indians.[20]

At this time parties of Delawares, Shawnees, Kickapoos, and some half dozen other bands migrated from the Indian territory

west of Arkansas and Missouri, and permanently established themselves in Texas. Parties of other tribes, including the Seminoles,
Creeks, and Cherokees, had acquired the habit of making extended sojourns in Texas and then returning to their homes.[21] In the
midst of these comings and goings appeared Wild Cat, the celebrated Seminole chief, with a plan for settling these bands along
the west bank of the Rio Grande. But his proposal created only
discord and confusion among the tribesmen.

Wild Cat was an unusual Indian. Although slight in person,
his shrewd countenance, fleetness of movement, and love of war
gave him the reputation of being one of the most dangerous chieftains in the field. In May, 1850, when Indian Agent John H.
Rollins met Wild Cat on the Llano River at the head of about 250
Seminoles and Kickapoos, the wily chieftain presented his grievances. On leaving Florida, he complained, the white man's government had promised to give him a country. Instead, it had
placed him and his people among the Creek Indians where they
had no voice in council and were greatly oppressed and abused.
Driven to seek a home elsewhere, he had gone into Mexico. Several months later he told Seminole and Creek tribesmen that he
had secured a grant of land from the Mexican government on the
Rio Grande opposite Eagle Pass where they would be allowed to
live "forever."[22] But the Creeks and Seminoles had little confidence
in Wild Cat and distrusted his movements. In November of the
same year, when Wild Cat with about half a dozen of his tribe
and one hundred Negroes left the Seminole country for the Rio
Grande, a company of Creek warriors pursued him and succeeded
in capturing some seventy or eighty of his followers.[23] The restlessness among these tribes reacted not too favorably on the frontier settlers.

Meanwhile, a new series of raids by Comanche and other bands,
which had begun in central Texas, shifted to the southward and
westward. In the spring of 1850, when Indians twice seized United
States mail and federal troops were unable to chastise the maraud-

ers, Ranger companies came to the rescue.[24] As the wild tribes continued their forays and settlers demanded greater protection, Major General George M. Brooke, the new commander of the Eighth Military Department, launched a vigorous campaign. Early in June he ordered all the disposable dragoons and Mounted Infantry stationed on the Nueces and lower Rio Grande, together with three companies of Rangers, to take the field and clear the country of hostile Indians. But Brooke's brave offensive accomplished little. Although some of the troops succeeded in engaging Indian bands at various points near Brownsville and on the San Antonio and Laredo road, the foe proved an elusive one. After much marching, scouting, and searching, he abandoned operations. The minor skirmishes had produced no definite result; the campaign was a failure.[25] Attempts of Congress to check Indian depredations by holding entire tribes responsible for acts of individual members proved no more effective.[26] Rumors of an alliance between the wild tribes of Texas and those of New Mexico caused great uneasiness.[27]

The government took other steps to combat the Indian menace in this region. In the fall of 1850 it appointed John A. Rogers, John H. Rollins, and Jesse Stem special agents for the Texas tribes, and Congress appropriated $30,000 for the Indian service of the southwestern tribes and $72,000 more to defray the expenses of the Rangers.[28] Since United States laws did not entirely extend over the Texas tribes, the Commissioner of Indian Affairs warned the new agents against the use of force and cautioned them not to interfere with the rights and dignity of a sovereign state (Texas). Moreover, while these officials were directed to use only kind, mild, and persuasive methods, they were, at the same time, to impress upon the natives that "our government was their best friend, with the will and power to protect . . . as well as to punish."[29] Thus the task of the agents was a difficult one.

The agents entered into their work with a will. Rollins traveled more than 1,100 miles in the Indian country and held "talks" with eight different bands. But to his disappointment the Comanches were not in attendance, for the Barnards had persuaded them to go to the Barnards' trading house[30] on the Brazos, where they could obtain plenty to eat and goods at a low price.[31] Here we have a striking example of the baleful influence of the traders on our Indian relations. Rogers, meanwhile, reported that some sixty different articles, mostly clothing, shoes, and household goods, at an estimated cost of more than $6,200, had been distributed among the Indians of the three agencies.[32]

Rollins made another attempt to win the good will of the natives. On December 10, 1850, he met the leaders of half a dozen tribes on Spring Creek near the San Sabá and negotiated an elaborate treaty consisting of twenty articles.[33] In the new agreement the chieftains again acknowledged the authority of the federal government. They promised to remain at peace, to deliver troublesome members of their tribes, as well as to restore white and Negro captives and stolen property, and not to go beyond the established line of military posts without permission from the Indian agent. This last provision of the treaty, it should be noted, was entirely one-sided, since whites were not prevented from entering the Indian country. The only concessions made by the government consisted of promises to establish trading houses, give presents, send blacksmiths and teachers, and later to establish a permanent boundary. But since Texas owned the soil, the last agreement was impossible of fulfillment. To the Indian, this furnished another example of broken faith.[34]

During the remainder of the decade no material change occurred in Texas Indian relations. Disgruntled warriors continued their forays; federal and state troops followed in pursuit; soldiers built additional military posts, and Indian officials negotiated new treaties. Rollins' treaty, signed by upwards of thirty chiefs, was broken five times within less than a month. To enforce treaty stipulations, in the spring of 1851 Brevet Lieutenant Colonel William Joseph Hardee, with a force of about 200 dragoons, accompanied by Indian Agents Rollins and Stem, held "talks" with Lipan and Comanche chiefs on the Llano and upper Brazos. Hardee, the agents, and the troops succeeded in persuading the Indians to restore seventeen Mexicans and one American boy held as captives. Strange as it may seem, some of the prisoners refused to leave their masters, preferring horses to ride and idleness among the Indians to work and servitude at home. The most important accomplishment of Hardee's expedition, perhaps, was the accurate knowledge it obtained of the true strength of the warlike tribes. For example, Hardee found that the Comanches, instead of possessing 10,000 to 20,000 warriors, could muster no more than 500 fighting men.[35] In October, 1851, Rogers negotiated another agreement on the San Sabá with the Southern Comanche, Lipan, and Mescalero tribes, who soon thereafter surrendered more than twenty white captives.[36]

Colonels Samuel Cooper and Oliver P. Temple,[37] meanwhile, met Wild Cat at Eagle Pass and held a "talk" with him. The crafty Seminole chieftain, who now appeared in a very humble and suppliant mood, expressed a desire to live at peace with the Americans and Mexicans, as well as the other Indians. Since he and his "Great Father, the President, had smoked the pipe of peace . . . and had buried the hatchet in the earth, no one was to dig it up." He fervently pleaded for a home in Texas for himself and his people.[38]

In Washington, Secretary of War Conrad added meaning to these "talks" when he ordered the movement of troops into Texas from Missouri, Arkansas, and Oregon, and the establishment of additional forts on the Texas frontier. Between the summer and fall of 1851 three new military positions—Forts Belknap, Phantom Hill, and Mason—were built and occupied by troops.[39] This display of energy seemed to restore confidence to the inhabitants of the Rio Grande Valley. Trade between Texas and Mexico soon flourished. Ranchers and merchants brought droves of mules and horses into the state almost daily, and commerce became more brisk than it had been for many a day. The roads appeared less dangerous. "In fact," declared Dr. (Captain) John S. Ford in his memoirs, "a good time seemed to be dawning upon the denizens of southern and southwestern Texas."[40]

But Ford's prophecy was short-lived. The year 1852 held fears and thrills for the settlements along the entire frontier. Except in the Rio Grande region, however, the excitement and alarms were greatly out of proportion to the real danger. An extremely dry summer and a diminishing food supply caused great suffering among the natives. To keep from starving, many, after feeding upon their animals, had to resort to plundering. The *Daily Missouri Republican* observed that unless the government furnished the Indians with food, all the troops in the Union could not keep them from stealing cattle. The Comanches harried the northern Mexican states.[41] Petitions and memorials to the governor of Texas and to Congress, although greatly exaggerating the danger and berating the federal government for its inadequate protection, brought some immediate action. Governor Bell dispatched three companies of Rangers to the Rio Grande country, and General Persifor F. Smith ordered five companies of Mounted Riflemen to the same region.[42] Six new military positions, built in 1852, extended the old inner line of defense about 150 miles.[43]

To deter the Comanches, Kiowas, and Kiowa-Apaches from raiding Texas and Mexico, the government once more resorted to treaty-making. In July, 1853, Thomas Fitzpatrick,[44] the celebrated Indian agent to the tribes of the upper Platte and Arkansas, met the principal chiefs of these tribes at Fort Atkinson and negotiated a treaty with them. By the terms of the agreement the government promised the Indians annuity goods valued at $18,000 each year for a period of ten years, as well as protection against white outlaws. The Indians, on their part, acknowledged the right of the government to lay out roads through their country and to establish military posts. They also promised to make restitution for past injuries, to discontinue raids into Mexico, and to restore captives. Sixteen prominent chiefs signed the agreement.[45]

But the Fort Atkinson treaty did little toward improving conditions on the Texan frontier. In fact, it seemed to make them worse. Being assured of annuity goods, including guns and ammunition, the northern tribes felt they could now embark on a grand career of plunder. The Northern Comanches exhibited extreme boldness. They sent word to Major Henry H. Sibley, commanding at Fort Phantom Hill, that as soon as the grass was good they would come down and whip the soldiers and destroy his post.[46]

When the United States secured the Gadsden Purchase the problem of defense became even more difficult. The wild tribes of Texas and New Mexico seemed to gain in boldness and vigor. The spring of 1854 ushered in a new period of excitement. During the next half dozen years marauding bands gave the settlers no peace. Repeatedly they raided and burned settlements, attacked wagon trains, drove off stock, and killed settlers. Frontiersmen, the press, and governors constantly called for greater protection; federal and state troops attempted to eliminate the Indian danger but were unable to secure a durable peace.

With the withdrawal of troops from some of the posts, the Indians, detecting the weakness of the garrisons, began to slip through the line of defense and raided the settlements. In the north former special agent Jesse Stem and a Mr. Lepperman were murdered by Kickapoo tribesmen within a few miles of Fort Belknap.[47] Along the Rio Grande, Mescalero, Comanche, and Apache raiders kept the settlers in a constant state of alarm. "Mustangers," traders, and government trains suffered at the hands of Wild Cat's followers and other bold and reckless braves bent on plunder.[48] There was no security for stock; what the raiders did not kill they drove off. To save some of their property, west Texas stockmen abandoned their ranches and drove the animals to San Antonio, where they tried to dispose of them.[49] Although detachments from Forts Ewell, Inge, and McIntosh pursued the pillagers and engaged them in several actions, they were able to inflict only minor losses.[50]

Throughout 1855-60 the Comanches continued their depredations, and army officers, settlers, and the frontier press recounted the all too familiar story of raids and ineffective punitive expeditions. During the early months of 1855 the frontier enjoyed a breathing spell, but the discharge of Mounted Rangers and the removal of regular forces into Kansas served as a signal for fresh Indian attacks. Raids again came thick and fast. The San Antonio *Texan* reported that the Comanches in the vicinity of Fort Belknap had burnt and torn up all the "papers"—agreements they had with Americans—and were preparing to join their northern kinsmen in a war against the white man.[51] In the fall of the year 1855, settlers of four southern counties complained to Governor Pease that the Indians were "killing, stealing, feasting upon the fruits of our labor." They begged for more adequate protection.[52] American citizens along the lower Rio Grande, meanwhile, had drawn up resolutions strongly protesting to the Mexican government for its failure to control the "almost daily . . . massacres and robberies" from across the border.[53] The *Daily Picayune* and the San Antonio *Ledger* urged strong punitive expeditions into Mexico.[54]

Late in December, 1855, Colonel Albert S. Johnston's regiment of Second Cavalry, after a march of a thousand miles, arrived in Texas.[55] But the peace that ensued was short-lived. Within a few months the whole Texan frontier was thrown into new alarms by reports of frequent and daring Indian attacks. Early in March, 1856, the *Texas State Gazette* reported: "We are pained to hear of more destruction of life and property by the Indians."[56] Several months later Major Henry Hill, paymaster of the United States army, and his guard, while transporting $10,000 in specie, were attacked at Devils' River by a band of fifty armed warriors and barely escaped alive.[57] Across northern and central Texas three new military camps—Cooper, Colorado, and Verde—were established. Federal troops were busy trailing Comanches in various parts of the state. But the raiders were not discouraged.[58]

Throughout 1857, raids continued. From the Brazos to the Rio Grande wild tribesmen spread fear and consternation among the settlers. "Our property is stolen and our citizens are scalped within hearing of the guns of the United States forts," wrote a prominent Texan to Governor Pease.[59] When Mescalero Apaches attacked the Texas-Santa Fe mail train, killed and scalped the escort, and destroyed the mail, scouting parties from Forts Lancaster and Davis succeeded in overtaking the marauders, but infantry could do little against a well-mounted foe armed with Sharps or Minié rifles.[60]

The frontier press was thoroughly disappointed. Failure to check Indian depredations, the *Daily Picayune* asserted, already was retarding western settlement. Surely, declared this champion of the frontiersman, "The emigrant will not readily go to a country where his seed must be put in the ground under protection of the musket and where he must nightly mount guard to protect his stock from a wary and treacherous foe."[61] The Indian excitement certainly did not encourage migration to west Texas. Writing from New Braunfels, the special correspondent of the *Picayune* lamented that whereas in the fall of 1852-54 the hotels had been crowded, the stages full to overflowing with prospective homeseekers, "this fall [1855] the tables are turned, and it is rare that we see a man making any inquiries for land; . . . a stranger at the hotels or a family of emigrants on our thoroughfares."[62] "When shall we have justice done us by the federal government?" asked the *State Gazette*. The San Antonio *Ledger* maintained that "the state of Texas can not . . . must not . . . longer rely upon the arm of the regular service with its ill-mounted men or worse than useless infantry force."[63]

Under such circumstances the frontiersmen regularly petitioned Governor Pease for Ranger companies, and the governor was obliging. In 1854 he authorized the Texans to "arm, pursue, overtake and punish" the robbers and send the bill to the federal government. At the same time he ordered six companies of

Mounted Rangers mustered into the service of the United States for a period of three months.[64] Early in July, 1855, he appointed Captain James H. Callahan to raise a company of mounted men for three months to protect the citizens of Bexar and Comal counties. Callahan's company, stationed near the head of the Guadalupe and the Blanco, temporarily put a stop to depredations by defeating and pursuing the raiders across the boundary line into Mexico.[65] Two years later Governor Pease again hearkened to public opinion by calling out a company of Rangers for sixty days. When these proved inadequate he tried a new plan—a combination of Ranger service and militia, which became known as "minute men."[66]

The frontiersmen, meanwhile, acting upon the suggestion of the governor, had taken the matter of local defense into their own hands. The settlers of Tarrant County raised a company of minute men to range the frontier; the citizens near Fredericksburg prepared " 'to beard the lion in his den,' and destroy every red devil without regard to age or sex, that crosses our vision."[67] A number of Texas towns organized volunteer companies and applied to the governor for uniforms and arms. Thus, many a young Texan found himself a member of the Galveston City Guards, the Washington Light Guards, or the Milam Rifles.[68]

The year 1858 witnessed more raids than ever before. The governor, the legislature, the press, the regular and state troops again grappled with the Indian problem. "The Indians are down on our defenceless citizens on the frontier committing murder and pillage on every hand," said the San Antonio *Texan*.[69] Early in January, Governor Runnels reported depredations in four north central counties,[70] and Runnels, like his predecessor, asked for a cavalry force or for authority to raise several mounted companies of state troops. Jesse Chisholm, the celebrated half-breed Cherokee trader, felt certain that the Mormons were tampering with the Camanches; he declared that this tribe spoke of a "Great Chief" (evidently Brigham Young) who was able to destroy the people of the whole United States.[71]

The Texas legislature, meanwhile, authorized the governor to call into service one hundred mounted volunteers, and appropriated $70,000 for the defense of the frontier. Captain John S. Ford was put in command of the Rangers.[72] From spring through fall of 1858, state and federal troops pursued and gave battle to Comanche and Kiowa warriors. Early in May Captain Ford, with a combined force of about 200 Rangers and Indian allies from the Brazos reservation, pursued some 300 Comanches under their chief Iron Jacket and defeated them near the Cherokee side of the Canadian.[73] A month later Lieutenant William B. Hazen of the Eighth Infantry led, from Fort Davis to the Guadalupe Mountains, a combined exploring and punitive expedition against Mescalero Apaches. This surprise attack failed, but Hazen succeeded in recovering stolen animals and capturing the band's entire equipment, including food, arms, ammunition, and fifty scalps.[74]

Sporadic activities of Rangers and regulars, however, meant little to the warlike Comanches and Kiowas, who continued to ravage the frontier. When settlers prepared "to abandon their homes and firesides,"[75] Governor Runnels became impatient. In a sharp letter to Secretary of War Floyd he declared, "The Indians have gone unpunished except only as Texas has administered it herself." He demanded action. Runnels wrote in a similar vein to President Buchanan.[76] Major Neighbors, too, was at a loss to understand why Washington did not heed the call for protection.[77]

But Runnels and Neighbors soon saw the federal government take vigorous action—Brevet Major Earl Van Dorn of the Second Cavalry led an elaborate punitive expedition into the Comanche country. On August 9, 1858, General Twiggs issued the orders.[78] Five weeks later Van Dorn left Fort Belknap with four companies of cavalry, a company of infantry, and a force of more than 130 friendly Indians. After a march northward of eleven days he arrived on the south bank of Otter Creek and established his base of operations—Camp Radziminski. Late in September Van Dorn set out with his mounted troops and Indian scouts for the Comanche village nearly a hundred miles to the eastward. Plodding over prairie, black creek bottoms, and treacherous dog towns, the troops finally sighted the hostile camp. At dawn on October 1, near the present town of Rush Springs, Oklahoma, a fierce fight began. For more than three hours some 400 warriors fought Van Dorn's men bravely and desperately, but superior weapons soon decided the issue. The Indians suffered the loss of some fifty warriors, women, and children, who were taken prisoner; 300 of their animals were captured, and 120 lodges burned. The troops lost five killed and nine wounded. Van Dorn received an arrow in the abdomen, but fortunately his wound did not prove fatal.[79]

Four days after the battle General Twiggs, with more enthusiasm than accuracy, referred to this engagement as "a victory more decisive and complete than any recorded in the history of our Indian warfare."[80] Captain George Frederic Price characterized the encounter as "one of the most important battles ever fought with the Comanches and the most complete victory ever achieved over them."[81]

Despite such optimism, the Comanches were not humbled. It was not long before Van Dorn was called upon to take the field against the same enemy. Pursuit and defeat by the white man's armies failed to divert the Comanches from their regular occupation of plunder and rapine. A portion of this tribe, after being defeated on the Canadian in the fall of 1858, had gone into Mexico, recrossed the Rio Grande in the following spring and resumed their practice of horse-stealing and of raiding the frontier settlements.[82] Once more the settlers, Texas congressmen, and Governor Runnels insisted that the Indians had not been sufficiently punished; once more General Twiggs yielded and issued orders for another campaign.[83] On the last day of April, 1859, Van Dorn with a large force of cavalry and friendly Indians from the Brazos Agency set out from Camp Radziminski and two weeks later, after marching northward about 200 miles, engaged a large force of Comanches and Kiowas south of old Fort Atkinson and decisively defeated them. According to Van Dorn's account, "The Comanches fought without asking or giving quarter until there was not one left to bend a bow."[84]

While Van Dorn was tracking down the Comanches, Lieutenant Hazen, with a small detachment from Fort Inge, pursued Kickapoo warriors to the headwaters of the Nueces, defeated them, and recovered stolen animals.[85] Between the winter of 1858 and spring of 1859 Captain Ford's company had made more than thirty scouting expeditions, performing active service of more than 200 days.[86]

In the spring of 1859 federal and state troops were dispatched to strategic positions along the El Paso mail route and the headwaters of the Red, Washita, and Canadian rivers. Additional military posts—Forts Stockton and Cobb—were established. But the warlike tribes were not deterred. Along the Canadian, Comanches pounced upon a party of United States public land surveyors and seized their equipment; in Comal County the settlements were "gradually thinning," and in Webb County no less than fifty ranches were being abandoned.[87] When outrages continued in the immediate vicinity of the military posts, frontiersmen again became panicky. In mass meetings held in different parts of Texas some pleaded for protection; others expressed a lack of faith in the central government. A public meeting at Weatherford, Parker County, roundly condemned the government's peace policy. In a resolution it declared: "The frontier has been abandoned to the merciless savage foes . . . . Until the Indians are taught that bullets are to be substituted for blankets there will be no peace on our borders." A large convention of citizens of seven northern counties assembling at Weatherford in the following month drew up similar resolutions and urged frontiersmen to take defense into their own hands.[88]

With the election of Sam Houston as governor of Texas in 1859, a change took place in the attitude of the state's chief executive toward the Indians, as well as in the means of dealing with them. A champion of the Indian's rights, Governor Houston believed that diplomacy, kindness, and moral influence would go a long way towards securing tranquillity. In letters to President Buchanan and Secretary of the Interior Jacob Thompson he urged the "importance of ordering a treaty and the payment of annuities directly from a Texas agency." Such a course, he felt confident, "will save many lives and millions of money."[89] At the same time, however, he tendered to Secretary of War Floyd the services of 5,000 Texas volunteers, ordered 300 Rangers into the field, and in counties suffering from Indian dangers, authorized the chief justices to organize detachments of minute men. By April, 1860, there was a "minute" detachment or company in nearly every Texas county.[90] When a rumor spread of a threatened invasion by confederated Indian bands, ten companies of state troops and twenty-three detachments of "minute men" were ready to take the field against the "red villains."[91] Within the next few months the "minute men" and state troops scouted for Indians in various parts of the state, but by the fall of the year the volunteers were ordered mustered out of service.[92]

The high military command in Washington, in the meantime, outlined an elaborate program of defense for the Southwest. On March 10, 1860, the commanders of the Departments of the West, Texas, and New Mexico (Sumner, Lee, and Fauntleroy), respectively, received orders to plan a vigorous spring offensive against the hostile Comanches and Kiowas. It was intended that a strong mounted force, comprising no less than eighteen companies of cavalry, dragoons, and mounted riflemen take the field and operate in three independent columns.[93] But the proposed spring offensive did not materialize. The Indians continued their attacks. In June, when the Comanches were reported on the Pecos River, Colonel Fauntleroy, commander of the New Mexico Military Department, sent three companies of infantry into the threatened area.[94] Despite vigorous scouting expeditions by state and federal troops, Governor Houston, as late as December, 1860, received information that the country was "full of Indians."[95] When pleas for protection were renewed, many "free lances" offered to raise volunteer companies. Houston, too, wrote and then telegraphed Secretary of War Floyd for permission to enroll a corps of Rangers into the service of the United States. But this request was refused.[96]

While whites and Indians were struggling for supremacy, a Texas frontiersman came forward with a unique solution. Saul Smith of Parker County proposed to Governor Houston that bloodhounds be used to track down Indians and thus secure peace on the frontier. With 1,000 or even 500 bloodhounds, Smith felt certain, a small ranging force would accomplish more than thousands of men. Smith's proposal does not seem to have been given a trial.[97]

White outlaws added to the danger and confusion. Organized bands of Americans and Mexican pseudo-patriots, occasionally mixed with Negroes and Indians, swooped down on frontier settlements, intercepted commercial caravans, stole stock, and terrorized the inhabitants.[98] The disturbances along the lower Rio Grande, accentuated by "Mustangers"[99] and white scalp-hunters,[100] centered mainly around four episodes: the Merchants' War,[101] the Callahan Expedition,[102] the Cart War,[103] and the depredations of Cortinas.[104] The "White Knives" proved a thorn in the side of frontiersmen.

For twelve years federal and state troops battled with Indians but without decisive result. Of the numerous military sorties of both regulars and Rangers, Major Van Dorn's two expeditions against the Comanches were the only ones of any appreciable size, and even they failed to achieve a permanent peace. Throughout this period, it was customary for partisans of state defense to discredit the service rendered by the United States army on the Texas frontier. Indignant Texans sometimes referred to federal troops as "sleepy soldiers who loaf around the posts." Such a characterization, of course, was as unfair as it was untrue. An examination of the reports of the secretaries of war during the years 1848-60 will show that federal forces engaged in more expeditions, fought more Indians, and recovered more property than did the state troops. The United States army represented the constant factor in the program of defense; the state troops were the varying element, and, therefore, the more spectacular. In 1860 nearly 3,000 regulars, or more than one-fifth of the entire United States army, were engaged in guarding a thousand miles of international border and an additional thousand miles of Indian frontier in the state. That is all that could have been reasonably expected.[105]

CHAPTER IX

New Mexico Tribesmen Go on the Warpath

BEYOND the Rio Grande the system of frontier defense was not radically different from that employed in Texas, nor were its achievements. In August, 1846, when General Kearny entered Santa Fe and proclaimed the authority of the United States, representatives of the Pueblos, Navahos, Utahs, and Apaches offered submission. Before long, however, the warlike tribes of New Mexico challenged the authority of the army by attacking military trains, driving off cattle, and even murdering Governor Charles Bent. Punitive expeditions served only to increase the contempt of the natives for the American soldier.[1]

While troops were moving westward and establishing military positions,[2] President Polk recommended fairness and leniency in dealing with the natives. He believed that the presence of agents among the tribes, the distribution of gifts, and the maintenance of a small military force would secure the Indians' good will and preserve the peace. The President was optimistic.[3]

In the spring of 1849 several Indian agencies were moved westward—the agency of the Upper Missouri was moved to Salt Lake City and the one at Council Bluffs to Santa Fe. James S. Calhoun was appointed Indian agent, and Washington Barrow of Tennessee was appointed subagent at the Santa Fe agency; John C. Hays of San Antonio was made subagent for the tribes on the Gila.[4] Calhoun was an excellent choice. A Southerner by birth, he had served with distinction in the Mexican War and his appointment as agent at Santa Fe was soon followed by promotion to the office of Superintendent of Indian Affairs and governor of the territory. Calhoun was thoroughly capable, honest, and intelligent—rare qualities in the Indian service of the period. Though occasionally maligned by his enemies, he accomplished a good deal for the frontier territory. And three years after his appointment, in June, 1852, when he died on the plains between Santa Fe and Kansas, his death was a great loss both to the Indian and the white man.[5]

Shortly after Calhoun arrived at Santa Fe to assume the duties of his office, he wrote to Commissioner of Indian Affairs William Medill that the Indians presumed a great deal upon their knowledge of a safe retreat into the mountains; that they could not be restrained until they were thoroughly chastised.[6] Calhoun was right about the Indians' retreat to the mountains, but he was too sanguine about the ease with which they could be punished. In the winter and spring of 1849 military units, plowing through deep mud and snow, tracked down and routed war parties of Utahs and Apaches but accomplished no definite results.[7]

To overawe the Navahos, Brevet Lieutenant Colonel John M. Washington, military commander and governor of the territory, led an elaborate expedition into their country. Washington's imposing army of 175 men, with its artillery wagons, and pack-mules, carrying thirty days' rations for 500 men, left Santa Fe the middle of August for Cañon de Chelly, the reputed stronghold of the Navahos. At Jemez the command was increased to 400 men. Marching westward, the army arrived at the Cañon early in September, but instead of chastising the Navahos, Washington and Calhoun entered into a treaty with them. Mariano Martinez and Chapitone, acting for the tribesmen, agreed to deliver captives, restore stock and other stolen property, permit passage through their country, and allow the establishment of military posts and agencies. The government on its part was to distribute gifts and fix the boundaries of the Navahos at an early date.[8]

Despite Washington's brave and imposing array of force his expedition did not accomplish a great deal. Some considered it a total failure. The *Daily Missouri Republican* characterized it as

"one of the most ridiculous set on foot by a military commander."
Its failure certainly did not surprise the *Republican*. Washington
was a man of peace who very much dreaded bloodshed of the
"poor Indian." The treaty proved a dead letter. While the troops
were still in the Navaho country, some of the tribe stole government mules almost in sight of the flagstaff in the plaza at Santa
Fe. A courier dispatched to Colonel Washington was killed within
a few miles of his camp.[9]

Apaches, meanwhile, in the vicinity of Las Vegas and the
Santa Rita Copper Mines terrorized the settlers.[10] In October Calhoun wrote to the Commissioner of Indian Affairs that not a day
passed without some fresh outrages. The *Daily Missouri Republican* declared that the Indian menace paralyzed industry and prevented the extension of western settlement. Discontent and confusion prevailed everywhere.[11]

Calhoun had a remedy—"compulsory enlightenment . . . enforced at the point of the bayonet."[12] His recommendation included an additional mounted regiment, military posts at Tunicha
and at Cañon de Chelly, and an Indian agent at every pueblo. The
citizens of Santa Fe eagerly approved Calhoun's proposals and
petitioned for a more vigorous military leader.[13] In September
Colonel John Munroe, a new commander, arrived with re-en-
forcements. By November troops occupied seven military positions in the department.[14] A month later Calhoun negotiated a
treaty with the Utahs at Abiquiu similar to the one agreed upon
by the Navahos. But again peace was not secured.[15]

Throughout the year 1850 raids continued. Navahos committed depredations near Cebolleta and on the Puerco; Kiowas
attacked peaceful Utah villages north of Taos, drove off stock,
and captured women and children; Apaches, in broad daylight
and within sight of the garrison at Doña Ana, drove off cattle
and captured Mexican citizens. Indians cut off an express party
from the States some forty miles east of Las Vegas, brutally murdered the entire party, and left their bodies to the wolves.[16]

Periodically, settlers filed claims with the territorial government for losses suffered at the hands of the Indians. Within a period of eighteen months property losses, mainly in sheep, mules, cattle, and horses, were estimated at more than $114,000.[17]

Frontiersmen did not lack champions in Congress. Speaking before the Senate in 1850, Benton of Missouri painted a harrowing picture. The desolation and ravages suffered by the inhabitants of New Mexico at the hands of the Indians during the first three years of American rule, Benton declared, far exceeded those in any other three years of New Mexico's entire existence. To defend this territory the United States had supplied a few companies of dragoons and stationary infantry, but within sight of their barracks the wild tribes murdered men and women, carried off children, and drove away flocks and herds reaching into the thousands. This small, inadequate force Benton considered "a reproach to us . . . and to our republican government." To turn a deaf ear to pleas for protection was "to draw upon our heads the censure of all good men."[18]

Suggestions for providing greater security were not wanting. David D. Mitchell of the Central Indian Superintendency proposed a treaty with all the tribes west of the Missouri River and the establishment of definite Indian boundaries; each tribe was to be held responsible for the conduct of its members.[19] Since among the wild tribes our government was labeled a "weak fellow," Hugh N. Smith, New Mexico's delegate to Congress, considered it high time for Indian agents to reside among the troublesome natives and have a strong military force to maintain order.[20] Commissioner of Indian Affairs Orlando Brown, Adjutant General Roger Jones, and officers in the field favored a periodic display of force among the dangerous tribes. John R. Bartlett, Commissioner of the United States-Mexican Boundary Survey Commission, contended that "the Indians must be annihilated or removed where they could do no harm."[21] The constant pressure for greater protection was followed by military reconnaissances, tours of inspection, and construction of additional forts. By 1852 seven new military posts were built in the territory.[22]

In the meantime, Colonel Edwin V. Sumner arrived with a considerable force from Fort Leavenworth and assumed command of the Ninth Military Department. Sumner's knowledge of New Mexico, his long experience on the frontier and in border camps, and his devotion to the service made him eminently qualified for the delicate task.[23] Sumner started with a blaze of energy to bring about reforms and to restore respect for the white man's government. In the middle of August, 1851, he left Santa Fe for the Navaho country with a large force of dragoons and artillery to punish the marauders. A week later he sent Brevet Major James H. Carleton with a company of dragoons to scour the plains between Fort Union and the Arkansas River. By October, having selected a site for a military post at Cañon Bonito, Sumner pushed forward to Cañon de Chelly. But the Navahos, having learned of his movements, drove off their cattle and sheep to more secure retreats in the interior. Sumner was unable to meet them in open battle. He had selected a site for Fort Defiance; he had penetrated Cañon de Chelly about a dozen miles; but he failed to chastise the Navahos.[24] In the Far Southwest, below the big bend of the Gila, Tonto Apaches had committed the atrocious Oatman massacre.[25]

It was at this time that Calhoun assumed his duties as the first territorial governor of New Mexico. Although his administration met with uniformly high praise, the conduct of some of his subordinates was severely criticized. Richard H. Weightman, one of Calhoun's Indian agents, who arrived at Santa Fe in July, 1851, was accused of doing nothing for two months but electioneer for the office of delegate to Congress. When he was elected, he left for Washington and took his colleague Edward H. Wingfield with him. Furthermore, as the limits of civil and military authority were not clearly defined, Calhoun's position was trying.[26] John Greiner, one of Calhoun's able assistants, writing from Santa Fe

in October, 1851, painted this realistic picture of the chaotic conditions prevailing in the territory: "Everybody and everything in
this . . . country appears at cross purposes. . . . Colonel Sumner re-
fuses to acknowledge the right of the Governor to send Indian
agents with him to the Indian country. . . . The Governor and
Secretary of the Territory can not hitch horses. The American resi-
dents are at war with the Governor while the Mexican population side with him. Even the missionaries [Baptist, Presbyterian,
Methodist] are at loggerheads. . . . The American troops are at
war with the Indians [Navahos]. . . ." But the soldiers were unable
to catch the elusive tribesmen.[27]

Such a state of affairs, coupled with a great need for food,
roused the bolder spirits to renew their attacks. Indian officials
and army leaders once more tried the standard remedies—treaties
and force. In the spring of 1851 Calhoun concluded a treaty with
Chacon and other Apache chiefs living east of the Rio Grande.
By this agreement the Indians pledged themselves to accept the
new lands to be assigned them and to settle down in pueblos; the
government agreed to furnish them facilities for tilling the soil.
Within less than a month, however, this treaty was violated. In
the fall of the year Greiner reported that the Utahs and Apaches
boasted of how many whites they had killed, and talked very
glibly of the scalps they intended to take.[28]

It was quite unfortunate that the New Mexican tribesmen
could not remain more peaceful, for the territory seemed on the
verge of a business boom. The report of the discovery of gold on
the headwaters of the Gila and on the Rio Conejos created a feverish spirit of buying. In the spring of the year many Mexican
and American merchants were on their way to the States to purchase supplies. If the Indians were suppressed and an adequate
system of roads or railroads from the States were built, the "58,000
greasers and 2,000 greasers' masters," it was believed, would grow
into a half a million prosperous inhabitants.[29]

Civil and military officers attempted to persuade or to intimi-

date the wild tribes into submission. In November, 1851, Calhoun
visited a band of Utahs at Abiquiu and distributed gifts among
them. And several months later, in an effort to keep the Navahos
at peace, Calhoun and Sumner met a large party of Navaho warriors at Jemez and submitted to them the alternative of peace and
plenty or wasted fields, torn lodges, and starving widows and
children. The Indians accepted the terms and gave hostages but
broke the pledge.[30] Early in the following May, Greiner had a
"talk" with the Navahos and told them to "speak straight." Several months later Sumner and Greiner met some Apache chiefs
at Santa Fe and Acoma and concluded new treaties. In November
Greiner held a grand council with about 500 Utahs at Abiquiu
and distributed about $3,000 worth of gifts.[31]

To make these "talks" and treaties effective in intimidating
the Apaches, who were terrorizing the Rio Grande Valley, Sumner made a grand display of energy. In February, 1852, he ordered
cavalry and infantry units into the Apache country and dispatched troops to the vicinity of Socorro and Valverde. He also
established a strong military force at Santa Fe, and formed a camp
at Albuquerque.[32]

But Sumner's very display of energy, especially in the early
months after his arrival, served only as a boomerang. His attempted reforms, like those of Calhoun, involved the movement
of troops from the settlements into the interior. As a result he
became quite unpopular with the merchants and traders, who resented the loss of the soldiers' business. A policy of retrenchment,
by which he discharged civilian employees from the military service, added to his unpopularity. This army of unemployed joined
the bands of thieves, cutthroats, and robbers who had been lib-
erated from the Santa Fe prison by Calhoun because of lack of
funds to maintain prisoners. Disguised as Indians, they terrorized
the settlements.[33] Although Sumner arrived promptly at Santa
Fe and restored order, the frontier press, ever a champion of disgruntled classes, took him to task. "The Big Bug of Albuquer-

que," ridiculed the Santa Fe *Weekly Gazette,* had bought a peace rather than obtained one by conquest. It was not Colonel Sumner, the *Gazette* continued, but the "red cloths and calico shirts" that had cowed the Indians. When Sumner-retaliated and characterized the New Mexican populace as "thoroughly debased and totally incapable of self government," he brought down greater abuse on his head. A writer under the name of "Justitia" called Sumner demented or besotted, and the *Gazette* declared "his every official act for two years . . . one series of blunders and absurdities." "He is too stupid and dishonest to acknowledge himself wrong," concluded the *Gazette.*[34] Sumner was removed.

Dr. William Carr Lane, who succeeded Calhoun, was a man of vision, vigor, and accomplishment. Before coming to New Mexico, he already had had experience as administrator, lawmaker, and soldier. He was the first mayor of St. Louis—having been elected to that office seven times, more often than any other man in the city's history. Handsome, warm-hearted, and high-spirited, he was an ardent champion of free schools and municipal waterworks. He served in the Missouri legislature and took part in expeditions against Tecumseh and Black Hawk. Above all, he was a humanitarian.[35]

Since his agents, John Greiner and Dr. Michael Steck, also felt kindly towards the red man and believed that the wild tribes could be trained to pueblo life, Lane tried the experiment of feeding, instead of fighting, the Indians. That the experiment would take time, patience, and money did not discourage the new Superintendent of Indian Affairs. In April, 1853, he made provisional treaties with some Apaches, agreeing to furnish food for five years and to give other aid to all who would work. Without waiting for the Senate's approval, Lane spent between $20,000 and $40,000 on the project. He fed about 1,000 natives on farms at Abiquiu and Fort Webster, but the experiment proved a failure. With suspension of the rations, the Apaches became bolder than ever.[36] Lane's policy, too, proved unpopular. He was succeeded by David Meriwether.[37]

Despite honest efforts of officials, the inhabitants of the territory considered themselves treated "like a step child . . . shamefully and inexcusably neglected by the General Government." The
settlers, the Santa Fe *Weekly Gazette* complained, were still "surrounded by barbarians some hundred of miles thick."[88] Indian
Agent Edward A. Graves characterized the New Mexican Indian
policy as a complete failure. Like many others, he attributed the
unfortunate state of affairs to the division of authority between
civil and military officers. Graves stoutly recommended concentration of power in the hands of one or the other. Unfortunately,
this sane advice was not heeded.[39]

In the half dozen years before the opening of the Civil War,
conditions in the territory became worse. Reports of rich silver
mines east of the Organ Mountains and gold in the vicinity of
Fort Webster attracted new streams of emigrants,[40] while the
California migration continued on a large scale. The Indian again
was pushed aside; the old story was repeated. Early in 1854 the
Indians of the territory declared they "must steal or starve." No
one realized the truth of this statement any better than Meriwether. He pointed out that the tribes would either have to be fed
for a time, or be exterminated; otherwise they might become masters of the whole country. When Meriwether's funds were exhausted and he could not relieve the suffering of the natives, the
disgruntled tribesmen took to the warpath.[41]

The Apaches now occupied the limelight, although the Navahos and other tribes contributed a good share to the general disorder. Early in February, 1854, Jicarilla braves ran off a herd of
cattle from the neighborhood of Barclay's Fort.[42] Lieutenant David
Bell with a party of dragoons gave pursuit. In the following month
federal troops from Cantonment Burgwin, serving as an escort to
the Santa Fe-Texas mail, encountered a strong force of about 250
Jicarilla Apache and Utah warriors near the Mexican village of
Cieneguilla, about twenty-five miles from Taos. In the fierce
three hours' struggle the troops barely escaped annihilation. Of

sixty dragoons, only seventeen men, mostly wounded, managed to escape to Taos.[43]

To prevent further disaster and to learn the truth about rumors that "the mountains around here [Taos] are completely covered with Indians," and that the savages were slaughtering women and children,[44] Lieutenant Colonel Philip St. George Cooke carried the war into the heart of the Indian country. Early in April, after tracking the enemy through snow and ice, over rugged mountains, and through dense forests, he succeeded in defeating Jicarilla Apache warriors on the upper branches of the *Agua* (or *Ojo*) *Caliente* and driving them beyond the Rio Grande. A month later a portion of Cooke's command pursued another band of Apaches into the Raton Mountains and inflicted defeat.[45] The Santa Fe *Weekly Gazette* hailed these expeditions as the dawn of a new day. The chastisement the Indian so long merited, jubilantly observed the *Gazette,* was about to be given him by a "hand that will not spare the rod."[46] The Jicarilla Apaches, to be sure, had been humbled and compelled to sue for peace, but many a year was yet to pass before they and their kinsmen were to be completely pacified.

The *Gazette* had been overoptimistic. Early in July, Judge Charles Beaubien wrote to Manuel Alvarez, former United States consul at Santa Fe and one-time acting governor, that the Apaches were committing depredations on all mountain roads. Near the Pima villages a party of fifty emigrants to California was reported murdered, and thousands of sheep and hundreds of oxen had been driven off near Fort Union.[47] Governor Meriwether stated that losses sustained by the white population of the territory during the current year amounted to about $112,000.[48] The territorial legislature, naturally, memorialized Congress to indemnify the settlers. The bloody incursions of the numerous roaming bands, the lawmakers declared, "had locked up and sealed the resources of the territory and reduced the citizens to lamentable indigence."[49]

Indian agents, meanwhile, again held "talks" with prominent

chieftains. In March, Kit Carson met Jicarilla Apache leaders at Cantonment Burgwin and learned that this tribe wanted a resident agent.[50] Three months later Henry L. Dodge, who lived among the Navahos and exercised considerable influence over them, arrived in Santa Fe with a deputation of about forty braves to hold a "talk" with acting-Governor Messervy. The council, held in the public square amid great ceremony, gave the chiefs such satisfaction that they promised not to steal and agreed to bring in all "bad men."[51] Congress, too, was trying to placate the Indians when in July, 1854, it appropriated $30,000 for new treaties.[52]

Warlike Apaches and Utahs, however, had little faith in "talks" and treaties, and early in 1855 again took to the warpath.[53] General John Garland, the new military commander, was now determined to teach these "bad Indians" a lesson they would not easily forget. In the spring of the year he had about a thousand troops in the field. Besides numerous minor skirmishes, two major punitive expeditions under Fauntleroy and Miles produced a temporary lull. When a band of Utahs committed murders and depredations along the upper Red River, Colonel Thomas T. Fauntleroy organized a force of about 500 regulars and volunteers and started in search of the enemy. Leaving Fort Massachusetts on March 15, he succeeded in overtaking a combined force of about 200 Apache and Utah warriors under their chieftains Huero and Blanco at Cochetopa Pass and routed them. A month later in a second engagement on the upper Arkansas near the Poncho Pass, Fauntleroy defeated another band under Chacon and recovered much plunder.

To break the power of the Apaches completely, Lieutenant Colonel Dixon S. Miles with a force of more than 300 men prepared for a three months' campaign through the White, Sacramento, and Guadalupe Mountains. But Miles did not measure strength with the enemy. Upon his arrival at the Bonita River, he hearkened to the pleas of Dr. Steck and held a "talk" in Dog Cañon with a dozen Mescalero chiefs. They sued for peace and promised to surrender stolen property and to deliver hostages. Miles's bloodless campaign temporarily humbled the Apaches and opened some 150 miles of wagon road.[54] In September the Santa Fe *Weekly Gazette* announced that " 'Order reigns in Warsaw.' " The territorial legislature passed laudatory resolutions thanking officers and men for their gallant conduct.[55] New treaties soon followed. The government promised new reservation boundaries and annuities; the principal chiefs assured Governor Meriwether of the red man's desire for peace and a "willingness to abandon his roving and predatory habits."[56]

The settlers violently opposed the treaties as being too favorable to the savages. The proposed Indian reserves, the frontiersmen contended, closed too much land to settlement and cut off too generous a slice of grazing land. The Senate rejected all the treaties.[57] But even if the agreements had been ratified, it is doubtful whether the Indians would have observed them. The tribes were suffering from hunger, some natives being reduced to eating horsehides. Fondness for firewater and gambling, for which the white man was largely responsible, left the tribes even more destitute, and goaded them on to new outbreaks.[58]

Reports on the Indian danger were conflicting. Governor Meriwether and Secretary of War Davis represented conditions as comparatively quiet and peaceful.[59] But Colonel James L. Collins,[60] Meriwether's successor,[61] wrote to Commissioner of Indian Affairs Charles E. Mix that more murders and robberies had been perpetrated in 1856 than in any previous year. The territorial legislature complained that no less than 30,000 savages roamed the country with but little restraint. In one foray alone Indian rustlers had driven off 10,000 head of sheep. A correspondent of the *Daily Missouri Republican* reported "nothing new in New Mexico except Indian depredations and murders."[62] The settlers felt themselves greatly aggrieved, and blamed their woes largely on Meriwether's "temporizing, weak, and imbecile" conduct. "The policy of waiting for those Indians to get *good,* may be pleasant enough for the functionaries of the Territory," declared the Santa Fe *Weekly Gazette,* "but it is not likely to afford much relief to our citizens."[63] Meriwether soon resigned and left for the States.[64]

While the press was busy heaping abuse on Meriwether, the troops built Forts Stanton and Buchanan.[65] Colonel Bonneville arrived with additional recruits. But the Mimbres, Gila, and Coyotero Apaches were not impressed; they terrorized the settlements west of the Rio Grande. In November, 1856, when Mogollon and Gila Apaches surprised Indian Agent Dodge a few miles from Zuñi and brutally murdered him,[66] the Gila expedition followed.

Colonel Benjamin L. E. de Bonneville, commander of the expedition, was one of the most picturesque figures in the United States army. Born in France in 1796, he came to the United States at an early age, entered West Point in 1813, and two years later graduated from there. His service of more than forty years had taken him to virtually every section of the United States. His tour of exploration of the Rocky Mountains in the thirties added to his fame. The "cheerful, debonair" Bonneville[67] soon mapped out a plan of campaign. Establishing his depot on the east bank of the Gila some fifteen miles from the Mogollon Mountains, he organized his forces into two main columns. The northern column, commanded by Colonel William L. Loring, struck out southeastward across a rough, mountainous, and deserted country. Upon crossing the San Vicente Mountains, it surprised a force of Apaches but succeeded in killing only some half dozen warriors, including their principal chief Cuchillo Negro. The troops recovered considerable plunder.[68]

Bonneville, meanwhile, accompanied the southern column under Lieutenant Colonel Miles to the Coyotero country. Marching southwestward from his camp on the Gila he encountered a large force of Coyotero and Mogollon Apaches in the present southeastern Arizona. On June 27 the fight began. From half past four till sundown a fierce battle raged. On a battlefield strung out for a mile on both sides of the Gila, Apache warriors fought valiantly and desperately but in the end were severely defeated. The troops suffered only half a dozen wounded and succeeded in taking prisoners and destroying considerable property. Shortly afterwards Coyotero chieftains came to Fort Thorn and promised to give up their lands, sheep, horses—everything—if only peace were granted.[69]

The Santa Fe *Weekly Gazette* characterized the Gila expedition as the most arduous, trying, and dangerous military operation projected since New Mexico had become a possession of the United States. Again the territorial legislature thanked officers and men for attaining their objective. They hailed Bonneville a hero, who had taught the Apaches a "most salutary lesson."[70]

In the midst of the celebration of victory Abraham R. Rencher, the new governor, arrived in Santa Fe.[71] Collins, the new Superintendent of Indian Affairs, had already visited the Navahos and found them friendly.[72] Now that the offices of governor and Superintendent were separated, it was believed that better times were at hand. But the change in civil administration failed to improve frontier conditions. The old spectre of hunger still haunted the Indian. In the winter of 1858, Cutera, one of the principal Mescalero chiefs, and a number of braves visited the superintendency at Santa Fe and begged for help. In the spring of the year when Kit Carson visited some Capote Utahs on the Conejos River he found them starving. "They must either starve or commit depredations," he wrote to Collins. At this agency Carson already was feeding 200 Utahs daily.[73] The Navahos, although still believing themselves the "greatest people living," were in a desperate plight.[74]

Added to the spectre of hunger at this time was a new danger. Vagabonds, ruffians, and filibusterers from California and elsewhere perpetrated deeds of violence on the sparsely settled white and Indian villages.[75] These undesirables readily preyed on the Indian and incited him to deeds of revenge and retaliation. A grave period of disorder followed. The Comanches and Apaches renewed their raids; the Mohaves were committing depredations; the Navahos again caused grave concern; and the Utahs, perhaps instigated by the Mormons, were not in too friendly a mood.

In the spring of 1858 Comanches attacked a white settlement on Red River about 130 miles from Fort Union and looted and burned the establishment. Later in the year Comanche and Kiowa warriors attacked the Overland Mail traveling eastward from Albuquerque to Neosho, Missouri, massacred the entire party and destroyed the mail. These Indians were determined that no road should ever be opened through their country as long as one of them was left alive. Apaches, meanwhile, drove off thousands of sheep in San Miguel County and terrorized settlers in the Tubac area. Captain Davidson's punitive expedition into the Piñal Indian country succeeded only in securing topographical information. The Indians, mounted on fleet horses, knew how to keep out of reach of the troops.[76]

For the enmity of Mangas Coloradas' band of Mimbreños Apaches, the whites had themselves to blame. Mangas Coloradas, or Red Sleeves, the greatest and most influential Apache of the nineteenth century, was a power to be reckoned with. A strong and magnificent physique, a keen and shrewd intelligence, coupled with daring courage and great wealth, gave him all the aspects of an ancient feudal baron. Surrounded by a large and influential following, he enjoyed prestige and wielded sway among the various branches of his race from the Colorado River to the Guadalupe Mountains. For half a century prior to the Civil War this robber baron was a veritable terror of the Southwest, ravaging and destroying the northern portions of Chihuahua and Sonora, large tracts of Durango, the whole of present Arizona, and a considerable part of New Mexico.[77]

In 1858 a crisis developed when about 150 desperate gold miners rushed into a new field discovered at Pinos Altos, near Santa Rita. When the Indian chief attempted to persuade the prospectors to go to other fields, they shamefully flogged him.[78] Apache anger and hatred toward the white man rose to feverish pitch. Mangas Coloradas soon assembled a large body of braves along the Overland Mail route and prepared for vengeance. The aggrieved chieftain now openly declared that if the government did not furnish him more beef and flour, he would permit his people to take what they pleased.[79] But the distribution of food and gifts was no assurance for security. Mangas Coloradas' desire for vengeance was never satiated. He was killed during the Civil War.

During 1859 and 1860 the Apaches continued their ravages. According to the *Daily Missouri Republican,* more depredations were being committed in New Mexico than in the rest of the Union combined. Stock was swept away; savages ran riot in the towns.[80] When Dr. Steck distributed beef, corn, cotton cloth, and fine blankets to a thousand Piñal Apaches assembled at Cañon del Oro, they promised to keep the peace; but only three days later, they attempted to run off the animals of the Santa Rita Copper Mining Company. During the summer Apache tribesmen robbed the Patagonia and Sonora mining companies of stock, stopped the Overland Mail, levied tribute of tobacco and corn upon the passengers, and burned the supplies of the Mexican fort at the head of the San Pedro. Punitive expeditions under Lieutenant Lazelle and Lieutenant Colonel Reeve into Dog Cañon and the Mescal Mountains were in vain.[81] During 1860, while the War Department was preparing for an active spring campaign, Indian outrages continued to be daring and numerous. Cochise and his band of Chiricahua Apaches spread terror along the Overland Mail route, by murdering about 150 Americans.[82]

The Mohaves, meanwhile, had decided to test the strength or weakness of American arms. In January, 1859, Mohave warriors attacked the camp of Brevet Lieutenant Colonel William Hoffman at Beaver Lake in the vicinity of the Colorado River near the thirty-fifth parallel. The Indians misjudged their opponent and were easily routed. Hoffman, a veteran of thirty years' service on the western frontier,[88] knew how to deal with the troublesome

Mohaves. To keep a watchful eye on this hostile tribe, he soon led more than 700 men from Fort Yuma to Beale's Crossing and established Fort Mojave. At the same time a command of dragoons was marching northeastward from San Bernardino to the new post. This show of military strength overawed the Indians. Six principal chiefs, wearing "old shirts, strings of beads around their necks, knives and scissors dangling from their sides, feathers in hair, faces painted but downcast and frightened," and about 500 tribesmen, mostly naked, appeared before the commander and humbly sued for peace.[84] When Hoffman told the chiefs that peace or war was in their hands, they accepted all the conditions. Their submission, however, was destined to be of short duration.[85]

But it was against the Navahos that the troops at this time exerted the greatest pressure, not because this tribe was any more guilty than its neighbors, but because it shielded wrongdoers and failed to exercise control over them. When a Navaho warrior had a domestic difficulty with his wife and was unable to bring her to do his will, the customs of his nation permitted him to kill some outsider. Thus, in July, 1858, at Fort Defiance, a Navaho shot and killed Jim, Major Brooks's Negro boy. Navaho failure to give up the murderer and a hasty and impolitic attack by Captain George McLane on Navaho warriors at *Ojo del Oso,* or Bear Spring, led to open hostilities.

To Lieutenant Colonel Miles was entrusted the task of chastising the Navaho. With a force of more than 300 men, he set out, early in September, from Fort Defiance for the Navaho country. Within the next three months practically the entire available military strength of the department was in the field. Miles's men penetrated Cañon de Chelly, fought seven or eight skirmishes, killed about 200 warriors, captured thousands of sheep, and destroyed about $100,000 worth of property. Late in November, S. M. Yost, Indian agent at Fort Defiance, proudly announced that the Navahos had been decisively conquered and, like the Santa Fe *Weekly Gazette* three years earlier, he, too, proclaimed the glad tidings that "peace reigneth in Warsaw."[86] Unfortunately, Yost, like many of his contemporaries, understood neither the Indian character nor the complexity of the Indian problem.

Outwardly, the Navahos seemed crushed. Old, iron-featured warriors, who once had considered their nation invincible, now embraced the Indian agent and hung their proud heads in humility and subjection. Armijo and Sarcillo Largo, two influential chieftains, pointed to the women and children and begged for peace in their behalf. A soldier at Fort Defiance, who composed a "Navajo War Song" in honor of the white man's victories, portrayed the red warriors in none too heroic a role. For, sang the trooper:

> They ran like very devils
> When our rifles we did show;
> Sent our lead into the heads
> Of Johnny Navajó.
> Then scouting we will go, my boys,
> Scouting we will go;
> We'll do our best to put to rest
> Poor Johnny Navajó.

The singer and his comrades felt very much elated. They had fought "And whipped poor Johnny Navajo."[87]

On Christmas Day, 1858, Superintendent Collins and Colonel Bonneville met Navaho chiefs in council at Fort Defiance and negotiated another treaty. The agreement once more provided for indemnification, liberation of captives, and the fixing of boundaries beyond which the Indians were not to pass. The federal government, of course, was to have freedom of passage through the Indian country and the privilege of establishing military posts.[88] But this treaty, too, accomplished nothing; the Navahos broke it before the Senate could ratify it. Punitive expeditions were again to follow.

The Navaho war was not without its critics. Although some felt that Bonneville had taught this tribe a lesson and brought it to its knees, others considered the venture a dismal failure. The New Mexico correspondent of the *Daily Missouri Republican* characterized it as a series of blunders from beginning to end. The expenditure of more than $1,000,000 to avenge the death of a Negro boy certainly was an expensive luxury, especially when it failed to accomplish its objective. The Santa Fe *Gazette* believed the Indians should have been pur. .ed more severely.[89]

In the summer and fall of 1859, when the Navahos again broke their pledges and committed new depredations, the military decided, once for all, to learn the real strength of the tribe and the true character of their country. Punitive-exploring expeditions were dispatched from Fort Defiance. These did not engage the Navahos in battle but succeeded in opening virgin trails and "sections of country never before known or attempted." Captain J. G. Walker of the Mounted Rifles, who also penetrated and explored Cañon de Chelly, once more dispelled the notion of its impregnability. Moreover, Walker found the Navahos desirous of peace and believed that another war against them would be a grave mistake. "Might not a little forbearance be the true part of wisdom?" queried this officer.[90]

But there is a limit to forbearance. Before long, hostile Navahos not only pillaged exposed settlements and drove off large herds of stock but even dared to attack Fort Defiance. Early in February, 1860, a force of 500 braves fell upon the cattle herd of the post but were repulsed. The raiders then threw all caution to the winds. At dawn of April 30 between 1,000 and 3,000 warriors attacked the post. It was only after a two-hour bitter fight that the small garrison of infantry succeeded in driving them off.[91]

As the summer advanced, outrages continued. One band of Navahos murdered settlers and seized stock within ten miles of Santa Fe; another band once more attempted to capture the mule herd of Fort Defiance and was again repulsed. To humble this stiff-necked tribe, Secretary of War Floyd ordered Colonel Fauntleroy to wage a winter campaign against them with secrecy and vigor. Troops from the East and Utah were soon marching toward New Mexico. By September Fauntleroy had fifteen companies of regulars in the Navaho country, as well as a command of friendly Utah Indians organized by Superintendent Collins.[92]

While preparations for the winter campaign were in progress a spirited quarrel developed between Fauntleroy, Governor Rencher, and the press. "The commander who sets snugly by the fire in his handsome quarters and issues warlike bulletins," declared the *Gazette,* "will never accomplish anything." The *Gazette* and the governor urged more vigorous action. Fauntleroy resented such imputations and criticized the civil authority for interfering with the military and unduly inflaming the inhabitants.[93]

In the spring the territorial legislature added to the confusion by authorizing an independent campaign. Fauntleroy vigorously opposed this movement. When Rencher ordered the formation of two companies of volunteers and supplied them with arms, Fauntleroy refused to furnish the ammunition. Fauntleroy declared, moreover, that if the governor authorized a campaign, the federal troops would be withdrawn from the Indian country.[94] Despite this threat a volunteer force of more than 400 men soon invaded the land of the Navahos, drove off considerable stock, slaughtered a great many animals, and returned to the settlements only when their ammunition gave out.

As a further complication, the citizens of Santa Fe decided to take the law into their own hands. A convention late in August urged independent expeditions against the Navahos. Unauthorized bodies of men were soon on the march. More than 300 mounted men penetrated the Navaho country, took possession of fields, captured large herds, and led away many captives, mostly women and children. Governor Rencher believed that these private military ventures were the work of a few interested speculators, backed by some federal officials, including Superintendent Collins. He tried to stop them, but in vain. The Santa Fe *Gazette,*

owned by Collins, naturally endorsed the white man's war.[95] Following the unauthorized military ventures, Colonel E. R. S.
Canby in the winter of 1860-61 led an expedition of regulars and
volunteers, which culminated in a three months' truce.[96]

Army officers and Indian agents, meanwhile, had learned that
Mormons were tampering with the tribes. Friendly Pah-Utes told
officials that the Mormons had invited the Navahos, Utahs, and
Mohaves to a council at Sierra Panoche, some eighty miles east of
the Colorado River, and promised to distribute arms and ammunition among the warriors. Commissioner of Indian Affairs
James W. Denver charged Brigham Young with poisoning the
minds of the natives. Unless the red man resisted, hinted the Mormons, the whole Indian country would soon be lost. The Mormon
"tata," or leader, was represented as the Indians' truest friend,
worth more than all the other "tatas," since he gave them kegs
of powder and guns, and could whip the whole world.[97] Con-
gressman John S. Phelps of Missouri, in a speech at Santa Fe, declared that the federal government had temporized too long. It
was high time for drastic action. In a fervent appeal Phelps insisted that "our armies must march through the Indian country
and leave trails of desolation." Superintendent Collins endorsed
Phelps's policy.[98]

The unsettled state of affairs was particularly annoying to
American merchants and traders who carried on an extensive
trade of approximately $10,000,000 a year with northern Mexican
states.[99] Moreover, rumors of gold discoveries in the gulches of
both sides of the Gila in the fall of 1858 attracted new emigrant
waves from Arkansas and Texas. The newly born Gila City with
its hotel and stores and rapidly growing population was doing a
thriving business. Silver mines near Tucson proved rich and promising, and silver mining companies near Tubac attracted the attention of capitalists.[100] But the Indian danger was a constant
menace to progress.

Unscrupulous white men intensified the danger. A self-styled

Dr. Lemon, alias Captain Bill Snooks, and his gang of outlaws devised an ingenious scheme of plundering the settlements.[101] William Ake and his California ruffians, acting as self-appointed "regulators," spread terror among the Mexican and Indian population in the Sonoita Valley.[102] The "Cebolleteños"[103] and the "Mesilla Guard"[104] fanned the flame of the Indian's hatred toward the white man.

The federal government had spent more than $3,000,000 a year on Indian affairs in the territory. The policy of fighting the Indians and of making treaties with them continued throughout the period but failed to stop depredations. Upon the outbreak of the Civil War the territory suffered a setback. The removal of federal troops for active service in the East served as a signal for the wild tribes to reassert their power. The achievements toward Indian control during the preceding period were now practically lost. The entrance of Confederate forces from Texas added to the confusion.[105]

CHAPTER X

Friction with the Mormons and Indians in the Great Basin

IN 1847, at the time of the great Mormon exodus, hundreds of the Saints passed through and settled beyond the Indian frontier; in the years following the discovery of gold in California, thousands of treasure-seekers on their way to the great El Dorado pushed the Indian aside mercilessly. The white man squatted in fertile spots; he killed the Indian's game; he cut down the pine and the nut tree; he spread disease and death. In the path of these migrations were the Utah tribes, who, like their kinsmen in other portions of the Far West, could not but regard the invasion of their country as a violation of their inalienable rights.[1] The state of affairs in the Great Basin was further complicated by the influence of the Mormons on the natives and the relations of the Saints with the gentile population and government officials.

But the Indians in Utah Territory were perhaps less troublesome than in any other portion of the trans-Mississippi country. The Mormons, no doubt, were partly responsible for this difference. Approaching the Indians as brothers and equals, without any desire to force civilization upon them, the Saints easily gained their friendship. Franklin D. Richards, the church historian of the Mormons, declared: "It has been our habit to shoot Indians with tobacco and bread and biscuits rather than with powder and lead, and we are most successful with them."[2] The shrewd Brigham Young, like many other Mormons as well as Americans, believing that it was cheaper to feed the natives than to fight them, advised his agents to teach the Indians agriculture so that they could raise their own food. And the Saints did teach the natives how to till their lands and assured them they would suffer no harm so long as they remained at peace.[3] How the Mormons influenced the Indians' attitude toward non-Mormons is another story.

In the beginning, it seems, the federal government concerned itself comparatively little with the Indians in Utah, and it was not until April, 1849, that John Wilson was appointed agent with headquarters at Salt Lake City. The new official was directed to secure all available information concerning the tribes dwelling in the country from the Rocky Mountains to the Sierra Nevada.[4] Wilson took his task seriously and in August and September submitted elaborate reports to the Secretary of the Interior. In these reports he listed the names, boundaries, and characteristics of the various tribes and bands inhabiting the territory. Foremost among their difficulties, he found, was their rapidly diminishing food supply, caused by the California migration. Wilson made many suggestions. He advised that the Utah tribes be treated entirely as wards of the government and that the execution of the law be entrusted to the "true philanthropist . . . not to the brawling and often bankrupt politician"; he suggested that the Shoshones and the Utahs be united into one nation and taught agriculture; he urged that horse trading with the Indians be prohibited, as well as the distribution of useless ornaments. The white man's shining gifts, Wilson contended, were primarily an invention "for cheating these poor people."[5] But despite the wisdom of Wilson's recommendations, they do not seem to have been taken seriously by the officials in Washington.

The first important change in the government's Indian policy came in September, 1850, when the Territory of Utah was created and the administration of the affairs of the Great Basin Indians was separated from those of the California tribes. In the same month Brigham Young was appointed governor of the new territory and ex-officio Superintendent of Indian Affairs.[6] Organizing the territory still further, Young, in July, 1851, established one general agency and two subagencies. He assigned the Parowan agency, including that part of the territory which later became Nevada, to Jacob H. Holeman; Subagents Stephen B. Rose and Henry R. Day had charge of the Uintah and Parvan agencies. Young personally directed the affairs of the Indians south and west of the Great Salt Lake.[7]

But despite the appointment of Indian officials and the good will and kind intentions of the Mormons, friction developed. When the great tide of gentile emigration began to sweep across the Mormon country, the Indians became desperate for food. They had little or no alternative; they either had to steal from emigrant trains and infant settlements or starve. Even before the arrival of the pioneers in the valley of the Great Salt Lake, the Utah Lake tribes had a reputation as "bad Indians."[8] Although at first friendly with the colonists, they began, in the summer or fall of 1849, stealing grain, cattle, and horses, and occasionally attacking isolated settlements. In the next two years, when the tribesmen became more troublesome, the Mormons organized punitive expeditions, tracked the cattle thieves to the ravines and mountains, and easily defeated them.[9]

Since the principal thoroughfares to California and Oregon passed through the Utah country, it was highly desirable for the government to win the friendship of the tribes. Indian Agent Holeman, therefore, in the summer of 1852, accompanied by a strong military escort, visited the various camps of the Shoshones or Snakes inhabiting the Humboldt and Carson River country. Holeman made no treaties but distributed gifts among the natives and advised them to move from the emigrant trails. Upon his return to Salt Lake City he urged the establishment of several military posts along the emigrant routes not only to subdue the restless tribesmen but also to check the "bad whites."[10]

In the summer of the following year Gwinn Harris Heap, a member of Beale's first expedition to California, recorded his impressions of the natives. Many of them seemed friendly, but during the entire trip the white men had to keep their rifles in readi-

ness for instant use. The Mormons, he found, had taught the natives to irrigate the fields and raise large quantities of corn, pump-
kins, melons, and squash. Heap also observed that New Mexicans
had been in the habit of making annual expeditions among the
Utes to capture children to be sold into slavery. This practice was
a sore grievance among the tribes.[11]

Still another disturbing element in the Indian affairs in Utah
was the mutual distrust between Mormon and non-Mormon Indian agents. This was no small handicap in securing harmonious
relations between the federal government and the Indians, for the
latter were bewildered by the opposing tactics of the two factions.
So annoying were the activities of the Mormon spies that the non-
Mormon agents had to mail their letters and reports outside the
territory. Holeman, a non-Mormon agent, found it very difficult
to continue in office under these circumstances.[12]

When Holeman in 1853 again visited the Humboldt and Carson River country, he found the Indians friendly, but discovered
that a new and more serious situation had arisen—California
traders, whose chief stock was whiskey, had come out on the trail
and set up temporary grog shops. These profit-seekers demoralized
the natives and committed more depredations than the Indians.
Until the government could protect the route by granting power
to its officers to enforce the law, Holeman felt that there could be
no safety. He also recommended Indian colonization and training in farming. Since little was done and since he disagreed with
Young and other Mormon agents, he resigned. He was suceeeded
by Edward A. Bedell and shortly afterward by Dr. Garland
Hurt.[13]

Meanwhile, a rumor spread that a horde of Mexicans or "out-
landish" men were infesting the settlements, stirring up the Indians, furnishing them with guns and ammunition, and urging
them to attack. Brigham Young immediately took steps to meet
the impending danger. On April 23, 1853, he issued a proclamation directing the inhabitants to remain quiet, and dispatched to

the southward a detachment of thirty men under Captain Wall of the Mormon militia to reconnoiter for troublemakers.[14] The Indians did not attack the settlements but they massacred a party of army explorers under Captain John W. Gunnison.

The Gunnison massacre stirred up much bitter feeling between gentiles and Mormons and complicated the problem of defense. The story of that incident is as follows: On October 26, 1853, when Captain Gunnison of the Topographical Engineers and a portion of his command, a dozen men in all,[15] were engaged in surveying for a central railroad route to the Pacific between the thirty-eighth and thirty-ninth parallels, they were ambushed near Sevier Lake by a band of Paiute Indians. Eight of the party, including Gunnison, were ruthlessly murdered and their bodies horribly mutilated. Gunnison fell with fifteen arrow wounds and with his left arm cut off at the elbow. F. Creutzfeldt, the botanist of the expedition, had both arms hacked off. When the bodies were recovered the next day, they were scarcely recognizable, having been partially eaten by wolves.[16]

Reports on the responsibility for the massacre were conflicting. The Mormons attributed the attack to the murder of an Indian by a group of California emigrants; others, however, asserted that the Saints themselves, disguised as Indians, were among those who committed the dastardly deed, or, at least, had incited the murderers.[17] The Mormons' failure to bring the guilty Paiutes to justice certainly placed the Saints in no enviable light. Lieutenant Colonel Edward J. Steptoe, who was then on his way to California with artillery and dragoon recruits, was ordered to winter in Salt Lake City to investigate the Gunnison massacre and enforce the apprehension and trial of the murderers. He persuaded chiefs War-Kar and Kin-o-sha to surrender six Indians for trial. The accused were found guilty of manslaughter and sentenced to imprisonment. Even this mild punishment was never enforced, for the Indians escaped from jail.[18]

The Walker Indian War of 1853-54 added to the difficulties.

Long before the coming of the Mormons, Walkara (or Walker), a celebrated Utah chieftain described as a "quarrelsome and bloodthirsty" savage, made frequent raids into the Mexican states, levied tribute on the people, and carried off persons of rank whom he held for ransom. When the Mormons settled in the territory, Walker was at first friendly toward them, but when white men started to take the best Indian lands, when game disappeared, and when his people were shot down without provocation and their cattle stolen by bands of emigrants, his friendship turned to hatred. Further increasing the friction was the presence of trading parties from New Mexico who supplied the Indians with horses, firearms, and ammunition in exchange for Indian women and children, whom they afterwards sold into slavery.[19]

In the summer of 1853 Walker led his braves on the warpath. Since there were no federal troops in Utah at this time,[20] the work of checking the uprising devolved upon the Mormons. Brigham Young acted with vigor and decision. His General Orders Number 1, issued on July 21, 1853, directed the military commandants to build "good and substantial" forts, to construct adequate corrals, to repair and put into complete order their arms and ordnance, and to procure ammunition and guns. The same order also forbade distribution or sale of arms or ammunition to Indians. Four days later Young issued Orders Number 2 in which he assigned Colonel George A. Smith to the command of all the military districts south of Great Salt Lake County and directed him to enforce the terms of the previous order.[21]

The war was brief but decisive. The Mormons easily defeated the Indians, losing only a dozen killed and a number wounded. In the spring of 1854 Walker sued for peace. During the summer Brigham Young met the chieftain at Chicken Creek, made a truce with him, gave him presents, and restored peace. Walker afterward became very friendly with the Mormons and in January, 1855, on his deathbed, he asked his people not to kill the cattle of the Mormons or steal from them.[22]

But Chief Walker's plea meant little to other tribesmen. In 1855 so many reports of Indian attacks came into Salt Lake City from the Humboldt trail that Young sent Garland Hurt to investigate. The agent took with him a large assortment of gifts, such as bright pieces of cloth, beads, rings, knives, and razors. Early in August, when Hurt met a number of Shoshone chiefs at the Humboldt River, he succeeded in making an agreement with them. After the distribution of gifts Nim-ah-tio-cah, an old chieftain, declared he was sorry that his people had ever been hostile to the white man but "now their hearts were good towards the white brothers." Contrary to Indian tradition, the grizzled warrior wiped away a tear as he shook hands with the Indian agent. But the treaty was held up in Washington and nothing was done about it.[23] In the fall of the same year Brigham Young wrote to Commissioner of Indian Affairs Manypenny that he had met a large number of Shoshones and Utahs in council at Salt Lake City and had made a "good peace" with them.[24]

But a "good" peace could not last long, for the Indians were suffering from hunger. Agent Hurt, on his tour to Carson Valley, found the natives quite destitute. On the northern trails the tribes were reported committing depredations, driving off stock, and killing settlers.[25] Captain Rufus Ingalls, writing from Benicia in August, 1855, attributed these attacks to the too conciliatory policy of the Mormons "towards the rude savages that surround them." By treating the Indians as "brethren," sending missionaries among them, and even counseling intermarriage, Ingalls asserted, "they [the Mormons] frequently suffer abuse and insolence in consequence." Garland Hurt, too, reported that Mormon missionaries taught the tribesmen that the only friends were Mormons, that the land belonged to the Indians, and that the Saints would help the natives recover their rights.[26]

Then came the Utah Expedition! A clash between Mormon leaders and United States civil officers began almost as soon as the Territory of Utah was organized. The close association be-

tween the Mormon church and state caused constant friction. The
Mormons, who had great confidence in their own strength, acted
in a highhanded fashion in the use of government funds. For example, Young was accused of spending $20,000 Congress had
appropriated for public buildings in the territory to pay off the
debts of the Mormon church.[27] The crux of the difficulty lay in
the character of the United States territorial officials. According to
the Mormons, these men were political adventurers of the lowest
grade—"men, eager to accept the crumbs of government patron-
age." The Mormons received them kindly. If they had been men
of tact and discretion, contenting themselves only with the discharge of their duties, all would have gone well.[28]

Judge Perry E. Brocchus, characterized as a vain, ambitious,
corrupt, and revengeful man, in a public meeting in Salt Lake
City shortly after his arrival, attacked the practice of polygamy
and at once aroused the ire of the Mormons. Secretary Harris and
United States Marshal Heywood also clashed with the Saints.
Within a few months after their arrival Secretary Harris and
Judges Brandebury and Brocchus set out for Washington, taking
with them the territorial seal, records, documents, and funds.[29]
A second and third group of government officials, who followed
in rapid succession, failed to establish harmony. Judge W. W.
Drummond, himself a rather dissolute character, a gambler and
a bully, attacked plural marriage; Judge George P. Stiles charged
the Mormons with destroying the United States records in his
office.[30] Early in December, 1854, President Pierce offered the
governorship of the territory to Lieutenant Colonel Steptoe, but
that officer declined and signed a petition for the reappointment
of Brigham Young. "None but Mormon officials could hope for
respect or obedience in Utah Territory," shrewdly observed Steptoe.[31]

When Brigham Young was reappointed governor, hostility
toward Mormon practices and defiance of federal authority gained
momentum. From Salt Lake City came reports of large numbers

of emigrants leaving the territory. "The Mormons are driving out the gentiles," reported the *Kansas Weekly Herald*. United States marshals, judges, and surveyors experienced difficulty in performing their duties.[32] Frequent disputes between conflicting territorial judiciaries—United States district courts and inferior Mormon tribunals—the pernicious influence of disgruntled mail contractors, and the niggardly Congressional appropriations for Utah fanned the flames of Mormon discontent. By the time President Buchanan came into office, practically all the federal officials had left the territory.[33]

Buchanan determined to act vigorously. Since, in his opinion, there no longer remained any government in Utah but the "despotism of Brigham Young," he felt it his solemn duty "to restore the supremacy of the Constitution and laws within its limits." He therefore appointed a new governor and other federal officials for Utah, and this time sent with them a "military force for their protection, and to aid . . . in the execution of the laws."[34] But Alfred Cumming, the new governor, and his colleagues, who accompanied the troops to Utah, found their lot no easier than that of their predecessors.[35]

Meanwhile, the Utah Expedition, with Brevet Brigadier General William S. Harney in command, was being organized. On May 28, 1857, General Winfield Scott issued an order for the organization of 2,500 men at Fort Leavenworth to march to Utah as soon as possible. Because of election disorders in Kansas, Harney was detained there,[36] and on August 29 Colonel Albert S. Johnston[37] of the Second Cavalry was appointed to take Harney's place.

Late in July, 1857, detachments under Colonel E. B. Alexander, who was in charge of the troops pending Colonel Johnston's arrival from Washington, began to leave Fort Leavenworth; during the rest of the summer, additional detachments left that post destined for service in Utah. The soldiers encountered tremendous difficulties. The march of more than 1,200 miles to Fort Bridger, which lasted almost four months, was one of great toil, pain, and hardship. On the last stages of the journey—thirty-seven miles in fifteen days—the snow was deep and the weather bitter cold, the thermometer sometimes registering twenty-five degrees below zero. Early in November a severe snowstorm raged for six days. Men suffered frostbite and cattle and mules perished by the score.[38]

The first detachment entered Utah about the middle of September. Captain Stewart Van Vliet, quartermaster of the expedition, who had been sent ahead to procure supplies in Salt Lake City, was told by Brigham Young that there was plenty but that none would be sold to the United States forces. The Mormons were ready to apply a scorched earth policy to their beautiful country. Van Vliet was of the opinion that the Mormons were in a fair way to prevent the United States troops from entering Salt Lake City.[39]

In the meanwhile, on July 24, when some 2,500 Mormons were assembled on the banks of Silver Lake celebrating the tenth anniversary of the entrance of the Saints into Salt Lake Valley, they received the news that a new governor and another set of federal officers had been appointed for Utah, and that these men were to be escorted to their new posts by the "flower of the American army." The Mormons felt outraged. Immediately, their "leaders preached war, prayed war, and taught war."[40] Heber C. Kimball, a member of the presidency of the Mormon church, exclaimed: "I will fight until there is not a drop of blood in my veins. Good God! I have wives enough to whip out the United States."[41] The "rotten hearted curses" (the new set of officials) the Mormon leaders would not have. They wanted men of their own choice, particularly Brigham Young.[42]

He accepted the challenge, declaring "he would ask no odds of Uncle Sam or the devil." On September 15 he issued his famous proclamation forbidding the entrance of armed forces into Utah Territory, declaring a state of martial law, and ordering the Mormon militia to be in readiness to march at a moment's notice to repel invasion. Young dispatched this vigorous proclamation, accompanied by a letter, to the commanding officer of the expedition, advising the troops to withdraw immediately, or, if they remained, to surrender their arms.[43]

Under Young's forceful leadership, the Mormons prepared for defense. He organized a secret cavalry company in Carson Valley. He had fortifications erected in Echo Cañon. He ordered firearms manufactured and repaired. He authorized arms and horses to be furnished to Indian allies. He summoned brethren from everywhere to the defense of Zion. If matters became too serious for the Mormons they were prepared to depart for a New Zion in the Russian possessions.[44]

The Mormons, of course, did not intend to meet the United States army in the open field or behind breastworks. They relied on guerrilla warfare and surprise. To stampede animals, to set fire to supply trains, to burn the whole country on the enemy's flank, and to blockade roads by felling trees was their strategy. In this, they succeeded admirably. Before Johnston arrived, the vanguard of the federal troops under Colonel Alexander suffered great humiliation and disaster. Early in October, the Mormons burned three government supply trains on the Green River and Big Sandy, destroying vital supplies and equipment valued at more than $1,000,000. At the same time they ran off a large herd of cattle and burned grain and forage stored at Fort Bridger; they set fire to the fort; they destroyed all the grass en route to and beyond the site of the fort.[45]

About the middle of November the vanguard of the tired and frozen army arrived at the ruins of Fort Bridger, where Johnston established his depot of supplies. The bulk of the army went into winter quarters a short distance above. Colonel Cooke and his dragoons took station about forty miles to the south.[46] The winter was bitter cold. The privations and sufferings of the troops were tremendous. Food was scarce, clothing and shelter were inadequate, and prices were exorbitant. It was not uncommon for a man to offer $2.00 for a single biscuit; tobacco sold for $1.50 a plug.

When the Indians saw the troops hard up for provisions, they commenced killing their dogs and bringing them in for sale under the name of mountain sheep. Cooke's men subsisted on tainted beef without salt. Brigham Young sent salt to Johnston's camp, but the commander would "not accept a present from an enemy of my Government." The many discomforts resulting from rude and hastily built shelters, scant and ill-matched clothing, and reduced rations failed to dampen the spirits of the soldiers. Seasoned veterans and their younger comrades celebrated the festivities of Christmas and New Year with song, dance, and martial music.[47]

The Mormon militia, meanwhile, had returned to the valley. The Saints regarded the disasters of the federal army as righteous judgment. They welcomed their returning warriors, openly announced their contempt for the United States government and its army, and proclaimed that "Israel should now be free." At the same time they made great preparations for defending all the passes to the valley, and manufactured all kinds of arms and ammunition.[48]

The War Department, meanwhile, ordered about 3,000 additional men to the scene of the conflict,[49] and Johnston sent Captain Marcy to New Mexico to buy mules to replace those the expedition had lost. In the fall and winter of 1857-58, Marcy and his gallant band of mountain men and soldiers, some sixty in all, plowed through a trackless wilderness, over lofty and rugged mountains, without a pathway and through deep snows, subsisting on the carcasses of their dead animals. But the ragged, half-frozen, and starving detachment succeeded in its hazardous mission. Late in the spring of 1858 it returned to Johnston's camp with a large number of horses, mules, and beef cattle, and several thousand sheep.[50] Early in June of the same year Brevet Lieutenant Colonel Hoffman, the commanding officer at Fort Laramie, also arrived at Camp Scott with a large mule train loaded with supplies. The Army of Utah, once more adequately equipped and provisioned, was eager for action.[51]

Governor Cumming, meanwhile, issued a proclamation from the Green River country, declaring the Mormons in a state of rebellion and commanding "all armed parties . . . to disband and to return to their respective homes."[52] Judge Eckles established his court, and indicted Brigham Young and several other prominent Mormon leaders for high treason.[53]

At this critical juncture there appeared at Salt Lake City a mysterious Dr. Osborne, a "self-appointed" peace-maker, who turned out to be Colonel Thomas L. Kane of Philadelphia, former friend of the Mormons. Through Kane's efforts Governor Cumming went to Salt Lake City without an escort and secured recognition as the lawful governor of Utah.[54] Early in June the two regularly appointed peace commissioners, former Governor L. W. Powell of Kentucky and Major Ben McCulloch of Texas, arrived in Salt Lake City, bringing President Buchanan's proclamation of pardon to the people of Utah.[55] On June 14, General Johnston and Governor Cumming issued proclamations announcing the restoration of peace. The Mormon war was ended.[56]

The Army of Utah, considerably strengthened by the arrival of additional troops, supplies, and animals,[57] set out for Salt Lake City. Despite favorable negotiations with the government, the Mormon leaders had ordered a new exodus to the south. In the spring of 1858, between 30,000 and 40,000 Mormons had left their homes in Salt Lake City and the northern settlements, taking with them their movable belongings. Now that peace was declared, a continual stream of Mormons, wagons, and stock returned by night and day to Salt Lake City and the deserted settlements.[58] A correspondent with Johnston's army thus describes the scene as the troops entered Salt Lake City. "All day long from dawn till sunset, the troops and trains poured through the city, the utter silence of the streets being broken only by the music of the military bands, the monotonous tramp of the regiments, and the rattle of the baggage wagons. . . . The only visible groups of spectators were on the corners near Brigham Young's residence. The stillness was so profound that during the interval between the passage of the columns, the monotonous gurgle of City Creek struck every ear."[59]

During the summer Johnston had his men erect Camp Floyd, named in honor of Secretary of War John B. Floyd. By September, 1858, the Army of Utah reached a peak strength of more than 3,400 men. While the army remained at Camp Floyd it surveyed new military roads, furnished dragoon escort for emigrants, and suppressed Indian disorders along the Snake and Humboldt rivers.[60]

An unsavory phase of the Utah Expedition was excessive profiteering. Russell, Majors, and Waddell came in for considerable criticism. As official army contractors, they transported about 16,000,000 pounds of supplies, requiring more than 4,000 wagons, 53,000 draft animals, and 4,000 men. Army sutlers and Mormon farmers and merchants, too, did not lose any opportunity to sell supplies at greatly inflated prices. Brigham Young himself furnished timber for the building of Camp Floyd at a profit of more than $50,000.[61] Traders in the vicinity of the army camps demanded prices which were quite reminiscent of the days of the California gold rush. But when the troops withdrew, army equipment sold for a song. Mules originally bought for $175 were available for $60, and wagons costing $130 went for $30. Altogether, the Mormons purchased government goods valued at $4,000,000 for $100,000.[62] The sale of surplus army supplies at the close of World War I and World War II certainly had precedent.[63]

President Buchanan and Secretary of War Floyd considered the Utah Expedition fairly successful. The "war," to be sure, had not accomplished its original purpose entirely; it had curbed the more open rebellion and had quieted Indian outrages. Others, however, regarded the expedition as a colossal failure. Brigham Young, they said, had "matched his wits against the might of the United States government and had not come off second best."[64]

In the meanwhile an incident occurred which embittered relations with the Mormons still further. It was the Mountain Meadows massacre. In the spring of 1857 a party of about 130 emigrants from Johnston County, Arkansas, and a few Missourians, with a train of thirty wagons, horses, mules, and 600 oxen, set out for southern California under the leadership of Charles Fancher. At Salt Lake City the emigrants found it difficult to purchase the supplies they needed, and in the other Mormon settlements to the southwest they encountered similar difficulties. At Parowan they finally succeeded in obtaining corn but could find no one willing to grind it for them until they reached Cedar City.[65] Early in September the caravan reached Mountain Meadows, about 320 miles to the southwest of Salt Lake City, and encamped near a spring. The encampment was almost midway between two ranges of hills, some fifty feet high and 400 yards apart. On either side of the camp, ravines connected with the bed of the stream.

At daybreak on September 7, while the men were lighting the camp fires, they were fired upon by Indians, and probably by some white men disguised as Indians, and more than twenty were killed or wounded. The survivors, having dug a rifle pit and having made a protective corral of their wagons, were able to defend themselves for several days. But their ammunition ran low and it became almost impossible for them to reach the spring for water. For four harrowing days the siege lasted. On the morning of the fifth day, William Bateman and John Doyle Lee, radical leaders of an armed band of Mormons encamped nearby, approached the emigrant camp with a white flag and the besieged "gave up all their arms with the expectation that their lives would be spared."

On September 11, after the disarmed band started on its line of march, it suffered a new attack. At the first fire most of the men fell. Three attempted to escape but their enemies quickly ran them down and slaughtered them. The women shared the same fate and of the children only seventeen survived. The Indians stripped the corpses completely and carried off the clothing, provisions, wagon-covers, and even the bedding of the emigrants.[66]

Reports of the tragedy were conflicting. The Mormons maintained that the members of the Fancher company, while on their way from Salt Lake City to Mountain Meadows, had roused antagonism by their lawless and cruel actions both toward the Mormon inhabitants and the Indians. The Mormons asserted that the emigrants abused women, poisoned wells and streams, destroyed fences and growing crops, violated city ordinances, and resisted officers. They also attributed the excitement of the Iron County Militia leaders and the restlessness of the Indians to the approaching forces of the United States army. Government officials, Indian agents, and others, however, pointed out the absurdity of such claims. Judge Cradlebaugh declared that "this massacre was concocted by white men and consummated by whites and Indians." Spoodes, a Ute warrior, told Agent Garland Hurt that the Mormons had incited the Paiutes to the attack.[67] Many eyewitnesses told of seeing property of the ill-fated emigrants in the hands of Mormons, and Superintendent of Indian Affairs Forney reported that a few days after the massacre some $30,000 worth of property was distributed among the leading church dignitaries. Judge Cradlebaugh estimated the value of the property at $70,000.[68]

In March, 1859, a year and a half after the Mountain Meadows massacre, when Judge Cradlebaugh held a session of court at Provo and tried to get the grand jury to find true bills against any of the accused, he had to discharge it as a "useless appendage to a court of justice." It was not until 1874, seventeen years after the incident, that the investigation of the massacre was reopened and a joint indictment for conspiracy and murder was found against John D. Lee and a number of associates. The trials held in 1875 and 1876 in the United States District Court at Beaver City in southern Utah resulted in the conviction of Lee. He was executed on March 23, 1877. The others arraigned for trial were soon afterwards discharged from custody.[69]

The Utah Expedition and the Mountain Meadows massacre certainly did not improve Indian relations in Utah. In the sum-

mer of 1857, when troops were marching into the Mormon country, Young was removed from the governorship and the supervision of Indian affairs. James W. Denver, the United States
Commissioner of Indian Affairs, censured Young severely, charging him not only with using his office to further personal ends
but with instigating a rebellion.[70] In the fall of 1857, Jacob Forney,
who succeeded Young as Superintendent of Indian Affairs, hastened to Salt Lake City to take charge of his work. In the following spring he visited the Goshoots who roamed in the western
part of the territory and made arrangements for them to be
placed on lands suitable for farming. He also held a council with
the Bannocks. The Carson Valley tribes he found exceedingly
destitute, living in a most depraved state of ignorance.[71]

The Comstock silver strike[72] in 1859 aggravated conditions in
western Utah. When the *Nevada Journal* reported that the Washoe
diggings were "fabulously rich, both in silver and gold," and that
the miners were making "from $100 to $400 per day," a great
number of adventurers—miners, professional men, swindlers, and
other dregs of humanity, as well as women and children—rushed
to the new El Dorado. Boom towns appeared and disappeared as
if by magic, and prices in the mining districts soared higher than
in the days of Forty-nine.[73] The disorder and confusion at the diggings have been graphically described by the adventurous J. Ross
Browne, who was present in Virginia City, capital of the Washoe
silver district in the spring of 1860. He wrote:

Frame shanties, pitched together as if by accident; tents of canvas,
of blankets, of brush, of potato-sacks and old shirts, with empty
whisky barrels for chimneys; smoky hovels of mud and stone;
coyote holes in the mountain-side forcibly seized and held by
men; pits and shafts with smoke issuing from every crevice; piles
of goods and rubbish on craggy points, in the hollows, on the
rocks, in the mud, in the snow, everywhere scattered broadcast in
pellmell confusion, as if the clouds had suddenly burst overhead
and rained down the dregs of all the flimsy, rickety, filthy little
hovels and rubbish of merchandise that had ever undergone the
process of evaporation from the earth since the days of Noah.[74]

And in the white man's feverish haste to stake out a rich claim the Indian was the principal sufferer.

Early in 1860, shortly after the Pony Express went into operation, hostilities broke out on a grand scale. An Indian revolt embracing Paiutes, Bannocks, and Shoshones extended across the entire territory of the present Nevada, eastern California, and Oregon. In addition to attacks on white settlements, the desperate warriors destroyed nearly every pony express station between the Great Salt Lake and California, murdered many of its employees, and ran off its horses.[75]

The whites, too, were not idle. In May, after a combined force of Paiute, Shoshone, and Pit River tribes had attacked settlers in Carson Valley, more than 100 volunteers from the Washoe silver mine district, under the command of Major William M. Ormsby, took the field. But the Indians, numbering between 500 and 800 warriors, well-mounted and armed with rifles, ambushed their pursuers near Pyramid Lake and killed Ormsby and sixty of his men. The Indian successes, however, were short-lived. Late in May Captain Joseph Stewart with a force of about 700 men and Lieutenant Stephen H. Weed with a detachment from Camp Floyd moved against the hostile Indians and early in June, near Pyramid Lake, defeated them.[76]

Lieutenant Colonel Charles F. Smith, commander of the Department of Utah,[77] felt quite certain that "white Indians" were constantly stirring up Indian unrest. Eight days after Ormsby and his men had been ambushed, Smith wrote to Lieutenant Colonel M. T. Howe: "Judging by the events of last summer there is a tribe of Indians who have blue eyes and light hair, who wear whiskers and speak good English."[78] The government took steps to eliminate the danger of further trouble with Indians—be they "white Indians" or red. Shortly after the attack in Carson Valley, troops established Fort Churchill on Carson River and scouting parties escorted emigrants on their way to Oregon.[79]

Several years previously the government had employed quite

different measures. Then, in an attempt to keep the Utah tribes contented, Indian Agent Garland Hurt had established a number of Indian farms. At one time five such farms were in operation—the Spanish Fork reserve and the San Pete, Corn Creek, Deep Creek, and Ruby Valley farms. But the experiment, like that in Texas and California, proved a failure. Some Indians worked but most of them were lazy. In fact, Hurt had to hire white labor or he would not have had any crops. The natives were interested in the harvest but not in tilling the soil.[80]

The Utah Expedition played havoc with the Indian-farm experiment. After the agency farms fell into neglect, the Indians would not co-operate to make a new start. They were demoralized and confused about contradictions in authority. Before the United States army entered Utah they had been aware of two groups of whites—the "Mericats" and the "Mormone." When harmony was restored, the Mormons were out of power and the Americans were in control but much divided. This state of affairs was quite confusing to the simple savage mind. Superintendent Forney still believed that the only solution of the Utah Indian problem was to put the Indians to work on farms, but he did not have the funds to revive the farm program.[81]

Forney, lacking the support of the Mormons and not enjoying the full confidence of the federal officials in Utah, was unable to cope with the situation. He was removed. From September, 1859, to November, 1860, Utah was left without a Superintendent because of the delay of Forney's successor, Benjamin Davies, in reaching his post.[82] But Frederick Dodge, who had been agent at Salt Lake City and later at Carson Valley, did yeoman work among the tribes. In Dodge, as in Neighbors, Calhoun, and Carson, the government had the ideal Indian agent. In a methodical way he visited the tribes, studied their condition, and attempted to alleviate their suffering and bring peace between them and the white man. During the fall and winter months of 1858-59 he made a perilous and toilsome journey to Pyramid Lake, where he found great suffering among the natives. In the course of his extensive travels among his charges, he distributed clothing and flour to more than 4,000 Indians, who hailed him as a great deliverer.[83]

Dodge was the first Indian agent in western Utah to select areas on which to settle the Indians. He set off three sections of fertile lands for their exclusive use, where they would be more or less isolated from the white settlements. On these beautiful grassy meadows Dodge had hoped to place the Washoes and some of the Paiute tribes, but the former had been so humbled and reduced by war and disease that only the Paiutes remained to settle there.[84]

In 1860, Dodge, in charge of the Carson agency, employed Warren Wasson, an energetic, fearless, and just man, to assist him in marking off the Walker and Lake Pyramid reservations. Dodge soon left for Washington and upon the outbreak of the Civil War joined the army, but Wasson continued the plan Dodge had evolved for establishing the Paiute reservations. Shortly after the Indians were defeated near Pyramid Lake, he gathered them together on the Pyramid Lake reservation. Then, on the last of July he posted notices warning squatters that they must leave the lands on the Truckee River. In December he gave every man in the Paiute tribe around Pyramid Lake a hickory shirt and a pair of blue overalls, and every woman some calico, needles, and thread. When an old Indian arrived after all the gifts had been distributed, Wasson pulled off his own shirt and gave it to the old warrior. He had gained the undying admiration of the tribesmen.[85]

With the advent of the Mormons to the valley of the Great Salt Lake the control of the Great Basin gradually began to slip from the hands of the Indian. In the Utah country, as in other portions of the Far West, the red man was compelled to make way for his stronger, white brother.

CHAPTER XI

California Indian Wars

ON THE Pacific coast the problem of frontier defense was slightly different. With the exception of some mountain tribes, the Indian was peaceful. The problem was really defense of the Indian against the white man. Nevertheless, the white man constantly called for aid. Thus the army and civil authorities found themselves obliged to perform a dual role: to protect the peaceful natives as well as to insure the safety of the settlers and prospectors. The government recognized the complexity of the problem and made honest efforts to maintain peaceful relations between the two races. How well the government succeeded is another story.[1]

During the Spanish regime the mission Indians had enjoyed the privilege of occupying as much land as they needed for homes, fields, and pasturage. Hence, the Indians regarded the American advance as an attempt to rob them of their legal rights. It was but a step from killing cattle of trespassers to killing trespassers.[2]

Shortly after federal troops entered California, military officers established machinery for handling Indian affairs. In April, 1847, General Kearny appointed John A. Sutter and Mariano G. Vallejo subagents for the Indians residing near the Sacramento and San Joaquin rivers and for those between San Francisco Bay and Clear Lake. Four months later Colonel Richard B. Mason, the military governor, appointed Captain J. D. Hunter Indian agent for the southern district. Lieutenant H. W. Halleck, secretary for the territory, sent a circular to the subagents suggesting that they hold councils with the leaders of the hostile tribes and encourage them to take their grievances to the government.[3] Some of the tribes readily pledged themselves to turn to the white man's government for protection and redress,[4] but when they received little of either, they sought justice in their own way.

When peace was made with Mexico, the United States government took definite steps toward a permanent and general Indian policy. The request of Congress on July, 1848, for specific information concerning conditions in Oregon, California, and New Mexico and the report of Commissioner of Indian Affairs Medill in November were followed by the appointment of additional agents and special investigating officers for California. John Wilson was to be Indian agent at Salt Lake; Adam Johnston of Ohio, subagent for the Sacramento-San Joaquin area;[5] and the famous "Jack Hays" of the Texas Rangers, subagent on the Gila. William Carey Jones, acting under instructions from the Secretaries of State and the Interior, was directed specifically to study land titles and to inquire into the nature of previous Indian rights.[6]

Meanwhile, additional detachments of dragoons and infantry arrived in California from New York and Mexico.[7] In the fall of 1848 federal troops were distributed between the coast towns extending from San Diego to Sonoma, and within a few months military units were also stationed at Camp Stanislaus, about twenty miles from Stockton and on Bear Creek, above Sutter's Fort. In the following April, Brevet Brigadier General Bennet Riley succeeded Colonel Mason to the military command. By the end of 1849 more than 500 men were stationed in the department.[8] The new commander urged his officers to deal strictly with the Indians —apprehend guilty individuals or tribes and punish them thoroughly and effectively. He ordered them to do little parleying and not to accept mere promises of better conduct—to deal with each case promptly and forcefully.[9]

The activities of Indian agents and the presence of troops, however, failed to preserve the peace. In the Clear Lake region, for example, peaceful tribes had taken refuge on an island to be safe from intrusion. Unscrupulous whites hunted them down and carried them away in large gangs to work. Island warriors, thereupon, sought revenge and murdered isolated parties of whites. In the fall of 1849, they ambushed Captain William H. Warner of the Topographical Engineers, who led an exploring expedition in the Sierra Nevada. Warner and several of his men lost their lives.[10] The subsequent punitive expeditions of Lieutenant John W. Davidson and Captain Nathaniel Lyon proved disastrous for the tribesmen but settled nothing.[11]

The creation of the state government of California made the lot of the Indian no easier. The philosophy of the state lawmaker readily coincided with that of the frontiersman: the white man's interest had to be protected at all cost. A law entitled "An act for the Government and Protection of the Indians," which went into effect in April, 1850, regulated the conduct of the natives by white men for the benefit of white men. In theory, the law gave the Indians certain protection: stealing of Indians by whites was punishable by fine and whipping; ill-treatment of Indian minors entrusted to a white man and forcing an Indian to work against his will were subject to fine; the Indian could not be driven from his land where he resided. But all these legal safeguards were of no avail. For, although the law provided that either whites or natives might make complaints, the testimony of an Indian against a white man was worthless. Furthermore, the enforcement of the law was placed in the hands of justices of the peace—local officers who were bound to be influenced by the attitude of the community. The law also declared it the duty of justices and other peace officers to give the Indians advice, punish guilty chiefs by reprimand, fine, or "otherwise reasonably chastise them," for failure to control unruly tribesmen. Actually, the state law did little or nothing to protect the Indian's rights.[12]

At best, the Indian had little faith in the white man's justice or in his courts. As a rule, when natives committed crimes against each other they preferred to administer the punishment themselves rather than turn the culprit over to the white man. Two examples will illustrate this point. On one occasion when a southern Indian became drunk and exceedingly quarrelsome and dangerous, Chief Juan Antonio ordered one of his tribesmen to administer a hundred lashes to the culprit in public instead of having him placed in jail by the white man. In the spring of 1852 Chief Juan Antonio played a most dramatic role. When one of his tribesmen was held for the murder of another Indian, the chieftain appeared before the justice of the peace and demanded that the prisoner be delivered to the Indians for punishment. Upon refusal, Juan Antonio soon returned with thirty braves, seized the prisoner and the body of the murdered man, and dashed away to safety. The chief then dug a grave and compelled the murderer to get into it. Placing the dead man on top of the hapless prisoner, Juan Antonio filled the grave with earth.[13]

Peace could not long prevail, especially in the mining districts. Desperate fortune-hunters, in their eagerness to become sole masters of the field, brutally brushed aside Indians and white men and instituted anti-foreign movements.[14] "Our countrymen," wrote David F. Shall, an Arkansan in California, "have proved themselves quite as great proficients as highwaymen as the cunningest and bloodiest Indians and Spaniards." Vagabond adventurers took great delight in abusing the natives. The policy of exterminating the California Indian had begun.[15]

Appeals for redress being disregarded, the head chiefs of the Sacramento Valley held a general council and urged extermination of the white man. An epidemic of raids from the head of the Sacramento southward soon broke out. When the alarm spread, the government ordered Sheriff Rogers of El Dorado County to call out 200 men. The militia succeeded in destroying Indian stores on some abandoned rancherias—an action that goaded the Indians to further depredations.[16]

In the fall of 1850 and winter of 1851 Indians fell upon the upper San Joaquin Valley. They ravaged settlements along the Stanislaus and Tuolumne within a few miles of Stockton and along the Merced streams southward. And on the Kaweah and Kern rivers and in the Owens Lake country, they attacked and demolished settlements and cattle stations. Volunteer companies, who took the field, returned with glowing reports of victory though, in reality, they secured only occasional advantage, such as the destruction of a deserted rancheria and the killing of a few warriors. Regulars did not distinguish themselves any more than the militia.[17] To placate the frontiersmen, troops were stationed in the reputed danger zones and several military posts were established.[18]

While the whites were clashing with the natives, Indian Agent Johnston traveled more than 800 miles through the Sacramento Valley in an attempt to understand the conflict and bring about harmony between the races. In his visits among many tribes and wandering families he found suffering and destitution. The starved and ill-clad natives complained that the palefaces were overrunning their country, destroying their means of subsistence, and trampling upon the graves of their ancestors. Sylvester Woolbridge, Jr., pastor of the Presbyterian Church at Benicia, wrote to President Taylor that the Sierra Nevada Indians had been driven from their usual haunts and compelled to steal to avoid starvation. Indian women and children, he said, had been slaughtered in cold blood.[19]

The President soon appointed three special agents for California, who were to go into the Indian country, study the Indian needs, select sites for agencies, and negotiate treaties. In the spring and summer of 1851, George W. Barbour, Redick McKee, and Dr. O. M. Wozencraft—the newly arrived Indian officials—proceeded energetically to carry out the President's orders. But the prospectors and miners readily thwarted the good work of the special agents, and the Indians rose to defend their rights. The agreements made with the natives were not always carried out, for some of the tribes feared to go on reservations, while others preferred their mountain homes. Catching the so-called hostiles and bringing them in constituted the war of 1851-52—a somber page in our Indian relations.[20]

During 1851 conditions in the Humboldt region became extremely serious. Packers and miners used little caution in their treatment of the natives, regarding them as natural enemies, to be shot down whenever opportunity offered. The Indian retaliated.

Early in January an express arrived at San Jose from Mariposa County calling upon the governor for men and arms. When alarming accounts spread to other southern settlements, frontiersmen lost no time in preparing to meet the reputed danger. The citizens of San Diego declared the town under martial law, formed a corps of volunteers, and petitioned General Hitchcock for arms. Los Angeles followed suit by appointing five commissioners to prepare for defense. The California legislature passed a law authorizing the governor to send into the field an armed force of 500 men.[21]

Volunteer companies and federal troops soon had the situation well in hand. The Mariposa Battalion operated in the San Joaquin Valley; Captain Kuykendall's company of militia brought in the Chowchillas, a tribe of the Kaweah family; Captain Boling's men brought in the Yosemites. The war in the south ended successfully when Major Heintzelman's troops defeated the Indians in the mountains near San Isabel. Four Indian ringleaders, tried by court-martial for the murder of American citizens at Agua Caliente, were found guilty, and were executed on Christmas morning, 1851. Chief Antonio Guerra's [Garra's] promise to the warriors that "he would charm the bullets of the white men so they would not harm them any more than water," proved of no avail. In the north volunteer companies from Yreka and Jacksonville, and a California company under Captain Ben Wright defeated the Pit and Rogue River tribes. Treacherous and inhumane treatment of natives in this campaign added little luster to the white man's arms.[22]

The California press sharply divided on the proper policy toward the Indian. The mountain journals demanded vigorous action. The San Francisco *Herald* declared that "any patching up of paper treaties with them now is mere moonshine"; it maintained that the only proper way to deal with the savages was to subdue them completely. Others suggested more caution. The *Daily Alta California,* for example, was against circulating exciting stories, and openly declared that white adventurers were to blame for Indian disturbances. It cautioned the public not to believe "one-seventh of the rumors" which they heard about Indian bandits. Moreover, it opposed the use of prejudiced frontiersmen as volunteers and recommended a "hands off Indian policy" for the state; it believed that only the national government should handle the Indian problem. The *Alta* definitely opposed incurring a state debt "under the pretense of Indian difficulties which never existed or had been actually provoked." Likewise, the *Daily Evening Picayune* was not at all impressed by the assertion that the "brawling patriots . . . desire to protect our people"; it characterized the war in the south as a "humbug."[23]

California governors, Indian commissioners, and military officers also disagreed about the extent of the Indian danger and the proper course to pursue. Peter H. Burnett, the first governor, though by nature a kindly and humane man, saw no good in Indians. In his annual message to the legislature, in January, 1851, he referred to them as murderers and robbers, and prophesied a war of extermination. To avert their inevitable destiny, he declared, was beyond the power or wisdom of man. And his successor, John McDougal, expressed similar views.[24] The Indian commissioners, on the other hand, blamed the white man. Most of the attacks, they contended, were induced by unprincipled white men seeking gain or political capital out of Indian disturbances. They openly condemned Governor McDougal for his belligerency, and disapproved of his order calling out volunteers, whom it was alleged he paid at the rate of five and ten dollars a day, thus piling up "another pretty little claim for Uncle Sam."[25] General Ethan Allen Hitchcock, commander of the Pacific Division, agreed with the commissioners.[26]

California, of course, was neither expected nor permitted to take over the entire duty of protection. Early in 1852 the federal government sent 500 troops, and six months later it dispatched the Fourth Infantry regiment. Between 1852 and 1854, it established new military posts but failed to secure peace.[27] Lack of funds by Indian officials, repeated sufferings of the tribes, and ruthless seizure of Indian lands again showed the need of a "more correct" Indian policy. The natives once more bitterly complained that the white man's government failed to keep the faith.[28]

Throughout the middle and latter fifties clashes continued. As in earlier years, white men in their eager search for gold invariably violated the Indians' rights, crowding them out of their homes. In business dealings the Indian often had to bow to the white man's cupidity and dishonesty. He had to accept the meager and often dishonest wage the white man paid for his labor. The natives, in sheer desperation, took vengeance and then retreated to the mountain fastnesses, where settlers and soldiers found it difficult to follow.[29]

In February, 1854, Brevet Major General John E. Wool, the new commander of the reorganized Department of the Pacific, arrived in California.[30] Within a few months Wool wrote to Secretary of War Davis that the Indians in his department were quiet and peaceably inclined and that he was favorably impressed with Superintendent Beale's plan of removing them to the military reserve at the Tejón Pass.[31] His problem was to be the control of the whites. In the spring of the year reckless prospectors attacked Indian rancherias on the Deer Creek, McCloud, and Pit rivers and killed more than a hundred inoffensive natives.[32]

It appeared as if the whites would be satisfied with nothing less than complete extermination of the natives. In the Klamath region lawless men, after driving off "hostiles," attacked the peaceable tribes; a group of miners made war on Indians of the King's River country, who at first fled to the mountains and later to Fort Miller for protection; a third force attacked two camps of friendly Indians in the immediate vicinity of the reserve near Fort Lane and ruthlessly killed men, women, and children. Driven to desperation, some of the peaceable tribes united with the more warlike bands and retaliated by murdering settlers and destroying everything in their path.[33]

The plight of the Indians in the northeastern counties of El Dorado, Placer, Amador, and Calaveras was very sad. In December, 1855, E. A. Stevenson, a special agent, wrote to Superintendent Henley that some 8,000 Indians already afflicted with the very worst vices of civilization—drink, prostitution, and disease—were aimlessly straggling about the mining camps. The "miserably degraded and wretched" Root Diggers constantly roamed the country.[34] Henley appointed a special agent to prevent kidnapping of Indian children. He also appointed four special agents, without compensation, to keep the natives quiet and submissive, so that they would "work well."[35]

Conditions in the south appeared to be more quiet. Early in November, 1855, J. Lancaster Brent, a prominent Los Angeles lawyer and member of the legislature, wrote to Senator Gwin: "Our southern country is now prospering; the 10,000 Indians surrounding us are quiet, our cattle and stock are secure, and our frontier settlements without fear."[36] But since the settlers as well as General Wool believed the situation on the Pacific coast serious, a regiment of the Ninth Infantry was dispatched from Fort Monroe to re-enforce Wool's command. The troops arrived in January, 1856, and two months later were strengthened by the arrival of about 400 additional infantry and artillery.[37]

When the settlers, meanwhile, steadily advanced into the upper San Joaquin Valley, the Indians once more resisted the relentless march of the whites into their domains. The Kern River War broke out in the spring of 1856. Indians raided the Kern River settlements and drove off hundreds of cattle. A company of mounted riflemen from Tulare County overtook the cattle thieves but retreated when they discovered the enemy numbered no less than 500 warriors. The *Daily Alta California* reported that the settlers in the Tulare Valley had all deserted their homes and had fled to Woodsville and Visalia for safety. The Indian danger, as usual, had been greatly magnified. According to the Los Angeles *Star,* not a miner had been killed and not a single cow had been lost; on the contrary, more cattle were lost each year through white thieves than through Indians. As for war, continued the *Star,* it was foolish, expensive, and benefited no one, "except a few favorites." In May, 1856, with the arrival of federal troops from Forts Tejón and Jones the Indians retreated to the mountains. The Kern River War was over.[38]

During the hostilities General Wool became involved in bitter quarrels both in Washington and in California. The Washington *Union,* a "hireling organ" of the administration, according to the *Alta,* criticized the military commander for permitting massacres while he frittered away his time with local duties at San Francisco and paid "overzealous attention to political prospects." Secretary of War Davis, too, took Wool to task for postponing military duties and attending to unnecessary matters. The general pointed to his accomplishments. Within less than a year, Wool insisted, he had restored peace and quiet in the Indian country, had erected batteries for the protection of the harbor of San Francisco, had ordered an arsenal building at Benicia, and had established a new post at Téjon Pass. Moreover he had prevented filibustering expeditions into Mexico and was responsible for the arrest, trial, and conviction of a number of adventurers implicated in such schemes. And this vigorous action, Wool contended, was in accordance with the express wish of the President as well as the Secretary of War himself.[39] Wool also clashed with Governor J. Neely Johnson, whom he refused to furnish arms and ammunition in the latter's controversy with the San Francisco Vigilantes.[40]

General Wool's troubles finally came to an end in February, 1857, when, at his own request, he was recalled to the Atlantic seaboard. During his three years' command of the department Wool had had no definite defense policy; he had disagreed with Secretary of War Davis and Governor Johnson. But the *Daily Alta California* stood by the "old veteran" and described his course as being so wise and judicious as to merit the esteem, confidence, and respect of the people. "We part with him with profound regret," declared the *Alta* upon the general's departure.[41]

The arrival of General Fauntleroy, followed shortly afterward by General N. S. Clarke,[42] witnessed the renewal of a more vigorous defense policy. To protect both Indians and whites in the north, Clarke established Camp Bragg and Fort Crook in the Pit River country.[43] Lalakas, chief of the Klamath tribe, came to Yreka with a number of his warriors and entered into a treaty to provide for perpetual peace.[44] In July, however, Lieutenant George Crook was dispatched to the Pit River country to defeat a large force of Indians.[45]

During the winter of 1858 the Indians on the Tuolumne lived under the most shocking conditions, suffering intensely from cold and hunger in their miserable huts. Intercourse with civilized communities had wrought destitution, intemperance, and vice, all in their most revolting aspects. Said the *Daily Alta California*: "As soon as the gray light of morning appears, they may be seen prowling around in search of miserable offal, for which they must compete with the dogs." The natives in the northeastern and central counties fared no better, since they were "entirely neglected" by Superintendent Henley.[46]

Summer and fall of 1858 witnessed more "wars." Some white men abducted squaws, maltreated them, and then drove them away. The northern tribes of the Humboldt, Klamath, Scott, and Trinity rivers held a war dance and resolved upon revenge. In August Shoshone warriors attacked the Placerville Mail Stage near Gravelly Ford in the Goose Creek Mountains and killed several of the guards. Two months later another band attacked an emigrant company of more that 200 men, women, and children near Beale's Crossing. The Indians killed nine of the company, wounded sixteen others, and drove off the greater part of the stock.[47]

These outbreaks furnished a golden opportunity for the *Daily Alta California* to take the federal government to task for its lack of a clear-cut defense policy. The settlers on the Pacific coast, in particular, suffered because of this neglect; Congress and the Cabinet, as well as the President, were all to blame; willful neglect of duty deserved nothing less than the "united condemnation of this people," stoutly declared the *Alta*. "Let the government awake," demanded this champion, "and devote . . . the army for . . . protecting the interests of the country and the lives of its citizens, who risk their all on the trackless plains."[48]

The whites, meanwhile, following a well-established custom, again took matters into their own hands and proceeded to put the Indian in his place. In September the citizens of Humboldt Bay drew up resolutions for a war of extermination against the Bear, Eel River, and neighboring tribes.[49] Bands of white men, supported by companies of volunteers under State Adjutant General William C. Kibbe, were soon on the march. At Nome Cult Valley, King's River, and Mattole Station, the whites cruelly slaughtered peaceable Indians for cattle stealing or because they considered them a burden. In the Humboldt Bay region the state militia harried the scattered Indians until they were "entirely starved out." The luckless natives, driven like sheep down to Humboldt Bay, were then placed on the bark "Fanny Major" and dispatched to Mendocino; those who refused to go were killed. Afterwards, when some of the tribesmen left Mendocino to go back to their old haunts, the settlers wreaked a terrible vengeance on the reserve Indians, wantonly killing some sixty men, women, and children.

Between the fall of 1858 and the spring of 1859 Kibbe, in his bloody campaign, killed more than 100 natives and captured some 300 prisoners. The zealous action of General Kibbe and Captain W. S. Jarboe, and the attacks and ravages of the settlers upon the peaceable tribes along the Mad, Eel, and Pit rivers in the fall of 1859 claimed the lives of fully 200 additional victims.[50] The victors in the "Pit River War" were hailed as heroes. In January, 1860, a bill for nearly $70,000 was before the California legislature, to be distributed, in part, among "these crimsoned murderers."[51] The campaign cost the state more than $121,000, which it promptly passed on to the national government.[52]

When depredations were reported in the San Fernando Valley, Lieutenant Colonel B. L. Beall, commanding at Fort Tejón, sent

Captain Davidson of the First Dragoons on a punitive-exploring expedition into Owens Lake Indian country. In July, 1859, a scouting party of dragoons with wagon, pack-train, howitzer, and thirty days' rations, set out in search of the "hostiles." On the march northward through Walker's basin, the Kern River mines, and along the eastern slope of the Sierra Nevada, Davidson found between 1,200 to 1,500 quiet, industrious, and friendly natives—"an altogether reliable lot." To the rough frontiersmen, bent on wiping out hostile Indians, the expedition proved a failure, but not so to the future traveler, merchant, and emigrant. In his 117 miles of travel Davidson had pioneered the way for a direct route between the Great Salt Lake and southern California. He discovered a pass through the mountains to the Salt Lake road, which not only shortened the distance from Fort Tejón but also avoided entirely the Mohave desert and secured for travelers an adequate supply of grass and water.[53]

But the most dastardly deed of the white man was the massacre on Indian Island. Opposite Eureka, for many years safely hidden away on what is now Gunther's Island, lived a group of peaceable, inoffensive natives, who supported themselves mainly by fishing. Being somewhat isolated and undisturbed, they kept old traditional customs—superstitious but harmless ceremonies and rites, consisting principally of dances and monotonous chants. Towards midnight of February 25, 1860, when the tired natives were resting from the excitement of their ceremonies and dancing, a number of boats silently approached the island and out of them leaped white men armed with axes, clubs, and knives. When the alarm was given, men, women, and children began to flee for their lives. The murderers mercilessly struck down everyone in their path, "splitting open skulls, beating out brains, cutting throats" of their helpless victims. Of the 200 Indians on the island only six or seven men escaped alive. On the same night as the Indian Island massacre and in a similar manner white men attacked two rancherias, one south of the entrance to Humboldt Bay and another near the mouth of Eel River, killing about a hundred Indians.

The heinous deeds were traced to a secret organization in Eel River Valley, said to include some of the most prominent men in Humboldt County. Bret Harte, who was temporarily in charge of the Uniontown *Northern Californian,* denounced the outrage. A meeting of citizens at Hydesville in March "deeply deplored the late unfortunate and indiscriminate destruction of Indian life." In the following month the Humboldt County grand jury expressed its "condemnation of the outrage," but regretted that its investigations had failed to secure the facts. The case was dropped. The white murderers were neither apprehended nor punished.[54]

Such treacherous conduct could not but rouse a spirit of retaliation and revenge among the Indians. In the spring of 1860 between 1,500 and 3,000 warriors of the northern and eastern bands assembled in the vicinity of Pyramid Lake and prepared to go on the warpath. After public meetings, calls to arms, the assembling of war supplies and concentration of some 7,000 miners in the Washoe region, Captain Joseph Stewart and his federal forces, supported by Colonel "Jack Hays" and his California and Nevada volunteers, disastrously defeated the Indians in June, 1860, and scattered them through the mountains.[55]

At the same time federal military officers attempted to mollify the disgruntled tribesmen by holding councils and distributing gifts. Early in July, Major Carleton met a deputation of Pah-Utes (twenty-three men and one woman) in council at Camp Cody on the Mohave River. There he told the warriors about the kindness and wisdom of the "Great Father," the earnest desire of the white man to be the friend of his red brother, and the power of the white man's government. The chieftains pledged friendship; they accepted the gifts, and the council disbanded.[56]

In the spring of 1861, when the tribes of Hoopa Valley had formed a conspiracy to exterminate the settlers, United States troops at Forts Gaston and Humboldt, who had hitherto kept out of the war, now harkened to the call for help. Supplemented by newly authorized state volunteer guides, the federal forces under Captains Underwood and Lovell, in a vigorous, three months' campaign, temporarily put an end to the Indian troubles.[57]

Thus, a one-sided contest was waged in California between the Indian and the white man. The age-old struggle between a strong, more civilized people and a weak, backward race for possession of the soil was reaching a climax. The Indian was being "crowded to the wall," but the impatient Californians were not satisfied. They constantly demanded of the federal government more vigorous action against the luckless tribesmen. Congress was truly in a dilemma. It was not unaware of the Indian's rights and attempted to be fair but this attitude bore little fruit; the white man's interest was considered paramount.[58] The Dallas *Herald* stated the crux of the problem thus: "While we have our sympathy for both parties [whites and Indians] all must see that *nothing can or must retard the march of our population,* for any considerable length of time."[59] The Indian was forced to make way for the march of empire.

CHAPTER XII

The Texas Reservation Experiment

IN THE mid-nineteenth century, while military officers and soldiers, governors, and agents were busily engaged in establishing a line of military posts, waging indecisive wars against the wild tribes, and negotiating makeshift treaties, the federal government supplemented its program of frontier defense in the Southwest by trying the experiment of placing some of the tribes on reservations. Many believed that collisions between the two races could be greatly lessened, if the Indians had a permanent location which they could consider their home.[1] This costly experiment was made in Texas and California.

As early as 1847, Governor Henderson proposed that Texas sell the federal government a portion of its public lands to be used exclusively for the settlement of the Indians,[2] and three years later Indian Agent Rollins advocated essentially the same plan. Secretaries of War Conrad and Davis, and Commissioners of Indian Affairs Medill, Brown, and Lea favored a reservation experiment.[3] Governors Bell and Pease pleaded the Indian's cause. "Humanity loudly demands that something of this kind [reservation] should be done . . . for the poor Indian, who now has no other alternative left than to perish by famine or the sword," declared Bell. Governor Pease spoke in a similar vein.[4]

Several Texas newspapers in the early years recommended a peace policy. The *Democratic Telegraph and Texas Register* felt confident that the expenditure of $50,000 to $100,000 annually by "discreet and faithful agents" would result in complete safety on the frontier. Similarly, the *Western Texan* believed that feeding the Indians would do far more towards securing peace than fighting them.[5] Other leading Texas, New Mexico, and California papers, while believing that the Indian should be dealt with vigorously, nevertheless recommended a reservation policy.[6]

The Indians themselves, whose poverty and misery became more acute from year to year, were not averse to the reservation idea. In the fall of 1852 some 700 Comanches under the Chieftains Ketumse and Senaco, while encamped near Camp Johnston on the Concho, pleaded for "a country we may call our own."[7] In the following spring when Robert S. Neighbors, special United States Indian agent for Texas, visited a band of Southern Comanches in the vicinity of Fort Chadbourne and submitted to them the proposal of "settling down," the chiefs appeared willing and even anxious to do so if furnished with land and necessary assistance.[8]

Action, however, was slow. The state of Texas consistently maintained that neither the Indians nor the United States had any property rights in the public lands of Texas. Furthermore, some members of the legislature opposed the reservation system on the grounds that it would extend the power of the federal government and endanger the sovereignty of the state.[9] These objections were finally overcome. By an act approved February 6, 1854, the Texas legislature authorized the federal government to select and survey, from vacant lands within the state, a maximum of twelve leagues, for the exclusive use of the Texas tribes.[10]

In April, Captain Marcy of the United States army and Major Neighbors, representing the Indian Office, were appointed to locate and survey suitable lands for Indian reservations. Two months later these officials, accompanied by a large military escort, set out on their mission from Fort Washita. After an extensive reconnaissance of the country along the upper Big Wichita and Brazos rivers, Marcy and Neighbors selected two tracts which came to be known as the Brazos agency and the Comanche reserve. The former, containing eight leagues, or some 37,000 acres, and situated on the main fork of the Brazos, was intended for the various smaller tribes; the second tract, comprising four leagues, or more than 18,500 acres, and located on the Clear Fork of the Brazos, was to be used by the Comanches exclusively.[11] In July, Congress appropriated some $86,000 for colonizing the tribes.[12]

Within the next few months the Comanche and other tribes, as well as the Indian agents, urged the government to hurry with its reservation program, since many of the natives were starving.[13] Anxious to see the plan in operation, Neighbors visited Washington in the spring of 1855. Early in April he was back in Texas with "full power and instructions for carrying out his part of the proposed Indian policy."[14] Assisted by subagents George W. Hill and George T. Howard, Neighbors was soon busy getting the reservation system under way. Together they collected most of the peaceable tribes in the state—about 1,100 persons—at the Brazos agency; they selected sites for buildings and shops; they contracted for beef and other supplies; they had quantities of land prepared for planting.[15] Within a few months the *Texas State Gazette* reported Neighbors' exertions successful. The reserve settlements on the Clear Fork of the Brazos were progressing "finely." Buildings were being erected and the land was being plowed; the Comanches had greased their rifles and hung them up. The lesser tribes at the Brazos agency were equally industrious. They built log houses and fences, planted peach trees, took good care of their cattle, and produced the finest corn crop in Texas. "A more beautiful situation can't be found in Texas," declared the *Gazette*. ". . . Comfort and happiness beam from every face."[16]

In this description the *Gazette* was too sanguine. Though Neighbors succeeded in placing the peaceful tribes on the Brazos agency, his efforts with the Comanches proved disappointing. Even before the Indians had been placed on the reservation an incident occurred which was prophetic of the difficulties yet to be encountered. In January, 1855, a German trader by the name of Leyendecker, near Fort Chadbourne, fearing that the reserve system would cause a loss in trade with the Indians, spread a rumor among the tribesmen of Buffalo Hump, Ketumse, and Senaco that the whites were planning to kill all their people. As a result about 800 Comanches became frightened and fled to the country of their northern kinsmen.[17] Less than 200 remained with Ketumse; these for the time being settled on the Brazos reservation. By June, 1855, Neighbors reported that only 249 Comanches had settled on the Clear Fork reserve. Most of Senaco's followers, Agent Hill reported, suffered much from cold and hunger; they ate all their dogs and many of their horses; they were naked, without ammunition and tobacco. But the doughty warriors, accustomed to a life of liberty and plunder, preferred to take to the warpath or to die in the mountains rather than to go on the reservation. About 600 Indians from the lesser tribes were colonized at the Brazos agency.[18]

An honest attempt was made to operate both reservations for the benefit of the Indians. On each reservation was a resident agent. Agents Hill and Shapley P. Ross resided at the Brazos agency, and John R. Baylor and Matthew Leeper served the Comanches. Neighbors was supervising agent for all Texas Indians during the entire period.[19] A farmer, a blacksmith, a teacher, a physician, and an interpreter were assigned to each reservation. Every Indian was allowed a daily ration of two pounds of beef and three-fourths of a pound of flour or corn meal, and, for each one hundred rations, four quarts of salt. Besides food, the Indians received shoes, clothing, household articles and utensils, and blacksmith tools.[20]

That the agents had many and difficult duties to perform is evident in the instructions of their superior officer. In July, 1857, Neighbors directed Leeper, in charge of the Comanches, to maintain order, to prevent the introduction of liquor, and to see that the Indians carry out treaty stipulations. Leeper was also responsible for the distribution of rations and presents, the construction of buildings, and the confiscation of stolen property. Moreover, he was expected to assist the head chief in all functions and to reconcile all differences arising on the reservation.[21] To perform the manifold duties successfully required energy, tact, and quick decision. The agent necessarily wielded the powers of a dictator. "He could put Indians in prison, determine their sentences, break up families, take children from their parents . . . and prescribe the daily routine." Although he could do all these things and sometimes did, he was usually content with keeping the Indians on the reservation and preventing them from killing each other and the white officials. On the Texas reservations the agents generally were good men—men of standing in their respective communities, usually selected because of special fitness.[22]

In the spring of 1856, Neighbors reported that the Indians at the Brazos agency, of whom there were about 1,200, were making important and valuable improvements. They had already erected some 150 houses; they were putting in about 800 acres of corn and were determined to become entirely self-supporting.[23] Several months later Colonel M. T. Johnson of the Texas Rangers gave a similar account based on his observations. The "feeding policy" of Uncle Sam, he said, was succeeding most admirably. The Indians were rapidly becoming semicivilized, building log cabins, raising stock, and cultivating grains. Although grasshoppers made it necessary for them to replant most of their fields three times, the tribesmen seemed contented and well pleased; many were becoming "sleek and fat."[24] And after two years had passed, Captain Ford of the Rangers, in a letter to Governor Runnels, expressed the belief that the tribes established on the Brazos had cut loose from the wild Indians for good and had identified themselves with the whites in every way. "The strides they are making in the way of becoming civilized are great and, I might say even astonishing," he observed. Industry, peace, and contentment prevailed everywhere. Certainly, he found "no disposition to give trouble to the Agent or the Government."[25]

But at the Comanche reservation conditions did not run smoothly. It was very difficult to interest the Indians in agriculture. The braves, to be sure, were glad to have the government farmer put in the crop and the squaws to cultivate it. For warriors to engage in such menial tasks as tilling the soil was considered effeminate and degrading. At best, the Indians made poor farmers. They would turn their horses into the cornfield or turn them loose where they easily strayed into the field. Moreover, the natives had a mania for picking crops before they were fully grown or ripened. They would pick melons no larger than a hen's egg and would consume their corn before it had grown to the size of a roasting-ear. Some refused to plant their crops until they had received presents.[26]

The sale and barter of liquor among the tribesmen caused reservation officials great anxiety. Indian agents had the right to exclude liquor from the reservations and Texas laws prohibited persons "from selling, bartering, or giving spirituous or vinous liquors to an Indian. . . ." It was extremely difficult, however, to apprehend the persons who carried on this illegal traffic, since little or nothing could be learned from the Indians. It was charged that certain soldiers as well as civilians engaged in this lucrative but demoralizing business. The agents frequently destroyed liquor stocks, but the traffic continued.[27]

Domestic difficulties and disputes among the reservation Indians, often resulting in death, taxed the patience of the agents to the utmost. At one time, when a chieftain stabbed his wife, her brother vowed to avenge the wrong. When the husband's friend then came to his side, a general fight seemed imminent. But when the irate husband came to the agent and pleaded guilty, the agent turned the matter over to the other chiefs. Fortunately, the woman recovered and the matter was dropped. On another occasion there was violence resulting in the death of one Comanche. When a chieftain engaged in intrigue with another man's wife, the injured husband, according to custom, demanded compensation of the guilty man to the amount of a horse. When the latter refused to pay for his infidelity he was slain by the sons of the injured man. Then father and sons, together with their families, fled and were not overtaken, although a detachment of troops pursued them for 150 miles.[28]

More serious trouble loomed. The Southern Comanches who refused to settle down, together with parties of their northern kinsmen, continued to harass the settlements. The year 1857 witnessed a new series of depredations in northern and eastern Texas —a region which previously had been comparatively free from attack. Indian bandits were realists. When they found the Rio Grande frontier too closely guarded they readily transferred the seat of operations. They attacked and plundered the more settled and peaceful districts, the region of the reservations.[29]

During 1858, when the wild tribes broke out in an orgy of horse-stealing and general murder, the Texans decided to take vengeance. They were determined that all Indians must be punished; they did not care to differentiate between wild and peaceable tribes. Once an Indian, always an Indian, whether on the plains, the mountains, or the reservations. The war was to be transferred from the frontier settlements to the villages of the natives wherever they might be found. This hostile attitude on the part of the Texans, now supported by the United States army, by the Indian agents, and, strange as it may seem, by the reserve Indians themselves,[30] was to sound the death knell of the reservations.

The peacefully inclined tribesmen found themselves in a precarious position. Their homes had been located directly in the path of the migratory horde of whites who had now come to the very edge of the plains. To the north and west roamed the wild Comanches and their untamed allies. Caught between these two relentless forces the weak bands of the reservation were unable to escape.

The Southern Comanches had good cause for bitterness. Their defeat at the hands of Ford's Rangers and Van Dorn's regulars in the spring and summer of 1858, in which the reservation warriors aided the troops,[31] led them to new acts of vengeance on both whites and reservation Indians. Mounted on swift horses, and traveling by night, they stole horses, took scalps, and made a trail that any Texan could follow to the very door of the reservations. By such tactics they led the frontiersmen to conclude that their

troubles came from the reserve Indians. It certainly was easy for
neighboring settlers, recent arrivals from the older states, to con-
fuse the friendly Indians with the hostile tribes.[32]

Gradually, as differences among the Indians, agents, and settlers multiplied, the Texas frontiersmen resolved to clear the state
of red men. And when reports circulated that the inhabitants of
the reservations fraternized with their wilder kinsmen, committing depredations and stealing stock, the occasion was at hand.
Ranchmen frequently came to the reservations to hunt their lost
or stolen stock. Although they rarely ever found their property
there, they believed the Indians guilty. Many felt convinced that
the braves of the upper, or Comanche, reserve either took active
part in the depredations, or at least aided the raiders by slipping
away and stealing horses from the settlements, and then making
their way to join their kinsmen in the north.[33]

Late in 1857 and again in 1858 citizens of three central counties sent petitions to the Secretary of the Interior asking for the
removal of Neighbors and the appointment of a more suitable
man. The petitioners alleged that Neighbors was shielding "the
very Indians we are taxed to feed and clothe . . . the ones who are
inflicting the greatest injury upon us."[34] Neighbors and the agents
stoutly denied that their wards had been guilty of any theft or un-
lawful act.[35]

The charges against the reservation Indians were, no doubt,
greatly exaggerated. Some of the citizens were sincere, but the
great majority were misinformed and influenced by a few designing men. Evidence seems to prove that an organization of unprincipled white men stole, plundered, and killed on a vast scale,
and that they completely camouflaged their operations and shifted
the blame to the Indians.[36]

Prejudice and personal hatred played no small part. For example, Baylor, the first agent of the Comanche reservation, who
at first championed the cause of the Indians, became, on dismissal
from the service,[37] the inveterate enemy of Neighbors; he did all
he could to undermine the power of his former chief. Baylor had

no scruples about the methods he employed. Early in 1858 he wrote
to James Buckner Barry: "I am collecting all the evidence I can
against the Indians and the agents. . . . I want everything that
can be brought forward. . . . We must not be careless or they will
outprove us. . . . I want [Allison] Nelson in the place of Neighbors
and will do all in my power to aid him."[38] Manufactured evidence,
lies, and forgery, Baylor used without any qualms.[39] Sewell Moore,
another disgruntled Texan, in a letter to the President characterized the Indian agents as "Robbers of the Government," and accused Neighbors of supplying goods to the Indians at a profit of
more than 400 per cent.[40]

Recognizing the hopeless situation of his Indians, Neighbors
went to Washington in May, 1858, to acquaint the government
with the real conditions in Texas. As a result, Thomas T. Hawkins,
a special agent, was sent there to investigate the administration of
affairs.[41] Though he stayed at Camp Cooper and the Brazos agency
for five weeks, and in that time invited complainants to appear
before him and testify, very few did so. No one came to present
evidence against Neighbors. In his report Hawkins commended
the agents very highly, and stated that the reservation Indians had
made "great moral and physical advancement."[42]

Hawkins was not alone in these conclusions. Many settlers living near the reservations did not believe the Indians guilty and
readily endorsed the administration of Neighbors. Ford and E. N.
Burleson of the Rangers, who had been directed by the state to
watch the Comanches closely, found no evidence of guilt.[43] But
the reports of the special agents and the officers of the Texas militia
as well as those of the frontiersmen did not satisfy the troublemakers. The unprincipled agitators continued their work of sow-
ing seeds of hatred.

Occasions for attacks on the reservation Indians soon presented
themselves. Late in December, 1858, a band of recently arrived
settlers led by Peter Garland, fired on a small hunting party of
friendly Indans from the Brazos agency, killing four men and
three women, and wounding most of the others. The frontiersmen

lauded this deed, but a wave of indignation swept the older part of the state. Judge N. W. Battle of Waco ordered the arrest of several citizens of Palo Pinto County for murder, but no state officer could be found willing to make the arrest.[44] The grand jury not only refused to indict the suspected murderers but glorified the deed as a "public act."[45] Hatred for the reservation Indians reached fever pitch. Mass meetings and frontier newspapers called for war "to the knife."[46]

The end of the reservations was approaching. In March, 1859, Judge Battle wrote to Governor Runnels: "If no steps are taken to arrest the present movement, the Reserves will unquestionably be 'broken up' and the inhabitants 'red and white will be wiped out.' "[47] Two months later Runnels learned about "a deep laid scheme," headed by Baylor and Garland, to wipe out the reservations and to kill Neighbors and Ross.[48] These rumors were not without foundation. General Twiggs, who recognized the true state of affairs, ordered federal officials to do all in their power to avoid a conflict, and level-headed citizens, such as George B. Erath and Colonel Johnson, went among the people and urged a policy of peace.[49]

The enemies of the reservations, meanwhile, had marshaled their forces and set March 20 as the date for the attack. But the firm attitude of Captain John King of Camp Cooper temporarily thwarted this plan. The citizens of Palo Pinto, Erath, and Jack counties in mass meetings also opposed violence. The would-be attackers, about a hundred strong under Baylor and Allison Nelson, had already gathered at Rock Creek some twelve miles from the Brazos agency, but in the face of such opposition they temporarily withdrew. Before disbanding, they had resolved to "suspend operations" only for six weeks to allow the general government "peaceably" to remove the Indians from the state.[50]

Long before this crisis developed, many realized that the Indians would have to be removed from Texas. For two years the people had been demanding such action. The legislature, the governor, the Texans in Congress, military officers, and Indian agents

—all had urged it.[51] Finally, on March 30, 1859, the Commissioner of Indian Affairs wrote to Neighbors that the Indians would have to be moved in the ensuing fall or winter, and issued instructions accordingly.[52]

But before peaceful removal was effected the vengeful Texans made a last attempt at extermination. In April more than 120 Texans signed a petition demanding that Neighbors and the resident agents resign.[53] Early in the following month the inflamed citizens, organized into "ranger companies," surrounded both reservations and threatened the Indians and their agents day and night.[54] A crisis developed on May 23 when Baylor at the head of 250 men came into the Brazos reservation, bent upon wiping out the Indians. Once more the determined resistance of the army officers at the reservation overawed the crowd and compelled them to withdraw.[55] Believing the "red roguish rascals . . . notoriously, criminally and unpardonably at fault," the settlers declared they would raise a thousand men and take the reservation by storm.[56] To prevent needless bloodshed, Governor Runnels appointed a board of five commissioners to visit the armed camp and work out a peaceful solution. At the same time, the governor assured Nelson, one of Neighbors' principal opponents, that the board would be composed of "men whose interests or sympathies are identified with the frontier."[57]

The tension at last was relieved when on June 11 the Department of the Interior issued orders for the removal of the Indians to the newly leased reservation north of the Red River.[58] In a heavy rainstorm on the last day of July, Neighbors, assisted by Agents Blain, Ross, and Leeper, gathered some 1,400 Indians from both reservations, and escorted by two companies of cavalry and one of infantry, started for the new home.[59] A week later Neighbors wrote to his wife from his camp on Red River: "I have this day crossed all the Indians out of the heathen land of Texas and am now, out of the land of the Philistines."[60] By the middle of August the picturesque cavalcade arrived at the banks of the Washita near the site of the present Anadarko, Oklahoma. Two weeks later Neighbors turned his charges over to Agent Blain.[61]

But Neighbors, who had been a champion of the Texas Indians from the days of the Texas Republic, was destined to pay with his life for his courageous stand. During the stormy years of the late fifties he had made many enemies and these now turned against him the hatred they had felt towards the Indians. While stopping at Fort Belknap, he was shot in the back by Ed Cornett, a man he did not know. In his untimely death the people of Texas lost a devoted public servant and the Indians a true friend.[62] For almost a quarter of a century he had championed the cause of both.[63]

The removal of the Texas tribes to a new home north of the Red River only created another sore spot. Indian raids instigated by "evil and designing" men soon broke out afresh.[64] When the Civil War began, the wild tribes renewed their attacks on a grander scale, wreaking vengeance on the white man who had robbed them of their hunting grounds. The Comanches continued to be the dread of the frontier settler.[65]

The establishment of the Texas reservations had been an experiment. But despite the expenditure of nearly half a million dollars,[66] the experiment failed. Many factors contributed to the failure. For one thing, some opposed government expenditure for the Indians. To this group, feeding the red man seemed an utter waste of good money. Failure to stop inroads into Texas of other warlike tribes proved a stumbling block in the path of the reservation policy. Moreover, the army's opposition to the olive branch, its perpetual conflict with Indian agents, and the incessant demands of selfish interests added to the confusion and discord.[67]

But the most important single cause of the failure of the reservation system is to be found in the rapid growth of the white population. Collision with reservation Indians was inevitable. To the frontiersman, a reservation warrior on a peaceful hunting expedition and a wild raider were one and the same. The white man readily believed that the inmates of the reservations were responsible for all the wrongs. The reservations had to go.[68]

CHAPTER XIII

California Indian Reservations

I N CALIFORNIA, as in Texas, the federal government hearkened to the advocates of an Indian peace policy and embarked on a reservation experiment.[1] Among these advocates was the *Daily Alta California,* which boldly declared that the Indian was the true owner of the soil, and since he was deprived of his heritage, some means of supporting him would have to be provided. To strengthen its position, the *Alta* reprinted an article from the *Morning Courier and New-York Enquirer* which severely criticized the government's Indian policy. This Atlantic seaboard journal asserted that natives on our frontiers had been treated like dogs; it was high time that they be treated more like men. In a similar vein, the *Alta* maintained that force or war was utterly futile; it was not human, politic, or Christian. The only economical and wise policy, this paper insisted, was one of peace.[2]

Voluminous reports to Congress showed that a general reservation system like that of the Spanish missionaries was quite feasible. Surely what the missionaries had accomplished the United States government could do.[3] Congress proceeded cautiously. Late in September, 1850, it passed laws authorizing the appointment of Indian agents in California and appropriated $25,000 to enable the President to make treaties with the various tribes in the territories.[4] In accordance with this plan the President appointed three special agents for California to serve as peace commissioners. Early in January, 1851, the newly arrived Indian officials—Colonel Redick McKee, George W. Barbour, and Dr. O. M. Wozencraft—entered upon their delicate mission by issuing an appeal to the people of California, urging mildness, moderation, and forbearance toward the natives. "The safety and security of every community," they declared, "demands that equal and exact justice be meted out to all alike." Domestication and not extermination was by far the wiser policy, they assured the settlers. The *Alta* praised the temperate and reasonable plea of the commissioners and urged that the Indians be given a fair chance.[6]

During the spring and summer the special agents entered upon their duties in earnest. With imposing caravans carrying provisions, munitions, and Indian goods, and protected by a large escort, they advanced into the Indian country to study conditions and to conciliate the tribes. Sending out runners to summon the red men, the commissioners held councils, distributed gifts, licensed traders, negotiated treaties, and established reservations. On this elaborate tour, covering hundreds of miles and extending from Scott's Valley in the north to Tulare Valley in the south, the commissioners learned that the size of California's Indian population had been greatly exaggerated, and that many of the natives were in a destitute condition. The mountain tribes along the San Joaquin had reached only a very low stage of civilization; they subsisted on rats, grasshoppers, acorns, and fish, and had practically no clothes and no weapons. Although many of them were thievish, they were for the most part docile and tractable. The commissioners believed that the best way to keep the natives quiet and contented was to give them plenty of food.

Between March and November, 1851, they negotiated eighteen treaties with more than 420 chiefs representing about 25,000 natives. The treaties were definite and simple. The Indians agreed to keep the peace, cede their land titles, and go on reservations; the government, on its part, agreed to set aside some 11,000 square miles for reservations, pay for the Indian land in goods, and furnish teachers, farmers, and mechanics.[7] Some of the tribesmen declared they were "mad, crazy with joy," that good white men had come at last and agreed that the Indian had a right to live somewhere. For a while the commissioners felt optimistic and even jubilant. But their plans were doomed to failure. Prospectors and miners paid little or no heed to treaties or reservations. They promptly invaded valuable mineral lands and brutally shoved

aside or killed protesting Indians.[8] California "politics," lavish expenditures by the commissioners, and the removal of large tracts
of land from public and private use were sufficient to overthrow
the commissioners' entire system.[9]

Influenced by special interests, the California legislature forthwith condemned the Indian treaties and recommended the removal of the wild tribes beyond the state.[10] Pleading the red man's
cause in the state senate, the celebrated Jonathan J. Warner pointed
out that to reject the treaties would greatly lessen the Indian's
faith in our government. If the treaties were unfair, they should
be amended, not rejected. Moreover, removal of the Indians from
the state was utterly impractical, for there was no other place
where they could be located. There was only one other solution:
"Drive them at once into the ocean or bury them in the land of
their birth." In conclusion Warner insisted that the "Indians must
be provided with a home." The *Alta* and the *Daily Evening Picayune* also defended the commissioners' policy.[11] When the California members convinced the Senate that "the whole army of the
United States could not expel the white intruders" from the mineral lands of the reservations, all the California Indian treaties
were rejected.[12]

Meanwhile, early in February, 1852, a convention of California
citizens, champions of the peace policy, assembled in Washington
and framed a memorial, including "some plan for colonizing them
[the Indians] satisfactorily to the people of the west coast and
beneficial to the Indians themselves."[13] The federal government
soon modified its California Indian policy. On March 3, 1852,
Congress created the office of Superintendent of Indian Affairs
for California. Some months later Lieutenant Beale, the new Superintendent, proceeded to the Pacific coast[14] to learn the true
causes of the difficulties. His tour of inspection among the tribes
of Upper California disclosed enormous waste and gross mismanagement in the Indian service.[15] He therefore recommended the
adoption of a modified plan, the military reservation. The Indians

were to be collected on reservations not for Indians but for the army. Here the natives would live under the protection of a military post and government agents would teach them to work. The Indians on these reserves would not receive title to the lands but would be considered merely as wards of the nation. Believing that California's Indian land problem might thus be solved, Beale asked for an appropriation of $500,000.[16]

A portion of Beale's plan was soon put into operation. On March 3, 1853, Congress authorized the President to establish five military reservations from the public domain in California, not to exceed 25,000 acres each, for the protection and improvement of the Indians, and appropriated $250,000 to carry out this program.[17] Beale proceeded energetically. He established an experimental farm on the San Juan River, and a reservation at Tejón Pass in the southern extreme of the San Joaquin Valley. By the spring of 1854 more than 400 Indians were at work tilling some 2,500 acres of land, grazing about 2,000 head of cattle, cultivating extensive gardens, and raising fruit trees. Headquarters were erected for the employees and large granaries were built for the crops. The Indians feasted on cattle, and the success of the program seemed to be assured.[18]

The new plan received considerable praise as being extremely humane and economical. A traveler, writing from Fort Miller in October, 1853, found the Tejón reservation entirely successful and the Indians "perfectly happy."[19] The San Francisco *Herald* reported that Beale's humane experiment was succeeding beyond its author's most sanguine expectations; one contemporary wrote that the Indians "could not be driven away with a 'Big Stick.' "[20] The *Alta* credited Beale not only with cementing a firm and faithful bond between himself and the Tejón tribes but also with working a complete moral reformation.[21] The *Daily California Chronicle* praised the Superintendent and his able assistant, Benjamin D. Wilson,[22] for transforming "a wilderness into a peaceful home, and wild men into quiet and contented cultivators."[23]

Beale, too, felt very hopeful and optimistic about his wards on the Tejón reserve. In his report to Commissioner of Indian Affairs Manypenny he painted a rosy picture. "It is impossible to do justice to the docility and energy which these poor people possess," he wrote. Since their tasks were never made laborious, they worked not only without murmur but with the most cheerful alacrity. They looked upon the results of their labor with amazement and delight. On Sundays they played at "Bandy and Ball" with the overseers. As for their attitude towards reservation life, Beale made this revealing comment: "Constantly they say to me: 'We have been asleep a long time. We are just beginning to awake, but our eyes are not yet wide open.' "[24]

But despite the favorable reports, the promises which the system held out at its inauguration did not materialize. Only a small percentage of Indians settled on the reservations. The Commissioner of Indian Affairs attributed the failure to mismanagement on the part of the government employees, to the interference of white settlers, and to the indolence of the natives. Beale's very energy, his courageous and ruthless campaign against corrupt and inefficient Indian agents and contractors served as a boomerang.[25] Politics and his seeming laxity in business matters contributed to his downfall.[26] Early in June, 1854, Thomas Jefferson Henley succeeded Beale and in the following month assumed the duties of his office.[27]

Henley, at this time, was a prominent figure in the business and political circles of California. A native of Indiana, he became active in Democratic politics of his state at an early age. He was elected to the Indiana legislature many times and to Congress for three successive terms. But he left his native state for California during the gold rush of 1849. There he became a member of the banking firm of Henley, Latham, and Hastings. In the early fifties he served as postmaster of San Francisco, a position he resigned to become Superintendent of Indian Affairs of California. A zealous and thorough partisan and an active stump speaker, he was commonly called the "War Horse of the Democracy."[28]

But Henley had no easy task ahead of him, especially since he followed a man who had created the impression of having done a revolutionary piece of work. The *Southern Californian,* an anti-administration paper, highly resentful of Beale's removal, severely denounced the system administered by Henley as a "stupendous fraud and humbug."[29] The Indians on the Tejón reserve, too, assumed a hostile attitude toward Beale's successor. About a hundred of them slipped away and went northward towards the Owens Lake country.[30]

Despite opposition Henley went ahead and modified the plan inaugurated by his predecessor. Instead of spending the entire appropriation for the maintenance of one Indian reservation, he used it for the support of several. The vast size of California, the large number of small scattered tribes in the state, and the reluctance of the Indians to move any great distance from their old homes—all these circumstances made Henley believe that more reservations were desirable. An increase in number, the new Superintendent pointed out, should also prove to be more economical.[31] Accordingly, by the fall of 1858 there were five permanent reservations in California. The Tejón reserve, started by Beale, which originally contained 75,000 acres, was reduced to one-third its size.[32] About 700 Indians cultivated the soil here. The Klamath reserve on the Klamath River was occupied by about 2,500 Indians of the extreme northern tribes, who were engaged chiefly in salmon fishing and berrying. And in Colusa County was the Nome Lackee reserve, containing between 2,000 and 3,000 natives. Some fifty miles south of Cape Mendocino was a fourth reserve, where about 500 Digger Indians had been settled. By the fall of 1858 a contemporary described the Mendocino reservation as the largest in the state, containing about 4,000 natives. The fifth was the Nome Cult reserve, located about sixty miles southwest of Nome Lackee. In time it became the chief reservation in the state.[33] Henley also established temporary reservations or Indian farms at Fresno, King's, Kern, and Tule River (or Madden). The Superintendent was thus enabled to reward additional friends with po-

sitions which the reservations proper did not provide. By the fall
of 1858, of the 61,000 Indians under Henley's jurisdiction, some
11,000 resided on reservations and Indian farms. Within a period
of five years, during the regimes of Beale and Henley, the reservation experiment in California cost the federal government $1,173,-
000.[34]

Official reports transmitted to Congress from time to time
gave glowing accounts of the progress of the system. According
to Henley and his agents "the extent and variety of the crops were
fabulously grand"; "immense numbers" of Indians were being
fed and clothed. The natives, they asserted, were cheerful workers,
making considerable progress in peaceful pursuits. To Commissioner of Indian Affairs Denver, Henley wrote that the reservation Indians appeared healthy, contented, and happy. Indeed, he
asserted, many of them had already learned to work like white
men.[35]

Indian officials were not alone in their praise. In the fall of 1855
the celebrated "Jack Hays," formerly of the Texas Rangers and
now Surveyor General of California, after a trip to the Tejón reservation, wrote to Henley that he had been "agreeably disappointed" to find the Indians quiet, contented, and industrious. Captain
E. D. Keyes, who visited Nome Lackee in the same year, found
the 1,000 natives well fed and clothed. The young squaws, under
the instruction of American women, had learned how to sew,
plait straw, and make hats. Three years later one of the editors of
the *Daily Alta California* also reported the natives "happy, contented . . . and living in genuine arcadian simplicity and enjoy-
ment."[36] A writer in *Hutchings' California Magazine* expressed
the opinion that the California reservation system was "the best
mitigation of existing evils."[37]

Despite the glowing reports of Indian officials and others, repeated charges of mistreatment of the natives and of graft and
corruption reached the federal authorities. The Tejón reserve, for
example, was represented as being in a state of decay and totally

useless. According to the *Southern Californian*, the reservation controlled nothing, gave security to no one, and benefited no one. Its failure, according to this paper, was due largely to the incompetence of Henley, who cared little for the Indians but devoted his time and attention to politics and lobbying in and about Sacramento.[38] The government, therefore, ordered J. Ross Browne, special agent of the Treasury Department, and Godard Bailey of the Department of the Interior, who had been on the Gila, to examine the California reservations. Their investigations disclosed glaring abuses. The reservations, they reported, were no better than almshouses where large numbers of Indians were insufficiently fed and clothed at great expense to the government.

Browne, who had a gift for satirical writing, told of blankets furnished the Indians that were so thin that they were practically transparent; shirts and pantaloons were equally transparent and readily cracked open at the seams. During the summer months the natives were encouraged to go about with red or green pantaloons painted on their legs, and Browne suggested with a chuckle that striped blue shirts artistically marked out on their bodies might be cool, economical, and picturesque. Sanitary conditions, he reported, were appalling and medical care was practically nonexistent. In the spring of 1858 when he visited the Mendocino reservation he found that all the able-bodied men had left. The remainder were lying on the bare ground "without a rag of clothing ... and dying of starvation." Joel Lewis, a farmer at Mendocino, in a letter to the United States deputy surveyor, made this complaint: "I am tired of Indian Reservations, particularly this one, as working naked and starved savages is anything but agreeable."[39] Conditions at the other reservations were no better. When the Indians refused to work they were beaten into submission.[40]

There were other abuses, too. Henley, it seems, misapplied reservation funds for private ventures. He built a sawmill, stocked his private farm with fine cattle, and employed Indian labor without pay. But for the reservations he purchased third-rate cattle, charging the government exorbitant prices. He also filled many offices with his own kinsmen. His overstaffed, overpaid corps of assistants spent most of its time in attending to private claims. In the fall of 1858, Bailey wrote to Commissioner of Indian Affairs Mix: "If Henley had accepted the office for the purpose of defrauding the government he could not have devised a system better calculated to baffle investigation than that which obtains in every branch of the business of this superintendency."[41]

Bailey made specific suggestions for improving Indian relations. He recommended that the California natives be divided into three groups: (1) The mountain tribes should be left undisturbed, since they did not come into direct contact with the whites. (2) The friendly agriculturalists, who lived in the vicinity of Owens Lake and to the southward should be secured in the possession of their land and aided in working out their own salvation. (3) The third group, those who loitered around the towns and mining communities, should be removed to a reservation and compelled to work for their support. Labor was to be performed exclusively by the natives; no whites except officials and instructors were to be allowed to come near, and Indians were not to be permitted to leave this reserve.[42]

In the spring of 1859, James Y. McDuffie succeeded Henley. The appointment of the new Superintendent, a former marshal of the Northern District of California and a resident of Georgia at the time of his appointment, evoked considerable difference of opinion. The San Francisco *Herald* considered his appointment most judicious, but the *Alta*, recalling that McDuffie had been the proprietor of a San Francisco gambling house, expressed grave doubts concerning his fitness.[43] McDuffie himself made a brave show of reform. His extensive visits to the reservations and farms led him to conclude that, with the exception of Klamath, all the reservations were in a deplorable condition.[44] With this opinion others concurred. A citizen of Humboldt County characterized the Mendocino reservation as an "abominable humbug and swindle."[45] And the Washington correspondent of the *Alta* reported the Indian service in California going from bad to worse. Under these circumstances the Commissioner of Indian Affairs recommended the abandonment of the existing system and the adoption of some other plan.[46]

The California legislature and others suggested that the federal government abolish the reservation experiment and cede to the state entire jurisdiction, management, and control of the California tribes. To be relieved of the Indian burden in California the government, of course, was expected to meet a number of conditions: it was to pay expenses incurred by the state or citizens in Indian wars; it was to cede all tracts of land originally designed for the colonization of Indians, as well as the personal property belonging to the reservations and farms; it was to pay the treasury of California $50,000 per annum for a period of twenty years.[47]

But the government did not choose to surrender its jurisdiction over the California tribes. Congress, acting upon the suggestion of the Secretary of the Interior, passed a law which provided for a new method of administering the Indian affairs of the state. According to this plan California was to be divided into a northern and southern district, each under a superintending agent.[48] The Indians who were to be placed on small reservations would go there by simple agreement and not by treaty; those not placed on reservations but requiring supervision, would be parceled out among farmers. Although less expensive, the new system, it was hoped, would prove more effective than the old.[49]

When the modified plan was put into execution several reservations were abandoned, and the Indians were no longer concentrated at a few places. In the northern superintendency Nome Lackee, Mendocino, and the Klamath reservations were sold, and about 2,000 Indians were removed to Smith River in Del Norte County, where farms were rented. In the south, the Fresno and King's River farms and the Tejón reservation were abandoned. The Tule River farm became the headquarters for a small portion of the neglected San Joaquin tribes, who in due time were cast adrift to starve.[50]

Despite the honest attempts of the federal government and its vast expenditure of money,[51] the California reservation experiment had proved a failure. For a number of years its champions in Congress and in the press had fought a valiant fight but finally bowed their heads in defeat. Designed as an asylum and protection for the Indian, as well as a bulwark of defense for the white man, the reservation system was doomed to failure from the outset. It could hardly be expected that the Indians, true lovers of freedom, would be willing to go on reservations or to remain after being taken there. In many instances they had to be driven by force. Whenever they attempted to escape they were forced back at the point of the bayonet. On the California reservations the Indians soon found themselves at the mercy of one of the most notorious "Indian rings" in American history. Robbed by government officials, debauched by men who claimed to be their superiors, and made desperate by poverty and disease, the Indians saw their days numbered. The government had been ardently desirous of promoting the Indians' welfare, but destiny was ever thwarting its labors.[52]

Although the reservation experiment did not solve the Indian problem in California, it had far-reaching results. The system as founded by Beale and extended by Henley ultimately became the accepted policy of the nation. It was the most definite and by far the most permanent single contribution to Indian policy of the century. In the seventies, when the federal government took definite steps to remedy its previous mistakes and established the modern reservation system, the red man received a square deal and the problem of frontier defense was solved.[53]

CHAPTER XIV

On the Eve of the Civil War

THE PERIOD from 1848 to 1860 was essentially a frontier epoch. During these years, when the federal government was seeking the proper method of dealing with the Indian, it was consciously paving the way for the transformation of the Far West from a sparsely settled country to one of thriving communities and settlements. In its quest for peace and security for the white man as well as for the Indian, the government carried on an extensive and varied program. Exploring for military and commercial roads, examining western streams, erecting military posts, building roads, dispatching punitive expeditions, and establishing Indian reservations—all these had but one aim—to make the Far West a peaceful and prosperous area. Thousands of men and millions of dollars played a part in these vast and varied undertakings. Permanent peace on the frontier was not attained until a quarter of a century later, but the government in its policy of frontier defense was building a firm foundation for the Greater Southwest of today.

The coming of the Civil War halted the completion of this program; and yet much had been achieved. The vast region beyond the Mississippi River was no longer an unknown land. In a little over a decade, government explorers, surveyors, engineers, and scientists had brought to light a wealth of accurate geographical information about sections of the country previously little known. At the close of the Mexican War many portions of the Far West had been as unknown as the interior of "darkest Africa." A trip to Santa Fe or to the Rocky Mountains was considered almost equal to a voyage to China.[1] Western Texas was pictured as a wild and undeveloped country—a land of the buffalo, the mustang, the rattlesnake, and the tarantula.[2] The Territory of New Mexico was considered by many a land of "burning deserts, parched mountains, dried rivers, . . . Greasers, and Apaches."[3] The Salt Lake country was characterized as an inhospitable and "mean land." But on the eve of the Civil War the true character of these and many other areas had been established.[4]

With the gradual disappearance of the blank spaces on the map of the Far West, the virgin lands and gold fields beyond the Mississippi, which in earlier years had beckoned only hardy pioneers, could now attract less bold and less adventurous spirits. Many of the grueling hardships and grave dangers incident to the overland journey of earlier days had disappeared or had considerably lessened. Soldiers, merchants, and emigrants and settlers could now travel with comparative ease and safety from one end of the country to the other over established routes, well supplied with grass and water and rendered safe by long lines of military posts. The Far West had been opened to greater trade, travel, and settlement; the delusion of the Great American desert had disappeared.[5]

In administering the manifold program of frontier defense, many a fledgling army officer had an excellent opportunity to secure practical military experience. Grant, McClellan, Sherman, and Pope served their apprenticeship on the western frontier. Likewise, Lee and the two Johnstons (Albert Sidney and Joseph Eggleston), together with a host of other officers,[6] secured valuable military training in the Far West. The frequent prairie and mountain travel trained the eye to take in at a glance the salient features of a country. Surveying western streams, building roads and forts, and leading punitive expeditions against Indians and white outlaws prepared these officers for military leadership in the War between the States.

Upon Grant and Lee, in particular, service on the western frontier was to have a profound influence. At Jefferson Barracks, in Texas, and in the Mexican War Grant already had learned about men and what they would do "in a pinch." At the distant, lonely frontier posts in Oregon and California he met men in the rough, saw life in the rough; and his spirit of tenderness became covered "as with a coat of steel, a coat he was to need time upon time in the Civil War."[7] Lee likewise gained strength, maturity, and wisdom on the frontier. In Texas he worked with and commanded many of the officers who were to become either Northern or Southern field commanders in the Civil War. To know these men, their strength and weakness, served him well in later military crises. In 1861, when Lee came from the Texas wilderness, he was prepared physically, mentally, and spiritually to assume the role of the South's peerless leader—as General Scott characterized him —"America's very best soldier."[8]

Frontier defense also stimulated growth in population and influenced general progress in the Southwest. In the decade 1850-60 the Texas population increased from some 212,000 to more than 604,000; in New Mexico Territory a population of less than 62,000 inhabitants had grown to more than 93,000 during the same period. Utah Territory and California experienced even larger gains—the former showing an increase from about 11,000 to more than 40,000, and the latter from less than 93,000 to nearly 380,000.[9] This rapid growth, accompanied by the occupation of large areas of Indian lands, brought forth new western territories[10] and a host of new counties.[11] Some of the older western settlements grew by leaps and bounds and many new ones were born.[12]

With the exception of backward New Mexico, the character of many of the western settlements had greatly changed—notably in Texas, in Utah, and especially in the larger coast towns in California. Tents and log houses gave way to comfortable buildings and well-fenced farms; in the cities fine edifices and spacious public buildings of brick and stone were erected. The quality of the streets and sidewalks was greatly improved. "The spirit of western progress was asserting itself."[13]

Moreover, the Southwest was amassing great wealth. Farmers, stockmen, and merchants, in addition to numerous tradesmen and professional classes, added materially to the wealth of their respec-

tive states and territories. The Texans, for example, had grown
rich fast. The value of property in the state in 1850 was about $52,-
000,000; ten years later it was nearly six times as great. California
showed even more remarkable progress—an increase in wealth of
more than 837 per cent. New Mexico and Utah Territories also
showed considerable gains.[14] In agriculture,[15] manufacture,[16] mining,[17] and grazing[18] the story was one of marked advance.

To meet the needs of a rapidly growing population, a network
of overland mail and passenger "stages"[19] radiated into the various
portions of the Far West in the later 1850's. And, in the absence of
a transcontinental railroad, overland freighting—precursor of
the modern trucking system—took on the character of a well-or-
ganized business. As military posts multiplied and mining camps
increased, the business of carrying provisions, supplies, and equipment to the outposts in the Indian and mining country grew enor-
mously. A high-water mark in freighting was reached during the
"Mormon War," when Russell, Majors, and Waddell, the official
army contractors, transported some 16,000,000 pounds of supplies
to Utah. In its heyday this firm owned and operated more than
6,200 wagons and about 75,000 oxen. The freighting companies,
both large and small, with their acres of wagons, huge herds of
oxen, and regiments of drivers and other employees penetrated the
far corners of the Far West. Overland freighting reached its peak
in the 1860's under the picturesque and dynamic Ben Holladay.
By 1865 the amount of merchandise carried across the plains
amounted to more than 31,000,000 pounds for the year. The needs
of the frontier soldier, the settler, and the prospector were being
supplied.[20]

The busy and rapidly growing Southwest was plagued with
lawlessness. Father Domenech, who traveled extensively through
the Southwest in the 1850's, characterized the Americans of the
Texan frontiers as "the very scum of society—bankrupts, escaped
criminals, old volunteers, who . . . came to seek adventure and illicit gains." Drinking, gambling, and duelling he found the order
of the day. San Antonio was notorious for assassinations.[21] W. W.

Mills, a prominent Texan, wrote that in El Paso, in the late fifties, "every citizen, whatever his age or calling, habitually carried a six-shooter at his belt and slept with it under his pillow."[22] Conditions in New Mexican towns were not much better. Wild, boisterous gamblers and outlaws frequently so ganged together as to place the lives and property of law-abiding citizens in grave danger.[23] In California the unsettled conditions of society and business and the feverish rush for gold brought forth, especially in the cities, a host of criminal classes. Gambling developed into a regular business; stealing of horses, cattle, and mules was carried on in such a way as to resemble a regular and legitimate trade.[24] Human life was the cheapest thing in Los Angeles; "Nigger Alley" was as tough a spot as could be found anywhere on the face of the earth.[25]

Despite the numerous "bad men," a large majority of the people of the Southwest were law-abiding citizens. When the lawless elements became too bold and the law-enforcement machinery was weak or too slow, the better class of settlers took the law into its own hands. From Texas to California, "Regulators," "Moderators," and "Vigilantes" meted out speedy and impartial justice. Whipping, branding, "mosquito treatment," and hanging had a salutary effect on the lawless elements of our last frontier.[26]

In the mid-nineteenth century the Southwest certainly showed marked influences and characteristics of the frontier. Here one found some of the conditions so graphically described by Professor Frederick Jackson Turner in his memorable essay, "The Significance of the Frontier in American History," and, perhaps, overzealously amplified by his admiring disciples.[27] Here one could discern the economic influence in full swing. For to the Southwest came trader, miner, cattle raiser, and farmer to seek economic security. Here, too, because of the Indian danger, frontiersmen regularly pooled their interests in the cause of common defense. Many of the frontier communities, protected by trading establishments and military posts, served as vanguards of civilization—nuclei for larger settlements into which civilizing influences gradually found their way.[28]

The southwestern frontier, like other American frontiers, was a veritable melting pot of classes, races, and cultures. To the land of opportunity came thousands from every walk of life and from everywhere. Since all faced the same dangers and battled together for a livelihood, every man felt as good as every other. Here all classes of society met on a common level. Anyone who "put on airs" did not belong.[29] Strength, courage, and hardihood were prime essentials. Resourcefulness was a cardinal virtue: the newcomer had to be resourceful in order to survive. Hospitality he practiced in full measure: on the trail, in the mining camp, in the frontier home, he received the respectable stranger or visitor with a genuine welcome. The frontiersman spoke "straight from the shoulder." Polite phrases or indirect speech found little favor among a busy, hard-working, vigorous people. Above all, the frontiersman was an optimist. He implicitly believed in the new country with its vast resources and boundless opportunities.[30] Such was the settler of the Southwest—the pioneer who built homes and roads, plowed and planted, prospected for precious metals, chastised the red man, and established civil order.[31]

A particular influence of the frontier was that exerted on literature. From early colonial days the frontier beckoned adventurous spirits, who subsequently left some account of the influence provided by their environment. But it was in the nineteenth century, in the trans-Mississippi country, that government explorers, soldiers, hunters, trappers, solitary pathfinders, and pioneers in their wanderings throughout the vast unknown region left their impress on American literature. The numerous reports of the official explorers, as well as the embellished oral accounts of the unofficial trail blazers, furnished a rich storehouse for novelists, dramatists, and poets. Cooper in *The Leatherstocking Tales* and Irving in *The Adventures of Captain Bonneville* opened new vistas for the literature of the frontier.[32]

The spirit of the frontier was popularized in the dime novels, published by the house of Beadle and Adams and read by millions. Trappers, ranchers, Indians, gold seekers, cowboys, road agents, and bad men were the subjects for an amazing number of sensational tales of adventure and combat.[33] On a higher literary level, men like Mark Twain and Bret Harte initiated the Wild West movement in American literature. Bret Harte's fiction breathed life and spirit into the California frontier; Mark Twain's hilarious sketches of California and Nevada created a "Psychic West"—an illusion of freedom, of irresponsibility, of buoyancy.[34] In the twentieth century John G. Neihardt, in *The Splendid Wayfaring* and especially in *A Cycle of the West*, portrayed the frontier spirit of the great American epic period, 1822-1890. Throughout the moving drama of his monumental epic of the West, he is deeply stirred by the irresistible urge of the western migrations. In the apparently unscrupulous, cold-blooded pushing of the tribesmen and in the clash of cultures the poet recognizes the inevitable outcome— physical prowess for the white man, spiritual triumph for the Indian.[35]

Long before Neihardt's day the inevitable character of the conflict was apparent to many people. During the period of the great migrations, in the late 1840's and 1850's, the clash between the races became more bitter. Many of the Indians, to be sure, were peaceable. But the warlike tribesmen, not adjusted to an agricultural life, were caught by the pressure of circumstances. For them, there was only one solution: to fight to the death to defend their natural "rights." Many of the whites, including government officials and military officers (among them Neighbors, Beale, Cooke, Marcy, and Manypenny) recognized the injustice done to the Indians and pleaded for fairness. But to the average pioneer and settler, who bore the brunt of the Indian attacks, there was only one kind of Indian: a savage murderer, who had to be exterminated. To be sure, the Indian suffered historical "wrongs." But the responsibility for these "wrongs" is difficult to assess. Doubtless, they were the inevitable product of the "March of Empire." Our government, as noted previously, had attempted to deal fairly with the Indian, but there were many hurdles in its path. Despite the many blunders, however, the federal Indian policy had a brighter side. The government could show a number of positive achievements for the benefit of the Indian.[36]

The last chapter of the Indian's story is well known. In the period following the Civil War he fought a valiant fight for survival but was compelled to bow his head in defeat—giving way to a stronger, more progressive civilization. In the inevitable, one-sided contest the Indian did not always receive a "square deal," but he probably secured no worse treatment than did backward natives in other parts of the world at the hands of empire builders. In any case, the Indian did not entirely capitulate. Although defeated on the field of battle, he retained his personality and his spirit—a spirit deeply rooted in social group life. This Indian group spirit has shown remarkable tenacity.[37] Despite depopulation[38] and loss of homeland, the Indian "was never inwardly defeated."[39] The will to live and the tenacity to save his culture has proved the Indian's salvation and secured him champions, among whom may be particularly mentioned one of the most recent, John Collier, President Franklin D. Roosevelt's Commissioner of Indian Affairs, who ushered in a new era for the red man. After centuries of exploitation by the white man, "the Indian is finding his place as a farmer, a teacher, a mechanic. His culture and handicrafts, once looked upon as crude and contemptible by his 'civilizers,' now are fostered and preserved."[40] The once "vanishing American" is coming into his own.[41]

Thus, on the eve of the Civil War, the government policy of frontier defense had already presaged a brighter tomorrow, a Greater Southwest. Many a link in the chain of peace and prosperity on the frontier had been forged. With the successful termination of the war, the coming of the Pacific railroads, and the gradual solution of the Indian problem, the knotty problem of frontier defense came to a close, and the Far Southwest took its place as a leader in the affairs of the nation. The march of empire in the continental United States was completed.

References

ABBREVIATIONS

Adjutant General's Office—A. G. O.
Army Commands, United States—A. C., U. S.
Commissioner of Indian Affairs—C. I. A.
Engineers, Office of the Chief—E., O. C.
General Orders—G. O.
Headquarters of the Army—H. A.
Indian Affairs Office—I. A. O.
Letters Received—L. R.
Letters Sent—L. S.
Library of Congress—L. C.
Missouri Historical Society—M. H. S.
National Archives—N. A.
Quartermaster General's Office—Q. G. O.
Secretary of the Interior—S. I.
Secretary of War—S. W.
State Department—S. D.
Surgeon General's Office—S. G. O.
Topographical Engineers Bureau—T. E. B.

I

1. *Congressional Globe, Appendix*, 30 Cong., 1 Sess., 420.
2. Frederick Law Olmsted, *A Journey through Texas or a Saddle-trip on the Southwestern Frontier* (New York, 1857), 411, 423-426; John Russell Smith, *North America* (New York, 1924), 246-248; St. Louis *Daily Missouri Republican*, June 27, 1855; W. B. Dewees, *Letters from an Early Settler of Texas* (Louisville, Ky., 1852), 299-300.
3. George Pierce Garrison, *Westward Extension, 1841-1850* (New York, 1906), 300.
4. George A. McCall, *Letters from the Frontiers Written during a Period of Thirty Years' Service in the Army of the United States* (Philadelphia, 1868), 490-493; New Orleans *Daily Picayune*, Dec. 12, 1855.
5. St. Louis *Daily Missouri Republican*, June 27, 1855.
6. Carl Coke Rister, *The Southwestern Frontier, 1865-1881* (Cleveland, 1928), 27.
7. Olmsted, 447-448; Smith, 430-431; Lydia Spencer Lane, *I Married a Soldier or Old Days in the Old Army* (Philadelphia, 1893), 16.
8. Joseph Schmitz, "Impressions of Texas in 1860," *Southwestern Historical Quarterly*, XLII (April, 1939), 344-345.
9. San Antonio *Western Texan*, Nov. 25, 1852.
10. Corpus Christi *Nueces Valley*, April 3, 1858.
11. New Orleans *Daily Picayune*, July 21, 1860.
12. Houston *Democratic Telegraph and Texas Register*, June 6, 1850.
13. Dallas *Herald*, July 3, 1858; John C. Hays, "Life and Adventures of a Texas Ranger . . .," 12, MS., Bancroft Library, University of California.
14. Washington (Tex.) *Texas Ranger*, May 11, 1854. (Prior to January, 1854, this paper was called *Texas Ranger & Lone Star*.)
15. William Curry Holden, "Frontier Problems and Movements in West Texas, 1846-1900," MS., Ph.D. dissertation, University of Texas, 1928, p. 43; Dudley G. Wooten, *A Comprehensive History of Texas, 1685-1897* (Dallas, 1898), I, 772.
16. William Watts Hart Davis, *El Gringo or New Mexico and Her People* (New York, 1857), 57, 58, 387, 551; Horatio O. Ladd, *The Story of New Mexico* (Boston, 1891), 256-257; *Senate Executive Documents*, 36 Cong., 2 Sess., I, No. 1, p. 53.
17. Sylvester Mowry, *Arizona and Sonora: the Geography, History, and Resources of the Silver Region of North America* (New York, 1864), 23; Helena (Ark.) *Southern Shield*, April 21, 1849; Charles P. Clever, *New Mexico: Resources; Necessities for Railroad Connection with Atlantic and Pacific; Her Great Future* (Washington, 1868), 5.

18. St. Louis *Daily Missouri Republican*, Oct. 14, 1859; Davis, 205.

19. Mowry, 24-28; St. Louis *Daily Missouri Republican*, April 17, 1853, May 10, 1859; "Cincinnatus" (Marvin Wheat), *Travels on the Western Slope of the Mexican Cordillera* (San Francisco, 1857), 339-340.

20. St. Louis *Daily Missouri Republican*, Jan. 31, 1849, April 23, 1851, April 26, May 3, 1852; Austin *Texas State Gazette*, May 26, 1855 (in September, 1855, the name was changed to *State Gazette*); Mowry, 37, 38, 193; Ladd, 446; *Senate Executive Documents*, 31 Cong., 2 Sess., III, No. 26, pp. 4-5.

21. Ladd, 262; Austin *Texas State Gazette*, May 26, 1855.

22. J. Ross Browne, *Adventures in the Apache Country: a Tour through Arizona and Sonora with Notes on the Silver Regions of Nevada* (New York, 1869), 11, 16, 27; Austin *State Gazette*, April 2, 1859; St. Louis *Daily Missouri Republican*, May 10, Sept. 4, 1859.

23. United States, *Census, 1850* (Washington, 1853), 993. (Hereafter the Census reports will be cited as *Census, 1850, Census, 1860*, etc.)

24. Mowry, 33-35.

25. St. Louis *Daily Missouri Republican*, Sept. 13, 1851; Davis, 181-189, 220-226; Ralph Emerson Twitchell, *The Leading Facts of New Mexican History* (Cedar Rapids, Iowa, 1912), II, 157-160, 164-167.

26. Richard Francis Burton, *The City of the Saints* (London, 1861), 343; George Wharton James, *Utah: the Land of Blossoming Valleys* (Boston, 1922), pp. x, 1-2, 6.

27. James, pp. x, 6; Burton, 33, 336-337, 339-340, 345; William Chandless, *A Visit to Salt Lake* (London, 1857), 138, 149; T. B. H. Stenhouse, *The Rocky Mountain Saints* (Salt Lake City, 1904), 734.

28. Rockwell D. Hunt and Nellie Van De Grift Sánchez, *A Short History of California* (New York, 1929), 9-10, 12, 58-63; John S. Hittell, *The Resources of California* (San Francisco, 1869), 1.

29. Walter Murray, "Narrative of a California Volunteer, July, 1846-Feb., 1848," p. 71, MS., Bancroft Library, University of California. (Hereafter cited as Murray, "Narrative," MS., Bancroft Library.)

30. Theodore Henry Hittell, *History of California* (San Francisco, 1897), II, 472-478; Hittell, *The Resources of California*, 151; Alexander von Humboldt (Baron Friedrich Heinrich Alexander), *Political Essay on the Kingdom of New Spain* (London, 1811, tr. by John Black), II, 443-444.

31. Hittell, *History of California*, II, 548-555; Hunt and Sánchez, 11-12.

32. Of this number about 4,000 were California descendants of Europeans and less than 400 had come from the United States. Hittell, *History of California*, II, 469.

33. Fayette Robinson, *California and Its Gold Regions* . . . (New York, 1849), 15.

34. *Census, 1850*, p. 969; *Census, 1860, Population* (Washington, 1864), 28.

35. Hittell, *History of California*, II, 471, III, 44, 175; Richard Henry Dana, Jr., *Two Years before the Mast* (New York, 1909), 81; Murray, "Narrative," 90-91, 94-95, MS., Bancroft Library; Henry Holbrook to Mrs. James Clarke, April 10, 1855, MS., California File, 1848-1860, Huntington Library, San Marino, Calif.

36. For the tribal divisions of each of these groups, see Frederick Webb Hodge, *Hand Book of American Indians North of Mexico* (Washington, 1907-10), I, 362-363, 385-386, 684-685, II, 530-536, 947-949.

37. Hodge, II, 179-182, 947-949.

38. *Ibid.*, II, 947; Randolph B. Marcy, *Thirty Years of Army Life on the Border* (New York, 1866), 160.

39. Hodge, I, 327-329; William Kennedy, *Texas: The Rise, Progress and Prospects of the Republic of Texas* (London, 1841), I, 344-345; Austin *Texas State Gazette*, June 21, 1851; Pope to Floyd, May 7, 1859: "A Military Memoir of the Country between the Mississippi River and the Pacific Ocean with Some Account of Frontier Defenses, May 7, 1859," pp. 14-15, MS., Letters Received, Topographical Engineers Bureau, Engineers, Office of the Chief, National Archives, Washington. (Hereafter cited as Pope, "Military Memoir," L. R., T. E. B., E., O. C., N. A.)

40. *Senate Executive Documents*, 31 Cong., 1 Sess., No. 1, p. 963.

41. James Lee Humfreville, *Twenty Years among Our Hostile Indians* (New York, 1899), 175.

42. *Ibid.*, 236; Hodge, I, 699-700; *Senate Executive Documents*, 31 Cong., 1 Sess., No. 1, p. 963.

43. Rister, 33.

44. *House Executive Documents*, 31 Cong., 1 Sess., III, No. 5, Pt. 2, pp. 998-999; Edward S. Curtis, *The North American Indian* (Cambridge, 1907-1926), I, 13-14.

45. For the chief tribal divisions of Texas Apaches—the Lipan, Mescalero, Natage, and Jumano—see Thomas Maitland Marshall, *A History of the Western Boundary of the Louisiana Purchase, 1819-1841* (Berkeley, Calif., 1914), 128; Hodge, I, 62-63, 846; Curtis, I, 83; *Senate Executive Documents*, 31 Cong., 1 Sess., No. 1 p. 963.

46. Woodworth Clum, *Apache Agent: the Story of John P. Clum* (Boston, 1936), 12; Ralph H. Ogle, "Federal Control of the Western Apaches, 1848-1886," *New Mexico Historical Review*, XIV, (Oct., 1939), 319-320, 322-324. For a comprehensive account of the Texas Apaches, see Frank D. Reeve, "The Apache Indians in Texas," *Southwestern Historical Quarterly*, L (Oct., 1946), 189-219.

47. *Senate Executive Documents*, 31 Cong., 1 Sess., No. 1, p. 963.

48. *Ibid.*, 31 Cong., 2 Sess., III, No. 26, p. 3; Adolf F. Bandelier, *Final Report of Investigations among the Indians of the Southwestern United States Carried on Mainly in the Years from 1880 to 1885* (Cambridge, 1890-92), I, 118-142; Santa Fe *Weekly Gazette*, May 21, 1853; J. H. Watts, "Santa Fe Affairs," 3, MS., Bancroft Library.

49. Hubert Howe Bancroft, *History of Arizona and New Mexico* (San Francisco, 1889), 671-672; Santa Fe *Weekly Gazette*, May 21, 1853; *House Executive Documents*, 31 Cong., 1 Sess., III, No. 5, Pt. 2, p. 997.

50. Bandelier, I, 102-103; Browne, 140-141, 276-277; Curtis, II, 27, 31-32.

51. Bandelier, I, 102-103; 110-111; Curtis, II, 4-8, 81-82; Browne, 107, 110-111; Benjamin Hayes, "Diary of a Journey Overland, 1849-1850," pp. 119-120, 128, MS., Bancroft Library. (Hereafter cited as Hayes, Diary.)

52. Bandelier, I, 106; Curtis, II, 48-52, 63-67; Julius Froebel, *Seven Years' Travel in Central America, Northern Mexico, and the Far West of the United States* (London, 1859), 527-528.

53. Curtis, I, 73-76, 81-83; Bandelier, I, 175; Bancroft, 673-674; Emmanuel Henri Dieudonné Domenech, *Seven Years' Residence in the Great Deserts of North America* (London, 1860), I, 184.

54. Bandelier, I, 174; Hodge, II, 874; St. Louis *Daily Missouri Republican*, Feb. 1, 1850, Dec. 8, 1851.

55. For the various Apache bands such as the Mescalero, Jicarilla, Chiricahua, Mimbre, Mogollon, Coyotero, Tonto, and White Mountain, see McCall, 517, 518, 519; Curtis, I, 53-54; St. Louis *Daily Missouri Republican*, Feb. 1, 1850, Dec. 8, 1851, Oct. 6, 1859.

56. Bandelier, I, 177-180; James Fowler Rusling, *The Great West and the Pacific Coast* (New York, 1877), 401; Hayes, Diary, 112, MS., Bancroft Library.
Cong., 2 Sess., VI, No. 13, p. 8; Santa Fe *Weekly Gazette*, Jan. 21, 1854.

58. *Senate Executive Documents*, 36 Cong., 1 Sess., I, No. 2, p. 733.

59. Jacob Platt Dunn, Jr., *Massacres of the Mountains: a History of the Indian Wars of the Far West* (New York, 1886), 275-276; *House Executive Documents*, 31 Cong., 1 Sess., III, No. 5, Pt. 2, pp. 1002-04.

60. Dunn, 276-277; *House Executive Documents*, 31 Cong., 1 Sess., III, No. 5, Pt. 2, p. 1003; James H. Simpson, *Report of Explorations across the Great Basin of the Territory of Utah for a Direct Wagon Route from Camp Floyd to Genoa in Carson Valley, 1859* (Washington, 1876), 34-36, 41-43, 459-462.

61. J. D. Borthwick, *Three Years in California* (London, 1857), 128; Effie Mona Mack, *Nevada* (Glendale, Calif., 1936), 42-43.

62. Mack, 44-47.

63. *House Executive Documents*, 31 Cong., 1 Sess., III, No. 5, Pt. 2, p. 1003.

64. Hodge, I, 190-191; John Walton Caughey, *California* (New York, 1940), 2-3.

65. Clark Wissler, *Indians of the United States* (New York, 1940), 184-185.

66. For the chain of prosperous missions—with their workshops, school rooms, storehouses, chapels, dormitories, extensive grain fields, groves and vineyards, and numerous herds of stock—established by the Spanish padres, see Hodge, I, 894-895; Fr. Zephyrin Engelhardt, *The Missions and Missionaries of California* (San Francisco, 1908-12), II.

67. Houston *Democratic Telegraph and Texas Register*, Dec. 27, 1850; Bancroft, *The Native Races* (San Francisco, 1882-83), I, 326-327, 337-341, 362-363, 402, gives the names and location of the numerous California tribal divisions.

68. William H. Ellison, "The Federal Indian Policy in California, 1846-1860," *Mississippi Valley Historical Review*, IX (June, 1922), 39-40; John Collier, *The Indians of the Americas* (New York, 1947), 220-223; *Census, 1850*, p. 982; *ibid., 1860, Population*, 27.

69. Warren K. Moorehead, *The American Indian in the United States, 1850-1914* (Andover, Mass., 1914), 325, 329.

70. *American State Papers, Indian Affairs* (Washington, 1832-34), II, 541-544.

71. The Indian Intercourse Act of 1834 did not give the Indians a perpetual guarantee to all the lands in the Indian Country. Actually, in this Indian Country there were three different kinds of lands. See J. C. Malin, *Indian Policy and Westward Expansion, 1770-1854*, University of Kansas, "Humanistic Studies," II, No. 3 (Lawrence, Kans., 1921), 55-57; United States, *Statutes at Large* (Boston, 1846-1873, Washington, 1875-1948), IV, 729-738. (Hereafter cited as *Statutes at Large*.)

72. For the anomalous situation of the "Indian Country" and the factors leading to the modification of this phase of the government's Indian policy, see Malin, 12-14. See also above, p. 20.

73. *Statutes at Large*, IV, 203-204; Santa Fe *Weekly Gazette*, Jan. 21, 1854, March 10, 1855.

74. For the gold fever, see St. Louis *Daily Missouri Republican*, Dec. 27, 1848, Jan. 20, 26, Nov. 21, 1849, Oct. 3, 1850; Alexandre Dumas, *Un Gil-Blas en Californie* (Paris, 1861), 315-317; Ralph P. Bieber, "California Gold Mania," *Mississippi Valley Historical Review*, XXXV (June, 1948), 3-28.

75. St. Louis *Daily Missouri Republican*, Nov. 21, 1849, Oct. 3, 1850; Van Vliet to Jesup, July 1, 7, 1850 (Enclosures: Fort Laramie), MSS., L. R., Quartermaster General's Office, N. A. (Hereafter Quartermaster General's Office will be cited as Q. G. O.)

76. For a description of these trails, see Bieber (ed.), *Southern Trails to California in 1849* (Glendale, Calif., 1937), 28-62; Grant Foreman, "Early Trails through Oklahoma," *Chronicles of Oklahoma*, III (June, 1925), 110-112; Octavius Thorndike Howe, *Argonauts of '49* (Cambridge, Mass., 1923), 16, 37-45.

77. Ruth A. Gallaher, "The Indian Agent in the United States since 1850," *Iowa Journal of History and Politics*, XIV (April, 1916), 174.

II

1. Frederick Jackson Turner, *The Frontier in American History* (New York, 1920), 10.

2. Gallaher, "The Indian Agent in the United States before 1850," *Iowa Journal of History and Politics*, XIV, 4-5; *Senate Executive Documents*, 31 Cong., 1 Sess., I, No. 1, Pt. 1, p. 114; *ibid.*, 33 Cong., 2 Sess., I, No. 1, p. 390.

3. George Dewey Harmon, *Sixty Years of Indian Affairs: Political, Economic, and Diplomatic, 1789-1850* (Chapel Hill, N. C., 1941), 94-133; *Statutes at Large*, I, 452, III, 641; Gallaher, "The Indian Agent in the United States before 1850," *Iowa Journal of History and Politics*, XIV, 34.

4. *Ibid.*, XIV, 5, 26.

5. It was not until much later, however, that any administrative work was taken up. The first act of Congress directly providing for Indian agents was approved on March 1, 1793. *Statutes at Large*, I, 50, 137, 331.

6. The number of Indian officials was constantly increasing. In 1802 the personnel of the Indian Department consisted of 1 superintendent, 4 agents, 1 assistant agent, and 7 interpreters. In January, 1824, Secretary of War Calhoun reported 18 agents and 22 sub agents. By 1850 there were 281 men employed in some phase of Indian service. *American State Papers, Miscellaneous* (Washington, 1834), I, 305, 313; *ibid., Indian Affairs*, II, 449, 450; Harmon, 173.

7. *Statutes at Large*, IV, 35, 36; Gallaher, "The Indian Agent in the United States before 1850," *Iowa Journal of History and Politics*, XIV, 33; Everett Dick, *Vanguards of the Frontier* (New York, 1941), 101-102.

8. *Statutes at Large*, IV, 564.

9. *Ibid.*, IV, 735-738.

10. The law of 1832 provided that "no ardent spirits shall be hereafter introduced into the Indian country." The law of 1834 provided a penalty of $500 fine, and the law of 1847 increased the penalty to two years' imprisonment. *Ibid.*, IV, 564, 732, IX, 203-204.

11. Laurence P. Schmeckebier, *The Office of Indian Affairs: Its History, Activities, and Organization* (Baltimore, 1927), 2.

12. Helen McCowen Carpenter, "Diary, May 26—Oct. 22, 1856," MS., California State Library, Sacramento.

13. *House Executive Documents*, 33 Cong., 1 Sess., I, No. 1, Pt. 1, p. 258. Foreman, *Advancing the Frontier* (Norman, Okla., 1933), 15, 17, 188, 191-193; Schmeckebier, 430-431, 450.

14. *Senate Executive Documents*, 32 Cong., 1 Sess., III, No. 1, Pt. 3, pp. 452-453; *ibid.*, 36 Cong., 2 Sess., I, No. 1, pp. 50-51; Santa Fe *Weekly Gazette*, May 21, 1853; Johnson and Graham's Lessee v. McIntosh, 8 Wheaton (21 U. S.), 543.

15. *Senate Executive Documents*, 32 Cong., 1 Sess., I, No. 1, p. 448.

16. Lena Clara Koch, "The Federal Indian Policy in Texas, 1845-1860," *Southwestern Historical Quarterly,* XXVIII (April, 1925), 267-268; San Francisco *Daily Alta California,* Nov. 13, 1852.

17. Schmeckebier, 10; Frederic Logan Paxson, *The Last American Frontier* (New York, 1918), 14,·31-32; Malin, 35-75.

18. Medill to Neighbors, Feb. 22, 1849, MSS., Letters Sent, Indian Affairs Office, N. A. (Hereafter cited as L. S., I. A. O., N. A.)

19. *Statutes at Large,* IX, 395.

20. Gallaher, "The Indian Agent in the United States before 1850," *Iowa Journal of History and Politics,* XIV, 54; *ibid.,* "The Indian Agent in the United States since 1850," XIV, 236; Malin, 15-75.

21. *House Executive Documents,* 31 Cong., 1 Sess., III, No. 5, Pt. 2, pp. 952-955; *ibid.,* 31 Cong., 2 Sess., No 25, pp. 1-4; St. Louis *Daily Missouri Republican,* Dec. 13, 1854.

22. *Statutes at Large,* IX, 586-587.

23. *House Executive Documents,* 32 Cong., 1 Sess., II, No. 2, Pt. 3, p. 411.

24. Tahlequah (Okla.) *Cherokee Advocate,* April 6, 1853.

25. *Senate Executive Documents,* 34 Cong., 3 Sess., II, No. 5, p. 571; *ibid.,* 36 Cong., 2 Sess., I, No. 1, pp. 235-236.

26. Emory Upton, *The Military Policy of the United States* (Washington, 1917), 224.

27. *Congressional Globe,* 34 Cong., 3 Sess., p. 483.

28. *Ibid.,* p. 533.

29. *Statutes at Large,* X, 2-3, 675, 698.

30. *Ibid.,* X, 239; Gallaher, "The Indian Agent in the United States since 1850," *Iowa Journal of History and Politics,* XIV, 176.

31. *Senate Executive Documents,* 34 Cong., 3 Sess., II, No. 5, p. 571.

32. *House Executive Documents,* 35 Cong., 2 Sess., II, No. 2, Pt. 1, pp. 649-657 (Bailey's report to Commissioner of Indian Affairs); Browne to Commissioner of Indian Affairs, July 2, 1858, and Browne, Abstract, "Condition of Indians in California," Sept. 18, 1858, MSS., L. R., I. A. O., N. A.

33. Bancroft, *History of California* (San Francisco, 1884-90), VII, 492.

34. St. Louis *Daily Missouri Republican,* Dec. 9, 1858.

35. Austin *State Gazette,* Sept. 11, 25, 1858.

36. Wissler, 260.

37. Fort Smith (Ark.) *Times* in San Francisco *Daily Alta California,* Nov. 9, 1858.

38. Davis, 251; San Francisco *Daily Alta California,* Dec. 2, 1851, Nov. 13, 1852, Sept. 30, 1859.

39. Dick, 107-111, 116-117.

40. Flora Warren Seymour, *Indian Agents of the Old Frontier* (New York, 1941), 1.

41. Samuel Houston, *The Writings of Sam Houston, 1813-1863* (Amelia W. Williams and Eugene C. Barker, eds., Austin, 1938-43), V, 343, 345; Schmeckebier, 47.

42. Henry Benjamin Whipple, *Lights and Shadows of a Long Episcopate* (New York, 1899), 511-512.

43. Gallaher, "The Indian Agent in the United States since 1850," *Iowa Journal of History and Politics,* XIV, 178; San Francisco *Daily Alta California,* Nov. 13, 1852.

44. *House Executive Documents,* 35 Cong., 1 Sess., I, No. 88, pp. 211-213; Dick, 120; "Reminiscences of Mendocino," *Hutchings' California Magazine,* III (Oct., 1858), 156.

45. W. S. Nye, *Carbine and Lance* (Norman, Okla., 1937), 15; Santa Fe *Weekly Gazette,* March 14, 1857; *Senate Executive Documents,* 35 Cong., 2 Sess., II, No. 1, Pt. 2, p. 279.

46. See above, pp. 109-113.

47. Alexander to President Buchanan, July 22, 1858, MSS., L. R., I. A. O., N. A.

48. Dallas *Herald,* Aug. 21, 1858.

49. *Congressional Globe*, 33 Cong., 2 Sess., XXX, 439-440; *ibid.*, 35 Cong., 1 Sess., XXXVI, Pt. 1, pp. 493, 672, 875.

50. San Francisco *Evening Picayune,* Jan. 30, 1851. (In September, 1851, the name was changed to *Daily Evening Picayune.*)

51. Domenech, *Missionary Adventures in Texas and Mexico, 1846-1852* (London, 1858), 176.

52. Turner to Houston, July 10, 1860, MSS., Governors' Letters, Archives, Texas State Library, Austin. (Hereafter cited as Governors' Letters.)

53. See above, Chapters VIII, IX, XI.

54. Joseph Ellison, *California and the Nation, 1850-1869* (Berkeley, Calif., 1927), 83; Sumner to Calhoun, Nov. 10, 1851, MSS., L. S., Department of New Mexico, Book 5, Army Commands, United States, N.A. (Hereafter Army Commands, United States, will be cited as A. C., U. S.)

55. St. Louis *Daily Missouri Republican,* Jan. 11, March 31, Oct. 1, 1848.

56. *Ibid.*, Dec. 9, 29, 1851; Santa Fe *Weekly Gazette*, Feb. 12, 19, 26, March 5, April 9, 1853.

57. William Preston Johnston, *Life of General Albert Sidney Johnston* (New York, 1879), 236-237.

58. San Francisco *Daily Alta California*, Sept. 20, Oct. 26, 1856.

59. *House Executive Documents*, 33 Cong., 1 Sess., I, No. 1, Pt. 1, pp. 243-264; *Senate Executive Documents*, 32 Cong., 1 Sess., III, No. 1, Pt. 3, pp. 271-272, 447-450; St. Louis *Daily Missouri Republican*, Dec. 20, 1849.

60. Mack, 287; Harmon, 363-366; Alban W. Hoopes, *Indian Affairs and Their Administration with Special Reference to the Far West, 1849-1860* (Philadelphia, 1932), 16-17, 235-238; Ford to Burleson, Aug. 11, 1859, MSS., Burleson, "Letters," Archives, University of Texas.

61. Schmeckebier, 11.

62. Harmon, 367-370; Edward Everett Dale, "The End of the Indian Problem," *The Quest for Political Unity in World History* (Stanley Pargellis, ed., Washington, 1944: Annual Report, *American Historical Association, 1942*, III), 314-315; Dougherty to Cass, Dec. 6, 1832 [Enclosure: Dr. Davis to Cass, Nov. 18, 1832, Dr. Martin to Cass, Nov. 27, 1832, names of Indians vaccinated], MSS., L. R., I. A. O., N. A.

III

1. *Senate Documents*, 29 Cong., 1 Sess., No. 1, pp. 220c-220g.

2. Beginning with Fort Jesup in Louisiana, the chain included Forts Towson, Washita, and Gibson in Oklahoma, Fort Smith in Arkansas, Forts Scott and Leavenworth in Kansas, Forts Des Moines and Atkinson in Iowa, Fort Snelling in Minnesota, and Fort Wilkins on Lake Superior. It should be noted, of course, that prior to the Mexican War some of these outposts were not located in the present-day states but rather in unorganized Indian country or in territories. *Ibid.*, 220d; *Senate Executive Documents*, 31 Cong., 2 Sess., No. 1, Pt. 2, p. 121. Additional information about the principal military posts mentioned in this and subsequent chapters will be found below, p. 285.

3. James S. Calhoun, *Official Correspondence of . . .* (Annie H. Abel, ed., Washington, 1915), 8.

4. Fort Mann, although not a military post, rendered important service as a depot "to repair wagons and recruit animals" for military and wagon trains en route between Fort Leavenworth and Santa Fe. It was discontinued in 1848. Santa Fe traders and emigrants, however, continued to camp at or near the depot until the fall of 1849 and possibly until the establishment of new Fort Atkinson on the Arkansas in 1850. Lewis H. Garrard, *Wah-To-Yah and the Taos Trail* (Bieber, ed., Glendale, Calif., 1938), 35-36, 331-338; Foreman, *Marcy & the Gold Seekers* . . . (Norman, Okla., 1939), 75; Charles Irving Jones, "William Kronig, New Mexico Pioneer, from his Memories of 1849-1860," *New Mexico Historical Review*, XIX (July, 1944), 188; St. Louis *Daily Missouri Republican*, July 3, 11, 19, Aug. 3, 24, Sept. 23, 1848, June 30, July 8, Sept. 12, Nov. 1, 1849.

5. In July, 1847, "Old Fort Kearny" was established on the west bank of the Missouri River, some 50 miles south of Omaha and in May of the following year was abandoned. "Fort Childs," built opposite Grand Island on the south side of the Platte, was renamed Fort Kearny in 1848 in honor of Major General Stephen Watts Kearny. The fort was one of the most important military posts on the Oregon trail. Eugene Bandel, *Frontier Life in the*

Army, 1854-1861 (Bieber, ed., Glendale, 1932), 78; Albert Watkins, "History of Fort Kearny," Nebraska State Historical Society, *Collections* (Lincoln, 1911), XVI, 240-242, 260-261; Woodbury to Totten, Dec. 7, 1848, Feb. 2, 1849, MSS., L. R., E., O. C., N. A.

6. For the history of Fort Laramie see Bandel, 88-91; LeRoy R. Hafen and Francis Marion Young, *Fort Laramie and the Pageant of the West, 1834-1890* (Glendale, 1938); "Medical History of Fort Laramie, 1849-1890," MSS., Adjutant General's Office, N. A. (Hereafter Adjutant General's Office will be cited as A. G. O.)

7. Fort Polk was abandoned in February, 1850. James Mooney, "Calendar History of the Kiowa Indians," Bureau of American Ethnology, *Seventeenth Annual Report* (Washington, 1898), Pt. 1, pp. 387-388.

8. *Senate Documents,* 29 Cong., 2 Sess., No. 1, pp. 46-47; Rister, 63-64; L. W. Newton, "Fort Brown," *Dictionary of American History* (New York, 1940), I, 244.

9. Ringgold Barracks, strategically located upon a commanding bluff on the east bank of the Rio Grande, was named in honor of Major Samuel Ringgold, who was killed at the battle of Palo Alto. The post was abandoned about 1857 and reoccupied in December, 1859. At the opening of the Civil War it was again abandoned and in 1865 was reoccupied. J. L. Rock and W. I. Smith, *Southern and Western Texas Guide, 1878* (St. Louis, 1878), 34; John S. Billings, *Report on Barracks and Hospitals with Descriptions of Military Posts* (Washington, 1870), 213.

10. George R. Gibson, *Journal of a Soldier under Kearny and Doniphan, 1846-1847* (Bieber, ed., Glendale, 1935), 220; New Orleans *Daily Picayune*, Nov. 6, 12, 1846; Billings, 257.

11. *House Executive Documents*, 31 Cong., 1 Sess., No. 17, p. 337; Kimball Hale Dimmick, "Diary," May 1, 7, 1848, MSS., California File, 1848-1860, Huntington Library.

12. *House Executive Documents,* 30 Cong., 2 Sess., No. 1, p. 161.

13. See above, pp. 44-49.

14. At the close of the Mexican War the United States was divided, for purposes of military administration, into three divisions—Eastern, Western, and Pacific—and eleven departments. Texas, the Territory of New Mexico, and California were designated as the Eighth, Ninth, and Tenth Military Departments, respectively. The Territory of Utah formed part of the Department of the West until June, 1857, when it became the independent Department of Utah. Raphael P. Thian, *Notes Illustrating the Military Geography of the United States, 1813-1880* (Washington, 1881), 8, 20, 25, 31, 40-51, 85-86, 100-105.

15. *House Documents*, 29 Cong., 2 Sess., No. 75, pp. 7-8; *Senate Executive Documents*, 31 Cong., 1 Sess., No. 1, Pt. 2, p. 963; Ford to Runnels, June 2, 1858, MSS., Governors' Letters.

16. Fort Mason, established in July, 1851, in the present Mason County, was occupied irregularly by troops until March, 1861, when it was abandoned. It was reoccupied after the Civil War and finally abandoned in 1869. Mooney, "Calendar History of the Kiowa Indians," Bureau of American Ethnology, *Seventeenth Annual Report*, Pt. 1, p. 387; *The War of the Rebellion: A Compilation of the Official Records of the Union and Confederate Armies* (Washington, 1880-92), Ser. 1, I, 502 (hereafter cited as *Official Records*); William G. Freeman, "Report of Inspection of Eighth Military Department, April 22, 1853, . . . ," pp. 63-64, MS., A. G. O., N. A. (Hereafter cited as Freeman, "Report," A. G. O., N. A.)

17. Fort Croghan in Burnet County and Gates in Coryell County were built in 1849. *Senate Executive Documents,* 34 Cong., 1 Sess., No. 96, p. 370; Freeman, "Report," 102, MS., A. G. O., N. A.

18. *Senate Executive Documents*, 32 Cong., 1 Sess., No. 1, Pt. 1, pp. 270-274; Whiting to Deas, Jan. 21, 1850, MSS., L. R., E., O. C., N. A.

19. *Senate Executive Documents*, 34 Cong., 1 Sess., No. 96, p. 373; John W. Forney, *What I Saw in Texas* (Philadelphia, 1872), 14; Rister, "Fort Worth," *Dictionary of American History*, II, 310.

20. St. Louis *Daily Missouri Republican*, March 19, 1851, Oct. 7, 1853; Washington (Ark.) *Telegraph*, Feb. 5, 1851; Neighbors to Manypenny, March 1, April 12, 1854, MSS., L. R., I. A. O., Texas, N. A.

21. Jefferson Barracks, named in honor of President Jefferson, was established in 1826 on the west bank of the Mississippi River, at that time about ten miles below St. Louis. Between July and October of the same year the post was known as "Cantonment Adams" and "Camp Miller." The original purpose of the Barracks—a "school for the instruction of infantry"—was short-lived, but its importance as a military station continued throughout the years. Soldiers and munitions generally were distributed to the frontier garrisons from the

Barracks; many important exploring and military expeditions started from this post; some of our most famous military leaders—Grant, Lee, Sherman, and Pershing—served here. Upon the outbreak of the Civil War it was transformed into a general military hospital; after the close of the war and until 1867, it was used as a garrison for troops. Then it became an engineers' and ordnance depot, a cavalry post, and recruiting depot. The Barracks figured prominently in World War I, and in World War II it served as a replacement center for the Army Air Corps, quartering as many as 40,000 men during the peak periods. Before the close of the War it became a separation center and by July 1, 1946, the historic Jefferson Barracks was officially closed. In January, 1951, the post was reactivated for aircraft warning drill by Missouri Air National Guard. *House Documents*, 19 Cong., 2 Sess., No. 2, pp. 173, 180e; Bandel, 73-74; "Jefferson Barracks through Five Wars," *Missouri Historical Review*, XXXVI (April, 1942), 339-341; "Barracks Fades out as Military Post," St. Louis *Post-Dispatch*, July 1, 1946; "Aircraft Warning Drill" and ". . . Air Guard Warning Squadron," *ibid.*, Jan. 22, March 1, 1951.

22. *Senate Executive Documents*, 32 Cong., 1 Sess., No. 1, Pt. 1, p. 106; St. Louis *Daily Missouri Republican*, March 14, April 29, June 13, 1851; General Orders No. 19, A. G. O., April 1, 1851, MSS., A. G. O., N. A. (Hereafter General Orders will be cited as G. O.)

23. H. H. McConnell, *Five Years a Cavalryman* (Jacksboro, Tex., 1889), 67; *Senate Executive Documents*, 34 Cong., 1 Sess., No. 96, pp. 371-372, 375; "Fort Belknap, Post Returns," June, 1851, April, 1860, MSS., A. G. O., N. A.

24. *Senate Executive Documents*, 34 Cong., 1 Sess., No. 96, pp. 371-372, 375; Thomas H. S. Hamersly, *Complete Regular Army Register of the United States for 100 years, 1779-1879, with a Military History of the Department of War* (Washington, 1880), Pt. 2, p. 125.

25. Fort Chadbourne was located on Oak Creek and Fort McKavett on the San Sabá River in present Menard County. *Ibid.*, Pt. 2, p. 127; M. L. Crimmins, "Fort McKavett, Texas," *Southwestern Historical Quarterly*, XXXVIII (July, 1934), 28, 29, 35; Freeman, "Report," 69, MS., A. G. O., N. A.

26. *Senate Executive Documents*, 36 Cong., 1 Sess., No. 52, pp. 185-186; Mooney, "Calendar History of the Kiowa Indians," *Bureau of American Ethnology, Seventeenth Annual Report*, Pt. 1, p. 387; Freeman, "Report," 55, MS., A. G. O., N. A.

27. At Camps Cooper and Colorado, established in 1856, the troops experienced considerable difficulty in obtaining healthful drinking water; at the latter post, liquor was peddled freely among the soldiers. *Senate Executive Documents*, 36 Cong., 1 Sess., No. 52, pp. 185-188; "Camp Colorado, Post Returns," 1856, 1861, MSS., A. G. O., N. A.

28. Paul I. Wellman, "Fort Cobb," *Dictionary of American History*, I, 406; Foreman, *Advancing the Frontier*, 250-254, 297; Foreman, *A History of Oklahoma* (Norman, Okla., 1942), 36, 96, 101; G. O. No. 34, A. G. O., June 25, 1851, MSS., A. G. O., N. A.

29. Austin *Texas State Gazette*, Feb. 7, 1857; Houston *Democratic Telegraph and Texas Register*, Aug. 7, 1850; St. Louis *Daily Missouri Republican*, Sept. 6, 1850.

30. *Ibid.*, April 1, 1851; Houston *Democratic Telegraph and Texas Register*, March 21, May 23, 1850; Neighbors to Manypenny, May 8, 1854, MSS., L. R., I. A. O., Texas, N. A.

31. Houston *Mercantile Advertiser*, Aug. 4, 1849; *House Journal*, 32 Cong., 1 Sess., p. 400; Rusk to Conrad, Feb. 28, 1852, MSS., L. S., Secretary of War, N. A.; (hereafter Secretary of War will be cited as S. W.); Johnston to Bee, Feb. 14, 1857, MSS., L. S., Department of Texas, A. C., U. S., N. A.

32. See above, p. 33.

33. Early in March, 1849, Lieutenant Egbert L. Vielé with a company of First Infantry established Camp Crawford about three-quarters of a mile above Laredo. In January of the following year the name of the camp was changed to Fort McIntosh. *House Executive Documents*, 32 Cong., 1 Sess., No. 2, Pt. 1, p. 280; Billings, 215; Mansfield to Thomas, Dec. 13, 1860, MSS., L. R., A. G. O., N. A.

34. Fort Duncan, situated at Eagle Pass, was considered one of the most commanding positions on the frontier. Although occupied by troops in 1849, buildings were not erected until the following year. For several years, the troops at this frontier outpost were very badly housed. *Senate Executive Documents*, 31 Cong., 1 Sess., No. 1, Pt. 1, p. 152; *ibid.*, 36 Cong., 1 Sess., No. 52, pp 179-181; Rock and Smith, 31.

35. Albert G. Brackett, *History of the United States Cavalry* (New York, 1865), 125-126.

36. Fort Merrill, some sixty miles northwest of Corpus Christi, was established in 1849, and Fort Ewell, about fifty miles beyond, was built three years later. Fort Inge, near the present town of Uvalde, was of major importance, since it was on the great inland

commercial route at the point where the principal road to El Paso branched off for Eagle Pass. *Senate Executive Documents,* 34 Cong., 1 Sess., No. 96, p. 352; Olmsted, 285-286; Freeman, "Report," 14, 22, MS., A. G. O., N. A.

37. *Ibid.,* Appendix, pp. v, 6, MS., A. G. O., N. A.

38. Fort Martin Scott, established in 1848, was located about two miles south of Fredericksburg; Fort Lancaster, situated on Live Oak Creek in the present Crockett County, was built in 1855 but not occupied by troops until the following year; Camp Wood, on the Nueces River, about fifty miles northwest of Fort Inge, was built in 1857. *Senate Executive Documents,* 36 Cong., 1 Sess., No. 52, pp. 192-193; "Outline Index of Military Forts and Stations," MSS., A. G. O., N. A.; "Fort Martin Scott, Post Returns," Dec., 1848, Dec., 1866. MSS., A. G. O., N. A.

39. The six other positions occupied by troops in this line included San Antonio; Fort Lincoln, about fifty miles west of San Antonio; Camp Verde, near Bandera Pass in Kendall County; Camp Hudson in Crockett County; Austin; and Fort Terrett on the Llano River. In this line, Fort Lincoln was established in 1849, Fort Terrett in 1852, Camp Verde in 1856, and Camp Hudson in 1857. *Senate Executive Documents,* 32 Cong., 1 Sess., No. 1, Pt. 1, pp. 277-280; *ibid.,* 34 Cong., 1 Sess., No. 96, p. 393; *ibid.,* 36 Cong., 1 Sess., No. 52, pp. 188, 191-192; Whiting to Deas, March 14, 1850, MSS., L. R., E., O. C., N. A.; "San Antonio and Austin, Post Returns," 1845-1875, MSS., A. G. O., N. A.

40. Austin *Texas State Gazette,* Aug. 27, 1857, Aug. 28, Sept. 4, 1858.

41. Billings, 223, 227-228, 231; *Official Records,* Ser. 1, I, 502, 594-596; Mansfield to Thomas, Oct. 31, Nov. 7, 17, 1860, MSS., L. R., A. G. O., N. A.

42. The "Post of El Paso," in the extreme northwest corner of the "Big Bend" sector, was established in February, 1848, but the official designation as Fort Bliss was not made until March, 1854. Like the other Texas posts it was evacuated during the Civil War but reoccupied in 1867. "Fort Bliss, Post Returns," Feb., 1848, March, 1854, March, 1867, Dec., 1870, MSS., A. G. O., N. A.; "Back to 1848," St. Louis *Post-Dispatch,* Nov. 21, 1948.

43. In addition to the regularly established posts, troops also occupied many temporary camps, such as Davis's Landing, McCulloch's Station, Ross's Station, Conner's Station, Camp Edinburg, Redmond's Ranch, Camp Rosario, Camp Barranca, Camp Johnston, and Camp Radziminski (Oklahoma). To avoid crowding and confusion, many of the temporary camps have not been shown on the map. *House Executive Documents,* 30 Cong., 2 Sess., I, No. 1, pp. 163-165; *ibid.,* 35 Cong., 2 Sess., No. 27, pp. 48-49; *Senate Executive Documents,* 32 Cong., 2 Sess., No. 1, Pt. 2, pp. 58-61; *ibid.,* 36 Cong., 1 Sess., No. 2, Pt. 2, p. 604.

44. See above, Chapter VIII, note 104.

45. The principal Texas posts abandoned during this period—some only temporarily—were Forts Belknap, Brown, Ewell, Graham, Lincoln, Martin Scott, Mason, McKavett, Worth, and Ringgold Barracks. *House Executive Documents,* 32 Cong., 2 Sess., No. 1, Pt. 2, p. 58; *Senate Executive Documents,* 33 Cong., 2 Sess., No. 1, Pt. 2, p. 58; Twiggs to Thomas, Feb. 7, 1859, MSS., L. R., Headquarters of the Army, N. A. (Hereafter Headquarters of the Army will be cited as H. A.)

46. *Senate Executive Documents,* 36 Cong., 2 Sess., No. 1, Pt. 2, pp. 218-220. For additional details relating to the Texas posts in the fifties, see Crimmins, "Colonel J. K. F. Mansfield's Report of the Inspection of the Department of Texas in 1856," *Southwestern Historical Quarterly,* XLII (Oct., 1938), 122-148, (Jan., 1939), 215-257, (April, 1939), 351-387.

47. Rister, *The Southwestern Frontier, 1865-1881,* p. 43.

48. St. Louis *Daily Missouri Republican,* Sept. 23, Nov. 14, 1848, Feb. 16, July 8, Aug. 6, 12, Dec. 9, 20, 1849, June 21, 23, 1850, March 22, May 18, 1851; Houston *Democratic Telegraph and Texas Register,* June 27, 1850.

49. The claim of the state of Chihuahua alone was more than $20,000,000. St. Louis *Daily Missouri Republican,* Nov. 4, 1851.

50. *House Executive Documents,* 31 Cong., 1 Sess., No. 5, Pt. 1, p. 112; *Senate Executive Documents,* 31 Cong., 1 Sess., No. 64, pp. 138-139; McCall, 526, 530-536.

51. *Senate Executive Documents,* 32 Cong., 1 Sess., I, No. 1, Pt. 1, pp. 203, 238; *House Executive Documents,* 32 Cong., 2 Sess., No. 1, Pt. 1, p. 80.

52. *Senate Executive Documents,* 36 Cong., 1 Sess., No. 52, pp. 221-222; William A. Bell, *New Tracks in North America: a Journal of Travel and Adventure* (London, 1869), I, 122; "Ancient Santa Fé," MS., Bancroft Library.

53. Fort Webster was established in 1852. In December of the following year it was abandoned and the troops were removed to the newly built Fort Thorn. *House Executive*

Documents, 32 Cong., 2 Sess., No. 1, Pt. 1, p. 80, Pt. 2, p. 60; Davis, 402-405; Calhoun, 418; Garland to Cooper, Jan. 27, 1854, MSS., L. R., A. G. O., N. A.

54. In 1858 Fort Massachusetts was moved six miles to the south and renamed Fort Garland. Crimmins, "Fort Massachusetts, First United States Military Post in Colorado," *Colorado Magazine*, XIV (July, 1937), 128-132.

55. Ogle, "Federal Control of the Western Apaches, 1848-1886," *New Mexico Historical Review*, XIV, 342; New Orleans *Daily Picayune*, Feb. 17, 1853; Santa Fe *Weekly Gazette*, Feb. 26, 1853.

56. San Francisco *Evening Bulletin*, May 12, 1858.

57. Forts Webster and Conrad were abandoned. *House Executive Documents*, 33 Cong., 2 Sess., No. 1, Pt. 2, p. 60; *Senate Executive Documents*, 34 Cong., 1 Sess., No. 96, p. 414; "Medical History of Fort Craig, 1854-1884," MSS., A. G. O., N. A.

58. *House Executive Documents*, 34 Cong., 1 Sess., No. 1, Pt. 2, p. 70; Mowry, 22.

59. *House Executive Documents*, 34 Cong., 3 Sess., No. 1, p. 3; *Senate Executive Documents*, 36 Cong., 1 Sess., No. 52, pp. 207, 210-211, 219-220; W. Clement Eaton, "Frontier Life in Southern Arizona, 1858-1861," *Southwestern Historical Quarterly*, XXXVI (Oct., 1932), 191.

60. St. Louis *Daily Missouri Republican*, Feb. 6, 1857; Santa Fe *Weekly Gazette*, March 14, 1857.

61. See above, pp. 161-162, 165-166.

62. Fort Garland was really not a new military post. See note 54. *Senate Executive Documents*, 35 Cong., 2 Sess., No. 1, Pt. 1, p. 559, Pt. 2, pp. 291-293, 297-298, Pt. 3, p. 778; John H. Nankivell, "Fort Garland, Colorado," *Colorado Magazine*, XVI (Jan. 1939), 14-23.

63. In May, 1859, Bonneville established a permanent camp on the San Pedro, but Fort Breckinridge was not officially established until May of the following year. It was abandoned in July, 1861. *Senate Executive Documents*, 36 Cong., 1 Sess., II, No. 2, Pt. 2, pp. 295, 301-307, 606-607; *ibid.*, 36 Cong., 2 Sess., II, No. 1, Pt. 2, pp. 222-223; *Official Records*, Ser. 1, IV, 1; "Fort Breckinridge, Post Return," May, 1860, MSS., A. G. O., N. A.

64. *Laws of the Territory of New Mexico, 1860* (Santa Fe, 1860), 130, 132, 134.

65. Fauntleroy to Cooper, Dec. 6, 1859, MSS., L. R., A. G. O., N. A.

66. G. O. No. 6, H. A., March 12, 1860, MSS., A. G. O., N. A.; Bancroft, *History of Arizona and New Mexico*, 497.

67. See above, pp. 179-184.

68. For the colorful history of Fort Bridger see J. Cecil Alter, *James Bridger* (Salt Lake City, 1925), 176-178, 244-247, 252-261, 315-328; *Senate Executive Documents*, 35 Cong., 2 Sess., II, No. 1, Pt. 2, p. 780; *ibid.*, 36 Cong., 1 Sess., No. 52, pp. 306-307.

69. In February, 1861, the name of Camp Floyd was changed to Camp Crittenden and in July of the same year the post was abandoned. G. O. No. 36, 37, 49, Department of Utah, July 7, 13, Aug. 24, 1858, and G. O. No. 21, Dept. of Utah, Sept. 9, 1859, MSS., A. G. O., N. A.; *Senate Executive Documents*, 36 Cong., 1 Sess., No. 52, pp. 288-300; *ibid.*, 36 Cong., 2 Sess., II, No. 1, p. 224.

70. Although Fort Churchill was situated in the Department of Utah, it was under the Military Department of California. *Ibid.*, 37 Cong., 2 Sess., II, No. 1, p. 35; *House Executive Documents*, 41 Cong., 2 Sess., II, No. 1, Pt. 2, p. 114; Mack, 311-313.

71. For the history of Benicia Barracks and the distinction between Benicia Barracks, Benicia Arsenal, and Benicia Ordnance Depot—all situated on the same property—see Bandel, 63-64, 309-310; *Senate Executive Documents*, 32 Cong., 1 Sess., No. 1, Pt. 1, pp. 309-310, 324; "Outline Index of Military Forts and Stations," MSS., A. G. O., N .A.

72. *House Executive Documents*, 31 Cong., 1 Sess., No. 17, pp. 905, 941-943; *Senate Executive Documents*, 31 Cong., 1 Sess., No. 47, Pt. 2, pp. 3-8.

73. See above, pp. 104-105.

74. Hooker to Riley, Feb. 26, 1850, MSS., L. R., H. A., N. A.

75. The widely known "Warner's Ranch," famous stopping place for emigrants who traveled the southern trails to California was established by Jonathan Trumbull Warner ("J. J. Warner" or "Juan José Warner"). A native of Connecticut, Warner arrived in California in 1831 and soon became a Mexican citizen and a successful merchant. In 1844 or 1845 he secured a grant of land from the Mexican government and built an adobe house on it. His establishment soon became the celebrated "Warner's Ranch." Jopseh J. Hill, *The History of Warner's Ranch and Its Environs* (Los Angeles, 1927), 94-111; H. D. Barrows,

"Memorial Sketch of Col. J. J. Warner," Historical Society, Southern California, *Publications* (Los Angeles, 1895), III, 23-29.

76. *Senate Executive Documents*, 31 Cong., 2 Sess., No. 1, Pt. 2, p. 116E; *ibid*., 32 Cong., 1 Sess., No. 110, pp. 2-16.

77. *House Executive Documents,* 34 Cong., 3 Sess., No. 76, p. 34; Bandel, 260; "Medical History of Fort Yuma, 1850-1873," MSS., A. G. O., N. A.

78. *Senate Executive Documents*, 33 Cong., Spec. Sess., No. 4, pp. 39, 81-256; Ellison, "The Federal Indian Policy in California, 1846-1860," *Mississippi Valley Historical Review*, IX, 57; Stuart to Barbour, McKee, and Wozencraft, Oct. 9, 1850, MSS., L. S., Secretary of the Interior, N. A. (Hereafter Secretary of the Interior will be cited as S. I.)

79. St. Louis *Daily Missouri Republican*, March 17, 19, 1851; San Francosco *Daily Alta California*, Jan. 14, Aug. 26, Dec. 12, 1851; Conrad to Gwin, Dec. 27, 1851, MSS., L. S., S. W., N. A.

80. Fort Miller, originally Camp Barbour, was established in 1851 in the mining district on the San Joaquin River, Fort Reading, situated on Cow Creek, and Fort Jones in Siskiyou County, were built in the spring and fall of 1852, respectively. In the following year Fort Lane was established near Jacksonville, Oregon. Fort Umpqua, the northernmost post in the department, about five miles below Gardiner City, Oregon, was built in 1856. *House Executive Documents*, 32 Cong., 2 Sess., No. 1, Pt. 2, pp. 62, 70, 86; *Senate Executive Documents*, 36 Cong., 1 Sess., No. 52, pp. 240-241; Helen S. Giffen, "Fort Miller and Millerton," *Historical Society, Southern California Quarterly*, XXI (March, 1939), 5-15; Mansfield to Thomas, April 23, May 16, 1859, MSS., L. R., A. G. O., N. A.

81. Rancho del Chino, situated about 120 miles north of San Diego, was occupied in 1851. In September, 1852, the troops were transferred to Rancho de Jurupa, some twenty miles eastward. *Senate Executive Documents*, 34 Cong., 1 Sess., No. 96, p. 439; William F. Edgar, "Historical Notes of Old Land Marks in California," Historical Society, Southern California, *Publications* (Los Angeles, 1893), III, 29.

82. *House Executive Documents*, 35 Cong., 1 Sess., No. 88, p. 103; *ibid*., 35 Cong., 2 Sess., No. 2, p. 784; Mildred Brooke Hoover, *Historic Spots in California: Counties of the Coast Range* (Stanford University, Calif., 1937), 132; H. E. and E. G. Rensch and Hoover, *Historic Spots in California: Valley and Sierra Counties* (Stanford University, Calif., 1933), 133-134.

83. San Francisco *Daily Alta California*, Oct. 9, 1854.

84. *House Executive Documents*, 35 Cong., 1 Sess., No. 2, Pt. 2, p. 78; Hoover, 210-211; "Outline Index of Military Forts and Stations," MSS., A. G. O., N. A.

85. George Crook, *General George Crook: His Autobiography* (Martin F. Schmitt, ed., Norman, Okla., 1946), 54-56.

86. Soon afterward troops also occupied Camp Prentiss near San Bernardino and Camp Cass, near Red Bluffs, northwest of Tehama. San Francisco *Daily Alta California*, Nov. 8, 1858; *Senate Executive Documents*, 36 Cong., 1 Sess., No. 2, Pt. 2, pp. 612-613; Billings, 448-451.

87. In April, 1859, when Hoffman arrived at Beale's Crossing and established a cantonment he called it "Camp Colorado." In the following month Major Lewis A. Armistead renamed the camp "Fort Mojave." The post was near the present Mohave City, Arizona. Although geographically in New Mexico Territory, Fort Mojave was in the Department of California. See above, pp. 164-165. *Senate Executive Documents*, 36 Congress., 1 Sess., No. 2, Pt. 2, pp. 387-395, 405, 417; *ibid., No. 52*, pp. 235-236; Bandel, 57, 60, 251, 258, 277.

88. Mansfield to McDowell, March 5, April 4, 16, 1859, Mansfield to Thomas, May 6, 1859, MSS., L. R., A. G. O., N. A.

89. Thian, 53-54, 85-86; Bancroft, *History of California*, VII, 467.

90. *Senate Executive Documents*, 32 Cong., 1 Sess., No. 1, Pt. 1, pp. 106, 225.

91. St. Louis *Daily Missouri Republican*, Feb. 23, 1856.

92. *Ibid*., April 22, 1850; *Senate Miscellaneous Documents*, 35 Cong., 1 Sess., II, No. 134, pp. 1-3, 10-15; Scott to Floyd, June 1, 1857, MSS., L. S., H. A., N. A.

93. *Senate Executive Documents*, 33 Cong., 1 Sess., No. 1, Pt. 2, p. 6; *ibid*., 34 Cong., 3 Sess., No. 5, Pt. 2, p. 6; Jesup to Conrad, Nov. 22, 1851, MSS., L. S., Q. G. O., N. A.

94. Whiting to Totten, June 19, 1849, Whiting to Deas, Jan. 21, March 14, 1850, MSS., L. R., E., O. C., N. A.; Worth to Wood, Feb. 15, 1849, MSS., Governors' Letters; Johnston to Thomas, Nov. 17, 1856, MSS., L. S., Department of Texas, A. C., U. S., N. A.

95. Tarver to Pease, June 22, 1857, MSS., Governors' Letters.

96. Pope, "Military Memoir," 37, MS., L. R., T. E. B., E., O. C., N. A.

97. *Ibid.*

98. *Ibid.,* 37-38; Houston *Democratic Telegraph and Texas Register,* Oct. 30, Nov. 6, 1850; Austin *State Gazette,* Sept. 11, 13, 1858; St. Louis *Daily Missouri Republican,* June 28, 1851, May 5, 1857, Sept. 3, 1859.

99. Victor Considerant, *Au Texas* (Paris, 1854), 74.

100. Conrad to Bell, Sept. 30, 1852, MSS., Governors' Letters.

101. Committee of Citizens to Governor Pease, March 13, 1854, MSS., Governors' Letters; Austin *Texas State Gazette,* Sept. 7, 1850, March 26, May 21, 1859.

102. Charles William Ramsdell, "The Frontier and Secession," *Studies in Southern History and Politics* (New York, 1914), 68-79; Ford to Runnels, June 2, 1858, MSS., Governors' Letters.

103. Pope, "Military Memoir," 42-43, MS., L. R., T. E. B., E., O. C., N. A.

104. Weightman to Alvarez, May 6, 1852, MSS., Ralph Emerson Twitchell, Collection, New Mexico Historical Society, Santa Fe. (Hereafter cited as Twitchell, Collection.)

105. McLaws to Alexander, June 6, 1850, MSS., L. S., Department of New Mexico, Book 6, A. C., U. S., N. A.; Graves to Manypenny, Nov. 29, 1853, MSS., L. R., I. A. O., New Mexico, N. A.; St. Louis *Daily Missouri Republican,* Dec. 8, 1851; Santa Fe *Weekly Gazette,* Nov. 26, 1853.

106. Traders in Indian children defended the pernicious practice by declaring that the native children were not sold as slaves but adopted by white families and freed upon reaching maturity— the girls at the age of sixteen and the boys at the age of twenty. Dunn, 372; Santa Fe *Weekly Gazette,* Nov. 20, 1852; Lafayette Head, "Statement in regard to Buying and Selling Paiute Indian Children, April 30, 1852," MSS., William G. Ritch, Collection, Huntington Library. (Hereafter cited as Ritch, Collection.)

107. Pope, "Military Memoir," 43-44, MS., L. R., T. E. B., E., O. C., N. A.; Russell to Greiner, July 29, 1852, Greiner, 1852, "Overawing the Indians," MSS., Ritch, Collection.

108. Pope, "Military Memoir," 44-45, MS., L. R., T. E. B., E., O. C., N. A.

109. *Ibid.,* 37-38; Rollins to Brooke, Oct. 4, 1850, MSS., Governors' Letters.

110. James L. Tyson, *Diary of a Physician in California* (New York, 1850), 62-63; San Francisco *Daily Evening Picayune,* Dec. 3, 1851.

111. Wilson to Brown, May 31, 1850, Johnston to Brown, July 6, 1850, MSS., L. R., I. A. O., California, N. A.; San Francisco *Daily Alta California,* Jan. 6, 1851, Sept. 5, 1853.

112. San Francisco *Daily Evening Picayune,* Dec. 5, 9, 11, 1851; San Francisco *Daily Alta California,* April 7, 1855, May 12, 1856; Wool to Henley, March 5, 1855, Henley to Manypenny, April 9, 1855, MSS., L. R., I. A. O., California, N. A.; Vallejo to Governor, Aug. 4, 1849, "Unbound Documents, Archives of California, 1846-1850," pp. 93-94, MS., Bancroft Library.

113. Pope, "Military Memoir," 29-32, 49, 57-58, MS., L. R., T. E. B., E., O. C., N. A.

114. San Francisco *Herald,* Aug. 21, Sept. 14, 1859.

115. Froebel, 323; Bell, I, 28; Abert to Marcy, Nov. 17, 1848, "United States Miscellaneous, California and New Mexico, 1846-1850," MSS., Library of Congress. (Hereafter Library of Congress will be cited as L. C.)

116. *Senate Executive Documents,* 36 Cong., 2 Sess., No. 1, Pt. 2, p. 32.

IV

1. George W. Fuller, *A History of the Pacific Northwest* (New York, 1931), 180-182; Bancroft, *History of Oregon* (San Francisco, 1886), I, 14-15, 59-70, 89-99; Robert G. Cleland, *A History of California: The American Period* (New York, 1922), 46-60, 67-74, 96, 461.

2. See above, Chapter 1, footnote 76.

3. Although this volume deals primarily with the period from 1848 to 1860, nevertheless the explorations of Colonel Kearny, Lieutenant Colonel Cooke, and Lieutenant Abert, which were made during the Mexican War, are included. The activities of these army officers formed such an integral part of the exploration policy of the government that they could hardly be omitted.

4. St. Louis *Daily Missouri Republican,* Nov. 2, 1848; Tahlequah (Okla.) *Cherokee Advocate,* Dec. 11, 1848; Marcy to Jones, Nov. 6, 1848, MSS., L. S., S. W., N. A.; "Journals of Stephen W. Kearny," July 2-Aug. 19, 1820, Sept. 17, 1824-May 10, 1826, March 10, 1831-Jan. 15, 1842, Kearny, "Diary and Letter Book, 1846-1847," MSS., Missouri Historical Society, St. Louis. (Hereafter the Missouri Historical Society will be cited as M. H. S.)

5. G. O. No. 15, H. A., May 29, 1846, MSS., A. G. O., N. A.

6. Gibson, 39-41, 45, 125-126.

7. Fort Leavenworth, originally known as Cantonment Leavenworth, was established in the spring of 1827 by Colonel Henry Leavenworth. Situated on the west bank of the Missouri River some 500 miles above its confluence with the Mississippi, it was intended primarily as a protection to traders along the Santa Fe trail. The post became important as a starting point for many military expeditions to the Far West, as a meeting place for Indian councils, and as a supply depot for other forts and camps on the frontier. It rose to national prominence during the Mexican War, and throughout the eighteen fifties it continued to be a point of departure for many military expeditions. During the Civil War it served at various times as headquarters of the Department of the West, the Department of Kansas, and the Department of Missouri. In the sixties and seventies Fort Leavenworth was for a time the seat of an arsenal and of the United States Disciplinary Barracks; today it includes, in addition to a military post, the United States Penitentiary and the Command and General Staff School. *Senate Executive Documents*, 34 Cong., 1 Sess., No. 96, p. 158; Bieber, "Fort Leavenworth," *Dictionary of American History*, III, 258; Elvid Hunt, *Fort Leavenworth, 1827-1927* (Fort Leavenworth, Kans., 1926); Erasmus T. Carr, "Reminiscences Concerning Fort Leavenworth in 1855-1856," Kansas State Historical Society, *Collections* (Topeka, Kans., 1912), XII, 375-383.

8. *Census, 1850*, p. 993; *Senate Executive Documents*, 33 Cong., 1 Sess., No. 1, Pt. 1, pp. 243-433; *ibid.*, 33 Cong., 2 Sess., VI, No. 13, p. 8; Philip St. George Cooke, *The Conquest of New Mexico and California* (New York, 1878), 49-50.

9. *Ibid.*, 69; *House Executive Documents*, 30 Cong., 1 Sess., No. 41, pp. 45-113; Kearny, "Diary and Letter Book, 1846-1847," pp. 75-85, MSS., M. H. S.; Swords to Jesup, Oct. 8, 1847, MSS., L. R., Q. G. O., N. A.

10. *House Exeuctive Documents*, 30 Cong., 1 Sess., No. 41, pp. 7-127, 567-614; Washington (D.C.) *National Intelligencer*, Nov. 18, 1846.

11. George W. Cullum, *Biographical Register of the Officers and Graduates of the U. S. Military Academy at West Point, N. Y. from its Establishment in 1802 to 1890* (Boston, 1891, Cambridge, 1901, Saginaw, Mich., 1910), I, 397-398; Cooke, *Scenes and Adventures in the Army* (Philadelphia, 1857), 40-109, 157-196, 219-220; Philip St. George Cooke, William Henry Chase Whiting, and François Xavier Aubry, *Exploring Southwestern Trails, 1846-1854* (Bieber, ed., in collaboration with Averam B. Bender, Glendale, 1938), 18-20, 65-240.

12. For the character and history of the Mormon Battalion see Frank Alfred Golder in collaboration with Thomas A. Bailey and J. Lyman Smith, *The March of the Mormon Battalion* (New York, 1928); Brackett, "Sketch of Mormon Battalion, No. 8, Miscellaneous Historical Papers," MS., Bancroft Library.

13. Cooke, *The Conquest of New Mexico and California*, 91.

14. *Ibid.*, 162-163; Golder, Bailey, and Smith, 184, 189; *House Executive Documents*, 30 Cong., 1 Sess., No. 41, pp. 51-62; Cooke, Whiting, and Aubry, 67-237.

15. Brackett, 124; Cooke, Whiting, and Aubry, 29; Bancroft, *History of Arizona and New Mexico*, 478; New Orleans *Daily Picayune*, May 25, 1847.

16. Marcy graduated from West Point in 1832. Except for two short periods of recruiting duty in the East, he spent thirteen years of service on the Michigan and Wisconsin frontiers. The decade following the Mexican War he served in the Southwest, principally in Indian Territory, Texas, and New Mexico Territory where he opened new trails, selected sites for military posts and Indian reservations. He rendered invaluable service during the Mormon War by going to New Mexico in the dead of winter and securing much-needed animals for the army. During the early years of the Civil War he served as chief of staff of his son-in-law, General McClellan. From 1863 to 1878 he was inspector in various departments. At the time of his retirement in 1881 he held the rank of brigadier general. He died at West Orange, New Jersey, on January 22, 1887. Cullum, I, 521-522; *Dictionary of American Biography* (New York, 1928-37), XII, 273-274; St. Louis *Daily Missouri Republican*, March 12, 16, April 12, 1858.

17. *House Executive Documents*, 31 Cong., 1 Sess., VIII, No. 45, pp. 26-27.

18. For the career and importance of Black Beaver, see Carolyn Thomas Foreman, "Black Beaver," *Chronicles of Oklahoma*, XXIV (autumn, 1946), 269-292.

19. Jesse Chisholm, celebrated half-breed Cherokee guide, trader, and interpreter was a factor in the affairs of the Southwest for nearly half a century. Coming west with the Cherokees from Tennessee about 1825 he made his home at Fort Gibson. His reputation among

the Indians as a "square shooter," "square dealer," and man with a "straight tongue" made it possible for him to exercise great influence among the red warriors. For more than twenty years, the Chisholm trail, running along the North Canadian River in the Indian Territory, northward into central Kansas, and south into northern Texas, was used by United States troops, army supply trains, Texas cattle drovers, and pioneers (including women and children). Joseph G. McCoy, *Historical Sketches of the Cattle Trade of the West and Southwest* (Bieber, ed., Glendale, 1940), 159-163; Thomas Ulvan Taylor, *Jesse Chisholm* (Bandera, Tex., 1939), 24-25, 81-82; St. Louis *Daily Missouri Republican*, July 25, 1858.

20. *House Executive Documents*, 31 Cong., 1 Sess., VIII, No. 45, pp. 23, 28, 30-48.

21. *Ibid.*, 52-77.

22. *Ibid.*, 19, 29, 80-82; Fort Smith (Ark.) *Herald*, Nov. 1, 1850; Simpson to Abert, May 15, 1849, MSS., L. R., T. E. B., E., O. C., N. A.

23. *House Executive Documents*, 31 Cong., 1 Sess., VIII, No. 45, pp. 80-82; St. Louis *Daily Missouri Republican*, March 31, 1853.

24. Fort Smith *Herald*, May 16, June 13, July 11, 25, Sept. 5, Nov. 2, 1849, May 4, 11, Nov. 8, 15, 22, 29, Dec. 6, 1850; Marcy, *Adventure on Red River: Report on the Exploration of the Headwaters of the Red River by Captain Randolph B. Marcy and Captain G. B. McClellan* (Grant Foreman, ed., Norman, Okla., 1937), p. vi.

25. Fort Smith *Herald*, May 30, Oct. 10, 1849, May 11, 1850; Houston *Democratic Telegraph and Texas Register*, Oct. 4, 1849.

26. Marcy, *Adventure on Red River*, pp. vi-vii.

27. See above, pp. 35, 37, 39.

28. John James Abert's name was linked with the Bureau of Topographical Engineers for more than a quarter of a century. A native of Virginia, he was graduated from West Point in 1811 and was employed by the government in the War Department at Washington, where he also studied law. In 1813 he resigned from the army and became counsellor at law in the District of Columbia. During the War of 1812 he served as a private soldier in the battle of Blandensburg, Maryland, August, 1814. Later in the same year he joined the Corps of Engineers with the rank of major, and during the next fifteen years he served as Assistant in Geodetic Survey of the Atlantic seaboard and as Superintending Topographical Engineer of Surveys of many rivers, islands, and canals. From 1829 to 1861 he was in charge of the Topographical Bureau, being in command of the corps of Topographical Engineers from 1838 to 1861. In 1832, as United States commissioner he conducted Indian emigration to the Missouri frontier and in the following year he served as commissioner to the Creek and Wyandotte tribes. As head of the corps of Topographical Engineers, Abert had an important role in the development of governmental engineering projects for more than a quarter of a century prior to the Civil War. His engineering reports are considered standard works. He was one of the founders of the National Institute of Science, since merged into the Smithsonian Institution. He was retired, September 9, 1861, and died in Washington, January 27, 1863. Francis B. Heitman, *Historical Register and Dictionary of the United States Army, 1789-1903* (Washington, 1903), I, 150; Cullum, I, 101; *Lamb's Biographical Dictionary of the United States* (J. H. Brown, ed., Boston, 1900), I, 13.

29. Thomas W. Symons, "The Army and the Exploration of the West," *The Journal of the Military Service Institution of the United States* (Sept., 1883), IV, 230; Abert to Stansbury, April 11, 1849, MSS., L. S., T. E. B., E., O. C., N. A.

30. *Senate Executive Documents*, 32 Cong., Spec. Sess., II, No. 3, pp. 75-76.

31. General John Wilson, a prominent lawyer of Fayette, Missouri, had been appointed Indian agent for "Salt Lake, California" and naval agent for the port of San Francisco. When the eastern boundary of California was determined it was found that his agency was in Utah. After a brief stay in Utah, Wilson spent the greater part of his career—more than twenty-five years—in California. *Senate Executive Documents*, 31 Cong., 1 Sess., 1, No. 1, pt. 1, pp. 11-12; *ibid.*, IX, No. 18, pp. 97-98; Hoopes, 39; Kate L. Gregg, "Boonslickers in the Gold Rush to California," *Missouri Historical Review*, XLI (July, 1947), 350-356.

32. *Senate Executive Documents*, 32 Cong., Spec. Sess., II, No. 3, pp. 85-86; St. Louis *Daily Missouri Republican*, Sept. 23, 1850.

33. *Senate Executive Documents*, 32 Cong., Spec. Sess., II, No. 3, pp. 87-95.

34. *Ibid.*, 98-119; St. Louis *Daily Missouri Republican*, July 7, 1850.

35. *Senate Executive Documents*, 32 Cong., Spec. Sess., II, No. 3, p. 120.

36. *Ibid.*, 101-110; St. Louis *Daily Missouri Republican*, July 7, 1850.

37. *Senate Executive Documents*, 32 Cong., Spec. Sess., II, No. 3, pp. 120-122, 149-150, 156-215.

38. *Ibid.*, 118-119, 216; Alter, 215, 221.

39. Abert to Simpson, May 5, 1849, MSS., L. S., T. E. B., E., O. C., N. A.

40. *Senate Executive Documents*, 32 Cong., 2 Sess., No 59, pp. 4, 11; St. Louis *Daily Missouri Republican*, June 11, 1851.

41. *Senate Executive Documents*, 32 Cong., 2 Sess., No. 59, pp. 5-20, 24-29.

42. *Ibid.*, 20-21; Frank C. Lockwood, *Pioneer Days in Arizona* (New York, 1932), 106-109.

43. *Senate Executive Documents*, 32 Cong., 2 Sess., No. 59, pp. 10-14, 17-20, 37.

44. *Ibid.*, 33-178.

45. Edward W. Callahan, *List of Officers of the Navy of the United States and of the Marine Corps from 1775 to 1900* (New York, 1901), 47; St. Louis *Daily Missouri Republican*, June 2, 1849; San Francisco *Call*, April 23, 1893; "Statement of General E. F. Beale," Biographical Sketch (typewritten copy for Bancroft, n.d.), MS., Bancroft Library.

46. San Francisco *Daily Alta California*, Nov. 26, 1857; San Francisco *Call*, April 23, 1893.

47. Bent's Fort was the famous outfitting and trading station on the Arkansas. For many years it was the headquarters of Bent, St. Vrain & Company, widely known as Indian traders, trappers, and Santa Fe traders. Built of adobe about 1833 and situated near the north bank of the Arkansas River in present Otero County, Colorado, the fort was known as Bent's Old Fort or Fort William. In 1849, William Bent, possibly fearing an Indian attack, destroyed the fort; in 1853, he built Bent's New Fort some thirty-eight miles to the eastward in present Bent County. Six years later, when the post was leased to the government, the name was changed to Fort Fauntleroy and shortly after to Fort Wise and Fort Lyon. James J. Webb, *Adventures in the Santa Fe Trade, 1844-1847* (Bieber, ed., Glendale, 1931), 59; George Bird Grinnell, "Old Bent's Fort and Its Builders," Kansas State Historical Society, *Collections* (Topeka, 1923), XV, 28-91; New York *Herald*, June 16, 1862; Warner to Meigs, Nov. 6, 1862, Fort Wise, MSS., L. R., Q. G. O., N. A.

48. Gwinn H. Heap, *Central Route to the Pacific from the Valley of the Mississippi to California: Journal of the Expedition* (Philadelphia, 1854), 32.

49. See above, p. 176.

50. Heap, 9-111, 123-127; *House Executive Documents*, 35 Cong., 1 Sess., No. 124, p. 15.

51. *Statutes at Large*, X, 639, XI, 162-163.

52. Floyd to Beale, April 22, 1857, MSS., L. S., S. W., N. A.

53. Beale tried the camel experiment in answer to the need for a more rapid and certain mode of transportation to the distant frontier posts. As early as 1836, Major George H. Crosman proposed the use of the camel. Twelve years later Major Henry C. Wayne suggested that the War Department send to the Near East for camels for use in frontier military service. In 1854 Lieutenant Beale suggested the organization of a camel corps for transport purposes. Secretary of War Davis approved these recommendations and Congress appropriated $30,000 for the "purchase and importation of camels and dromedaries." On May 14, 1856, thirty-three camels were landed at Indianola, Texas. Another herd of forty-four was brought over in February of the following year. The first experiment with camels was made in the fall of 1857 by Lieutenant Beale in his reconnaissance of a wagon road from Fort Defiance to the eastern frontier of California. After this expedition the camels were used in various capacities during the time of the overland stages. Despite their efficiency as beasts of burden, the camels ultimately proved a failure, probably because they were handled by inexperienced men. The westerners had no use for them, and the packers and soldiers detested them. In 1863 the remnant of the herd, about fourteen, was turned loose in Arizona and left to shift for itself. *Senate Executive Documents*, 34 Cong., 3 Sess., No. 62, pp. 1-238; *Statutes at Large*, X, 639; Stephen Bonsal, *Edward Fitzgerald Beale: A Pioneer in the Path of Empire, 1822-1903* (New York, 1912), 199-207; Lewis Burt Lesley (ed.), *Uncle Sam's Camels: the Journal of May Humphreys Stacey Supplemented by the Report of Edward F. Beale, 1857-1858* (Cambridge, 1929), 4-13; "Camels," 1848-1866, MSS., L. R., Q. G. O., N. A.

54. In addition to the regular articles of food, Beale's traveling commissariat included 10 barrels of vinegar, 335 pounds of salt, 100 pounds of pepper, and 100 pounds of saleratus. The absence of refrigeration facilities necessitated the extensive use of condiments. Floyd to Beale, April 24, 1857, MSS., L. S., S. W., N. A.

55. Between July, 1853, and March, 1854, Lieutenant A. W. Whipple of the Topographical Engineers conducted a survey for a railroad route to the Pacific. The survey, embracing the country between Fort Smith and Los Angeles, extended along the Canadian, across the Panhandle of Texas and New Mexico, westward to the Great Colorado, across the Mohave Valley and the California desert. George L. Albright, *Official Explorations for Pacific Railroads* (Berkeley, 1921), 105-117.

56. *House Executive Documents*, 35 Cong., 1 Sess., No. 124, pp. 2, 38, 44-76.

57. *Ibid.*, 76-87; St. Louis *Daily Missouri Republican*, Jan. 19, 1858.

58. *House Executive Documents*, 36 Cong., 1 Sess., VI, No. 42, pp. 8-53; Floyd to Beale, Aug. 5, 1858, MSS., L. S., S. W., N. A.; Beale to Floyd, May 16, 1859, MSS., L. R., A. G. O., N. A.; Beale (Enclosure, Steen to Jesup, Oct. 15, 1858), MSS., L. R., Q. G. O., N. A.

59. *House Executive Documents*, 36 Cong., 1 Sess., VI, No. 42, pp. 40-45, 48; San Antonio *Texan*, May 28, 1859.

60. Beale to Floyd, July 16, Dec. 15, 1859 (Enclosure, Crump to Beale, n. d.), MSS., L. R., S. W., N. A.

61. St. Louis *Daily Missouri Republican*, Sept. 4, 1859; San Francisco *Daily Alta California*, July 19, 1859.

62. *Ibid.*, Nov. 9, 1858, Jan. 30, June 26, Aug. 31, 1859.

63. Simpson, 13-14, 489-495.

64. *Ibid.*, 16-25.

65. Mack, 342; Symons, "The Army and the Exploration of the West," *The Journal of the Military Service Institution of the United States*, IV, 237.

66. *Senate Executive Documents*, 35 Cong., 2 Sess., No. 40, pp. 3-39; *ibid.*, 36 Cong., 1 Sess., No. 2, Pt. 3, pp. 847-848; Simpson to Porter, Dec. 28, 1858 (Simpson's Report), MSS., L. R., T. E. B., E., O. C., N. A.

67. Simpson, 3, 7, 25-148, 217; *Senate Executive Documents*, 36 Cong., 1 Sess., No. 1, Pt. 1, p. 106, No. 2, Pt. 2, pp. 15, 221; San Francisco *Daily Alta California*, July 20, 1859; Salt Lake City *Deseret News*, July 20, 1859.

68. Simpson, 3; Simpson to Abert, Aug. 9, Sept. 6, 1859, MSS., L. R., T. E. B., E., O. C., N. A.

69. The explorations of John Charles Frémont, "the Pathfinder," are not included in this study. His first three expeditions to the Far West were made prior to the Mexican War; the fourth (1848-49) and fifth (1853-54)—primarily private ventures—were concerned with finding a practical railroad route to the Pacific. See John Charles Frémont, *Memoirs of My Life . . .* (Chicago, 1887); Allan Nevins, *Frémont, the West's Greatest Adventurer* (New York, 1928), I, II; St. Louis *Daily Missouri Republican*, March 7, 25, 30, April 19, 22, 24, Nov. 23, 1849, May 30, July 12, 1854.

70. Between 1845 and 1851 the Quartermaster General's Office reported an increase in transportation costs of more than 1,600 per cent. *Senate Executive Documents*, 32 Cong., 1 Sess., I, No. 1, Pt. 1, p. 110; *ibid.*, 33 Cong., 1 Sess., No. 1, Pt. 2, p. 24; Abert to Marko, May 18, 1849, Abert to Rockwell, June 30, 1849, MSS., L. S., T. E. B., E., O. C., N. A.

71. *Senate Journal*, 31 Cong., 1 Sess., 625; *Senate Reports*, 31 Cong., 2 Sess., No. 240; *House Journal*, 32 Cong., 2 Sess., 210; *ibid.*, 34 Cong., 1 Sess., Pt. 1, p. 490; *House Reports*, 32 Cong., 2 Sess., No. 2; St. Louis *Daily Missouri Republican*, Feb. 8, 12, 1855, May 6, 1856; California, *Statutes, 1855* (Sacramento, 1853), 308.

72. *House Reports*, 34 Cong., 1 Sess., No. 355.

73. *Statutes at Large*, XI, 27, 162-163.

74. *Senate Executive Documents*, 35 Cong., 2 Sess., No. 36, pp. 7-36, 75-76.

75. *Statutes at Large*, IX, 439, 306, X, 151, 168, 203, 303, 306, 603, 604, 641; *Senate Executive Documents*, 34 Cong., 3 Sess., II, 390; *House Executive Documents*, 34 Cong., 1 Sess., No. 1, Pt. 2, pp. 43-44, 273, 468, 475-483; *ibid.*, 35 Cong., 1 Sess., No. 79, p. 3; St. Louis *Daily Missouri Republican*, Aug. 25, 1855.

76. *Senate Executive Documents*, 35 Cong., 2 Sess., III, No. 1, Pt. 3, pp. 1032, 1206-1209; *ibid.*, 36 Cong., 1 Sess., II, No. 2, Pt. 2, p. 693; Macomb to Abert, Oct. 30, 1860, MSS., L. R., T. E. B., E., O. C., N. A.

77. When Texas entered the Union she was permitted to keep all her public lands. In the fifties Texas roads were still most primitive. One contemporary described them thus: "In the woods, simple notches in the trees indicate the route. In the prairies and open country there is no marked path; . . . everyone proceeds, according to his taste, along a flat, unbroken surface." Domenech, *Missionary Adventures in Texas and Mexico*, 26. See also Olmsted, 93, 239, 246.

78. San Francisco *Daily National*, Sept. 24, 1858; A. J. Bledsoe, *Indian Wars of the Northwest* (San Francisco, 1885), 218; California, *Assembly Journal, 1855* (Sacramento, 1855), 426-427; *Senate Miscellaneous Documents*, 33 Cong., 1 Sess., No. 53, p. 1.

79. *Statutes at Large*, X, 151, 303, 603-604, XI, 168, 337, XII, 19; *House Executive Documents*, 36 Cong., 2 Sess., VIII, No. 44; *ibid.*, No. 64, pp. 3-17; *Senate Executive Documents*, 37 Cong., 2 Sess., II, No. 1, pp. 124, 548.

80. Santa Fe *Weekly Gazette*, April 11, 1857.

81. *House Executive Documents*, 35 Cong., 1 Sess., No. 2, Pt. 2, p. 14; Sumner to Jesup Jan. 21, 1856, MSS., L. R., Q. G. O., N. A.

82. *La Jornada del Muerto* ("Dead Man's Journey" or "Journey of Death") was a noted ninety-mile belt of desert country in the Rio Grande Valley. Situated in south-central New Mexico it extended in a strip five to thirty miles wide from Valverde to El Paso, Texas. In the mid-nineteenth century this inhospitable wasteland was the dread of travelers. Julius Froebel, a German naturalist who crossed the *Jornada* in the fall of 1852, believed that it had a worse reputation than it deserved, for the barren stretch of country was seldom entirely without water, and the road for the most part was good. Davis, 371-372; Froebel, 317; George Wilkins Kendall, *Narrative of an Expedition across the Great Southwestern Prairies from Texas to Santa Fe* (London, 1845), I, 430-431; Carl L. Cannon, "Jornada del Muerto," *Dictionary of American History*, III, 181-182.

83. *House Miscellaneous Documents*, 33 Cong., 1 Sess., No. 49; *Senate Journal*, 33 Cong., 1 Sess., 297; New Orleans *Daily Picayune*, June 11, 1857; Johnston to Brooke, Jan. 9, 1850, MSS., L. R., T. E. B., E., O. C., N. A.

84. *Statutes at Large*, XI, 203.

85. St. Louis *Daily Missouri Republican*, March 27, 1858, Aug. 15, 1859; *Senate Executive Documents*, 36 Cong., 1 Sess., II, No. 2, Pt. 2, pp. 544-548; Pope to Abert, March 1, 24, 1855, Feb. 2, May 4, July 5, 1856, Feb. 1, 1858, Jan. 1, July 9, Nov. 7, 1859, MSS., L. R., T. E. B., E., O. C., N. A.

86. In the late fifties artesian wells in the Carson River Valley supplied United States troops with water. In Southern California the water from artesian wells sunk by the Overland Mail company was "damnably bad" and insufficient in quantity. In the seventies artesian wells were successfully located in northern Texas and in southern California. Bandel, 55-56, 61, 65, 235, 259; Homer S. Thrall, *A Pictorial History of Texas* (St. Louis, 1879), 59.

87. *Senate Executive Documents*, 37 Cong., 2 Sess., II, No. 1, p. 545; St. Louis *Daily Missouri Republican*, Oct. 30, 1856.

V

1. Stella M. Drumm, "Robert E. Lee and the Improvement of the Mississippi River," Missouri Historical Society, *Collections*, VI (Feb., 1929), 161.

2. *Ibid.*, 161, 166-167.

3. Norman Caldwell, "The Red River Raft," *Chronicles of Oklahoma*, XIX (Sept., 1941), 257-259; Henry Putney Beers, *The Western Military Frontier, 1815-1846* (Philadelphia, 1935), 136-137; Walter Prichard, "Red River Raft," *Dictionary of American History*, IV, 432.

4. Jesup to Crawford, Nov. 10, 1849, Jesup to Conrad, Nov. 22, 1851, MSS., L. S., Q. G. O., N. A.

5. Ramsdell, "Internal Improvement Projects in Texas in the Fifties," Mississippi Valley Historical Association, *Proceedings*, IX (April, 1917), Pt. 1, p. 99; Houston *Democratic Telegraph and Texas Register*, Aug. 3, 1848.

6. Francis White Johnson, *A History of Texas and Texans* (Chicago, 1914), I, 505; Houston *Democratic Telegraph and Texas Register*, Aug. 3, 1848; St. Louis *Daily Missouri Republican*, May 22, Aug. 21, 1852; New Orleans *Daily Picayune*, Aug. 19, 1853.

7. San Antonio *Ledger*, May 26, July 21, 1853; New Orleans *Daily Picayune*, Aug. 19, 1853; S. G. Reed, *A History of Texas Railroads . . .* (Houston, 1941), 53-117.

8. Abert to Kauffman, July 23, 1850, MSS., L. S., T. E. B., E., O. C., N. A.

9. New Orleans *Daily Picayune*, March 10, 1852; Abert to Johnston, June 10, 1850, MSS., L. S., T. E. B., E., O. C., N. A.

10. Whiting to Totten, March 2, 18, April 26, 30, 1853, Stevens to Totten, June 10, July 8, 1854, H. L. Smith to Totten, June 22, Aug. 15, 1853, Feb. 4, 1854, MSS., L. R., E., O. C., N. A; New Orleans *Daily Picayune*, Nov. 29, 1853; *Senate Executive Documents*, 33 Cong., 2 Sess., No. 1, Pt. 2, p. 167.

11. During this period troops at the Texas posts received supplies overland from long distances and at considerable expense. The garrison at Laredo, for example, was being supplied from Ringgold Barracks over a tedious route of 120 miles; the post at Eagle Pass was being supplied from the same point, a distance of 224 miles; El Paso received its supplies from Port de La Vaca, 850 miles overland, at an annual cost of $200,000. Johnston to Abert, April 27, 1850, Jan 7, 1851, MSS., L. R., T. E. B., E., O. C., N. A.; New Orleans *Daily Picayune*, Oct. 3, 1849.

12. Melinda Rankin, *Texas in 1850* (Boston, 1850), 172-173.

13. Bryant P. Tilden, Jr., *Notes on the Upper Rio Grande* (Philadelphia, 1847), 7-32.

14. Whiting to Worth, Jan. 24, 1849, MSS., L. R., E., O. C., N. A.

15. In the early forties Love served at Forts Gibson, Scott, and Leavenworth. In 1843 he commanded a company of Captain Cooke's dragoons from Fort Leavenworth to protect the annual caravan of traders on the Santa Fe trail. Two years later he accompanied Kearny to South Pass; he distinguished himself in the battle of Santa Cruz de Rosales in the Mexican War. Cullum, II, 79-80; William E. Connelley (ed.), "A Journal of the Santa Fe Trail," *Mississippi Valley Historical Review*, XII (June, 1925), 73-74.

16. *Senate Executive Documents*, 31 Cong., 2 Sess., No. 1, Pt. 2, pp. 324-329; St. Louis *Daily Missouri Republican*, Nov. 8, 1850.

17. *Senate Executive Documents*, 31 Cong., 2 Sess., No. 1, Pt. 2, pp. 324-326; *ibid.*, 33 Cong., 2 Sess., No. 78, p. 62; Johnston to Abert, Jan. 7, 1851 (Enclosures: William E. Smith to Johnston, Oct. 26, 1850, Jan. 6, Feb. 28, 1851), MSS., L. R., T. E. B., E., O. C., N. A.

18. Harvey Fergusson, *Rio Grande* (New York, 1933), 3-4.

19. Washington (Ark.) *Telegraph*, Jan. 23, March 27, 1850, Feb. 12, 1851, Oct. 26, 1853, March 29, 1854; New Orleans *Daily Picayune*, Jan. 13, 1859; *Congressional Globe*, 35 Cong., 1 Sess., Appendix, 478; Jesup to Conrad, Dec. 20, 1851, MSS., L. S., Q. G. O., N. A.

20. By this time Congress already had appropriated more than one-half million dollars for the removal of the great raft of Louisiana. *Senate Bills and Resolutions*, 30 Cong., 1 Sess., Bill 307; *Statutes at Large*, X, 57; *House Executive Documents*, 32 Cong., 2 Sess., I, No. 1, Pt. 2, p. 72.

21. Washington (Ark.) *Telegraph*, Nov. 22, 1854, Dec. 3, 1856; Fuller to Abert, Sept. 30, Oct. 4, 1854, Long to Abert, Oct. 3, 1855, Feb. 7, 19, May 17, July 24, 1856, Feb. 7, Nov. 2, 1857, Jan. 10, Oct. 10, 1858, April 11, 1859, MSS., L. R., T. E. B., E., O. C., N. A.

22. New Orleans *Daily Picayune*, March 17, July 10, 1860; Caldwell, "The Red River Raft," *Chronicles of Oklahoma*, XIX, 263-266.

23. St. Louis *Daily Missouri Republican*, April 5, 1853; Abert to Marcy, Nov. 17, 1848, "United States Miscellaneous, California and New Mexico, 1846-1850," MSS., L. C.

24. Sebastian to Conrad, Feb. 11, 1852, Borland to Conrad, Feb. 23, 1852, MSS., L. R., T. E. B., E., O. C., N. A.

25. *Senate Executive Documents*, 32 Cong., 2 Sess., No. 54, p. 1; Special Orders No. 33, March 5, 1852, MSS., A. G. O., N. A.

26. The command included Captain George B. McClellan of the Engineers, who made observations and acted as quartermaster and commissary; Lieutenant Joseph Updegraff; Dr. George G. Shumard of Fort Smith, who was surgeon and geologist of the expedition; Captain J. H. Strain of Fort Washita; J. H. Suydam of New York. Five Delaware Indians acted as guides and herders. Marcy, *Thirty Years of Army Life on the Border*, 139; George B. McClellan to John McClellan, April 21, 1852, John McClellan to Thomas English, July 27, 1852, McClellan, "Letters," III, MSS., L. C.

27. St. Louis *Daily Missouri Republican*, Aug. 27, 1852, April 5, 1853; Marcy, *Thirty Years of Army Life on the Border*, 119-139; McClellan to mother, May 7, 1852, McClellan to John McClellan, May 14, 1852, McClellan to sister Maria, Sept. 6, 1852, McClellan, "Letters," III, IV, MSS., L.C.

28. Marcy, *Thirty Years of Army Life on the Border*, 140-157; *Senate Executive Documents*, 32 Cong., 2 Sess., No. 54, p. 51.

29. St. Louis *Daily Missouri Republican*, July 24, 28, Aug. 7, 12, 1852; Marcy, *Thirty Years of Army Life on the Border*, 164; John McClellan to Mrs. English, July 27, 1852, McClellan, "Letters," III, MSS., L. C.

30. *Senate Executive Documents*, 32 Cong., 2 Sess., No. 54, appendix, contains much valuable scientific data; Marcy, *Adventure on Red River*, pp. xiv-xvii; McClellan to mother, Aug. 23, 1852, McClellan, "Letters," IV, MSS., L. C.

31. Edwin Bryant, *What I Saw in California* (New York, 1848), 275-276; *House Miscellaneous Documents*, 41 Cong., 3 Sess., No. 12, p. 11.

32. Lewis R. Freeman, *The Colorado River: Yesterday, Today, and Tomorrow* (New York, 1923), 142.

33. Samuel Peter Heintzelman had a long and distinguished career in the army. Born in Lancaster County, Pennsylvania, in 1805, he entered West Point in 1822, and upon graduation four years later was commissioned second lieutenant, Second Infantry. During the next twenty-five years he served successively on the Northern Frontier at Forts Gratiot, Mackinac, and Brady, in Florida and the Creek country, and on the staff in the quartermaster's department. In 1847 he joined Scott's expedition against Mexico City and was brevetted major for "gallant and meritorious conduct in the battle of Huamantla." In 1848-49 he accompanied his regiment around Cape Horn to California and for several years was busily engaged in the Territory of New Mexico, being brevetted lieutenant colonel for his conduct in the campaign against the Yuma Indians. He founded Fort Yuma. Along the Rio Grande border, he rendered valuable service against the organized marauders under Cortinas. During the Civil War he advanced rapidly in rank, holding high and important commands throughout the entire war. He was brevetted brigadier general in 1862 and major general in 1865. He was retired from active service in February, 1869, and died at Washington, D. C., on May 1, 1880. The commander-in-chief of the army described General Heintzelman as "a man of an intense nature, of vehement action, guided by sound judgment and a cultivated taste." *Dictionary of American Biography*; Cullum, I, 372-374; Washington (D. C.) *Evening Star*, May 1, 1880; Samuel Peter Heintzelman, "Papers," MSS., L. C.

34. *Senate Executive Documents*, 32 Cong., 1 Sess., IX, No. 81, pp. 2-22.

35. *House Executive Documents*, 35 Cong., 2 Sess., No. 114, pp. 23-24; Freeman, 146-147; Bancroft, *History of Arizona and New Mexico*, 490; "Medical History of Fort Yuma, 1850-1873," MSS., A. G. O., N. A.

36. *House Executive Documents*, 32 Cong., 2 Sess., No. 1, Pt. 2, pp. 30-31; *ibid.*, 34 Cong., 3 Sess., No. 76, p. 38; Freeman, 147.

37. *House Miscellaneous Documents*, 34 Cong., 1, Sess., II, No. 86.

38. Forty thousand dollars was set aside to defray the expenses of the expedition. *House Executive Documents*, 36 Cong., 1 Sess., No. 90, p. 6; Freeman, 147; Floyd to Ives, May 15, 1857, MSS., L. S., S. W., N. A.

39. In the more important exploring expeditions of the period, the personnel included not only military officers and engineers but also surveyors, topographers, naturalists, geologists, and artists. Louise Rasmussen, "Artists of the Explorations Overland, 1840-1860," *Oregon Historical Quarterly*, XLIII (March, 1942), 56-62.

40. *House Executive Documents*, 36 Cong., 1 Sess., No. 90, pp. 5-25.

41. *Ibid.*, 21, 36; Frederick Samuel Dellenbaugh, *The Romance of the Colorado River* (New York, 1902), 160.

42. *House Executive Documents*, 36 Cong., 1 Sess., No. 90, pp. 38-43.

43. *Ibid.*, 43-61; Dellenbaugh, 164; San Francisco *Daily Alta California*, May 12, 1858.

44. *House Executive Documents*, 36 Cong., 1 Sess., No. 90, pp. 43-44, 54-55, 66-72.

45. Freeman says that Ives was wrong about the head of navigation, for within a few years occasional cargoes were being sent through by steamer to the little Mormon colony of Callville founded in 1864, almost within sight of Las Vegas Wash where Ives turned back. Freeman, 167.

46. Dellenbaugh, 167; *House Executive Documents*, 36 Cong., 1 Sess., No. 90, pp. 75-84.

47. *Ibid.*, 85-89.

48. *Ibid.*, 91-130.

49. *Ibid.*, 87-89; Dellenbaugh, 150-151, 154-155.

50. *House Executive Documents*, 36 Cong., 1 Sess., No. 90, pp. 2-5; Freeman, 170; Bell, I, p. xlii.

51. *Senate Executive Documents*, 35 Cong., 2 Sess., No. 1, Pt. 2, p. 584; *House Miscellaneous Documents*, 41 Cong., 3 Sess., No. 12, pp. 1, 2, 4, 12; Rusling, 357.

52. In the latter half of the nineteenth century the Great Colorado served as a medium of transportation for the mining settlements along its banks. Towards the close of the century its waters irrigated the land. In the most recent period the Boulder Dam project has proved invaluable. An excellent treatment of the uses of the Colorado River is given by

Edwin Truesdell Force, "The Use of the Colorado River in the United States, 1850-1933," MS., Ph.D. dissertation, University of California, 1937; E. D. Tuttle, "The River Colorado," *Arizona Historical Review*, I (July, 1928), 54-68.

VI

1. Josiah Gregg, *Commerce of the Prairies*, in *Early Western Travels* (R. G. Thwaites, ed., Cleveland, 1905), XX, 222; Webb, 28.

2. Gregg, XIX, 254-255; Ellen C. Semple, *American History and Its Geographic Conditions* (Boston, 1903), 191, 194-198.

3. Froebel, 204; New Orleans *Daily Picayune*, Oct. 18, 1848; John S. Ford, "Memoirs," II, 248. MSS., Archives, University of Texas. (Hereafter cited as Ford, "Memoirs.")

4. Clarksville (Tex.) *Northern Standard*, Sept. 2, 1848 (by October, 1852, the name was changed to the *Standard*); Victoria *Texian Advocate*, Aug. 24, Nov. 2, 9, 1848.

5. Frank Triplett, *Conquering the Wilderness* (New York, 1883), 601-608; Thrall, 550; John C. Caperton, "Sketch of Colonel John C. Hays, Texas Ranger," MS. (typewritten copy), Archives, University of Texas. (Hereafter the last reference will be cited as Caperton, "Sketch of Colonel Hays," MS., Archives, University of Texas); Ford, "Memoirs," II, 241, 247a, III, 499-502.

6. For the career of this picturesque Texan, see Thrall, 552; Wooten, II, 338-339.

7. The Norteños, as the townsmen of Presidio del Norte were called, were considered a bad lot. To hold their ground between hostile Comanches and Apaches, they became "allies, spies, powder purveyors, receivers and buyers of stolen goods of the Texan Comanche." This alliance with the Comanches seemed advantageous to the Mexicans, for by this means they assisted in keeping the Apaches in check. Froebel, 408-409.

8. Fort Leaton was not a fort but a ranch and trading post. Situated about five miles below Presidio del Norte on the American side of the Rio Grande, it was established in 1846 by a frontiersman named Ben Leaton. Clarksville (Tex.) *Northern Standard*, Feb. 10, 1849; Mooney, "Calendar History of the Kiowa Indians," Bureau of American Ethnology, *Seventeenth Annual Report*, Pt. 1, p. 387; Alice Jack ("Mrs. O. L.") Shipman, *Taming the Big Bend* (Austin, 1926), 6, 10, 11, 18, 199.

9. Cooke, Whiting, and Aubry, 31-33; Clarksville (Tex.) *Northern Standard*, Feb. 10, 1849; Caperton, "Sketch of Colonel Hays," 67-75, MS., Archives, University of Texas; John C. Hays, "Life and Adventures of a Texas Ranger . . . ," 60-67, MS., Bancroft Library.

10. *Ibid.*, 68.

11. St. Louis *Daily Union*, Jan. 11, 1849.

12. Thian, 46-47; Marcy to Worth, Dec. 10, 1848, MSS., L.S., S. W., N. A.

13. St. Louis *Daily Missouri Republican*, Jan. 10, 1849; Worth, Order No. 10, Feb. 9, 1849, MSS., L. R., E., O. C., N. A.

14. *Senate Executive Documents*, 31 Cong., 1 Sess., XIV, No. 64, pp. 4-7; Cooke, Whiting, and Aubry, 34-36, 243-350 (Whiting's Journal); Whiting to Totten, May 17, June 10, 1849 (Whiting's Report), MSS., L. R., E., O. C., N. A.

15. Besides Neighbors and Ford, the motley crowd included: D. C. ("Doc.") Sullivan, Alpheus D. Neal, Jim Shaw (Delaware), Patrick Goin (Choctaw), Joe Ellis, Tom Coshatee (Shawnee), an Anadarko, and Buffalo Hump (Guide). Mackall to Brooke, July 22, 1849 (Enclosure: Neighbors' Report, June 4, 1849), MSS., L. R., H. A., N. A.; Ford, "Memoirs," III, 504-506.

16. The Waco Tanks consisted of an old camping ground of Mexicans and Indians. One tank situated in a cave was said to have contained 50,000 gallons of pure water. McKall to Brooke, July 22, 1849 (Enclosure: Neighbors' Report, June 4, 1849), MSS., L. R., H. A., N. A.

17. *Ibid.*; Ford, "Memoirs," III, 503-525.

18. *Ibid.*, III, 514, 520.

19. *Senate Executive Documents*, 31 Cong., 1 Sess., XIV, No. 64, pp. 14-25, 26-29, 40-54.

20. *Ibid.*, 42, 53; St. Louis *Daily Missouri Republican*, Feb. 12, March 14, May 22, June 20, 1850; Austin *Texas State Gazette*, June 1, Sept. 28, 1850, May 1, 1852; San Antonio *Ledger*, April 14, Oct. 16, 1851, April 14, 1853; Brooke to Jones, June 13, 1850, MSS., L. R., H. A., N. A.

21. *Senate Executive Documents*, 31 Cong., 1 Sess., XIV, No. 64, pp. 13, 23, 26-27;

Brooke to Freeman, Jan. 13, 1850 (Enclosure: Smith to Johnston, Oct. 3, 1849), MSS., L. R., H. A., N. A.

22. *Senate Executive Documents*, 31 Cong., 1 Sess., XIV, No. 64, pp. 237-250; Whiting to Totten, March 25, 1850 (Enclosure: Whiting's Journal, Jan. 21, March 14, 1850), MSS., L. R., E., O. C., N. A.

23. *Senate Executive Documents*, 31 Cong., 1 Sess., XIV, No. 64, pp. 7-12; Special Orders No. 50, Sept. 11, 1849, Eighth Military Department, Book 250, MSS., A. G. O., N. A.; Johnston to Abert, Dec. 8, 1849 (Enclosure: Michler's Report, July 31, 1849), MSS., L. R., T. E. B., E., O. C., N. A.

24. *Senate Executive Documents*, 33 Cong., 2 Sess., No. 78, p. 62; Special Orders No. 52, Nov. 21, 1850, Eighth Military Department, Book 250, MSS., A. G. O., N. A.; Smith to Johnston, Jan. 6, 1851, Johnston to Abert, Jan. 10, 1851 (Enclosure: Bryan's Report, Dec. 23, 1850), MSS., L. R., T. E. B., E., O. C., N. A.

25. A. B. Bender, "The Texas Frontier, 1848-1861," *Southwestern Historical Quarterly*, XXXVIII (Oct., 1934), 138-139; Green to Cooper, Dec. 16, 1852, MSS., L. R., H. A., N. A.

26. *Senate Executive Documents*, 33 Cong., 2 Sess., No. 78, p. 62; Bender, "The Texas Frontier, 1848-1861," *Southwestern Historical Quarterly*, XXXVIII, 137-138; George McClellan to John McClellan, Sept. 3, Oct. 25, 1852, Totten to George McClellan, Sept. 25, 1852, George McClellan to sister Maria, Oct. 9, 1852, Smith to George McClellan, Oct. 11, 1852, McClellan, "Letters," IV, MSS., L. C.

27. Marcy, *Thirty Years of Army Life on the Border*, 171-180; William B. Parker, *Notes Taken during the Expedition Commanded by Captain R. B. Marcy, U. S. A., through Unexplored Texas in the Summer and Fall of 1854* (Philadelphia, 1856), 10, 67-72.

28. Marcy, *Thirty Years of Army Life on the Border*, 181-216; Parker, 130-201.

29. In making the surveys of the different tracts, Marcy ran and marked the boundary lines, both in American and Spanish measurement so that either form could be adopted. Randolph B. Marcy, "Field Notes, Dec., 1854," Pt. 1, pp. 1, 9, Pt. 2, p. 1, MS., Q. G. O., N. A.

30. Parker, 173; R. C. Crane, "Some Aspects of the History of West and Northwest Texas since 1845," *Southwestern Historical Quarterly*, XXVI (July, 1922), 36.

31. For details of these explorations, see Bender, "The Texas Frontier, 1848-1861," *Southwestern Historical Quarterly*, XXXVIII, 140-148.

32. *House Executive Documents*, 30 Cong., 1 Sess., No. 41, pp. 43-44, 460-511; Bender, "Government Explorations in the Territory of New Mexico, 1846-1859," *New Mexico Historical Review*, IX (Jan., 1934), 5-6.

33. See above, pp. 150-151.

34. *Senate Executive Documents*, 31 Cong., 1 Sess., XIV, No. 64, pp. 56-138; Fort Smith *Herald*, Dec. 5, 1849; Calhoun, 77; Simpson to Abert, April 11, 1850 (Enclosure: Abert's Journal, Sept. 28, 1849), MSS., L. R., T. E. B., E., O. C., N. A.

35. Pierre Melicourt Papin was the son of Pierre Melicourt Papin, prominent Indian trader and wealthy St. Louisan, and Mitishais, an Indian woman of the Osage nation. "Will of Pierre Melicourt Papin, July 7, 1849," MS., No. 2,800, Probate Court, St. Louis.

36. *Senate Executive Documents*, 33 Cong., 2 Sess., XIII, No. 78, Pt. 11, p. 62; McCall, 509; Munroe to Freeman, April 6, 1850 (Enclosure: Judd to McLaws, March 30, 1850), MSS., L. R., H. A., N. A.

37. John C. Cremony, *Life among the Apaches* (Santa Fe, 1868), 198-199; Bancroft, *History of Arizona and New Mexico*, 661-662.

38. See above, pp. 61-63.

39. *Senate Miscellaneous Documents*, 33 Cong., 2 Sess., No. 24, p. 298.

40. *Ibid.*, 315-316.

41. *Ibid.*, 296-316; Garland to Thomas, Jan. 20, 1854 (Enclosure: Nichols to Carleton, Dec. 3, 1853), MSS., L. R., A. G. O., N. A.

42. *Senate Miscellaneous Documents*, 33 Cong., 2 Sess., No. 24, pp. 306, 310-312.

43. See above, pp. 65-67.

44. Abert to Cooper, June 29, 1854, MSS., L. S., T. E. B., E., O. C., N. A.

45. *Senate Executive Documents*, 36 Cong., 2 Sess., II, No. 1, pp. 146-151; J. N. Macomb, *Report of Exploring Expedition from Santa Fe, New Mexico to the Junction of Grand and Green Rivers of the Great Colorado of the West, 1859* (Washington, 1876); Humphreys to Macomb, April 6, 1859, MSS., L. R., A. G. O., N. A.; John S. Newberry, "Notes on San Juan (Macomb's) Expedition, July 13-Sept. 28, 1859," MS., E., O. C., N. A.

46. Macomb, 1.

47. *Senate Executive Documents*, 36 Cong., 1 Sess., II, No. 2, Pt. 2, pp. 294-295, 312-313, 330-331.

48. *Ibid.*, 313, 328-330.

49. *Ibid.*, 313; Bonneville to Thomas, Sept. 25, 1859 (Enclosure: Jackson to Wilkins, Sept. 8, 1859), MSS., L. R., A. G. O., New Mexico, N. A.

50. *Senate Executive Documents*, 36 Cong., 1 Sess., II, No. 2, Pt. 2, pp. 313-315.

51. Bonneville to Thomas, Aug. 12, 1859 (Enclosure: Gordon to Wilkins, July 28, 1859), MSS., L. R., A. G. O., New Mexico, N. A.

52. *Senate Executive Documents*, 36 Cong., 1 Sess., II, No. 2, Pt. 2, pp. 325-327, 351-354.

53. *Ibid.*, 31 Cong., 1 Sess., No. 18, pp. 504-511.

54. Cleland, 268-269; Marcy to Wetmore, Nov. 24, 1848, William L. Marcy, "Correspondence," XV, MSS., L. C.

55. Cleland, 270; Howe, 8, 11; Mason to Jones, Aug. 17, 1848, "United States Miscellaneous, California and New Mexico, 1846-1850," MSS., L. C.

56. Carolyn Thomas Foreman, "General Bennet Riley," *Chronicles of Oklahoma*, XIX (Sept., 1941), 225-244; Fort Smith *Herald*, Oct. 4, 1848; St. Louis *Daily Missouri Republican*, Jan. 20, 1852, June 15, 1853; San Francisco *Daily Alta California*, July 17, 26, 1853.

57. *House Executive Documents*, 31 Cong., 1 Sess., No. 17, pp. 941-943; Riley to Freeman, Sept. 20, 1849 (Enclosure: Derby's Journal), MSS., L. R., H. A., N. A.

58. *Senate Executive Documents*, 31 Cong., 1 Sess., No. 47, Pt. 2, pp. 16-22; Walter E. Stoddard, "William H. Warner, Soldier and Engineer," *Engineerogram* (Sacramento), Oct., 1939; St. Louis *Daily Missouri Republican*, Nov. 21, Dec. 17, 1849; St. Louis *Daily Union*, Dec. 19, 1849.

59. *Senate Executive Documents*, 31 Cong., 1 Sess., No. 47, Pt. 2, pp. 4-16; Abert to Derby, Aug. 8, 1848, Feb. 5, 1849, MSS., L. S., T. E. B., E., O. C., N. A.

60. In the fifties there were between 4,000,000 and 5,000,000 acres of tule or flooded lands in California which were practically useless. The state offered them for sale at $1.00 per acre on condition that purchasers reclaim them. Marysville *Weekly California Express*, Jan. 30, 1858; Hittell, *History of California*, II, 558.

61. *Senate Executive Documents*, 32 Cong., 1 Sess., No. 110, pp. 2-17; Derby to Canby, July 10, 1850 (Derby's Report), MSS., L. R., T. E. B., E., O. C., N. A.

62. See above, pp. 58-69.

VII

1. Bandel, 19; Symons, "The Army and the Exploration of the West," *The Journal of the Military Service Institution of the United States*, IV, 210.

2. *Senate Documents*, 29 Cong., 1 Sess., I, No. 1, pp. 193, 220a-220f.

3. The army at this time consisted of eight regiments of infantry, two of dragoons, and four of artillery. *Ibid.*; William A. Ganoe, *The History of the United States Army* (New York, 1942), 196.

4. *Statutes at Large*, IX, 11, 13-14, 123-124, 184; *House Executive Documents*, 30 Cong., 2 Sess., I, No. 1, pp. 160, 184f, 184g.

5. The authorized strength was 10,317, but the actual force consisted of a little over 8,000. *Ibid.*, 184a; Ganoe, 230.

6. See above, chapter III, Note 14.

7. *House Executive Documents*, 30 Cong., 2 Sess., I, No. 1, pp. 164-165.

8. St. Louis *Daily Missouri Republican*, April 29, 1851, July 10, 21, 1854, Nov. 12, 19, 22, 1857; *Senate Executive Documents*, 33 Cong., 1 Sess., II, No. 1, Pt. 2, pp. 3, 13, 95; *ibid.*, 33 Cong., 2 Sess., II, No. 1, p. 6.

9. Corpus Christi *Star*, May 26, 1849.

10. *House Executive Documents*, 31 Cong., 1 Sess., III, No. 5, Pt. 1, pp. 98-100.

11. *Ibid.*, 30 Cong., 2 Sess., No. 1, pp. 162-163, 166.

12. *Congressional Globe*, 31 Cong., 1 Sess., XXI, Pt. 2, p. 1049.

13. Bounties varied according to place of enlistment. For example, in the Eighth Military Department, the bounty was $26; in the Ninth, $52; in the Tenth, $117; in the Eleventh, $142. *Statutes at Large*, IX, 438-439; G. O. No. 20, A. G. O., June 22, 1850, MSS., A. G. O., N. A.

14. *Senate Executive Documents*, 31 Cong., 1 Sess., I, No. 1, pp. 90-91.

15. *Ibid.*, 33 Cong., 1 Sess., No. 1, Pt. 2, p. 3.

16. New York *Daily Times* in St. Louis *Daily Missouri Republican*, July 21, 1854.

17. St. Louis *Daily Missouri Republican*, July 10, 1854.

18. Austin *Texas State Gazette,* April 14, 1855.

19. *Ibid.*

20. *Congressional Globe*, 33 Cong., 2 Sess., XXX, 498.

21. *Ibid.*, 441-443, 461, 498.

22. *Ibid.*, 437, 440, 462, 465-466, 497-498.

23. Austin *State Gazette*, June 20, 1857, June 18, 1859.

24. *Senate Executive Documents*, 34 Cong., 1 Sess., II, No. 1, Pt. 2, pp. 3, 31; *Statutes at Large*, X, 639.

25. St. Louis *Daily Missouri Republican*, Nov. 12, 19, 22, 1857.

26. *Congressional Globe*, 35 Cong., 1 Sess., XXXVI, Pt. 1, pp. 492-497, 646-647, 669-673, 873-875.

27. *Senate Executive Documents*, 35 Cong., 2 Sess., II, No. 1, Pt. 2, p. 3, III, Pt. 3, p. 769.

28. *Ibid.*, 36 Cong., 2 Sess., II, No. 1, pp. 3, 189, 213.

29. For the location of the various military units in 1860, see *ibid.*, 214-229.

30. *House Executive Documents*, 30 Cong., 2 Sess., I, No. 1, pp. 164-165; *Senate Executive Documents*, 34 Cong., 1 Sess., II, No. 1, Pt. 2, pp. 126-127; *ibid.*, 36 Cong., 2 Sess., II, No. 1, pp. 212-213.

31. St. Louis *Daily Missouri Republican*, Aug. 25, 1849, Jan. 18, 1855; Austin *State Gazette*, Sept. 11, 1858; Twiggs to Thomas, July 1, 1857, MSS., L. R., A. G. O., N. A.

32. St. Louis *Daily Missouri Republican*, Aug. 25, 1849.

33. *Ibid.*, Sept. 15, 1854.

34. Austin *State Gazette*, Dec. 24, 1856.

35. Brownsville (Tex.) *American Flag*, in Austin *State Gazette*, July 1, 1854.

36. *Congressional Globe*, 31 Cong., 1 Sess., XXI, Pt. 2, pp. 1051, 1052; Houston, V, 157.

37. *Congressional Globe*, 31 Cong., 1 Sess., XXI, Pt. 2, pp. 1048-1049; *ibid.*, 33 Cong., 2 Sess., XXX, 440; Heap, 33; Scott to Cooper, Oct. 3, 1859, MSS., L. R., H. A., N. A.

38. Frontier garrisons usually were classified into three categories—commands, cantonments, and forts. See Dick, 75-76.

39. *Senate Executive Documents*, 36 Cong., 1 Sess., No. 52, pp. 290, 298; Ford, "Memoirs," IV, 670, 672; Mansfield to Thomas, Oct. 13, 1860, MSS., L. R., A. G. O., N. A.

40. Gibson, 122-123; Percival G. Lowe, *Five Years a Dragoon* (Kansas City, Mo., 1906), 29-32.

41. Dick, 77; Santa Fe *Weekly Gazette,* Jan. 8, 1859; "Medical History of Fort McKavett, 1852-1872," MSS., A. G. O., N. A.; Abadie to Lawson, Nov. 2, 1854, MSS., L. R., Surgeon General's Office, N. A. (hereafter Surgeon General's Office will be cited as S. G. O.); Kearny, "Journal," Jan. 17, 20, 1841, MSS., M. H. S.

42. Cooper to Lawson, April 4, June 12, 1849, MSS., L. R., S. G. O., N. A.; Mansfield to Thomas, Nov. 7, 1860, MSS., L. R., A. G. O., N. A.

43. Dick, 77; R. H. McKay, *Little Pills* (Pittsburg, Kans., 1918), 26; Sumner to Jesup, Jan. 21, 1856 (Enclosure: Fort Leavenworth, Artesian Wells), Bell to Jesup, Jan. 25, 1859 (Enclosure: Fort Riley), MSS., L. R., Q. G. O., N. A.

44. St. Louis *Daily Missouri Republican*, Feb. 10, July 11, 1848, Dec. 22, 1849; *Statutes at Large*, IX, 149-150.

45. Dana to Jesup, Feb. 28, 1850 (Enclosures: Fort Gaines), Hackney to Jesup, Oct. 21, 1856 (Enclosures: Mounted Volunteers), Brent to Jesup, Nov. 30, 1856 (Enclosures: Fort Riley, Hay Contracts), MSS., L. R., Q. G. O., N. A.

46. *Senate Executive Documents*, 34 Cong., 1 Sess., II, No. 1, Pt. 2, pp. 539-551; *ibid.*, 34 Cong., 3 Sess., III, No. 5, pp. 373-404; *ibid.*, 36 Cong., 1 Sess., III, No. 2, pp. 1106-1107.

47. *Ibid.*, 32 Cong., 1 Sess., I, No. 1, Pt. 1, pp. 295-296; St. Louis *Daily Missouri Republican*, Aug. 17, 1848, Sept. 11, 1855, Nov. 13, 1859; San Francisco *Daily Alta California*, Oct. 10, 1855; see also above, Chapter IV, note 53.

48. Twiggs to Gibson, June 19, 1857, MSS., L. S., Department of Texas, A. C., U. S., N. A.; McCall to Scott, June 14, 1852 (Enclosure: Fort Yuma), MSS., L. R., Q. G. O., N. A.; "U. S. Army, Ninth Military Department, Memorandum Concerning Thefts from Military Stores, 1852," MSS., Ritch Collection.

49. The cost of army transportation in the fifties averaged about $2,000,000 annually.

This represented about 13 per cent of the total expenditures for all military purposes. Upton, 224; Letters and Reports, Q. G., 1848-1861, MSS., L. S., Q. G. O., N. A.

50. Register of Contracts, Book 7 (1848-1863), MSS., Commissary-General of Subsistence, Office, N. A.; *Handbook of Subsistence Stores* (Washington, 1896).

51. John Davis Billings, *Hardtack and Coffee or the Unwritten Story of Army Life* (Boston, 1888), 110-116, 134-135.

52. Gibson to Twiggs, June 19, 1857, MSS., L.S., Department of Texas, A. C., U. S., N. A.; Mansfield to Thomas, Sept. 27, Oct. 9, 13, Nov. 7, 17, 1860, MSS., L. R., A. G. O., N. A.

53. Dick, 80-81; William B. Morrison, *Military Posts and Camps in Oklahoma* (Oklahoma City, 1936), 95; Freeman, "Report," Appendix V, 6, Appendix W, 11, 14-15, MS., A. G. O., N. A.

54. Pope, "Military Memoir," 52-53, MS., L. R., T. E. B., E., O. C., N. A.

55. Rodney Glisan, *A Journal of Army Life* (San Francisco, 1874), 111-112; "Ancient Santa Fé," 3-4, MS., Bancroft Library; G. O. No. 1, A. G. O., Jan. 8, 1851, No. 3, Feb. 9, 1854, MSS., A. G. O., N. A.

56. *Uniform of the Army of the United States (Illustrated from 1774 to 1907* (New York, 1907), I, 31-45; William Walton, *The Army and the Navy of the United States, 1776-1891* (Philadelphia, 1890), III, Pt. 2, p. 46, V, Pt. 4, p. 66.

57. Freeman, "Report," Appendix W, 9-12, MS., A. G. O., N. A.

58. Bandel, 124-125; Teresa Vielé, *Following the Drum* (New York, 1858), 224-225.

59. Lowe, 45-46; Bandel, 128, 184; St. Louis *Daily Missouri Republican*, Sept. 24, 1856; Mansfield to McDowell, March 5, 1859, MSS., L. R., A. G. O., N. A.

60. Bandel, 102-103; *Senate Reports*, 30 Cong., 2 Sess., No. 295, pp. 1-16; *ibid.*, 31 Cong., 2 Sess., No. 257, pp. 1-7.

61. H. L. Scott, *Military Dictionary* (New York, 1861), 510-512, 515.

62. For the historical development, character, and effectiveness of the Colt revolver see *Senate Reports*, 30 Cong., 2 Sess., No. 295, pp. 1-16; *ibid.*, 31 Cong., 2 Sess., No. 257, pp. 1-7; Walter Prescott Webb, *The Great Plains* (Boston, 1931), 167-179; *Armsmear: The Home, the Arm, and the Armory of Samuel Colt* (Henry Barnard, ed., New York, 1866), 159-200.

63. Charles B. Norton, *American Inventions and Improvements in Breech-loading Small Arms* (Boston, 1882), 165-166; *Senate Executive Documents*, 36 Cong. (erroneously numbered 35 Cong), Spec. Sess., No. 2, pp. 1-2.

64. *House Executive Documents*, 33 Cong., 2 Sess., No. 1, Pt. 2, pp. 351-352; *ibid.*, 34 Cong., 3 Sess., No. 1, Pt. 2, p. 2.

65. Between 1861 and 1866, however, the government purchased no less than nineteen different systems of breech loaders. Norton, 14.

66. Emory to Assistant Adjutant General, Feb. 8, 1858, MSS., L. R., Department of the West, A. C., U. S., N. A.

67. St. Louis *Daily Missouri Republican*, Oct. 4, 1859; Eaton, "Frontier Life in Southern Arizona, 1858-1861," *Southwestern Historical Quarterly*, XXXVI, 191.

68. Dick, 73; George A. Forsyth, *The Story of the Soldier* (New York, 1900), 86; *Senate Executive Documents*, 31 Cong., 2 Sess., I, No. 1, Pt. 2, p. 144.

69. Cooke, *Scenes and Adventures in the Army*, 201-224; Murray, "Narrative," 23-24, MS., Bancroft Library.

70. Gibson, 270; Vielé, 221; Foreman, *Advancing the Frontier*, 61.

71. St. Louis *Daily Missouri Republican*, May 27, June 6, 1850, Sept. 15, 16, 17, 22, 24, 1851, Jan. 26, 1854, Jan. 18, 1855; Bonneville to Thomas, Oct. 27, 1858, MSS., L. R., A. G. O., N. A.

72. *Senate Executive Documents*, 34 Cong., 1 Sess., No. 96, pp. 54, 415; *ibid.*, 36 Cong., 1 Sess., No. 52, pp. 186, 235-236, 264, 287, 309.

73. *Ibid.*, 34 Cong., 1 Sess., No. 96, pp. 52-54, 353, 452; *ibid.*, 36 Cong., 1 Sess., No. 52, pp. 187, 214, 215, 218, 224.

74. *Ibid.*, 34 Cong., 1 Sess., No. 96, pp. 52-54, 58, 60, 438.

75. *Ibid.*, 74-75; *ibid.*, 36 Cong., 1 Sess., No. 52, pp. 39-40, 98, 216, 298; Edwards to Lawson, Feb. 2, 1849, MSS., L. R., S. G. O., N. A.

76. St. Louis *Daily Missouri Republican*, Jan. 10, 23, 24, April 13, May 13, 26, June 10, 1849, June 16, 25, 1851, Sept. 9, 1855; *Senate Executive Documents*, 36 Cong., 1 Sess., No 52, p. 183.

77. *Ibid.*, 34 Cong., 1 Sess., No. 96, p. 160.

78. *Ibid.*, 415; Edwards to Lawson, Feb. 2, 1849, Bill to Lawson, Feb. 1, 1860, MSS., L. R., S. G. O., N. A.

79. *Senate Executive Documents*, 36 Cong., 1 Sess., No. 52, p. 284.

80. *Ibid.*, 272, 297, 298; Abadie to Nichols, Dec. 9, 1855, MSS., L. R., S. G. O., N. A.; Morris to Lawson, Feb. 9, 1860 (Enclosure: Fort Ridgely), MSS., L. R., Q. G. O., N. A.

81. Scott to Cooper, Oct. 3, 1859 (Enclosure: Johnston to Assistant Adjutant General, Aug. 27, 1859), Mansfield to Thomas, Oct. 31, 1860, MSS., L. R., A. G. O., N. A.

82. Deyerle to Hitchcock, April 20, 1852, Alexander to Lawson, Jan. 16, 1857, Engle to Lawson, Jan. 2, 1859, MSS., L. R., S. G. O., N. A.

83. *House Executive Documents*, 32 Cong., 2 Sess., I, No. 1, Pt. 2, p. 136; Heiskell to Edwards, Feb. 25, 1850, MSS., L. S., S. G. O., N. A.; DeLeon to Lawson, June 15, Aug. 28, 1856, MSS., L. R., S. G. O., N. A.

84. *House Executive Documents*, 31 Cong., 2 Sess., I, No. 1, Pt. 2, p. 134; *Senate Executive Documents*, 35 Cong., 2 Sess., II, No. 1, Pt. 2, p. 806; Lowe, 42.

85. *Ibid.*, 42; Ford, "Memoirs," IV, 663.

86. In 1858 no less than six military posts in a single department were without a medical officer. *House Executive Documents*, 35 Cong., 2 Sess., II, No. 2, Pt. 2, p. 762; *Statutes at Large*, XI, 151; Lawson to Davis [n. d.] 1856, MSS., L. S., S. G. O., N. A.

87. When a medical officer was not assigned to a military post the commanding officer generally hired a private physician. During this period some thirty civilian doctors supplemented the work of the army surgeons. *House Executive Documents*, 32 Cong., 2 Sess., I, No. 1, Pt. 2, p. 138; *Senate Executive Documents*, 34 Cong., 1 Sess., II, No. 1, Pt. 2, pp. 174-175; Heiskell to McCalla, Sept. 11, 1848, MSS., L. S., S. G. O., N. A.

88. For the mortality rates at the various military posts see *Senate Executive Documents*, 36 Cong., 1 Sess., No. 52, p. 325.

89. *Statutes at Large*, XI, 151; St. Louis *Daily Missouri Republican*, Jan. 18, 1855; Lee to Jesup, Jan. 29, 1853 (Enclosures: Forts Snelling, Ripley, and Ridgely), MSS., L. R., Q. G. O., N. A.

90. For the pay schedule of commissioned officers of the United States army, 1783-1873, see *House Reports*, 33 Cong., 2 Sess., No. 40, p. 42; St. Louis *Daily Missouri Republican*, Jan. 13, 1857; T. M. Exley, *A Compendium of the Pay of the Army from 1785 to 1888* (Washington, 1888).

91. New York *Evening Post*, in St. Louis *Daily Missouri Republican*, Jan. 27, 1857.

92. *Statutes at Large*, XI, 163.

93. Bandel, 105, 122; *House Executive Documents*, 31 Cong., 2 Sess., I, No. 1, Pt. 2, p. 333; Mansfield to McDowell, March 5, 21, 1859, MSS., L. R., A. G. O., N. A.

94. For the character and importance of the sutler or military storekeeper at the frontier posts, see Dick, 81-82; McConnell, 208.

95. Johnston, 169-179; Arrie Barrett, "Federal Military Outposts in Texas, 1846-1861," MS., M. A. thesis, University of Texas, 1927, pp. 50-53.

96. *Senate Executive Documents*, 34 Cong., 3 Sess., II, No. 5, p. 7.

97. New York *Daily Times* in St. Louis *Daily Missouri Republican*, July 21, 1854.

98. *Congressional Globe*, 32 Cong., 2 Sess., XXVI, 795; *ibid.*, 33 Cong., 1 Sess., XXVIII, Pt. 1, p. 695.

99. *Statutes at Large*, X, 575; Exley, 40-51.

100. Enlisted men employed as laborers and teamsters at posts east of the Rocky Mountains were allowed extra pay of twenty-five cents per day; as mechanics, forty cents; west of the Rocky Mountains the corresponding rates were thirty-five and fifty cents, respectively. The additional payment was a substitute for the extra "gill of whiskey or spirits" which had been allowed the men on fatigue duty by the law of March 2, 1819. G. O. No. 16, A. G. O., Sept. 13, 1854, MSS., A. G. O., N. A.; New Orleans *Daily Picayune*, Aug. 24, 1854.

101. Lowe, 49, 124; L. B. Bloom (ed.), "Bourke on the Southwest," *New Mexico Historical Review*, IX (Jan. 1934), 41; Santa Fe *Weekly Gazette*, Jan. 30, 1858.

102. Beall, Orders No. 5, April 14, 1849, MSS., L. R., Ninth Military Department, A. C., U. S., N. A.; Connelley, *Doniphan's Expedition and the Conquest of New Mexico and California* (Topeka, 1907), 90-92; St. Louis *Daily Missouri Republican*, Oct. 15, 1848; "Life of Jesse Sumpter, the Oldest Citizen of Eagle Pass, Texas," 26-27, MS., Archives, University of Texas.

103. G. O. No. 7, A. G. O., April 11, 1859, MSS., A. G. O., N. A.; McKay, 23.

104. Olmsted, 286; Harris Newmark, *Sixty Years in Southern California, 1853-1913* (New York, 1916), 157.

105. St. Louis *Weekly Reveille*, Dec. 21, 1846; Richard S. Elliott, *Notes Taken in Sixty Years* (St. Louis, 1883), 250; Lowe, 97.

106. St. Louis *Daily Missouri Republican*, Dec. 13, 1858.

107. *Senate Executive Documents*, 36 Cong., 1 Sess., No. 52, pp. 32, 188, 240, 300, 307.

108. Glisan, 82, 456-457.

109. Lowe, 24, 124.

110. *Laws of the Territory of New Mexico, 1860*, p. 66.

111. St. Louis *Daily Missouri Republican*, July 11, 1848; Beall, Special Order No. 5, April 27, 1849, MSS., L. R., Ninth Military Department, A. C., U. S., N. A.

112. Bandel, 265; Kearny, "Journal," July 4, 1825, MSS., M. H. S.; G. O. No. 9, A. G. O., June 23, 1857, No. 7, April 11, 1859, MSS., A. G. O., N. A.

113. St. Louis *Daily Missouri Republican*, Feb. 2, 1848; Fort Smith *Herald*, Jan. 26, 1850.

114. St. Louis *Daily Missouri Republican*, March 26, 1853; *Laws of the Territory of New Mexico, 1853*, p. 97.

115. *Senate Executive Documents*, 34 Cong., 3 Sess., II, No. 5, p. 3; *House Executive Documents*, 35 Cong., 1 Sess., No. 2, Pt. 2, p. 58.

116. *Ibid.*, 31 Cong., 1 Sess., III, No. 5, Pt. 1, p. 90; Dimmick, "Diary," May 28, June 11, 17, 26, 1848, MSS., California File, Huntington Library.

117. McDougal to Fillmore, March 1, 1851, MSS., L. R., S. W., N. A.

118. Hitchcock's Proclamation, July 9, 1851, Orders, Pacific Division, MSS., A. G. O., N. A.

119. Van Vliet to Jesup, July 23, 1850 (Enclosure: Fort Laramie), MSS., L. R., Q. G. O., N. A.

120. Glisan, 105-106; St. Louis *Daily Missouri Republican*, Feb. 19, 1853, May 15, Aug. 27, Sept. 3, 1858.

121. *Senate Executive Documents*, 34 Cong., 3 Sess., III (erroneously numbered II), No. 5, p. 7; Mansfield to Thomas, Dec. 6, 1860, MSS., L. R., A. G. O., N. A.

122. Froebel, 323.

123. Dick, 86-87; Foreman, *Advancing the Frontier*, 61, 67-68; Orders No. 8, 10, Ninth Military Department, Jan. 11, 25, 1852, MSS., L. S., Department of New Mexico, Book 5, A. C., U. S., N. A.

124. Vielé, 222; Domenech, *Missionary Adventures in Texas and Mexico*, 69.

125. Vielé, 117.

126. "Bucking" was abolished in 1853. G. O. No. 3, A. G. O., Jan. 27, 1853, MSS., A. G. O., N. A.; Edward S. Farrow, *A Dictionary of Military Terms* (New York, 1918), 91; San Francisco *Daily Alta California*, Feb. 2, 1851, March 31, 1852.

127. By an act approved August 5, 1861, flogging was abolished in the army. *Statutes at Large*, XII, 317.

128. St. Louis *Daily Union*, May 27, 1850; Clinton E. Brooks and Frank D. Reeve (eds.) "James A. Bennett: a Dragoon in New Mexico, 1850-1856," *New Mexico Historical Review*, XXII (Jan., 1947), 55, 88; Orders No. 43, Ninth Military Department, Dec. 2, 1851, No. 8, Jan. 11, 1852, MSS., L. S., Department of New Mexico, Book 5, A. C., U. S., N. A.

VIII

1. It is interesting to note that the almost extinct buffalo—less than 1,000 head half a century ago—has now increased to more than 20,000 in our national parks and on the open range. Rister, *Border Captives: the Traffic in Prisoners by Southern Plains Indians, 1835-1875* (Norman, 1940), 36; Clarksville (Tex.) *Standard*, May 28, 1853; St. Louis *Post-Dispatch*, Sept. 14, 1934; Howard to Lea, June 1, 1852, MSS., L. R., I. A. O., Texas, N. A.

2. St. Louis *Daily Missouri Republican*, Dec. 17, 1852; Austin *Texas State Gazette*, Feb. 26, 1853.

3. Houston *Democratic Telegraph and Texas Register*, Dec. 10, 1845.

4. Austin *Southern Intelligencer*, Jan. 26, 1859.

5. *House Executive Documents*, 30 Cong., 1 Sess., No. 8, pp. 751-752, 892-906.

6. Rupert N. Richardson, *The Comanche Barrier to South Plains Settlement: a Century and a Half of Savage Resistance to the Advancing White Frontier* (Glendale, 1933), 146-158; Henderson to Butler, Lewis, and Smith, May 5, 1846, MSS., Governors' Letters; Neighbors to Medill, Nov. 18, 1847, Oct. 23, 1848, MSS., L. R., I. A. O., N. A.

7. Austin *Texas Democrat*, April 22, 1848; Henderson to Secretary of War, Aug. 7, 1848, MSS., Governors' Letters; Jones to Taylor, June 26, 1848, MSS., L. R., I. A. O., Texas, N. A.

8. Fort Smith *Herald*, Nov. 22, 1848; Tahlequah (Okla.) *Cherokee Advocate*, Dec. 4, 1848; St. Louis *Daily Missouri Republican*, Oct. 25, Nov. 2, 1848.

9. Houston *Democratic Telegraph and Texas Register*, Feb. 17, Dec. 14, 1848.

10. Corpus Christi *Star*, Oct. 3, 1848.

11. *Ibid.*, Nov. 14, Dec. 5, 16, 1848; St. Louis *Daily Missouri Republican*, Nov. 16, 18, 1848; *House Executive Documents*, 30 Cong., 2 Sess., I, No. 1, pp. 163-165.

12. Victoria *Texian Advocate*, Oct. 19, Nov. 9, 1848.

13. Harmon, "The United States Indian Policy in Texas, 1845-1860," *Mississippi Valley Historical Review*, XVII (Dec., 1930), 382-383.

14. Rister, *Border Captives,* 104-106; Domenech, *Missionary Adventures in Texas and Mexico,* 118.

15. In January, 1855, Senator Houston declared in the United States Senate that no less than 2,000 persons were held captive by the Comanches. White captives were especially prized, since they were more marketable than the darker-skinned Mexicans. Their treatment, however, was most cruel and inhumane. The ransom of white captives ranged from $100 to $2,000. Mexican slaves were usually sold for tobacco, knives, blankets, corn, cotton goods, etc. Attempts of the government to halt the Comanche captive traffic by treaty proved vain. *Congressional Globe,* 33 Cong., 2 Sess., XXX, 501; *Senate Executive Documents,* 31 Cong., 1 Sess., II, No. 1, Pt. 2, pp. 136-137; Rister, *Border Captives,* pp. vii-ix, 65-102, 112-113.

16. Clarksville (Tex.) *Northern Standard*, July 21, 1849; St. Louis *Daily Missouri Republican*, June 3, 10, 1849; *House Reports*, 31 Cong., 1 Sess., Report 280, pp. 2-3; Governors' Message, Nov. 30, 1849, MSS., Governors' Letters.

17. *House Executive Documents*, 31 Cong., 1 Sess., No. 5, Pt. 1, pp. 140, 142, 151; Clarksville (Tex.) *Northern Standard*, July 14, 21, 1849; St. Louis *Daily Missouri Republican*, Oct. 29, 1849; Brooke to Jones, Sept. 6, Nov. 29, 1849, MSS., L. R., H. A., N. A.

18. Corpus Christi *Star*, Aug. 25, 1849; Department Returns, Eighth Military Department, Dec., 1849, MSS., A. G. O., N. A.

19. Domenech, *Missionary Adventures in Texas and Mexico,* 176.

20. Austin *Texas State Gazette*, May 25, July 20, 1850.

21. Catlett to Bell, May 3, 1851, MSS., Governors' Letters.

22. Washington (Ark.) *Telegraph*, Nov. 20, 1850, March 12, 1851; Rollins to Bell, Oct. 30, 1850, Brooke to Bell, Nov. 12, 1850, MSS., Governors' Letters.

23. Fort Smith *Herald*, Oct. 4, 11, Nov. 8, 1850.

24. Austin *Texas State Gazette*, May 18, 1850; New Orleans *Daily Picayune*, May 18, 1850; St. Louis *Daily Missouri Republican*, July 7, 25, Sept. 3, 15, 1850.

25. Houston *Democratic Telegraph and Texas Register*, May 23, June 13, Aug. 7, 1850; St. Louis *Daily Missouri Republican*, July 15, Sept. 15, 1850; *House Executive Documents*, 31 Cong., 2 Sess., I, No. 1, Pt. 2, pp. 23-52, 56-62, 66-67, 124.

26. *Senate Bills and Resolutions*, 30 Congress, 2 Sess., Senate Bill 239; Holden, "Frontier Defense, 1846-1860," *West Texas Historical Association Year Book* (Abilene, Tex., 1930), VI, 45-46.

27. St. Louis *Daily Missouri Republican*, Oct. 25, 1850; Catlett to Hayney, Sept. 14, 1850, MSS., Governors' Letters.

28. *Statutes at Large*, IX, 556, 559; Lea to Rogers, Rollins, and Stem, Nov. 2, 5, 1850, MSS., L. S., I. A. O., N. A.; Clayton to Bell, Feb. 26, 1851, MSS., Governors' Letters.

29. Lea to Rogers, Rollins, and Stem, Nov. 25, 1850, MSS., L. S., I. A. O., N. A.

30. Barnards' establishment was an Indian trading post on the Brazos River, a few miles north of Waco in the present Hood County, Texas. It was under the control of George and Charles E. Barnard and David and John Torrey. Friendly Indians came here to trade animals, buffalo robes, deerskins, and such skins as they manufactured for provisions, clothing, and cutlery. Richardson, *Texas, the Lone Star State* (New York, 1943), 198; Ford, "Memoirs," III, 504.

31. *House Executive Documents*, 31 Cong., 2 Sess., I, No. 1, Pt. 1, pp. 143-145; Rollins to Commissioner of Indian Affairs, Sept. 30, 1850, MSS., L. R., I. A. O., Texas, N. A.

32. Rogers to Lea, Nov. 16, 1850, MSS., L. R., I. A. O., Texas, N. A.

33. The Spring Creek Indian council was probably the best attended and most satisfactory Indian gathering ever held in Texas. Rollins, who suffered from tuberculosis, was

carried to the field for the purpose of signing the treaty, but he was a mere figurehead; Major Neighbors and Dr. John S. Ford, special agents for the Texas tribes, carried on most of Rollins' Indian business. Houston, V, 345.

34. Richardson, *The Comanche Barrier to South Plains Settlement*, 162; Texas Indian Treaty, Dec. 10, 1850, MSS., L. R., I. A. O., N. A.

35. St. Louis *Daily Missouri Republican*, Jan. 18, May 24, July 2, 1851; Fort Smith *Herald*, March 21, 1851; *House Executive Documents*, 32 Cong., 1 Sess., No. 2, Pt. 1, pp. 118-124; Orders No. 31, Headquarters, Eighth Military Department, April 20, 1851, MSS., Governors' Letters.

36. Richardson, *The Comanche Barrier to South Plains Settlement*, 163; Rogers to Lea, Nov. 25, 1851, MSS., L. R., I. A. O., Texas, N. A.

37. Oliver P. Temple, C. S. Todd, and Robert B. Campbell had been appointed by the Department of the Interior to procure information, collect statistics, and make treaties with the tribes on the borders of Mexico. Loughery to Todd, Campbell, and Temple, Oct. 15, 1850, MSS., L. S., I. A. O., N. A.

38. Austin *Texas State Gazette*, June 21, 1851.

39. See above, p. 35.

40. Ford, "Memoirs," III, 596.

41. St. Louis *Daily Missouri Republican*, Oct. 5, 1851, Feb. 24, 1852; *House Executive Documents*, 32 Cong., 2 Sess., No. 1, Pt. 2, p. 80; Holden, "Frontier Defense, 1846-1860," *West Texas Historical Association Year Book*, VI, 47; Capron to Lea, May 24, 1852, MSS., L. R., I. A. O., Texas, N. A.

42. Austin *Texas State Gazette*, Jan. 22, 1853; *House Executive Documents*, 32 Cong., 2 Sess., No. 1, Pt. 2, pp. 17-20; Memorial to Bell, Aug. 5, 1852, Stem to Bell, Feb. 20, 1852, Parker to Bell, May 16, 1852, Smith to Bell, Aug. 9, 1852, MSS., Governors' Letters.

43. The six new posts comprised Camp Johnston, Forts Chadbourne, McKavett, Clark, Terrett, and Ewell. *House Executive Documents,* 32 Cong., 2 Sess., No. 1, Pt. 2, p. 58; *ibid.,* 33 Cong., 1 Sess., No. 1, p. 118.

44. For Fitzpatrick's career and influence among the tribes, see Hafen and W. J. Ghent, *Broken Hand. The Story of Thomas Fitzpatrick, Chief of the Mountain Men* (Denver, 1931), 128-265.

45. The signers included Shaved Head (principal chief of the Comanches), White Eagle, Ten Bears, "One Who Rides the Clouds," Little Mountain, and Satanta. *Statutes at Large*, X, 165-169; Richardson, *The Comanche Barrier to South Plains Settlement*, 184-185.

46. *Ibid.*, 190; Foreman, *A History of Oklahoma*, 83.

47. New Orleans *Daily Picayune*, March 11, 1854; Merrill to Neighbors, March 30, 1854, MSS., Governors' Letters.

48. New Orleans *Daily Picayune*, March 20, 30, July 19, Sept. 13, Oct. 12, 1854; Washington (Tex.) *Texas Ranger*, June 8, 1854; St. Louis *Daily Missouri Republican*, Jan. 19, 1855; Neighbors to Manypenny, May 8, 1854, MSS., L. R., I. A. O., Texas, N. A.

49. New Orleans *Daily Picayune*, July 17, 1854.

50. *Ibid.*, May 25, 1854; Austin *State Gazette*, Aug. 19, 1854; *House Executive Documents*, 33 Cong., 2 Sess., I, No. 1, Pt. 2, pp. 28-30.

51. St. Louis *Daily Missouri Republican*, Sept. 15, 1855; San Antonio *Texan*, Feb. 8, 1855; Austin *Texas State Gazette*, Sept. 8, 15, 22, 29, 1855; New Orleans *Daily Picayune*, Feb. 17, 1855.

52. Petitions to Pease, Sept. 1, 15, Oct., 1855, Indian Affairs, 1846-1860, MSS., Archives, Texas State Library.

53. New Orleans *Daily Picayune*, June 2, July 1, 1854.

54. *Ibid.*, July 19, 1854; San Antonio *Ledger*, Oct. 13, 1855.

55. St. Louis *Daily Missouri Republican*, March 9, 1856; Foreman, *A History of Oklahoma*, 85-86.

56. *Senate Executive Documents*, 34 Cong., 3 Sess., No. 5, Pt. 1, p. 725; Austin *Texas State Gazette*, March 8, 1856.

57. New Orleans *Daily Picayune*, June 22, 1856.

58. *House Executive Documents*, 35 Cong., 1 Sess., No. 2, Pt. 2, pp. 51-55; Austin *State Gazette*, May 31, Dec. 20, 1856.

59. Tarver to Pease, June 22, 1857, MSS., Governors' Letters.

60. St. Louis *Daily Missouri Republican*, Aug. 28, Nov. 22, 1857; Twiggs to Thomas, Aug. 9, 1857, MSS., L. R., A. G. O., N. A.

61. New Orleans *Daily Picayune*, July 19, 1854.

62. *Ibid.,* Dec. 12, 1855.

63. Austin *State Gazette,* Nov. 14, 1857; San Antonio *Ledger,* July 21, 1855.

64. Petitions to Pease, March 13, April 14, 15, 20, 29, May 8, 24, 1854, Pease to Smith, Aug. 8, 1854, MSS., Governors' Letters; New Orleans *Daily Picayune,* Aug. 12, 1854.

65. Austin *Texas State Gazette,* July 11, Nov. 10, 1855; Pease to Callahan, July 5, 1855, Pease to Smith, Sept. 5, 1855, MSS., Governors' Letters.

66. Instructions: Pease to Carmack, Conner, Robison, and Lieutenants, Nov. 23, 1857, MSS., Governors' Letters.

67. Austin *Texas State Gazette,* April 15, 1854; New Orleans *Daily Picayune,* Feb. 24, 1855.

68. Committees from "W. L. Guards," "Milam Rifles," "Galveston Artillery," "Richmond Company" to Pease, April 9, 1857, MSS., Governors' Letters.

69. San Antonio *Texan,* Jan. 28, 1858; Carmack to Governor, Jan. 7, 11, 1858, Frost to Governor, Jan. 8, 1858, MSS., Governors' Letters.

70. These were Erath, Bosque, Palo Pinto, and Comanche counties. *House Executive Documents,* 35 Cong., 2 Sess., No. 27, pp. 3-4.

71. McKisick to Pulliam, April 15, 1858, MSS., L. R., I. A. O., N. A.

72. Austin *State Gazette,* Jan. 30, 1858; Runnels to Ford, Jan. 28, 1858, MSS., Governors' Letters.

73. *House Executive Documents,* 35 Cong., 2 Sess., No. 27, pp. 17-20; Ford to Runnels, May 22, 1858, MSS., Governors' Letters.

74. Hazen to Dye, June 22, 1858, MSS., L. R., H. A., N. A.

75. Austin *State Gazette,* Sept. 25, 1858.

76. Runnels to Floyd, Aug. 9, 1858, Runnels to Buchanan, Sept. 17, 1858, MSS., Governors' Letters.

77. Neighbors to Runnels, Sept. 8, 1858, MSS., Governors' Letters.

78. Special Orders No. 71, Headquarters, Department of Texas, Aug. 9, 1858, Orders and Special Orders, Department of Texas, Book 519, MSS., A. G. O., N. A.

79. *House Executive Documents,* 35 Cong., 2 Sess., No. 27, pp. 48-52; Nye, 23-30.

80. Quoted in Richardson, *The Comanche Barrier to South Plains Settlement,* 239.

81. George Frederic Price, *Across the Continent with the Fifth Cavalry* (New York, 1883), 70.

82. *Senate Executive Documents,* 36 Cong., 1 Sess., No. 2, Pt. 2, pp. 358, 360, 378; Austin *State Gazette,* March 26, 1859; Blain to Rector, March 3, Aug. 15, 1859, MSS., L. R., I. A. O., N. A.; Pendarvis to Runnels, April 9, 1859, MSS., Governors' Letters.

83. Austin *State Gazette,* March 26, 1859.

84. *Senate Executive Documents,* 36 Cong., 1 Sess., II, No. 2, pp. 368-370; Joseph B. Thoburn, "Indian Fight in Ford County, 1859," Kansas State Historical Society, *Collections,* XII, 316-321.

85. Hazen to Maclay, May 23, 1859, MSS., L. R., A. G. O., N. A.

86. Austin *State Gazette,* April 30, 1859.

87. San Francisco *Daily Alta California,* March 2, 1859; Santa Fe *Gazette,* July 30, 1859; Austin *State Gazette,* Oct. 22, 1859; Jones to Runnels, Sept. 3, 1859, MSS., Governors' Letters.

88. *House Miscellaneous Documents,* 36 Cong., 1 Sess., No. 38, p. 2; Dallas *Herald,* Feb. 22, April 11, 1860; Austin *State Gazette,* Feb. 25, 1860.

89. Houston, VII, 480-484.

90. Johnson, I, 519; *House Executive Documents,* 36 Cong., I Sess., No. 81, p. 105; Houston, VII, 480-482, 511- 512, 536-537.

91. *Ibid.,* VIII, 16; Houston to Burleson, April 21, 23, 1860, MSS., Burleson, "Letters," Archives, University of Texas; Johnson to Conner, April 23, 1860, MSS., Governors' Letters.

92. Houston to chief justices, June 23, 25, July 10, 16, 1860, Houston to state military officers, June 25, Aug. 6, 21, Sept. 12, 13, 29, Oct. 10, 1860, Executive Record Book, 1859-1861, MSS., Archives, Texas State Library.

93. Scott to Sumner, Lee, and Fauntleroy, March 10, 1860, MSS., L. S., H. A., N. A.

94. Townsend to Fauntleroy, June 18, 1860, MSS., L. R., H. A., N. A.

95. San Francisco *Herald,* Sept. 24, 1860; Houston, VIII, 221-222.

96. Dallas *Herald,* Dec. 19, 1860; *House Miscellaneous Documents,* 36 Cong., 1 Sess., No. 38, pp. 6-7; McKee, Cochran, Hood, and Norton to Houston, Dec. 15, 16, 18, 1860, MSS., Governors' Letters.

97. Smith to Houston, Jan. 14, 1860, MSS., Governors' Letters.

98. Rister, *Border Captives*, 37; St. Louis *Daily Missouri Republican*, Feb. 4, July 12, Nov. 2, 1848, June 10, 1849, Jan. 12, 1850; Houston, VIII, 116.

99. The "Mustangers" consisted of a large body of well-armed runaway vagabonds, outlaws, and other adventurers of many nations. Operating between the Nueces and the Rio Grande, they organized ostensibly for the purpose of catching "mustangs" or wild horses; in reality, they often engaged in robbery and plunder, murdering travelers and making descents upon wagon trains and border settlements. Olmsted, 443-444; J. Frank Dobie, Mody C. Boatright, and Harry H. Ransom (eds.,), *Mustangs and Cow Horses* (Austin, 1940), 5-11; Humphreys to Deas, Dec. 1, 1849, Crawford to Pease, March 2, 1854, MSS., Governors' Letters; Smith to Davis, Dec. 22, 1853, Jefferson Davis, "Correspondence," MSS., L. C.

100. In 1849 the state of Chihuahua hired American mercenaries to kill dangerous Indians, paying $50 to $500 per scalp. When these hunters of Indian scalps crossed into Texas and plied their unsavory trade, killing peaceable and friendly tribesmen, the Indians along the whole frontier were roused to fury. St. Louis *Daily Missouri Republican*, Aug. 12, 25, Oct. 29, 1849; New Orleans *Daily Picayune*, Oct. 31, 1849; Crawford to Clayton, Nov. 8, 1849, MSS., L. S., S. W., N. A.

101. Between 1848 and 1853 American merchants in Texas, resenting the severe tariff policy of the Mexican government, resorted to smuggling on a grand scale, invaded Mexico, and assisted with arms and money filibustering expeditions led by such self-appointed Mexican liberators as José Maria Jesus Carabajal. The Merchants' War, however, only boomeranged against the Texas traders. J. Fred Rippy, "Border Troubles along the Rio Grande, 1848-1860," *Southwestern Historical Quarterly*, XXIII (Oct., 1919), 94-97; Domenech, *Missionary Adventurers in Texas and Mexico*, 327-328; St. Louis *Daily Missouri Republican*, Nov. 24, 29, 1851, April 15, 30, 1853; Ford, "Memoirs," IV, 629-638.

102. In 1855, belligerent Texans, in an attempt to recover runaway slaves, organized a foray into Mexico under the leadership of James H. Callahan, a prominent slave owner and noted Indian fighter. But Callahan and his army of more than 500 men suffered defeat. Forced to retreat, the filibusterers fell back on Piedras Negras, which they pillaged and burned. The Texans barely managed to return safely to United States soil. The Callahan expedition proved a fiasco. Its leader was later assassinated. Rippy, "Border Troubles along the Rio Grande, 1848-1860," *Southwestern Historical Quarterly*, XXIII, 101; Dobie, *A Vaquero of the Brush Country* (Dallas, 1929), 48; John Henry Brown, *History of Texas* (St. Louis, 1893), II, 370-371; New Orleans *Daily Picayune*, Oct. 24, Nov. 4, 11, Dec. 12, 1855; "Life of Jesse Sumpter, the Oldest Citizen of Eagle Pass, Texas," 31, MS., Archives, University of Texas; Pease to Callahan, Oct. 10, 1855, Pease to Smith, Oct. 13, 1855, MSS., Governors' Letters.

103. The Cart War began in 1855 when a secret organization of Texan teamsters instituted a veritable reign of terror among competing Mexican cartmen. Attacks on cartmen soon gave way to wholesale and bold robberies, including attacks on United States supply trains. Mounted Rangers and lynch law put an end to the disorders. Rippy, "Border Troubles along the Rio Grande, 1848-1860," *Southwestern Historical Quarterly*, XXIII, 103-104; New Orleans *Daily Picayune*, Oct. 4, 1857; Corpus Christi *Nueces Valley*, Oct. 24, Nov. 14, 1857, Jan. 5, 1858; Special Orders, No. 122, Headquarters, Department of Texas, Sept. 19, 1857, MSS., Governors' Letters.

104. In 1859 the cunning, picturesque Mexican bandit Juan Eponucena or Nepomuceno Cortinas, "The Red Robber of the Rio Grande," like his prototype Carabajal half a dozen years earlier, set himself up as a champion of his downtrodden countrymen in Texas, and proceeded to redress grievances. The pseudo-patriot, after terrorizing the American settlers in Brownsville, set up his headquarters nearby and entered on a grand career of banditry. He stopped and cut open the mail; he plundered ranches; and for several months he kept the lower Rio Grande country in a state of alarm and terror. Late in December Major Samuel P. Heintzelman with a large force of regulars and Texas volunteers decisively defeated the bandit, and in the following spring a large force of Mexican soldiers defeated the main body of the outlaws near Tamaulipas. Cortinas escaped to the Burgos Mountains. The Cortinas War was over. This episode cost Texas and its citizens nearly half a million dollars. Rippy, "Border Troubles along the Rio Grande, 1848-1860," *Southwestern Historical Quarterly*, XXIII, 104-111; Walter Prescott Webb, *The Texas Rangers* (Boston, 1935), 175-192; Houston, VII, 392-394; *House Executive Documents*, 36 Cong., 1 Sess., No. 52, pp. 33-43; *ibid.*, 36 Cong., 1 Sess., No. 81, pp. 75-77, 83-85, 100-104; *Senate Executive Documents*, 36 Cong., 2 Sess., No. 1, Pt. 2, pp. 194-195; Texas, *Senate Journal*, 8

Session [Extra], 15; Austin *State Gazette*, Nov. 12, Dec. 31, 1859, Jan. 27, 1860; Champion to Fenn, Dec. 16, 1859, Report of the Grand Jury on the Disturbances of the Country, Brownsville, Dec. 27, 1859, MSS., Governors' Letters; Cortinas to Stillman, Oct. 26, 1859, Heintzelman, "Papers," MSS., L. C.

105. Holden, "Frontier Defense, 1846-1860," *West Texas Historical Association Year Book*, VI, 63; *Senate Executive Documents*, 36 Congress, 2 Sess., II, No. 1, pp. 189, 213, 220-221; Austin *Texas State Gazette*, April 14, 1855.

IX

1. See Bender, "Frontier Defense in the Territory of New Mexico, 1846-1853," *New Mexico Historical Review*, IX (July, 1934), 251-252; St. Louis *Daily Missouri Republican*, July 11, 19, 26, Aug. 3, 19, 1848.

2. *Ibid.*, April 17, Oct. 31, Nov. 19, 23, Dec. 19, 1848.

3. *House Executive Documents*, 30 Cong., 2 Sess., No. 1, pp. 19-20.

4. Ewing to Medill, March 29, April 5, 7, 1849, Medill to Calhoun, April 7, 1849, MSS., L. S., I. A. O., N. A.

5. Calhoun, pp. xi-xiii.

6. *Ibid.*, 17-19.

7. St. Louis *Daily Missouri Republican*, March 29, May 17, July 2, 1849; Beall to Dickerson, Jan. 16, March 11, 19, 1849, Whittlesey to Beall, March 15, 1849, MSS., L. R., H. A., N. A.

8. *Senate Executive Documents*, 31 Cong., 1 Sess., No. 64, pp. 56-139; *Statutes at Large*, IX, 974-975.

9. St. Louis *Daily Missouri Republican*, Nov. 14, Dec. 18, 19, 1849.

10. *Ibid.*, Sept. 12, Nov. 4, 1849, Feb. 1, March 26, 1850; *House Executive Documents*, 31 Cong., 1 Sess., No. 5, Pt. 1, pp. 108-111; Steen to Dickerson, Sept. 1, 1849, MSS., L. R., T. E. B., E., O. C., N. A.; Steen to Dickerson, Oct. 20, 1849, MSS., Ritch, Collection.

11. *House Executive Documents*, 31 Cong., 1 Sess., III, No. 5, Pt. 2, p. 998; St. Louis *Daily Missouri Republican*, Dec. 18, 20, 1849.

12. *House Executive Documents*, 31 Cong., 1 Sess., III, No. 5, Pt. 2, p. 998.

13. *Ibid.*, 1001; St. Louis *Daily Missouri Republican*, May 17, Aug. 25, Nov. 14, 1849.

14. *Ibid.*, Sept. 29, Dec. 19, 1849; *House Executive Documents*, 31 Cong., 1 Sess., No. 5, Pt. 1, p. 188D.

15. *Statutes at Large*, IX, 984-985.

16. St. Louis *Daily Missouri Republican*, May 20, July 8, Aug. 18, 1850; McCall, 493-494; John Greiner, "Overawing the Indians, 1852," MSS., Ritch, Collection.

17. McCall, 526-527; *Senate Executive Documents*, 35 Cong., 2 Sess., No. 1, Pt. 1, p. 558; "Depositions by Settlers to Governor Calhoun, *re* Stolen Stock, 1847-1851," "Petition to Governor Lane for Indemnities for Stolen Stock, 1852," MSS., Ritch, Collection.

18. Quoted in Santa Fe *Weekly Gazette*, Dec. 20, 1856.

19. *Senate Miscellaneous Documents*, 31 Cong., 1 Sess., No. 70, pp. 4-5.

20. *House Executive Documents*, 31 Cong., 2 Sess., No. 1, Pt. 1, pp. 142-143.

21. *Ibid.*, 293-296; Brown to Calhoun, April 24, 1850, MSS., L. S., Commissioner of Indian Affairs, I. A. O., N. A. (hereafter Commissioner of Indian Affairs will be cited as C. I. A.); Jones to Deas, June 5, 1850, MSS., L. R., T. E. B., O. C., N. A.; Bartlett to Stuart, Feb. 19, 1852, MSS., L. R., S. I., I. A. O., N. A.

22. See above, pp. 37-38.

23. St. Louis *Daily Missouri Republican*, Aug. 9, Oct. 1, 1850, April 25, June 16, 1851; William Hutchinson, "Sketches of Pioneer Kansas Experience," Kansas State Historical Society, *Transactions* (Topeka, 1902), VII, 393.

24. St. Louis *Daily Missouri Republican*, Sept. 1, 13, Oct. 2, 24, 28, 30, Dec. 29, 1851, May 5, 1852; Calhoun, 417.

25. Dunn, 158-184.

26. The other two Indian agents, John Greiner and A. R. Wooley, were stationed at Taos and Anton Chico, respectively. Like Calhoun, Greiner was a capable and honest official, held in high esteem both by Americans and Indians. Between July, 1851, and May, 1853, he served as Indian agent, Acting Superintendent of Indian Affairs, and secretary of the territory. St. Louis *Daily Missouri Republican*, May 19, Nov. 29, Dec. 29, 1851; Bieber, "Letters of William Carr Lane, 1852-1854," *New Mexico Historical Review*, III (April, 1928), 189.

27. Greiner, "Private Letters of a Government Official in the Southwest," *Journal of American History*, III (Oct., 1909), 546.

28. St. Louis *Daily Missouri Republican*, April 28, May 19, 28, 1851; Greiner, "Private Letters of a Government Official in the Southwest," *Journal of American History*, III, 546; Calhoun to Munroe, May 7, 1851; MSS., L. S., Department of New Mexico, Book 7, A. C., U. S., N. A.

29. St. Louis *Daily Missouri Republican*, May 25, Sept. 13, Dec. 7, 1851, Jan. 5, 30, Feb. 28, March 4, April 26, May 3, 1852.

30. *Ibid.*, Sept. 1, 8, Oct. 1, 1851, Jan. 5, 1852; *Senate Executive Documents*, 35 Cong., 2 Sess., No. 1, Pt. 1, p. 541.

31. St. Louis *Daily Missouri Republican*, Aug. 28, 1852; Santa Fe *Weekly Gazette*, Nov. 20, 1852; Greiner, "Talk with Navajo," May 9, 1852, MSS., Ritch, Collection; Lane to Lea, Dec. 31, 1852 (the date on the jacket is 1853), MSS., L. R., I. A. O., New Mexico, N. A.

32. Ogle, "Federal Control of the Western Apaches, 1848-1886," *New Mexico Historical Review*, XIV, 342; Sumner to Jones, Feb. 3, 1852, Sumner to Calhoun, March 21, 1852, MSS., Territorial Papers, New Mexico, State Department, N. A. (State Department will be cited as S. D.)

33. St. Louis *Daily Missouri Republican*, Aug. 28, Sept. 1, 13, Oct. 13, Nov. 6, 13, Dec. 9, 1851, May 5, 30, 1852.

34. Santa Fe *Weekly Gazette*, Feb. 19, 26, March 5, April 9, 1853.

35. In 1943 a Liberty freighter launched at Portland, Oregon, was named in Dr. William Carr Lane's honor. *Ibid.*, Dec. 18, 1852; Bieber, "Letters of William Carr Lane, 1852-1854," *New Mexico Historical Review*, III, 180-182, 197-201; Twitchell, II, 293; see also "In Honor of the First His-Honor," St. Louis *Post-Dispatch*, July 30, 1943; Dr. William Carr Lane, "Papers," MSS., M. H. S.

36. Santa Fe *Weekly Gazette*, Feb. 19, May 21, Dec. 31, 1853; *Senate Executive Documents*, 33 Cong., 1 Sess., No. 1, Pt. 1, p. 432; *ibid.*, 33 Cong., 2 Sess., No. 1, Pt. 1, p. 374; Lane to Manypenny, May 28, 1853, and Treaty, MSS., L. R., I. A. O., New Mexico, N. A.

37. For the previous career of Meriwether, see Twitchell, II, 296-297.

38. Santa Fe *Weekly Gazette*, Feb. 12, 19, April 30, 1853.

39. *Senate Executive Documents*, 33 Cong., 1 Sess., No. 1, Pt. 1, p. 437; Graves to Meriwether, Aug. 31, 1853, MSS., L. R., I. A. O., New Mexico, N. A.

40. St. Louis *Daily Missouri Republican*, Jan. 16, 26, 1854, Jan. 1, 1856.

41. *Ibid.*, Jan. 26, June 28, 1854; *Senate Executive Documents*, 33 Cong., 1 Sess., No. 1, Pt. 1, p. 430.

42. Barclay's Fort was a private trading post located between Fort Union and Santa Fe. It was built during the Mexican War. Judge Davis, who visited the establishment in 1854, described it thus: "It is a large *adobe* establishment. . . . From the outside it presents rather a formidable as well as a neat appearance, being pierced with loopholes and ornamented with battlements." Davis, 51.

43. St. Louis *Daily Missouri Republican*, March 28, April 29, May 1, 27, 1854; *House Executive Documents*, 33 Cong., 2 Sess., I, No. 1, Pt. 2, pp. 33-34.

44. Santa Fe *Weekly Gazette*, April 8, 1854.

45. *House Executive Documents*, 33 Cong., 2 Sess., IV, No. 1, Pt. 2, pp. 33-34, 36; Santa Fe *Weekly Gazette*, June 17, 24, 1854; Garland to Thomas, April 30, June 30, 1854, MSS., L. R., A. G. O., N. A.; James H. Quinn, "Journal of a Spy Company in Expeditions vs. the Indians under Colonel Cooke, Majors Brooke and Carleton, April 4-June 5, 1854," MSS., Ritch, Collection.

46. Santa Fe *Weekly Gazette*, April 22, 1854.

47. Twitchell, II, 126, 137-138, 273; Santa Fe *Weekly Gazette*, July 15, 1854; New Orleans *Daily Picayune*, Oct. 29, 1854; St. Louis *Daily Missouri Republican*, Feb. 2, 1855.

48. *Senate Executive Documents*, 33 Cong., 2 Sess., I, No. 1, Pt. 1, p. 222.

49. *Laws of the Territory of New Mexico, 1854*, pp. 16, 115, 117, 119, 121.

50. Carson to Messervy, March 27, 1854, MSS., L. R., I. A. O., New Mexico, N. A.

51. Santa Fe *Weekly Gazette*, June 17, 1854; New Orleans *Daily Picayune*, Aug. 2, 1854.

52. *House Executive Documents*, 34 Cong., 1 Sess., No. 1, Pt. 1, p. 326.

53. St. Louis *Daily Missouri Republican*, Feb. 24, 1855; Meriwether to Manypenny, Jan. 31, 1855, Carson to Meriwether, March 1, 1855, MSS., L. R., I. A. O., New Mexico, N. A.

54. *House Executive Documents*, 34 Cong., 1 Sess., No. 1, Pt. 2, pp. 56-57, 62, 69-70; Santa Fe *Weekly Gazette*, March 10, April 28, 1855; St. Louis *Daily Missouri Republican*,

March 28, April 27, 1855; "Minutes of a 'talk' held at Dog Cañon between Colonel Miles.
. . and several chiefs of the Mescalero Apache, April 3, 1855," MSS., L. R., I. A. O., New
Mexico, N. A.

55. Santa Fe *Weekly Gazette*, Sept. 1, 1855, Jan. 26, 1856; Meriwether to Manypenny,
May 1, 1856 (Enclosure: Resolutions, New Mexico Legislature), MSS., L. R., I. A. O., New
Mexico, N. A.

56. *House Executive Documents*, 34 Cong., 1 Sess., No. 1, Pt. 1, pp. 506-510; Meriwether to Manypenny, July 27, Aug. 14, Sept. 15, Dec. 18, 1855, MSS., L. R., I. A. O., New
Mexico, N. A.

57. Santa Fe *Weekly Gazette*, Oct. 18, 1856; Reeve, "The Government and the Navaho,
1846-1858," *New Mexico Historical Review*, XIV (Jan., 1939), 109-110; Beaubien and
others: Memorial to President, April 21, 1856, MSS., L. R., I. A. O., New Mexico, N. A.

58. *Senate Executive Documents*, 34 Cong., 2 Sess., No. 1, Pt. 1, p. 542; Miles to
Nichols, Oct. 11, 1855, MSS., L. R., I. A. O., New Mexico, N. A.; Quinn, "Journal of a Spy
Company in Expeditions vs. the Indians. . ., 1854," MSS., Ritch, Collection.

59. *Senate Executive Documents*, 34 Cong., 3 Sess., II, No. 5, Pt. 2, p. 4.

60. James L. Collins, usually known as "Squire Collins," was a justice of the peace in
Franklin, Missouri, in the early twenties. Between 1827 and the opening of the Mexican War
he was engaged in the Santa Fe trade. In January, 1847, he was appointed interpreter and
dispatch bearer for Colonel Doniphan's command, which he accompanied to Chihuahua.
During the spring of the same year he carried important dispatches from Doniphan to General Wool, stationed at Saltillo. In the fifties and sixties he was the principal owner of the
Santa Fe *Gazette*, and during most of that time was also its editor. From 1857 to 1863 he
likewise served the Territory of New Mexico as Superintendent of Indian Affairs. Gibson,
361; Webb, *The Great Plains*, 77; Connelley, 91, 99, 108, 453-463; Douglas C. McMurtrie,
"The History of Early Printing in New Mexico," *New Mexico Historical Review*, IV (Oct.,
1929), 398-404.

61. Upon the organization of the Territory of New Mexico the governor became *ex-
officio* Superintendent of Indian Affairs. This position was held successively by Calhoun
(1851-52), Lane (1852-53), and Meriwether (1853-57). In 1857 the two offices were separated: James L. Collins became Superintendent and W. W. H. Davis acted as governor until
the arrival of Abraham R. Rencher. Twitchell, II, 314; Bancroft, *History of Arizona and
New Mexico*, 662.

62. *Senate Executive Documents*, 35 Cong., 2 Sess., No. 1, Pt. 1, p. 542; Twitchell, II,
300; St. Louis *Daily Missouri Republican*, Aug. 26, 1856; Legislative Memorial, Jan. 1857,
MSS., Territorial Papers, New Mexico, S. D., N. A.

63. St. Louis *Daily Missouri Republican*, Feb. 28, 1855; Santa Fe *Weekly Gazette*, Nov.
5, 8, 29, Dec. 20, 27, 1856.

64. *Ibid.*, May 16, June 6, Oct. 31, 1857.

65. See above, pp. 39-40.

66. *Senate Executive Documents*, 35 Cong., 2 Sess., No. 1, Pt. 2, pp. 279-280; St. Louis
Daily Missouri Republican, April 27, 1857; Santa Fe *Weekly Gazette*, Nov. 13, 1858.

67. Prior to the Mexican War Colonel Bonneville was stationed first at New England
posts, in the South, and then in the Far West. He also participated in the Florida Wars and
distinguished himself in the war with Mexico. In the early fifties he performed frontier
duty at Forts Kearny, Howard, Benicia, and Vancouver. From October, 1856, to May, 1857,
he was in temporary command of the Department of New Mexico. In September, 1858,
he resumed command of the department and held this post until October, 1859, when he
was succeeded by Colonel Thomas T. Fauntleroy. During the Civil War he served as superintendent of the recruiting service in Missouri and in 1865 was brevetted brigadier general
"for long and faithful services in the army." He died at Fort Smith on June 12, 1878. Thian,
71; Cullum, I, 144-150; Washington Irving, *The Adventures of Captain Bonneville, U. S.
A. in the Rocky Mountains and the Far West* (New York, 1859).

68. Santa Fe *Weekly Gazette*, Oct. 31, 1857.

69. *Ibid.*, Oct. 31, 1857, Jan. 23, 1858; *House Executive Documents*, 35 Cong., 1 Sess.,
No. 2, Pt. 2, pp. 55-56, 60, 137.

70. Santa Fe *Weekly Gazette*, Oct. 31, 1857; *Senate Executive Documents*, 35 Cong., 2
Sess., No. 1, Pt. 2, pp. 279-280.

71. Governor Rencher, who served until the close of 1861, was a lawyer; he had been a
member of Congress and also had served as minister to Portugal. Twitchell, II, 314.

72. Santa Fe *Weekly Gazette*, Oct. 31, 1857.

73. *Ibid.*, Jan. 16, Feb. 27, 1858; Carson to Collins, May 27, 1858, MSS., L. R., I. A. O., New Mexico, N. A.

74. Santa Fe *Weekly Gazette*, Feb. 20, April 17, 1858.

75. See above, pp. 169-170, and notes 101-104, inclusive.

76. Santa Fe *Weekly Gazette*, April 10, 17, 1858; St. Louis *Daily Missouri Republican*, Dec. 20, 1858; Davidson to Lord, March 20, 1858, MSS., L. R., A. G. O., N. A.; Collins to Mix, Nov. 22, 1858 (Photostat), MSS., Twitchell, Collection.

77. St. Louis *Daily Missouri Republican*, April 18, 1854; Austin *State Gazette*, April 2, 1859; Cremony, 30, 47-48, 172-178; Greiner, Report to Luke Lea, July 31, 1852, MSS., Ritch, Collection.

78. Ogle, "Federal Control of the Western Apaches, 1848-1886," *New Mexico Historical Review*, XIV, 341; Clum, 29-32.

79. St. Louis *Daily Missouri Republican*, May 28, 1859.

80. *Senate Executive Documents*, 36 Cong., 1 Sess., I, No. 2, Pt. 1, pp. 97-98; *ibid.*, 36 Cong., 1 Sess., II, No. 2, Pt. 2, pp. 313-314; St. Louis *Daily Missouri Republican*, Nov. 23, 1859.

81. *Senate Executive Documents*, 36 Cong., 1 Sess., II, No. 2, Pt. 2, pp. 292-293, 298-299, 309; St. Louis *Daily Missouri Republican*, March 3, 30, April 26, July 17, Oct. 9, 1859; Bonneville to Thomas, Feb. 27, 1859, MSS., L. R., A. G. O., N. A.

82. San Francisco *Daily Alta California*, Feb. 7, 1860. For the difficulties with Cochise and his band of Apaches see Wellman, *Death in the Desert* (New York, 1935), 59-65.

83. William Hoffman, a native of the state of New York, graduated from the United States Military Academy in 1829. Stationed successively at Jefferson Barracks, Forts Leavenworth, Jesup, and Smith, he saw extensive service on the frontier. He took part in the Black Hawk and Florida Wars. He participated in many battles during the Mexican War. He served under Harney in the Sioux Expedition and played a prominent part in the "Mormon War." Hoffman had an intimate knowledge of the Indian and his mode of fighting and knew how to deal with him. He served with distinction during the Civil War, being brevetted major general in March, 1865. In May, 1870, he retired from active service voluntarily. He died on August 12, 1884. Bandel, 256; Cullum, I, 433-434.

84. *Senate Executive Documents*, 36 Cong., 1 Sess., II, No. 2, Pt. 2, pp. 387- 395, 401; San Francisco *Daily Alta California*, May 7, 1859.

85. *Senate Executive Documents*, 36 Cong., 1 Sess., II, No. 2, Pt. 2, pp. 410, 419-420; San Francisco *Daily Alta California*, Aug. 21, 1859; San Francisco *Herald*, Aug. 21, Sept. 14, 1859.

86. *Senate Executive Documents*, 35 Cong., 2 Sess., No. 1, Pt. 2, pp. 294-314; St. Louis *Daily Missouri Republican*, Feb. 3, 1859; Santa Fe *Weekly Gazette*, Nov. 27, Dec. 4, 1858.

87. *Ibid.*, Dec. 4, 1858.

88. *Senate Executive Documents*, 36 Cong., 1 Sess., II, No. 2, Pt. 2, pp. 273-276; Dunn, 271; Navaho Treaty, 1858, MS., L. R., I. A. O., New Mexico, N. A.

89. *House Executive Documents*, 36 Cong., 2 Sess., VI, No. 24; St. Louis *Daily Missouri Republican*, June 26, 1859; Santa Fe *Gazette*, Aug. 20, 1859.

90. *Senate Executive Documents*, 36 Cong., 2 Sess., II, No. 1, Pt. 2, pp. 199-200; *ibid.*, 36 Cong., 2 Sess., II, No. 2, Pt. 2, pp. 316-323, 325-327, 332-333, 345, 349-354; Bonneville to Thomas, Aug. 31, 1859 (Enclosure: Walker's Report), Fauntleroy to Thomas, Dec. 3, 1859, MSS., L. R., A. G. O., N. A.

91. *Senate Executive Documents*, 36 Cong., 2 Sess., II, No. 1, Pt. 2, pp. 3, 52-56, 190, 204.

92. *Ibid.*, 60, 200-204; San Antonio *Ledger and Texan*, Aug. 11, 1860; Floyd to Nichols, July 14, 1860, MSS., L. R., A. G. O., N. A.; Collins to Greenwood, Sept. 16, 1860, MSS., L. R., I. A. O., New Mexico, N. A.

93. Santa Fe *Gazette*, Oct. 20, 1860; Rencher to Cass, May 15, 1860, MSS., Territorial Papers, New Mexico, S. D., N. A.

94. Resolution, New Mexico Legislature, Jan. 4, 1861, MSS., Twitchell, Collection; Fauntleroy to Cass, May 7,1860, Rencher to Cass, May 15, 1860, MSS., Territorial Papers, New Mexico, S. D., N. A.

95. *House Executive Documents*, 36 Cong., 2 Sess., VI, No. 24, pp. 16-17; Rencher to Cass, Sept. 4, Nov. 10, 1860, Jan. 10, 1861, Rencher to Black, Feb. 16, 1861, MSS., Territorial Papers, New Mexico, S. D., N. A.

96. *House Executive Documents*, 36 Cong., 2 Sess., VI, No. 24, pp. 8-10; Bancroft, *History of Arizona and New Mexico*, 655-656, 677.

97. *Senate Executive Documents*, 36 Cong., 1 Sess., II, No. 2, Pt. 2, pp. 339-340; San Francisco *Daily Alta California*, Jan. 3, 1858; Santa Fe *Weekly Gazette*, Jan. 2, 16, March 13, April 10, 1858.

98. St. Louis *Daily Missouri Republican*, Oct. 14, 1859; *House Executive Documents*, 36 Cong., 1 Sess., No. 69, p. 49.

99. St. Louis *Daily Missouri Republican*, Nov. 4, 1859.

100. *Ibid.*, Sept. 10, Dec. 3, 10, 11, 1858, Jan. 3, 5, 7, 28, March 10, 30, 1859.

101. Assuming the role of captain in the United States army, Snooks made requisitions on the inhabitants for horses and mules on the promise of payment by the Quartermaster's Department. Failure to comply was followed by a threat of a $500 fine or punishment. At Laguna, when the demand for livestock and grain was refused, the bandits tied up the alcalde and carried him off to Zuñi. William G. Ritch, *Illustrated New Mexico* (Santa Fe, 1883), 22; *House Executive Documents*, 31 Cong., 1 Sess., III, No. 5, Pt. 2, pp. 997-998; St. Louis *Daily Missouri Republican*, July 10, 1849.

102. *Ibid.*, June 6, 26, 1859.

103. The "Cebolleteños" were an organization of Mexican bandits on the Navaho frontier who developed a regular and lucrative business of stealing Indian children and selling them to the Mexicans. Twitchell, II, 203.

104. In the spring of 1858 armed Mexican bands from the Mesilla Valley, styling themselves the "Mesilla Guard," wantonly murdered innocent natives at Doña Ana and at Fort Thorn Indian agency. The Santa Fe *Weekly Gazette* painted a sensationally horrible picture of the Doña Ana massacre. The bodies of the murdered women, it reported, were brutally mutilated by "cutting off their breasts, tearing out their tongues, and slicing up their hearts." Some thirty Mexican bandits were captured, indicted for murder and brought to trial at Socorro, but they were ultimately released, apparently without any punishment. *Senate Executive Documents*, 35 Cong., 2 Sess., II, No. 1, Pt. 2, pp. 283-289; Santa Fe *Weekly Gazette*, Feb. 20, March 6, May 1, 1858; St. Louis *Daily Missouri Republican*, Aug. 15, 1858.

105. *Ibid.*, Nov. 23, 1859; *Senate Executive Documents*, 37 Cong., 2 Sess., I, No. 1, pp. 448, 636, 732-737.

X

1. Mack, 289-290; St. Louis *Daily Missouri Republican*, March 3, 14, May 29, 30, Nov. 8, 1848, June 21, Nov. 14, 1850; *House Executive Documents*, 32 Cong., 2 Sess., No. 1, Pt. 1, p. 299.

2. Dunn, 277; Leland Hargrave Creer, *Utah and the Nation* (Seattle, 1929), 166.

3. Mack, 291; Bancroft, *History of Utah* (San Francisco, 1889), 471-472.

4. *Senate Executive Documents*, 31 Cong., 1 Sess., IX, No. 18, pp. 97-98.

5. *Ibid.*, 99-114; Mack, 290.

6. Young received his appointment as governor on September 20, 1850; he took the oath of office on January 3, 1851. James Buchanan, *Messages of . . .*(J. Buchanan Henry, comp., New York, 1888), 39; Stenhouse, 275.

7. Mack, 29-291. For the Indian agents and subagents of Utah in the fifties see Dale L. Morgan, "The Administration of Indian Affairs in Utah, 1851-1858," *Pacific Historical Review*, XVII (Nov., 1948), 384-406.

8. Mack, 291; St. Louis *Daily Missouri Republican*, June 21, 1850.

9. Orson F. Whitney, *History of Utah* (Salt Lake City, 1892), I, 423; St. Louis *Daily Missouri Republican*, June 17, 21, 1850, Aug. 2, Sept. 4, Nov. 24, 1851.

10. Utah Territory, too, had its share of "bad whites." On May 8, 1852, Indian agent Holeman wrote to United States Commissioner of Indian Affairs Luke Lea: " 'The White Indians' . . . are more dangerous than the red. The renegades, deserters, and thieves who had fled justice in California have taken refuge in the mountains, and having associated themselves with the Indians are more savage than the Indians themselves. By their cruelty to the whites they have stimulated the Indians to acts of barbarity which they were never known to be guilty of before." *House Executive Documents*, 32 Cong., 2 Sess., I, No. 1, Pt. 1, pp. 299-300, 437-438, 442-443; *ibid.*, 35 Cong., 1 Sess., X, No. 71, p. 153.

11. Heap, 73-78, 98-100.

12. Mack, 293.

13. *Ibid.*, 293-294; *Senate Executive Documents*, 33 Cong., 1 Sess., No. 1, Pt. 1, pp. 442, 446-447.

14. Salt Lake City *Deseret News,* April 30, 1853.

15. The personnel of the expedition is given in Whitney, I, 521, and in San Francisco *Daily Alta California,* Dec. 24, 1853.

16. In commemoration of the massacre of Gunnison and his seven luckless comrades a monument was erected in 1927 near Deseret, Millard County, Utah. *House Executive Documents,* 33 Cong., 1 Sess., V, No. 18, pp. 5-6; Bancroft, *History of Utah,* 470-471. Josiah F. Gibbs, "The Gunnison Massacre, 1853 . . . Indian Mareer's Version of the Tragedy, 1894," *Utah Historical Quarterly,* I (July, 1928), 67-75.

17. Whitney, I, 522-523; Bancroft, *History of Utah,* 470; Gibbs, "The Gunnison Massacre, 1853 . . . ," *Utah Historical Quarterly,* I, 67-75.

18. *Senate Executive Documents,* 34 Cong., 1 Sess., II, No. 1, Pt. 2, p. 167; *House Executive Documents,* 35 Cong., 1 Sess., X, No. 71, p. 178; Dunn, 278.

19. Whitney, I, 397-398; Bancroft, *History of Utah,* 473-475.

20. *Senate Executive Documents,* 33 Cong., 1 Sess., II, No. 1, Pt. 2, pp. 112-122.

21. St. Louis *Daily Missouri Republican,* Sept. 6, 1853; Creer, 179.

22. Salt Lake City *Deseret News,* July 3, 1853; St. Louis *Daily Missouri Republican,* March 12, May 17, June 2, Aug. 13, 1854; Bancroft, *History of Utah,* 474, 476-477, 479.

23. Mack, 294; Bancroft, *History of Utah,* 477; *Senate Executive Documents,* 34 Cong., 1 Sess., I, No. 1, Pt. 1, pp. 517-521.

24. *House Executive Documents,* 34 Cong., 1 Sess., No. 1, Pt. 1, p. 516.

25. St. Louis *Daily Missouri Republican,* May 4, 11, 1856; *House Executive Documents,* 34 Cong., 3 Sess., No. 1, pp. 778-783.

26. *Senate Executive Documents,* 34 Cong., 1 Sess., II, No. 1, Pt. 2, p. 168; *ibid.,* 35 Cong., 1 Sess., II, 593-595.

27. St. Louis *Daily Missouri Republican,* Nov. 3, 6, 1851, April 6, 1852.

28. Bancroft, *History of Utah,* 456, 486.

29. *Ibid.,* 456-461; Stenhouse, 276-278; St. Louis *Daily Missouri Republican,* Jan. 20, 1852.

30. Besides Judges Drummond and Stiles, other government officials in the territory during the early turbulent years included Secretary Benjamin G. Ferris, Chief Justices Lazarus H. Reed and John F. Kinney and Associate Justice Leonidas Shaver. Bancroft, *History of Utah,* 461-462, 488-491; Stenhouse, 279-281; *Senate Executive Documents,* 34 Cong., 1 Sess., II, No. 1, Pt. 2, p. 168.

31. *Ibid.,* 168.

32. Leavenworth City *Kansas Weekly Herald,* May 30, 1857, in St. Louis *Daily Missouri Republican,* June 2, 5, 1857; Buchanan, *Works of . . .* (John Bassett Moore, ed., Philadelphia, 1910), X, 203.

33. Bancroft, *History of Utah,* 485-486, 500-504; *Daily Missouri Republican,* Jan. 31, 1858; *House Executive Documents,* 35 Cong., 1 Sess., X, No. 71, pp. 114-115.

34. Buchanan, *Messages of . . . ,* 39-40.

35. Alfred Cumming of Georgia had been Superintendent of Indian Affairs in the upper Missouri. Cumming's colleagues comprised the following: Secretary John Hartnett, Chief Justice D. R. Eckles, Associate Justices John Cradlebaugh and Charles E. Sinclair, Marshal Peter K. Dotson, United States Attorney Alexander Wilson, and Superintendent of Indian Affairs Jacob Forney. Bancroft, *History of Utah,* 500, 539-540.

36. *Senate Executive Documents,* 35 Cong., 1 Sess., III, No. 11, Pt. 2, pp. 21-24; St. Louis *Daily Missouri Republican,* July 6, 1857; Bandel, 46-47.

37. Albert Sidney Johnston, a native of Kentucky, was educated at West Point, from which he graduated with distinction in 1826. He served in the Black Hawk War in 1832, but resigned from the army two years later. In the summer of 1836 he went to Texas, where he joined the Texan army as a private. He was soon appointed adjutant general of the army and in 1838 secretary of war of the Texas republic. Upon the outbreak of the Mexican War he enlisted in the first regiment of Texas volunteers, but returned to his home in Brazoria County in the latter part of the same year. In 1849 he re-entered the United States army with the rank of major and for five years served as paymaster on the Texas frontier. He was promoted to the rank of colonel, Second Cavalry, in 1855, commanded the Department of Texas in 1856 and 1857, and in the latter year assumed command of the Army of Utah. For his "ability, zeal, energy, and prudence" as commander of the Army of Utah he was brevetted brigadier general. Between November 1, 1860, and April 10, 1861, he was in command of the Department of the Pacific. He joined the Confederate forces and served with distinction during the early years of the Civil War. He was killed at the battle of Shiloh on

April 6, 1862. Johnston was an able soldier and accomplished civilian; he possessed prudence, courage, and foresight. Cullum, I, 368; Bandel, 224; St. Louis *Daily Missouri Republican,* Aug. 7, 1857; Johnston, 1-249.

38. *Senate Executive Documents,* 36 Cong., 1 Sess., No. 52, pp. 281-288; T. F. Roden-bough (comp.), *From Everglade to Cañon with the Second Dragoons* (New York, 1875), 185-191, 218; Dickerson to Jesup, Nov. 20, 1857 (Enclosure: Utah Expedition), MSS., L. R., Q. G. O., N. A.

39. *Senate Executive Documents,* 35 Cong., 1 Sess., III, No. 11, Pt. 2, pp. 8-9, 26, 36-38.

40. Whitney, I, 600-604; Stenhouse, 349-350; Creer, 134.

41. Parley Rex Syndergaard, "The United States Military Expedition to Utah, 1857-1858," MS., M. A. thesis, Washington University, St. Louis, 1941, p. 11.

42. St. Louis *Daily Missouri Republican,* Oct. 25, 1857.

43. *Senate Executive Documents,* 35 Cong., 1 Sess., III, No. 11, Pt. 2, p. 33; Marcy, *Thirty Years of Army Life on the Border,* 269-270; St. Louis *Daily Missouri Republican,* Nov. 24, 1857.

44. Bancroft, *History of Utah,* 505-509; San Francisco *Daily Alta California,* Oct. 12, 1857; St. Louis *Daily Missouri Republican,* Nov. 7, 21, 1857; Caleb Green, 1862, Journal Containing "A Visit to the Great Salt Lake or Observations during a five month's [*sic*] residence in Utah," MSS., Caleb Green, Collection, M. H. S.

45. Bancroft, *History of Utah,* 510-511, 520; St. Louis *Daily Missouri Republican,* Nov. 11, 16, Dec. 9, 13, 27, 1857, Jan. 1, 1858; *Senate Executive Documents,* 35 Cong., 1 Sess., III, No. 11, Pt. 2, pp. 29, 35. The list and amount of quartermaster's stores destroyed by the Mormons is found in Dickerson to Jesup, Nov. 30, 1857 (Enclosures: Utah Expedition), MSS., L. R., Q. G. O., N. A.

46. St. Louis *Daily Missouri Republican,* Jan. 10, 12, 1858.

47. *House Executive Documents,* 35 Cong., 1 Sess., X, No. 71, pp. 92-111; Bancroft, *History of Utah,* 523; Rodenbough, 192-221, 225; Johnston, 217-220.

48. Bancroft, *History of Utah,* 523-524; St. Louis *Daily Missouri Republican,* March 12, June 12, 1858.

49. Stenhouse, 380-381.

50. *Senate Executive Documents,* 35 Cong., 2 Sess., II, No. 1, Pt. 2, pp. 7-8; Marcy, *Thirty Years of Army Life on the Border,* 224-264; Samuel W. Ferguson, "With Albert Sidney Johnston's Expedition to Utah, 1857," Kansas State Historical Society, *Collections,* XII, 310-312.

51. *Senate Executive Documents,* 35 Cong., 2 Sess., II, No. 1, Pt. 2, pp. 108-109, 177-181; Bandel, 49-54.

52. St. Louis *Daily Missouri Republican,* Jan. 12, 1858.

53. *Ibid.,* Feb. 7, March 1, 1858; Stenhouse, 377.

54. New Orleans *Daily Picayune,* May 18, 1858; St. Louis *Daily Missouri Republican,* June 23, July 30, 1858; Bancroft, *History of Utah,* 526-527.

55. Buchanan's proclamation is given in full in Buchanan, *Works of . . .,* X, 202-206, and in *House Executive Documents,* 35 Cong., 2 Sess., II, No. 2, Pt. 1, pp. 69-72.

56. *Senate Executive Documents,* 35 Cong., 2 Sess., II, No. 1, Pt. 2, pp. 113-122.

57. By June, 1858, more than 5,600 officers and men had arrived in Utah or were en route, in addition to about 1,900 employees, 300 servants, and 200 women—making a total of 8,000. *House Executive Documents,* 35 Cong., 2 Sess., II, No. 2, Pt. 2, pp. 31-32; *Senate Executive Documents,* 35 Cong., 2 Sess., II, No. 1, Pt. 2, pp. 68-71; Bancroft, *History of Utah,* 497-528; St. Louis *Daily Missouri Republican,* July 4, 1858.

58. *Senate Executive Documents,* 35 Cong., 2 Sess., II, No. 1, Pt. 2, pp. 121-122, 172-173; St. Louis *Daily Missouri Republican,* June 15, July 2, 5, 13, Aug. 7, 1858; Little Rock (Ark.) *True Democrat,* Aug. 4, 1858; Bancroft, *History of Utah,* 535.

59. Quoted in Creer, 158-159.

60. *Senate Executive Documents,* 35 Cong., 2 Sess., II, No. 1, Pt. 2, pp. 122-123, 158-159; Marguerite Mott, "Activities in the Northwest, 1848-1861, under the Direction of the United States War Department," MS., M. A. thesis, Washington University, 1932, pp. 101-103; Department Returns, Department of Utah, Sept., 1858, MSS., A. G. O., N. A.

61. Alexander Majors, *Seventy Years on the Frontier* (New York, 1893), 142-144; Horace Greeley, *An Overland Journey* (New York, 1860), 246, 253-258; St. Louis *Daily Missouri Republican,* May 30, June 12, Aug. 27, 1858; Jesup to Floyd, Nov. 13, 1858, MSS., Letters Sent (Letters and Reports), Book 4, Q. G. O., N. A.

62. Frank J. Cannon and George L. Knapp, *Brigham Young and His Mormon Empire* (New York, 1913), 320; Whitney, I, 726.

63. St. Louis *Post-Dispatch*, March 16, Sept. 5, Oct. 19, 1944, July 14, 1946, May 1, 1947.

64. *Senate Executive Documents*, 36 Cong., 1 Sess., II, No. 2, pp. 14-15; Buchanan, *Messages of . . .*, 63-64; Cannon and Knapp, 10; Bancroft, *History of Utah*, 538.

65. *Senate Executive Documents*, 36 Cong., 1 Sess., XI, No. 42, p. 83; Gibbs, *The Mountain Meadows Massacre* (Salt Lake City, 1910), 18; Stenhouse, 431-435.

66. *Senate Executive Documents*, 36 Cong., 1 Sess., XI, No. 42, pp. 75-89; John D. Lee, *Mormonism Unveiled* (St. Louis, 1877), 237-245; Gibbs, *The Mountain Meadows Massacre*, 32-36; Bancroft, *History of Utah*, 550-557.

67. *Senate Executive Documents*, 36 Cong., 1 Sess., XI, No. 42, pp. 15, 75-83, 88, 96-97; James A. Little, *Jacob Hamblin* (Salt Lake City, 1909), 48-49; Bancroft, *History of Utah*, 548-549; Mott, "Activities in the Northwest, 1848-1861,. . .," MS., M.A. thesis, Washington University, 1932, pp. 89-92.

68. *Senate Executive Documents*, 36 Cong., 1 Sess., XI, No. 42, p. 53; *Congressional Globe*, 37 Cong., 3 Sess., Appendix, 123.

69. In his confession before his death, John D. Lee named fifty-two persons, including himself, who had been participants in the Mountain Meadows massacre. Lee's principal associates consisted of William H. Dame, Isaac C. Haight, John M. Higbee, and Philip Klingensmith. *Senate Executive Documents*, 36 Cong., 1 Sess., II, No. 2, pp. 139-146; *ibid.*, XI, No. 42, pp. 86-87; 100-103; Lee, 32-34, 302-380; Bancroft, *History of Utah*, 559-568.

70. *House Executive Documents*, 35 Cong., 1 Sess., X, No. 71, pp. 186-188; Mack, 295.

71. *Senate Executive Documents*, 35 Cong., 2 Sess., I, No. 1, Pt. 1, pp. 561-565; Mack, 296; St. Louis *Daily Missouri Republican*, Nov. 24, 1858.

72. For a brief account of the discovery and naming of the Comstock Lode, see Mack, 200-207.

73. Nevada City (Calif.) *Journal*, July 9, 1859, quoted in Mack, 209; New Orleans *Daily Picayune*, April 27, 1860; Browne, "A Peep at Washoe," *Harper's New Monthly Magazine*, XXII (Dec., 1860), 2-7, (Feb., 1861), 298.

74. *Ibid.*, XXII, 154.

75. Glenn D. Bradley, *The Story of the Pony Express* (Chicago, 1913), 171; Mack, 299-300.

76. The major part of Captain Stewart's force consisted of California and Nevada volunteers under the celebrated Colonel "Jack Hays." See above, p. 204. *Senate Executive Documents*, 36 Cong., 2 Sess., II, No. 1, pp. 4, 73-79, 89-92, 190-191; Bradley, 171-172.

77. Johnston was relieved of his command at his own request on February 29, 1860. Lieutenant Colonel Smith, his successor, was followed by Lieutenant Colonel P. St. George Cooke, who commanded the department from August, 1860, until the spring of 1861. Johnston, 241; Thian, 100-101.

78. *Senate Executive Documents*, 36 Cong., 2 Sess., II, No. 1, p. 80.

79. *Ibid.*, 100-105; Mack, 311-313.

80. *Senate Executive Documents*, 36 Cong., 1 Sess., I, No. 2, Pt. 1, pp. 735-737; Morgan, "The Administration of Indian Affairs in Utah, 1851-1858," *Pacific Historical Review*, XVII, 397-404; Nels Anderson, *Desert Saints* (Chicago, 1942), 203.

81. *Ibid.*, 202-203; Creer, 171-173.

82. Anderson, 204; *Senate Executive Documents*, 37 Cong., 2 Sess., I, No. 1, p. 750.

83. Mack, 296; St. Louis *Daily Missouri Republican*, Feb. 7, 1859.

84. *Senate Executive Documents*, 37 Cong., 2 Sess., I, No. 1, p. 739; Mack, 296-297.

85. *Ibid.*, 297-298, 314.

XI

1. Ellison, "The Federal Indian Policy in California, 1846-1860," *Mississippi Valley Historical Review*, IX, 41; California, *Senate Journal*, 1852 (San Francisco, 1852), 708; San Francisco *Daily Evening Picayune*, Dec. 3, 1851; John T. Little, "Statement of Events in the first years of American Occupation of California," 5, 6, 10, MS., Bancroft Library.

2. *Senate Executive Documents*, 31 Cong., 2 Sess., No. 18, pp. 2-35; *Congressional Globe*, 31 Cong., 1 Sess., XXI, Pt. 2, p. 1816; Hallie Mae McPherson, "William McKendree Gwin," MS., Ph.D. dissertation, University of California, 1932, p. 152.

3. *House Executive Documents*, 31 Cong., 1 Sess., No. 17, pp. 287, 294-296, 349, 382-383; Bancroft, *History of California*, V, 568.

4. Treaty between General Vallejo, Major Hardie, and eleven Indian chiefs of the Big Lakes near Sonoma, June 1, 1848, MSS., L. R., Tenth Military Department, A. C., U. S., N. A.

5. *House Executive Documents*, 30 Cong., 2 Sess., No. 1, pp. 20, 407-408; *Senate Executive Documents*, 31 Cong., 1 Sess., IX, No. 18, pp. 60, 97-98.

6. The special investigating officers were Thomas Butler King and William Carey Jones. *Ibid.*, pp. 9-11, 60, 226-228.

7. St. Louis *Daily Missouri Republican*, Oct. 25, 31, Nov. 23, 1848.

8. *Senate Executive Documents*, 31 Cong., 1 Sess., No. 52, p. 51; *House Executive Documents*, 31 Cong., 1 Sess., No. 17, p. 942; Bancroft, *History of California*, VI, 275; Department Returns, Tenth Military Department, Dec. 1849, MSS., A. G. O., N. A.

9. *Senate Executive Documents*, 31 Cong., 1 Sess., No. 52, p. 84.

10. For the Warner massacre, see above, p. 105.

11. *Senate Executive Documents*, 31 Cong., 1 Sess., No. 47, Pt. 2, pp. 16-33; *House Executive Documents*, 31 Cong., 2 Sess., No. 1, Pt. 2, pp. 78-83; Smith to Freeman, Jan. 12, 1850 (Enclosure: Davidson's Report, Jan. 6, 1850), MSS., L. R., H. A., N. A.

12. California, *Statutes, 1849-1850* (San Jose, 1850), 408-409; San Francisco *Daily Evening Picayune*, Dec. 20, 1851, Jan. 14, March 2, 1852; Charles Berdan Leonard, "The Federal Indian Policy in the San Joaquin Valley: Its Application and Results," MS., Ph. D. dissertation, University of California, 1928, pp. 91-92.

13. Kimball H. Dimmick to Sarah [Dimmick], June 10, 1852, MSS., California File, 1848-1860, Huntington Library.

14. The anti-foreign movements brought forth a crop of pseudo-patriots. Cunning Mexican brigands, posing as champions of their persecuted countrymen living in California, determined to take vengeance on the *Americanos*. Waves of lawlessness and brigandage followed. For the marauding exploits of Joaquín Carillo or Joaquín Murieta [Murrietta], Tiburcio Vasquez, and kindred spirits, see John A. Henshall, "A Bandit of the Golden Age," *Overland Monthly*, LIII (April 1909), 313-319, 403-404; Ireneo Paz, *Life and Adventures of the Celebrated Bandit Joaquín Murrieta: His Exploits in the State of California* (Chicago, 1925, tr. Frances P. Belle); Hittell, *History of California*, III, 712-726; Richard Gerald Mitchell, "Joaquín Murieta," MS., M.A. thesis, University of California, 1927, pp. 39-69, 89-107.

15. St. Louis *Daily Missouri Republican*, June 30, July 2, Aug. 15, 1849; Little Rock *Arkansas Banner*, Aug. 20, 1850; William Christie Macleod, *The American Indian Frontier* (London, 1928), 487.

16. Bancroft, *History of California*, VI, 319, VII, 480; St. Louis *Daily Missouri Republican*, Oct. 27, 1850; Sacramento *Transcript*, June 29, 1850; Smith to McDowell, June 30, 1850, MSS., L. R., H. A., N. A.

17. Bancroft, *History of California*, VII, 481; St. Louis *Daily Missouri Republican*, Dec. 30, 1850, Jan. 30, Feb. 16, March 17, 19, 1851.

18. See above, pp. 41-42.

19. *House Executive Documents*, 31 Cong., 2 Sess., I, No. 1, Pt. 1, pp. 122-125; *Senate Executive Documents*, 33 Cong., Spec. Sess., No. 4, p. 43; *Sacramento Transcript*, Feb. 28, 1851; Woolbridge to Taylor, Jan. 23, 1850, MSS., L. R., I. A. O., N. A.

20. Dunn, 133-135.

21. San Francisco *Daily Alta California*, Jan. 14, Dec. 2, 4, 12, 1851; San Francisco *Daily Evening Picayune*, Dec. 5, 1851; Hoover, 131-132.

22. Dunn, 133-135, 192-193; Lafayette Houghton Bunnell, *Discovery of the Yosemite and the Indian War of 1851* (New York, 1892), 30-148, 163-167; San Francisco *Daily Alta California*, Aug. 21, 1853; San Francisco *Daily Evening Picayune*, Jan. 15, 1852; O. M. Wozencraft, "Indian Affairs, 1849-1850," pp. 9-11, MS., Bancroft Library.

23. Ellison, *California and the Nation, 1850-1869*, pp. 84-85; San Francisco *Daily Alta California*, Jan. 6, 21, 31, June 12, 19, Sept. 9, 1851; San Francisco *Daily Evening Picayune*, Dec. 5, 1851, Jan. 3, 15, 1852; San Francisco *Herald*, Mar. 14, 1851.

24. Hittell, *History of California*, III, 899, 904; California, *Senate Journal, 1851* (San Jose, 1851), 13-16, 601-602; *ibid., 1852*, pp. 703-704, 714-716.

25. Hittell, *History of California*, III, 907-911; *Senate Executive Documents*, 33 Cong., Spec. Sess., No. 4, pp. 53, 56-59, 115, 248.

26. San Francisco *Daily Alta California*, Oct. 16, 1851; California, *Senate Journal, 1852*, p. 707.

27. San Francisco *Daily Alta California*, March 31, June 17, Sept. 19, 1852; San Francisco *Daily Evening Picayune*, March 8, 1852; Bancroft, *History of California*, VII, 460-461.

28. San Francisco *Daily Alta California*, Sept. 16, Dec. 2, 1851, Sept. 5, 1853; St. Louis *Daily Missouri Republican*, March 22, 1853.

29. *Senate Executive Documents*, 34 Cong., 3 Sess., II, No. 5, p. 151; Hittell, *History of California*, III, 897; Browne, "The Coast Rangers," *Harper's New Monthly Magazine*, XXIII (Aug., 1861), 306-307.

30. Thian, 86; San Francisco *Daily Alta California*, Feb. 18, 1854.

31. Davis to McClelland, June 22, 1854, MSS., L. S., S. W., N. A.

32. *Senate Executive Documents*, 33 Cong., 2 Sess., VI, No. 16, pp. 14-15; San Francisco *Daily Alta California*, March 29, April 12, 1854.

33. *Senate Executive Documents*, 34 Cong., 1 Sess., No. 26, p. 21; *House Executive Documents*, 34 Cong., 3 Sess., IX, No. 76, pp. 136-139; San Francisco *Daily Alta California*, Feb. 3, 20, Oct. 18, 1855; St. Louis *Daily Missouri Republican*, Nov. 16, Dec. 15, 1855.

34. Stevenson to Henley, Dec. 31, 1855, MSS., L. R., I. A. O., California, N. A.; San Francisco *Daily Alta California*, Sept. 29, 1856.

35. Henley to Manypenny, July 22, Sept. 19, 1855, June 3, 1856, Henley to McDaniel, Oct. 22, 1855, Henley to Sutter, Feb. 3, 1856, MSS., L. R., I. A. O., California, N. A.

36. Newmark, 35, 47, 105, 178, 295; Gwin to McClelland, Dec. 5, 1855 (Enclosure: Brent to Gwin, Nov. 2, 1855), MSS., L. R., I. A. O., Miscellaneous, N. A.

37. *House Executive Documents*, 34 Cong., 1 Sess., I, No. 1, Pt. 2, p. 89; San Francisco *Daily Alta California*, March 2, 6, 1856.

38. Bancroft, *History of California*, VII, 486; San Francisco *Daily Alta California*, May 6, 26, 1856; Los Angeles *Star*, May 17, 1856, in Hayes, "Indians," II, 83, MSS., Bancroft Library.

39. *House Executive Documents*, 35 Cong., 1 Sess., No. 88, pp. 1-213; San Francisco *Daily Alta California*, Dec. 24, 1854; St. Louis *Daily Missouri Republican*, Jan. 18, 1855; New Orleans *Daily Picayune*, Jan. 16, 1855.

40. San Francisco *Daily Alta California*, Sept. 20, Oct. 26, 1856.

41. *Ibid.*, Feb. 16, 18, 20, 1857.

42. Thian, 86; San Francisco *Daily Alta California*, April 30, 1857.

43. See above, p. 44.

44. San Francisco *Daily Alta California*, March 23, 1857.

45. *Ibid.*, Aug. 5, 1857. For the career of this rugged soldier, see Crook, 3-309.

46. San Francisco *Daily Alta California*, Feb. 8, May 12, 1858.

47. St. Louis *Daily Missouri Republican*, Sept. 16, Nov. 14, 1858; San Francisco *Daily National*, Aug. 17, Nov. 8, 1858.

48. San Francisco *Daily Alta California*, Aug. 17, 1858.

49. Browne to Mix, Sept. 29, 1858, MSS., L. R., I. A. O., California, N. A.

50. Dunn, 138-141; San Francisco *Daily Alta California*, Oct. 11, 19, Nov. 10, 1858, March 22, 1859, Jan. 22, 26, 1860; Browne, "The Coast Rangers," *Harper's New Monthly Magazine*, XXIII, 312; California, *Assembly Journal, 1860*, pp. 165-170, 318-325.

51. San Francisco *Daily Alta California*, Jan. 26, 1860.

52. California, *Statutes, 1859*, p. 295.

53. St. Louis *Daily Missouri Republican*, Sept. 21, 1859; San Francisco *Daily Alta California*, Sept. 3, 1859.

54. Hittell, *History of California*, III, 920-922; Bledsoe, 302-313; Hoover, 133-134.

55. San Francisco *Daily Alta California*, May 14, June 9, 1860; New Orleans *Daily Picayune*, June 23, 1860.

56. Carleton to Mackall, July 2, 1860, MSS., L. R., A. G. O., N. A.

57. Hittell, *History of California*, III, 923-924; Bledsoe, 340-346.

58. San Francisco *Daily Alta California*, Jan. 22, 1860; Kenneth W. Colgrove, "The Attitude of Congress toward the Pioneers of the West, 1820-1850," *Iowa Journal of History and Politics*, IX (April, 1911), 301-302.

59. Dallas *Herald*, Feb. 2, 1859.

XII

1. Richardson, *The Comanche Barrier to South Plains Settlement*, 211; Houston, V, 475-476; Butler and Lewis to Medill, April 1, 1846, MSS., L. R., I. A. O., N. A.

2. Governor Henderson's message in Clarksville (Tex.) *Northern Standard*, Jan. 22, 1848.

3. Malin, 81-88; St. Louis *Daily Missouri Republican*, Dec. 17, 1852; Rollins to Lea, March 20, 1851, MSS., L. R., I. A. O., Texas, N. A.; Davis to Bell, Sept. 19, 1853, MSS., Governors' Letters.

4. Bell's and Pease's messages in Austin *Texas State Gazette*, Nov. 15, Dec. 27, 1853.

5. Houston *Democratic Telegraph and Texas Register*, Aug. 9, 1849; San Antonio *Western Texan*, Nov. 25, 1852.

6. Austin *Texas State Gazette*, April 7, 1855; Austin *Southern Intelligencer*, Nov. 11, 1857; Santa Fe *Weekly Gazette*, March 10, 1855, Oct. 18, Dec. 20, 27, 1856, Feb. 20, Aug. 7, 1858; San Francisco *Daily Alta California*, Jan. 15, 31, May 31, June 19, July 26, 1851; San Francisco *Evening Picayune*, Sept. 13, 1851.

7. Richardson, *The Comanche Barrier to South Plains Settlement*, 212-213; Capron to Howard, Sept. 30, 1852, MSS., L. R., I. A. O., N. A.

8. *Senate Executive Documents*, 33 Cong., 1 Sess., No. 1, Pt. 1, p. 426.

9. Austin *Texas State Gazette*, Jan. 3, 1854.

10. Hans P. N. Gammel (ed.), *The Laws of Texas, 1822-1902* (Austin, 1898-1902), III, 1495.

11. In February, 1856, "A third Indian reservation to consist of five leagues of land was set apart by the state 'for the use and benefit of the several Indians residing west of the Pecos River, and within the limits of Texas.'" This grant was never actually colonized. Marcy, *Thirty Years of Army Life on the Border*, 170-223; *House Executive Documents*, 34 Cong., 1 Sess., No. 1, Pt. 1, pp. 497-506; Harmon, "The United States Indian Policy in Texas, 1845-1860," *Mississippi Valley Historical Review*, XVII, 395; Marcy and Neighbors to Manypenny, Sept. 30, 1854, MSS., L. R., I. A. O., Texas, N. A.

12. *Statutes at Large*, X, 331.

13. Neighbors to Manypenny, Jan. 8, 1855, Hill to Neighbors, Jan. 25, 1855, MSS., L. R., I. A. O., Texas, N. A.

14. Austin *Texas State Gazette*, April 7, 1855.

15. *Ibid.*; *St. Louis Daily Missouri Republican*, May 12, 1855; Neighbors to Manypenny, March 20, 1855 (Enclosure: proposals for fresh beef), MSS., L. R., I. A. O., N. A.

16. Austin *Texas State Gazette*, July 7, Aug. 25, Sept. 1, 22, 1855; New Orleans *Daily Picayune*, July 17, 1855; Ross to Neighbors, Jan. 1, 1856, MSS., L. R., I. A. O., Texas, N. A.

17. Austin *Texas State Gazette*, April 7, 1855; Hill to Neighbors, Jan. 25, 1855, MSS., L. R., I. A. O., N. A.

18. Foreman, *A History of Oklahoma*, 88; New Orleans *Daily Picayune*, July 30, 1855; Hill to Neighbors, April 3, 1855, Neighbors to Manypenny, June 10, 1855, MSS., L. R., I. A. O., N. A.

19. Virginia P. Noël, "United States Indian Reservations in Texas, 1854-1859," MS., M.A. thesis, University of Texas, 1924, pp. 144-146.

20. *Ibid.*, 167, 169, 178; Neighbors to Leeper, July 16, 1857 (Instructions), Abstract of Articles for Indians, Nov. 20, Dec. 31, 1857, Coombes to Ross, Dec. 31, 1858 (Teacher's Report), Shirley to Neighbors, March 29, 1858 (Medical Bill), MSS., L. R., I. A. O., N. A.

21. Neighbors to Leeper, July 16, 1857, MSS., L. R., I. A. O., N. A.

22. Wissler, 284; Noël, "United States Indian Reservations in Texas, 1854-1859," MS., M.A. thesis, University of Texas, 1924, pp. 146-148.

23. Austin *State Gazette*, March 29, 1856.

24. San Antonio *Texan*, July 31, 1856; Neighbors to Pease, June 4, 1856, MSS., Governors' Letters.

25. Ford to Runnels, April 7, 1858, MSS., Governors' Letters.

26. Richardson, *The Comanche Barrier to South Plains Settlement*, 228; Dick, 114; Baylor to Neighbors, July 6, 1856, MSS., L. R., I. A. O., N. A.

27. Harmon, "The United States Indian Policy in Texas, 1845-1860," *Mississippi Valley Historical Review*, XVII, 395-396; *House Executive Documents*, 34 Cong., 3 Sess., I, No. 1, p. 730; Ross to Neighbors, May 1, 1856, MSS., L. R., I. A. O., N. A.

28. Richardson, *The Comanche Barrier to South Plains Settlement*, 228; Baylor to Neighbors, June 8, 1856, Leeper to Neighbors, April 9, 1858, MSS., L. R., I. A. O., N. A.

29. Noël, "United States Indian Reservations in Texas, 1854-1859," MS., M.A. thesis, University of Texas, 1924, pp. 89-92; Ross to Neighbors, March 31, 1857, Leeper to Neighbors, Nov. 20, 1857, MSS., L. R., I. A. O., N. A.

30. Richardson, *The Comanche Barrier to South Plains Settlement*, 232, 233, 243; Clarksville (Tex.) *Standard*, Nov. 6, 1858.

31. See above, pp. 143-144.

32. Richardson, *The Comanche Barrier to South Plains Settlement*, 244; Lucy A. Erath, "Memoirs of George Bernard Erath," *Southwestern Historical Quarterly*, XXVII (Oct., 1923), 151.

33. Austin *State Gazette*, June 11, 1859; Preston and others to Leeper, Feb. 1, 1858, Preston and others to Givens, Feb. 9, 1858, Barry to Hawkins, Nov. 2, 1858, MSS., L. R., I. A. O., N. A.; James Buckner Barry, "Papers," Dec., 1857, April, 1858, MS. (typewritten copy), Archives, University of Texas.

34. "Petitions from Williamson and Lampasas Counties, Dec. 15, 1857," "Petition from Bosque County, Aug. 25, 1858," MSS., L. R., I. A. O., Texas, N. A.

35. Neighbors to Mix, Jan. 17, 1858, Leeper to Neighbors, Feb. 12, 1858, MSS., L. R., I. A. O., Texas, N. A.; Neighbors to Gibson, Jan. 21, 1858, MS., Neighbors, "Papers" (typewritten copy), Archives, University of Texas.

36. Holden, "Frontier Defense, 1846-1860," *West Texas Historical Association Year Book*, VI, 58-60; Dallas *Herald*, Sept. 1, 1858, June 29, 1859.

37. Neighbors to Manypenny, Feb. 20, March 19, 1856, Swindells to Neighbors, June 10, 1858, MSS., L. R., I. A. O., Texas, N. A.

38. Baylor to Barry, Aug. 2, 1858, MS., Barry, "Papers," Archives, University of Texas.

39. Swindells to Neighbors, June 10, 1858; Certificates concerning forged signatures (Chandler, Hawkins, Olephant, Peterson, Seal), Jan. 31, March 27, Nov. 6, 1858, MSS., L. R., I. A. O., Texas, N. A.

40. Moore to President, Dec. 2, 1857, MSS., L. R., I. A. O., Miscellaneous, N. A.

41. Mix to Hawkins, Sept. 4, 1858, MSS., L. S., I. A. O., N. A.

42. Dallas *Herald*, Dec. 22, 1858; *Senate Executive Documents*, 36 Cong., 1 Sess., I, No. 2, pp. 659-662; Hawkins to Mix, Oct. 30, 1858, MSS., L. R., I. A. O., Texas, N. A.

43. Van Hagan to Neighbors, March 27, 1858, "Petition of citizens of Young County, Jan. 20, 1857," "Petition of citizens of Clear Fork Ranch, March 30, 1858," "Affidavits of Ford and Burleson, Nov. 22, 1858," MSS., L. R., I. A. O., Texas, N. A.

44. Holden, "Frontier Defense, 1846-1860," *West Texas Historical Association Year Book*, VI, 55-56; Sturm to Runnels, Dec. 30, 1858, Neighbors to Runnels, Jan. 9, 10, 1859, Gurley to Runnels, Feb. 3, 1859, MSS., Governors' Letters.

45. Clarksville (Tex.) *Standard*, June 11, 1859.

46. *Ibid.*; Austin *State Gazette*, April 9, May 7, 28, 1859.

47. Battle to Runnels, March 14, 1859, MSS., Governors' Letters.

48. Barnard to Runnels, May 4, 1859, MSS., Governors' Letters.

49. Holden, "Frontier Defense, 1846-1860," *West Texas Historical Association Year Book*, VI, 57; Gurley to Runnels, May 5, 1859, MSS., Governors' Letters.

50. Richardson, *The Comanche Barrier to South Plains Settlement*, 253; Dallas *Herald*, March 9, 1859; Ross to Neighbors, March 25, 1859, Neighbors to Denver, March 28, 1859, MSS., L. R., I. A. O., N. A.

51. Austin *State Gazette*, March 27, 1858, June 18, 1859; Neighbors to Denver, Aug. 5, 1857, Neighbors to Twiggs, March 29, 1858, MSS., L. R., I. A. O., Texas, N. A.; Twiggs to Thomas, Oct. 20, 1857, MSS., L. R., H. A., N. A.

52. *Senate Executive Documents*, 36 Cong., 1 Sess., I, No. 2, pp. 631-632.

53. "Resolution," April 25, 1859, MSS., L. R., I. A. O., N. A.

54. Richardson, *The Comanche Barrier to South Plains Settlement*, 255; Neighbors to Mix, May 12, 1859, Leeper to Neighbors, May 12, 1859, MSS., L. R., I. A. O., N. A.

55. *Senate Executive Documents*, 36 Cong., 1 Sess., II, No. 2, Pt. 2, pp. 363, 371-372; St. Louis *Daily Missouri Republican*, May 29, 1859.

56. Richardson, *The Comanche Barrier to South Plains Settlement*, 256; Thomas to Runnels, April 15, 1859, MS., Neighbors, "Papers," Archives, University of Texas.

57. Instructions to Peace Commissioners, June 6, 1859, Runnels to Nelson, June 6, 1859, MSS., Governors' Letters.

58. *Senate Executive Documents*, 36 Cong., 1 Sess., I, No. 2, pp. 650-651. For an account of the "Leased District " in the present state of Oklahoma and the establishment of Fort Cobb, see Foreman, *A History of Oklahoma*, 38, 85, 89, 95-96.

59. *Senate Executive Documents*, 36 Cong., 1 Sess., II, No. 2, pp. 696-701; Neighbors, "Memorandum Travel Book from Brazos Agency, Texas, to the False Ouachita Agency," C. N., July 31-Aug. 30, 1859, MS., I. A. O., N. A. (Hereafter cited as Neighbors, "Memorandum Travel Book. . .," MS., I. A. O., N. A.)

60. Neighbors to Lizzie A. Neighbors, Aug. 8, 1859, MS., Neighbors, "Papers," Archives, University of Texas.

61. Nye, 35; Neighbors, "Memorandum Travel Book. . .," MS., I. A. O., N. A.

62. Nye, 35; Brown to Runnels, Sept. 5, 1859, MSS., Governors' Letters; Burkett to Mrs. Neighbors, Sept. 14, 1859, MS., Neighbors, "Papers," Archives, University of Texas.

63. Robert Simpson Neighbors, a native of Virginia, arrived in Texas in the spring of 1836 and soon became a member of the Texas Rangers. Three years later he joined the regular Texas army. In 1842 he was among the prisoners taken by the Mexican General Adrian Woll in the raid upon San Antonio and carried off to Mexico, where he remained a prisoner for two years. After his release he served the republic of Texas as subagent for the Lipan and Tonkawa tribes. From 1847 until his death in 1859 he devoted most of his time to Indian affairs, serving as United States special agent and supervising agent for the Texas tribes. He was removed from office as Indian agent by the Whig administration in 1849, but he continued to champion the cause of the Indian. As a member of the lower house of the Texas legislature his committee work resulted in the establishment of the Texas reservations. Neighbors was the ideal Indian agent. A man of imposing personality, he was notable for his courage, energy, fairness, and strength of character. The Indians trusted him. Houston, V, 165-166; Parker, 116, 130-131, 237-238; Marcy, *Thirty Years of Army Life on the Border*, 174, 178-179, 189-190; Neighbors, "Papers," MS., Archives, University of Texas.

64. Erath, "Memoirs of George Bernard Erath," *Southwestern Historical Quarterly*, XXVII, 155; Houston, VIII, 21-22; Blain to Rector, May 5, 1860, MSS., Governors' Letters.

65. Noël, "United States Indian Reservations in Texas, 1854-1859," MS., M.A. thesis, University of Texas, 1924, pp. 185-188.

66. The cost of maintaining the Texas Indian reservations during 1855-59 was $429,-872.63. Estimates, Neighbors' Reports, 1855-59, MSS., L. R., I. A. O., Texas, N. A.

67. Noël, "United States Indian Reservations in Texas, 1854-1859," MS., M.A. thesis, University of Texas, 1924, pp. 185-188; Dallas *Herald*, Dec. 22, 1858, Oct. 12, 1859; Neighbors to Runnels, Jan. 20, 1858, MSS., Governors' Letters; Neighbors to Twiggs, March 29, 1858, MSS., L. R., I. A. O., N. A.

68. Austin *Southern Intelligencer*, Jan. 26, 1859; Austin *State Gazette*, June 18, 1859.

XIII

1. In Utah and New Mexico Territories, where the reservation experiment also had its champions, a number of tribes were placed on "farms" or reservations. They were, however, not nearly so elaborate as those in Texas and in California. The Utah tribes were colonized on five farms in Utah, San Pete, and Ruby valleys. In New Mexico, Indians occupied farms on the Puerco, some twenty-five miles west of Abiquiu, on the Mimbres near the Copper Mines, and on the Gila. *Senate Executive Documents*, 36 Cong., 1 Sess., I, No. 2, pp. 735-737; *ibid.*, 36 Cong., 2 Sess., 1 No. 1, pp. 244, 393-395; Santa Fe *Weekly Gazette*, May 21, June 25, 1853, Oct. 18, Dec. 20, 1856, Feb. 20, April 10, Aug. 7, 1858; *Statutes at Large*, XI, 79, 184, 330, 400.

2. San Francisco *Daily Alta California*, Jan. 12, 15, May 31, June 19, 1851; *Morning Courier and New York Enquirer* in San Francisco *Daily Alta California*, Dec. 30, 1854.

3. *Senate Executive Documents*, 33 Cong., Spec. Sess., No. 4, p. 380; Browne, "The Coast Rangers," *Harper's New Monthly Magazine*, XXIII, 308.

4. *Statutes at Large*, IX, 519; Stuart to Barbour, McKee, and Wozencraft, Oct. 9, 1850, Loughery to *ibid.*, Oct. 15, 1850, MSS., L. S., I. A. O., N. A.

5. One group of Indian commissioners, consisting of Messrs. Gaines, Skinner, and Allen, had also been sent to Oregon Territory, and another, composed of Robert B. Campbell, C. S. Todd, and Oliver P. Temple, was dispatched to the Mexican border. The appointment of the latter commission was part of a plan to study the Indian problem and secure territory, probably in west Texas, on which all southern border tribes might be consolidated. George W. Manypenny, *Our Indian Wards* (Cincinnati, 1880), 151-153; *Senate Executive Documents*, 31 Cong., 2 Sess., No. 1, Pt. 1, pp. 153-155; *ibid.*, 32 Cong., 1 Sess., No. 1, Pt. 3,

pp. 302-306; Loughery to Todd, Campbell, and Temple, Oct. 15, 1850, MSS., L. S., I. A. O., N. A.

6. San Francisco *Daily Alta California*, Jan. 14, 15, 31, 1851.

7. The goods promised, consisting of food, clothing, tools, and work animals, were worth about $1,000,000 at that time. Moorehead, 330.

8. *Senate Executive Documents*, 33 Cong., Spec. Sess., No. 4, pp. 39-260; Manypenny, 154; Ellison, "The Federal Indian Policy in California, 1846-1860," *Mississippi Valley Historical Review*, IX, 55, 57; St. Louis *Daily Missouri Republican*, June 6, 1851; San Francisco *Daily Alta California*, May 10, 24, 31, Sept. 13, 1851.

9. Ellison, "The Federal Indian Policy in California, 1846-1860," *Mississippi Valley Historical Review*, IX, 58; *Senate Executive Documents*, 33 Cong., Spec. Sess., No. 4, p. 248; San Francisco *Daily Alta California*, Oct. 10, 1851, Feb. 9, 15, July 10, 1852.

10. McPherson, "William McKendree Gwin," MS., Ph.D. dissertation, University of California, 1932, pp. 155-156; *Congressional Globe*, 32 Cong., 1 Sess., XXIV, Pt. 2, pp. 1121-1122.

11. California, *Senate Journal, 1852*, pp. 602-604; San Francisco *Daily Alta California*, Jan. 31, May 31, July 26, 1851; San Francisco *Evening Picayune*, Sept. 13, 1851, April 5, 1852.

12. *Congressional Globe, 32* Cong., 1 Sess., XXIV, Pt. 3, pp. 890, 1121-1122.

13. San Francisco *Daily Alta California*, April 19, 1852.

14. *Statutes at Large*, X, 2; *Senate Executive Documents*, 33 Cong., Spec. Sess., No. 4, p. 361; Stuart to Commissioner of Indian Affairs, March 11, 1852, MSS., L. R., I. A. O., California, N. A.

15. *Senate Executive Documents*, 33 Cong., Spec. Sess., No. 4, pp. 361-366, 367; Bancroft, *History of California*, VII, 485.

16. *Senate Executive Documents*, 33 Cong., Spec. Sess., No. 4, pp. 361, 373-374, 379-380.

17. *Ibid.*, 33 Cong., 1 Sess., No. 1, Pt. 1, p. 258; *House Executive Documents*, 34 Cong., 3 Sess., No. 76, p. 79; *Statutes at Large*, X, 238.

18. Ellison, "The Federal Indian Policy in California, 1846-1860," *Mississippi Valley Historical Review*, IX, 63; Browne, "The Coast Rangers," *Harper's New Monthly Magazine*, XXIII, 308; St. Louis *Daily Missouri Republican*, April 15, 1854.

19. San Francisco *Daily Alta California*, Nov. 2, 1853.

20. San Francisco *Herald*, Jan. 23, 1854.

21. San Francisco *Daily Alta California*, June 25, 1854.

22. Benjamin D. Wilson, a wealthy and prominent Californian, was one of the few Indian officials who did not seek office for personal gain. He "only consented to serve as Indian agent from a sincere desire to benefit the country and the Indians." His great knowledge of the country and Indian character made him an ideal assistant to Beale in setting up the reservation system. He resigned, since he "could not continue in office in harmony with the superintendent and others, especially in regard to monies appropriated by the government." *Senate Executive Documents*, 33 Cong., Spec. Sess., No. 4, pp. 28-29; *ibid.*, 33 Cong., 1 Sess., No. 1, pt. 1, p. 468; Benjamin D. Wilson, "Observations in Early Days in California and New Mexico," 112, MS., Bancroft Library.

23. San Francisco *Daily California Chronicle*, July 11, 1854, quoted in Leonard, "The Federal Indian Policy in the San Joaquin Valley . . .," MS., Ph.D. dissertation, University of California, 1928, pp. 288-289.

24. *Senate Executive Documents*, 33 Cong., 2 Sess., I, No. 1, pp. 506-508.

25. *Ibid.*, 33 Cong., Spec. Sess., No. 4, pp. 372, 404-405; *House Executive Documents*, 35 Cong., 2 Sess., II, No. 2, Pt. 1, pp. 357-358; Bonsal, 186.

26. An investigation of Beale's accounts and a report on the subject by the Comptroller to the Secretary of the Treasury, April 9, 1855, completely vindicated Beale and partially restored him to public confidence. *Congressional Globe*, 33 Cong., 1 Sess., Pt. 2, pp. 1027, 1028, 1041-1051; *Senate Executive Documents*, 34 Cong., 3 Sess., No. 69, pp. 1-7; San Francisco *Daily Alta California*, June 2, 1876; Ellison, "The Federal Indian Policy in California, 1846-1860," *Mississippi Valley Historical Review*, IX, 63.

27. *Senate Executive Documents*, 33 Cong., 2 Sess., I, No. 1, p. 508.

28. San Francisco *Daily Alta California*, May 4, 26, 1875.

29. Los Angeles *Southern Californian*, June 20, 1855, in Hayes, "Indians," II, 178, 188, MSS., Bancroft Library.

30. San Francisco *Daily Alta California*, July 30, 1854.

31. Bancroft, *History of California*, VII, 490; Manypenny to McClelland, Jan. 31, 1855, (Enclosure: Henley to Manypenny, Dec. 18, 1854), MSS., L. R., I. A. O., N. A.

32. *House Executive Documents*, 35 Cong., 2 Sess., II, No. 2, Pt. 1, p. 357, 364; Charles C. Royce, "Indian Land Cessions in the United States," Bureau of American Ethnology, *Eighteenth Annual Report* (Washington, 1899), Pt. 2, pp. 782, 788-789.

33. Dunn, 135-137; *Senate Executive Documents*, 36 Cong., 1 Sess., No. 46, pp. 3-6; "Reminiscences of Mendocino," *Hutchings' California Magazine*, III, 157-159, 177; San Francisco *Daily Alta California*, Jan. 9, 1857.

34. *House Executive Documents*, 35 Cong., 2 Sess., II, No. 2, Pt. 1, pp. 357, 364; Bancroft, *History of California*, VII, 491; Annie Eikel Whittaker, "The Frontier Policy of the United States in the Mexican Cession, 1845-1860," MS., M. A. thesis, University of Texas, 1927, pp. 198, 207.

35. *Senate Executive Documents*, 35 Cong., 1 Sess., II, No. 11, pp. 677-678; *ibid.*, 35 Cong., 2 Sess., I, No. 1, Pt. 1, pp. 635-637; Browne, "The Coast Rangers," *Harper's New Monthly Magazine*, XXIII, 310; San Francisco *Daily Alta California*, April 20, 1856, April 14, 1857, May 4, 1858; Campbell to Henley, May 3, 1855, Henley to Denver, July 4, 1857, MSS., L. R., I. A. O., California, N. A.

36. San Francisco *Daily Alta California*, Oct. 15, 1855, May 28, 1858.

37. "Reminiscences of Mendocino," *Hutchings' California Magazine*, III, 157.

38. Los Angeles *Southern Californian*, June 27, 1855, in San Francisco *Daily Alta California*, July 6, 1855; Los Angeles *Southern Californian*, Oct. 24, 1855, in Hayes, "Indians," II, 194, MSS., Bancroft Library.

39. Browne, "The Coast Rangers," *Harper's New Monthly Magazine*, XXIII, 309-310; *House Executive Documents*, 35 Cong., 2 Sess., II, No. 2, Pt. 1, pp. 649-657 (Bailey's Report); Browne, Abstract, "Condition of Indians in California, Sept. 18, 1858," Lewis to Greene, April 14, 1858, Quinan to Smith, Oct. 1, 1860, MSS., L. R., I. A. O., California, N. A.

40. San Francisco *Daily Alta California*, March 5, 1858; Cooper to Floyd, April 14, 1857, MSS., L. R., I. A. O., California, N. A.; Browne to Thompson, July 2, 1858, MSS., L. R., I. A. O., miscellaneous, N. A.

41. Browne, "The Coast Rangers," *Harper's New Monthly Magazine*, XXIII, 310; Browne to Mix, Aug. 2, Sept. 4, 1858 (Browne's Report), Bailey to Mix, Aug. 30, Oct. 27, 1858 (Bailey's Final Report), MSS., L. R., I. A. O., California, N. A.

42. *Senate Executive Documents*, 35 Cong., 2 Sess., I, No. 1, Pt. 1, pp. 656-657.

43. *Ibid.*, 36 Cong., 1 Sess., No. 46, p. 2; San Francisco *Herald*, March 30, 1859; San Francisco *Daily Alta California*, March 30, April 18, 1859.

44. McDuffie to Greenwood, Aug. 9, Sept. 4, 30, 1859, MSS., L. R., I. A. O., California, N. A.

45. Conklin to Denver, Feb. 15, 1859, MSS., L. R., I. A. O., California, N. A.

46. *Senate Executive Documents*, 36 Cong., 1 Sess., No. 46, pp. 3-23; San Francisco *Daily Alta California*, Dec. 15, 1859.

47. *House Miscellaneous Documents*, 36 Cong., 1 Sess., No. 94, pp. 1-2; *Congressional Globe*, 36 Cong., 1 Sess., XXIX, Pt. 2, p. 1549; San Francisco *Daily Alta California*, Feb. 26, 1860.

48. *Statutes at Large*, XII, 57; *Senate Executive Documents*, 36 Cong., 2 Sess., No. 1, pp. 244-245; Greenwood to Dreibelbis, July 30, 1860, Greenwood to McDuffie, July 31, 1860, MSS., L. S., I. A. O., N. A.

49. *Senate Executive Documents*, 36 Cong., 2 Sess., No. 1, pp. 244-245; Bancroft, *History of California*, VII, 492.

50. *Ibid.*, VII, 493.

51. Between 1850 and 1859 the federal government spent more than $1,737,000 on Indian affairs in California. In addition Congress appropriated almost $1,000,000 to reimburse California for its Indian wars. These amounts were exclusive of expenses incurred by the United States army in policing the Indian country and in suppressing uprisings. Ellison, "The Federal Indian Policy in California, 1846-1860," *Mississippi Valley Historical Review*, IX, 67; San Francisco *Daily Alta California*, June 26, 1859.

52. Dunn, 137; Hittell, *History of California*, III, 916-917; *Congressional Globe*, 33 Cong., 1 Sess., XXVIII, Pt. 2, p. 1043; *ibid.*, 35 Cong., 2 Sess., pp. 694-698; San Francisco *Daily Alta California*, Dec. 21, 1854, Oct. 13, 1855, June 24, 1857.

53. Hoopes, 54, 68.

XIV

1. *House Executive Documents*, 30 Cong., 2 Sess., I, No. 1, 48 and map; *Senate Executive Documents*, 34 Cong., 3 Sess., II, 359-360; St. Louis *Daily Missouri Republican*, Aug. 11, 1851.

2. Kendall, I, 85, 94, 99; Olmsted, 308-313.

3. Browne, *Adventures in the Apache Country*, 11, 27; Mowry, 176-177; Austin *State Gazette*, April 2, 1859.

4. John G. Neihardt, *The Splendid Wayfaring, 1822-1831* (New York, 1920), 4; Symons, "The Army and the Exploration of the West," *The Journal of the Military Service Institution of the United States*, IV, 209.

5. *Senate Executive Documents*, 36 Cong., 2 Sess., No. 1, pp. 9-10; Randall H. Hewitt, *Across the Plains and over the Divide: a Mule-Train Journey from East to West in 1862 and Incidents Connected Therewith* (New York, 1906), 101; William Barrows, "The Great American Desert: There is None," *Magazine of Western History*, II (June, 1885), 132.

6. Among the less prominent Civil War leaders who had gained experience on the western frontier were: Philip St. George Cooke, Randolph B. Marcy, Benjamin L. E. Bonneville, and Samuel P. Heintzelman.

7. Cullum, II, 170-178; Lloyd Lewis, *Captain Sam Grant* (Boston, 1950), 100-338; William E. Brooks, *Grant at Appomattox* (Indianapolis, 1942), 41-55; A. L. Conger, *The Rise of U. S. Grant* (New York, 1931), 1-3; Ulysses Simpson Grant, *Personal Memoirs of U. S. Grant* (New York, 1885), I, 45-209; Thomas Maitland Marshall, "An Early Chapter in the Life of General Grant," MS., Ulysses S. Grant Papers, 1791-1932, M. H. S.

8. Cullum, I, 420-421; Rister, *Robert E. Lee in Texas* (Norman, Okla., 1946), pp. vii-viii, 10-167; Douglas Southall Freeman, *R. E. Lee: a Biography* (New York, 1936), I, 360-378, 406-412.

9. *Census, 1850*, pp. 504, 893, 969, 996; *ibid., 1860, Population*, 28, 483, 572, 573, 575, 595.

10. By 1861 the territories of Nevada, Colorado, and Arizona had been carved out of portions of Utah, Nebraska, and New Mexico. For the peculiar status of Arizona Territory in the early 1860's, see Twitchell, II, 362-363, 409.

11. Between 1850-60, inclusive, 71 new counties were created in Texas, 17 in California, and 14 in Utah; only 4 new counties were organized in New Mexico. *Census, 1850*, pp. 503-504, 966, 988, 1000; *ibid., 1860, Population*, 28, 472-476, 572, 574.

12. For examples of the growth of settlements in the Southwest during the decade 1850-60, see *Census, 1850*, pp. 504, 970–971; *ibid., 1860, Population*, 29-32, 576-577; Bancroft, *History of Utah*, 590-601; Mack, 56-57; Cleland, 263-264; Mowry to Cooper, May 1, June 25, July 23, 1855, MSS., L. R., A. G. O., N. A.

13. Bancroft, *History of North Mexican States and Texas* (San Francisco, 1889), II, 553; Bancroft, *History of Utah*, 581-583; Newmark, 211; Richardson, *Texas, the Lone Star State*, 224.

14. *Census, 1850*, pp. 514-520; *ibid., 1860, Mortality, Property, etc.*, (Washington, 1866), 294-295.

15. Improved Texas farm lands increased from approximately half a million acres to more than fivefold, representing a cash value of more than $88,000,000. In Utah the rate of agricultural progress was about the same—the number of improved farms increased from about 16,000 acres to more than 77,000 acres. The cash value of California farms, during the same period, increased more than twelvefold—from less than $4,000,000 to more than $48,000,000. *Ibid., 1860, Agriculture* (Washington, 1864), p. vii; Cleland, 445; Hittell, *History of California*, III, 866-872, IV, 178.

16. In 1850 the annual value of Texas manufactures was about $1,000,000; ten years later it increased to more than $6,500,000. In New Mexico and Utah Territories the rate of progress was about the same. California showed astonishing progress in manufacture. In 1860 it produced articles valued at more than $68,000,000 annually—an increase of more than 800 per cent in number of establishments and 600 per cent in value of products within a ten-year period. *Census, 1860, Manufactures* (Washington, 1865), 35-36, 594, 667, 670, 729-730; Davis, 211-214; Wallace Stegner, *Mormon Country* (New York, 1942), 67-70; Burton, 346-348, 384-387; Green, Journal, MSS., Caleb Green, Collection, M. H. S.

17. California was the greatest producer of precious metals in the 1850's—producing during the decade nearly one half billion dollars in gold. *Census, 1860, Manufactures*, 66;

Twitchell, II, 324; Marcy to Wetmore, Nov. 24, 1848, Marcy, "Correspondence," XV, MSS., L. C.

18. *Census, 1860, Agriculture*, pp. cviii-cxxviii. Of course, it was in the period following the Civil War that ranching became one of the great industries of the Far West.

19. For the provisions of the mail contracts and description of the various overland mail routes and schedules, see *House Executive Documents*, 32 Cong., 1 Sess., No. 56, VIII, 398-399; *ibid.*, 33 Cong., 2 Sess., No. 86, IX, 711, 714; *ibid.*, 34 Cong., 1 Sess., No. 122, XIII, 401; *ibid.*, 35 Cong., 1 Sess., No. 96, p. 353; St. Louis *Daily Missouri Republican*, Oct. 17, Nov. 10, 1858, Feb. 6, April 26, May 28, 1859; Hafen, *The Overland Mail, 1849-1869: Promoter of Settlement, Precursor of Railroads* (Cleveland, 1926), 53-159.

20. Majors, 142-144; Greeley, 47-48; Dick, 342-367; Frank A. Root and William Elsey Connelley, *The Overland Stage to California* (Topeka, Kans., 1901), 308; D. P. Rolfe, "Overland Freighting from Nebraska City," Nebraska State Historical Society, *Proceedings and Collections* (Lincoln, Nebr., 1902), Ser. 2, V, 286.

21. Domenech, *Missionary Adventures in Texas and Mexico*, 175, 222, 228.

22. W. W. Mills, *Forty Years at El Paso, 1858-1898* (Chicago, 1901), 15.

23. Richardson and Rister, *The Greater Southwest* (Glendale, Calif., 1934), 401.

24. Hittell, *History of California*, II, 719, III, 175-176, 460-649; Newmark, 29-30.

25. *Ibid.*, 31; Caughey, 355-356.

26. This phase of frontier justice continued into the latter nineteenth century. Samuel A. Hammett ("Philip Paxton," pseud.), *A Stray Yankee in Texas* (New York, 1853), 321-325; Richardson and Rister, 404-409; Richardson, *Texas, the Lone Star State*, 230; Wayne Gard, *Frontier Justice* (Norman, Okla., 1949), 23-39, 149-167, 271-273.

27. For almost half a century the Turner thesis remained unchallenged. Then, in the early 1930's the champions and opponents of the frontier hypothesis began a battle royal concerning the influence of the frontier in American history. Now it is usually felt that though clarification is desirable the Turner thesis does provide a useful approach. George Rogers Taylor (ed.), *The Turner Thesis Concerning the Role of the Frontier in American History* (Boston, 1949): II, *Problems in American Civilization*, eds., Earl Latham, George Rogers Taylor, and George F. Whicher (Boston, 1949).

28. Turner, 12-17.

29. Richardson and Rister, 483; Domenech, *Missionary Adventures in Texas and Mexico*, 227-228; Borthwick, 148-149; Dick, 516.

30. Richardson and Rister, 484-486; Dick, 511-515; Taylor, *The Turner Thesis*, 39-40; Emerson Hough, *The Passing of the Frontier* (New Haven, Conn., 1921), 2-3.

31. Lockwood, 123.

32. Lucy Lockwood Hazard, *The Frontier in American Literature* (New York, 1927), 96-125.

33. Edmund Pearson, *Dime Novels or Following an Old Trail in Popular Literature* (Boston, 1929), 5-268; Albert Johannsen, *The House of Beadle and Adams and Its Dime and Nickel Novels* (Norman, Okla., 1950), I, II.

34. Hazard, 182-201.

35. *Ibid.*, 126-137; Neihardt, *The Splendid Wayfaring*; Neihardt, *A Cycle of the West: the Song of Three Friends, the Song of Hugh Glass, the Song of Jed Smith, the Song of the Indian Wars, the Song of the Messiah* (New York, 1949); Howard Derrickson, "Monumental Epic of Our West," St. Louis *Post-Dispatch*, July 10, 1949.

36. See above, Ch. II.

37. Collier, 15-22, 27.

38. The Indian population reached the lowest ebb in its history in 1870 when it dwindled to 25,731. *Census, 1940, Population* (Washington, 1943), II, Pt. 1, p. 19.

39. Collier, 27, 176.

40. Although the new policy of regeneration of the Indian was introduced under the Hoover administration, it was the spirit and guiding hand of Collier that fostered self-reliance for the tribesmen. In his administration of the Howard-Wheeler Act of 1934, Collier made it possible for the Indian to attain greater economic security, racial integrity, and self-dependence. *Statutes at Large*, XLVI, Pt. 1, pp. 147, 1129, 1135, 1160; *ibid.*, XLVIII, Pt. 1, pp. 596, 984-988; Collier, 171, 261-287; "New Deal Policy Offers Indian Self-Government in Place of a Century of Dishonor," St. Louis *Post-Dispatch*, Oct. 20, 1934; "A New Day for the Indian," *ibid.*, May 12, 1940; "Navajo School," *ibid.*, March 18, 1951; "John Collier, Indians' Friend," St. Louis *Star-Times*, March 29, 1945.

41. The Indian population of continental United States as of January, 1948, numbered approximately 400,000. *The New International Year Book for 1949* (New York, 1950), 254; "Comeback of the Indian," St. Louis *Post-Dispatch*, Dec. 20, 1939; "Comeback of the Redskin," *ibid.*, Dec. 22, 1940; "No Longer the Vanishing American," *ibid.*, Sept. 25, 1943; Dick Terry, "The American Indian and His Future," *ibid.*, Oct. 7, 1945; "Navajo Tribal Custom Respected . . . 1950 Agenda," *ibid.*, Jan. 5, 1950.

PRINCIPAL MILITARY POSTS IN THE SOUTHWEST, 1848-60

Name	Location	Established	Abandoned[1]
Fort Arbuckle	On Wild Horse Creek, near present Davis, Okla.	1851	*
Fort Belknap	About one mile south of the site of Newcastle, Tex.	1851	*
Benicia Barracks	Benicia, Calif.	1849	*
Fort Bliss	About two miles below El Paso, Tex.	1848	
Fort Bridger	Green River, Uinta County, Wyo.	1858	*
Fort Brown	Brownsville, Tex.	1846	*
Fort Buchanan	About forty-five miles southeast of Tucson, Ariz.	1856	*
Cantonment Burgwin	About nine miles north of Taos, N. Mex.	1852	1860
Fort Clark	About forty-five miles above Eagle Pass, Tex.	1852	*
Fort Craig	About twelve miles above Fra Cristobal, N. Mex.	1854	*
Fort Davis	Presidio County, Tex.	1854	*
Fort Defiance	Cañon Bonito, Ariz.	1851	*
Fort Duncan	Eagle Pass, Tex.	1849	*
Camp Far West	About thirty-five miles north of Sutter's Fort, Calif.	1849	1852
Fort Fillmore	On Rio Grande, south of Las Cruces, N. Mex.	1851	*
Fort Gibson	On Grand River, Okla.	1824	*
Fort Humboldt	Near Bucksport, Calif.	1853	*
Fort Inge	Near present Uvalde, Tex.	1849	*
Jefferson Barracks[2]	Below St. Louis, Mo.	1826	*
Fort Kearny	Opposite Grand Island, on south bank of Platte River, Nebr.	1848	*
Fort Laramie	Goshen County, Wyo.	1849	*
Fort Leavenworth	On Missouri River about three miles above Leavenworth City, Kans.	1827	
Fort Marcy	Santa Fe, N. Mex.	1846	*
Fort Massachusetts	Utah Creek, San Luis Valley, Colo.	1852	*
Fort McIntosh	Above Laredo, Tex.	1849	*
Fort Mojave	Near Mohave City, Ariz.	1859	*
Fort Quitman	About eighty miles below El Paso, Tex.	1858	*
Fort Riley	On north bank of Kansas River, Kans.	1853	
Ringgold Barracks	Below Rio Grande City, Tex.	1848	*
Fort Smith	At Junction of Poteau and Arkansas rivers, Ark.	1817	*
Fort Stanton	On Bonita River, N. Mex.	1855	*
Fort Stockton	About 140 miles northeast of Presidio del Norte, Tex.	1859	*
Fort Tejón	Near Tejón Pass, Calif.	1854	*
Fort Thorn	Santa Barbara, N. Mex.	1853	1859
Fort Union	About 100 miles northeast of Santa Fe, N. Mex.	1851	*
Fort Worth	Site of present Fort Worth, Tex.	1849	1853
Fort Yuma	Mouth of the Gila River, Imperial County, Calif.	1850	*

[1] The posts abandoned after 1860 are designated by an asterisk. Where neither asterisk nor date is indicated the post was in existence as of October, 1951. The locations refer to present-day states. Additional pertinent details, including citations, will be found in the text and footnotes of Chapter III.

[2] Jefferson Barracks was reactivated in January, 1951. See above, Chapter III, note 21.

Bibliography

This is a select bibliography. Only those materials have been listed which have been actually used in the preparation of this study and cited in the footnotes.

PRIMARY MATERIALS
MANUSCRIPTS

BANCROFT LIBRARY, University of California
  "Ancient Santa Fé."
  BEALE, E. F., "Statement of General E. F. Beale,"
    Biographical Sketch [n. d.] written by Beale for H. H. Bancroft.
  HAYES, BENJAMIN, "Diary of a Journey Overland, 1849-1850." "Indians."
  HAYS, JOHN C., "Life and Adventures of a Texas Ranger ... as Furnished by Hays and Major John Caperton to Bancroft in 1879."
  LITTLE, JOHN T., "Statement of Events in the First Years of American Occupation of California, 1849-1861."
  "Miscellaneous Historical Papers (Brackett's Sketch of Mormon Battalion)."
  MURRAY, WALTER, "Narrative of a California Volunteer, July, 1846-Feb., 1848."
  "Unbound Documents, Archives of California, 1846-1850."
  WATTS, J. H., "Santa Fe Affairs."
  WILSON, BENJAMIN D., "Observations in Early Days in California and New Mexico."
  WOZENCRAFT, O. M., "Indian Affairs, 1849-1850."
CALIFORNIA STATE LIBRARY, Sacramento
  CARPENTER, HELEN McCOWEN, "Diary, May 26-Oct. 22, 1856."
HUNTINGTON LIBRARY, San Marino, California
  California File, 1848-1860.
  RITCH, WILLIAM G., Collection, 1848-1860.
LIBRARY OF CONGRESS
  DAVIS, JEFFERSON, "Correspondence, 1840-1877."
  HEINTZELMAN, SAMUEL PETER, "Papers, 1848-1860."
  McCLELLAN, GEORGE B., "Letters, 1848-1860."
  MARCY, WILLIAM L., "Correspondence, 1848-1857."
  "United States Miscellaneous, California and New Mexico, 1846-1850."
MISSOURI HISTORICAL SOCIETY, St. Louis
  GRANT, ULYSSES SIMPSON, "Papers, 1791-1932."
  GREEN, CALEB, 1862, Journal Containing "A visit to the Great Salt Lake or Observations during a five month's [sic] residence in Utah," Green, Collection.
  KEARNY, STEPHEN WATTS, "Journals, Diary and Letter Books, 1820-1847."
  LANE, WILLIAM CARR, "Papers, 1815-1881."
NATIONAL ARCHIVES
  Adjutant General's Office (Record Group No. 94) Department Returns, 1848-1861; Division Returns, 1848-1861; Freeman, William G., "Report of Inspection of Eighth Military Department, April 22, 1853";

General Orders, 1847-1861; Letters Received, 1848-1861; Letters Sent, 1848-1861; Medical History of Posts; Post Returns, 1848-1861; Special Orders, 1848-1862; General Orders, Orders, and Special Orders, 1848-1861, Headquarters of the Army; Orders, 1854-1857 and Special Orders, 1857-1860, Department of New Mexico (Ninth Military Department); Orders, 1848-1852, 1854-1861, and Special Orders, 1849-1852, 1854-1858, Department of the Pacific (Pacific Division); Orders, 1853-1858, and Special Orders, 1853-1860, Department of Texas (Eighth Military Department); General Orders, 1858-1860, Department of Utah, Orders and Special Orders, 1849-1852, Department of the West (Western Division).

Army Commands, United States (Record Group No. 98) Letters Received 1848-1861, Department of California (Tenth Military Department); Letters Received and Letters Sent, 1848-1861, Department of New Mexico (Ninth Military Department); Letters Received and Letters Sent, 1848-1861, Department of Texas (Eighth Military Department); Letters Received, 1848-1861, Department of the West (Western Division).

Commissary-General of Subsistence, Office (Record Group No. 192) Register of Contracts, 1848-1863.

Engineers, Office of the Chief (Record Group No. 77) Letters Received, 1846-1861; Letters Sent, 1846-1861; Letters Received, 1846-1861, and Letters Sent, 1845-1861, Topographical Engineers Bureau; NEWBERRY, JOHN S. "Notes on San Juan (Macomb's) Expedition, July 13-Sept. 28, 1859"; POPE, JOHN, "A Military Memoir of the Country between the Mississippi River and the Pacific Ocean with some Account of Frontier Defenses, May 7, 1859."

Headquarters of the Army (Record Group No. 108) Letters Received, 1848-1861; Letters Sent, 1848-1861.

Indian Affairs Office(Record Group No. 75) Letters Received and Letters Sent, 1848-1861, Commissioner of Indian Affairs; Letters Received, 1848-1861, California; Letters Received, 1848-1861, Miscellaneous; Letters Received, 1848-1861, New Mexico; Letters Received, 1848-1861, Texas; Neighbors, Robert S., "Memorandum Travel Book, from Brazos Agency, Texas, to the False Ouachita," C. N., July 31-Aug. 30, 1859.

Quartermaster General's Office(Record Group No. 92) "Camels," 1848-1866; Letters Received, 1848-1861; Letters Sent (Letters and Reports), 1848-1861; MARCY, RANDOLPH B., "Field Notes, Dec., 1854."

Secretary of the Interior, Office (Record Group No. 48) Letters Received, 1848-1861; Letters Sent, 1848-1861.

Secretary of War, Office (Record Group No. 107) Letters Received, 1848-1861; Letters Sent, 1848-1861.

State Department, General Records (Record Group No. 59) Territorial Papers, New Mexico, 1848-1861.

Surgeon General's Office (War) (Record Group No. 112) Letters Received, 1848-1861; Letters Sent, 1848-1861.

New Mexico Historical Society, Santa Fe
 Twitchell, Ralph Emerson, Collection, 1848-1860.
Probate Court, St. Louis
 "Will of Pierre Melicourt Papin, July 7, 1849."
Texas State Library, Austin
 Executive Record Books (Letters Sent), 1846-1861.
 Governors' Letters (Letters Received), 1846-1861.
 Indian Affairs, 1846-1860.
University of Texas Library, Austin
 Barry, James Buckner, "Papers, 1848-1860" (typewirtten copy).
 Burleson, Ed., "Letters, 1848-1860."
 Caperton, John C., "Sketch of Col. John C. Hays, Texas Ranger."
 Ford, John S., "Memoirs, 1848-1860."
 Neighbors, Robert S., "Papers, 1852-1859."

UNITED STATES GOVERNMENT PUBLICATIONS

Congressional Documents
 Congressional Globe, 30-37 Cong. (1847-1863).
 House Documents, 29 Cong., 2 Sess. (1846-1847).
 House Executive Documents, 30-36 Cong. (1847-1861); 41 Cong., 2 Sess.
  (1869-1870); 44 Cong., 1 Sess. (1875-1876).
 House Journal, 32 Cong. (1852-1853); 34 Cong. (1855-1857).
 House Miscellaneous Documents, 33-34 Cong. (1853-1857); 36 Cong.
  (1859-1861); 41 Cong., 3 Sess. (1870-1871).
 House Reports, 31-34 Cong. (1849-1857).
 Senate Bills and Resolutions, 30 Cong. (1847-1849).
 Senate Documents, 29 Cong., 1 Sess. (1845-1846); 56 Cong., 1 Sess.,
  (1899-1900).
 Senate Executive Documents, 30-37 Cong. (1847-1863).
 Senate Journal, 31 Cong. (1849-1851); 33 Cong. (1853-1855).
 Senate Miscellaneous Documents, 33 Cong. (1853-1855).
 Senate Reports, 30-31 Cong. (1847-1851).
Other Government Publications
 American State Papers, Indian Affairs. 2 vols. Washington, 1832-1834.
 American State Papers, Miscellaneous. 2 vols. Washington, 1834.
 Billings, John S., *Report on Barracks and Hospitals with Descriptions of
  Military Posts.* Washington, 1870.
 Handbook of Subsistence Stores. Washington, 1896.
 Macomb, John N., *Report of Exploring Expedition from Santa Fe, New
  Mexico to the Junction of Grand and Green Rivers of the Great Colo-
  rado of the West in 1859.* Washington, 1876.
 Royce, Charles C., "Indian Land Cessions in the United States," Bureau
  of American Ethnology, *Eighteenth Annual Report,* Part 2. Washing-
  ton, 1899.
 Simpson, James H., *Report of Explorations Across the Great Basin of the
  Territory of Utah for a Direct Wagon Route from Camp Floyd to
  Genoa in Carson Valley, 1859.* Washington, 1876.
 Uniform of the Army of the United States (Illustrated) from 1774-1907.
  2 vols. New York, 1907.

United States, *Census, 1850*. Washington, 1853.
    Census, 1860, 5 vols. Washington, 1862-1866.
    Census, 1940, Population, Characteristics of the Population, II, Pts. 1-7. Washington, 1943.
    Statutes at Large. 61 vols. Boston, 1846-1873, Washington, 1875-1948.
    The War of the Rebellion: A Compilation of the Official Records of the Union and Confederate Armies. Series 1. 39 vols. Washington, 1880-1892.

STATE DOCUMENTS

CALIFORNIA, *Assembly Journal, 1849-1861*. 13 vols. San Jose, 1850-1851, San Francisco, 1852-1853, Sacramento, 1854-1861.
    Senate Journal, 1849-1861. 13 vols. San Jose, 1850-1851, San Francisco, 1852-1853, Sacramento, 1854-1861.
    Statutes, 1850-1861. 12 vols. San Jose, 1850-1851, San Francisco, 1852-1853, Sacramento, 1854-1861.
GAMMEL, HANS P. N. (ed.), *The Laws of Texas, 1822-1902*. 10 vols. Austin, 1898-1902.
Laws of the Territory of New Mexico, 1846, 1847, 1851-1861. 13 vols. Santa Fe, 1847-1848, 1852-1861.
Texas, *Senate Journal*, 8 Sess. [Extra]. Austin, 1861.

NEWSPAPERS

ARKANSAS
    Fort Smith *Herald*, 1848-1851, 1856.
    Helena *Southern Shield*, 1849-1853.
    Little Rock *Arkansas Banner*, 1847-1851.
    Little Rock *True Democrat*, 1852-1860.
    Washington *Telegraph*, 1849-1856.
CALIFORNIA
    Los Angeles *Star*, 1851-1852.
    Marysville *Weekly California Express*, 1857-1859.
    Sacramento *Transcript*, 1850-1851.
    San Francisco *Daily Alta California*, 1850-1860.
    San Francisco *Daily California Chronicle*, 1854.
    San Francisco *Daily Evening Picayune*, 1851-1852.
    San Francisco *Daily National*, 1858.
    San Francisco *Evening Bulletin*, 1858.
    San Francisco *Evening Picayune*, 1851.
    San Francisco *Herald*, 1854, 1859-1860.
DISTRICT OF COLUMBIA
    Washington *National Intelligencer*, 1846.
KANSAS
    Leavenworth City *Kansas Weekly Herald*, 1854-1859.
LOUISIANA
    New Orleans *Daily Picayune*, 1846-1860.
MISSOURI
    St. Louis *Daily Missouri Republican*, 1847-1860.
    St. Louis *Daily Union*, 1849-1850.

St. Louis *Weekly Reveille*, 1846.
NEW MEXICO
Santa Fe *Gazette*, 1859-1860.
Santa Fe *Weekly Gazette*, 1852-1859.
OKLAHOMA (Indian Territory)
Tahlequah *Cherokee Advocate*, 1847-1853.
TEXAS
Austin *Southern Intelligencer*, 1856-1860.
Austin *State Gazette*, 1855-1860.
Austin *Texas Democrat*, 1848.
Austin *Texas State Gazette*, 1849-1855.
Clarksville *Northern Standard*, 1848-1852.
Clarksville *Standard*, 1852-1860.
Corpus Christi *Nueces Valley*, 1857-1858.
Corpus Christi *Star*, 1848-1849
Dallas *Herald*, 1858-1860.
Houston *Democratic Telegraph and Texas Register*, 1848-1850.
Houston *Mercantile Advertiser*, 1849.
San Antonio *Ledger*, 1851-1859.
San Antonio *Ledger and Texan*, 1860.
San Antonio *Texan*, 1855-1859.
San Antonio *Western Texan*, 1851-1854.
Victoria *Texian Advocate*, 1848, 1850-1851.
Washington, *Texas Ranger*, 1854.
UTAH
Salt Lake City *Deseret News,* 1851-1859.

OTHER PRIMARY MATERIALS

BANDEL, EUGENE, *Frontier Life in the Army, 1854-1861* (Ralph P. Bieber, ed.). Glendale, Calif., 1932.

BANDELIER, ADOLF F., *Final Report of Investigations among the Indians of the Southwestern United States Carried on Mainly in the Years from 1880-1885.* 2 vols. Cambridge, 1890-92.

BELL, WILLIAM A., *New Tracks in North America: A Journal of Travel and Adventure.* 2 vols. London, 1869.

BIEBER, RALPH P. (ed.), "Letters of William Carr Lane, 1852-1854," *New Mexico Historical Review*, III (April, 1928), 179-203.
Southern Trails to California in 1849. Glendale, 1937.

BILLINGS, JOHN DAVIS, *Hardtack and Coffee or the Unwritten Story of Army Life.* Boston, 1888.

BLOOM, LANSING B. (ed.), "Bourke on the Southwest," *New Mexico Historical Review*, VIII (Jan., 1933), 1-30, IX (Jan., 1934), 33-77, (April, 1934), 159-183, (July, 1934), 273-289, (Oct., 1934), 375-435.

BORTHWICK, J. D., *Three Years in California.* London, 1857.

BRACKETT, ALBERT G., *History of the United States Cavalry.* New York, 1865.

BROOKS, CLINTON, E. AND REEVE, FRANK D. (eds.), "James A. Bennett: A Dragoon in New Mexico, 1850-1856," *New Mexico Historical Review*, XXII (Jan., 1947), 51-97, (April, 1947), 140-176.

BROWNE, J. ROSS, *Adventures in the Apache Country: a Tour through Arizona and Sonora with Notes on the Silver Regions of Nevada.* New York, 1869.

"The Coast Rangers," *Harper's New Monthly Magazine,* XXIII (Aug., 1861), 306-316.

"A Peep at Washoe," *Harper's New Monthly Magazine,* XXII (Dec., 1860), 1-17, (Jan., 1861), 145-162, (Feb., 1861), 289-305.

BRYANT, EDWIN, *What I Saw in California. Journal of a Tour by Immigrant Route and South Pass of the Rocky Mountains, across the Continent of North America, the Great Desert Basin and through California in the Years, 1846-1847.* New York, 1848.

BUCHANAN, JAMES, *Messages of James Buchanan* (J. Buchanan Henry, comp.). New York, 1888.

Works of James Buchanan (John Bassett Moore, ed.). 12 vols. Philadelphia, 1908-11.

BURTON, RICHARD FRANCIS, *The City of the Saints.* London, 1861.

CALHOUN, JAMES S., *Official Correspondence of James S. Calhoun* (Annie H. Abel, ed.). Washington, 1915.

CARR, ERASMUS T., "Reminiscences Concerning Fort Leavenworth in 1855-1856," Kansas State Historical Society, *Collections,* XII. Topeka, Kans., 1912.

CHANDLESS, WILLIAM, *A Visit to Salt Lake.* London, 1857.

"Cincinnatus" (WHEAT, MARVIN), *Travels on the Western Slope of the Mexican Cordillera.* San Francisco, 1857.

CLEVER, CHARLES P., *New Mexico: Resources: Necessities for Railroad Connection with Atlantic and Pacific: Her Great Future.* Washington, 1868.

CONNELLEY, WILLIAM E. (ed.), *Doniphan's Expedition and the Conquest of New Mexico and California.* Topeka, 1907.

"A Journal of the Santa Fe Trail," *Mississippi Valley Historical Review,* XII (June, 1925), 72-98, (Sept., 1925), 227-255.

CONSIDERANT, VICTOR, *Au Texas.* Paris, 1854.

COOKE, PHILIP ST. GEORGE, *The Conquest of New Mexico and California.* New York, 1878.

Scenes and Adventures in the Army. Philadelphia, 1857.

COOKE, PHILIP ST. GEORGE, WHITING, WILLIAM HENRY C., AND AUBREY, FRANÇOIS XAVIER, *Exploring Southwestern Trails, 1846-1854* (Ralph P. Bieber, ed., in collaboration with Averam B. Bender). Glendale, 1938.

CREMONY, JOHN C., *Life among the Apaches.* Santa Fe, 1868.

CRIMMINS, M. L., "Colonel J. K. F. Mansfield's Report of the Inspection of the Department of Texas in 1856," *Southwestern Historical Quarterly,* XLII (Oct., 1938), 122-148, (Jan., 1939), 215-257, (April, 1939), 351-387.

CROOK, GEORGE, *General George Crook: His Autobiography* (Martin F. Schmitt, ed.). Norman, Okla., 1946.

DANA, JR., RICHARD HENRY, *Two Years Before the Mast.* New York, 1909.

DAVIS, WILLIAM WATTS HART, *El Gringo or New Mexico and Her People.* New York, 1857.

DEWEES, W. B., *Letters from an Early Settler of Texas.* Louisville, Ky., 1852.

DOBIE, J. FRANK, BOATRIGHT, MODY C., AND RANSOM, HARRY H. (eds.), *Mustangs and Cow Horses.* Austin, 1940.

DOMENECH, EMMANUEL HENRI DIEUDONNÉ, *Missionary Adventures in Texas and Mexico, 1846-1852.* London, 1858.

Seven Years' Residence in the Great Deserts of North America. London, 1860.

ELLIOTT, RICHARD S., *Notes Taken in Sixty Years.* St. Louis, 1883.

FOREMAN, GRANT, *Marcy & the Gold Seekers: the Journal of Captain R. B. Marcy, with an Account of the Gold Rush over the Southern Route.* Norman, Okla., 1939.

FORNEY, JOHN W., *What I Saw in Texas.* Philadelphia, 1872.

FORSYTH, GEORGE A., *The Story of the Soldier.* New York, 1900.

FRÉMONT, JOHN CHARLES, *Memoirs of My Life. Including in the Narrative Five Journeys of Western Exploration, during the Years 1842, 1843-4, 1845-6-7, 1848-9, 1853-4...* Chicago, 1887.

FROEBEL, JULIUS, *Seven Years' Travel in Central America, Northern Mexico, and the Far West of the United States.* London, 1859.

GARRARD, LEWIS H., *Wah-To-Yah and the Taos Trail* (Ralph P. Bieber, ed). Glendale, 1938.

GIBSON, GEORGE R., *Journal of a Soldier under Kearny and Doniphan, 1846-1847* (Ralph P. Bieber, ed.). Glendale, 1935.

GLISAN, RODNEY, *A Journal of Army Life.* San Francisco, 1874.

GOLDER, FRANK A., in collaboration with BAILEY, THOMAS A., AND SMITH, J. LYMAN, *The March of the Mormon Battalion from Council Bluffs to California, Taken from the Journal of Henry Standage.* New York, 1928.

GRANT, ULYSSES SIMPSON, *Personal Memoirs of U. S. Grant.* 2 vols. New York, 1885.

GREELEY, HORACE, *Overland Journey from New York to San Francisco.* New York, 1860.

GREGG, JOSIAH, *Commerce of the Prairies; or, The Journal of a Santa Fé Trader.* 2 vols. New York, 1845. Reprint, *Early Western Travels,* XIX, XX (R. G. Thwaites, ed.). Cleveland, 1905.

GREINER, JOHN, "Private Letters of a Government Official in the Southwest," *Journal of American History,* III (Oct., 1909), No. 4, pp. 541-554.

HAMMETT, SAMUEL A. ("Philip Paxton"), *A Stray Yankee in Texas.* New York, 1853.

HEAP, GWINN H., *Central Route to the Pacific from the Valley of the Mississippi to California: Journal of the Expedition.* Philadelphia, 1854.

HOUSTON, SAMUEL, *The Writings of Sam Houston, 1813-1863* (Amelia W. Williams and Eugene C. Barker, eds.). 8 vols. Austin, 1938-43.

HUMBOLDT, VON, BARON FRIEDRICH HEINRICH ALEXANDER, *Political Essay on the Kingdom of New Spain* (John Black, tr.). 4 vols. London, 1811.

HUMFREVILLE, JAMES LEE, *Twenty Years among Our Hostile Indians.* New York, 1899.

IRVING, WASHINGTON, *The Adventures of Captain Bonneville, U. S. A. in the Rocky Mountains and the Far West.* New York, 1859.

KENDALL, GEORGE WILKINS, *Narrative of an Expedition across the Great Southwestern Prairies from Texas to Santa Fé.* 2 vols. London, 1845.

KENNEDY, WILLIAM, *Texas: The Rise, Progress, and Prospects of the Republic of Texas.* 2 vols. London, 1841.

LANE, LYDIA SPENCER, *I Married a Soldier; or, Old Days in the Old Army.* Philadelphia, 1893.

LEE, JOHN DOYLE, *Mormonism Unveiled.* St. Louis, 1877.

LESLEY, LEWIS BURT (ed.), *Uncle Sam's Camels: The Journal of May Humphreys Stacey Supplemented by the Report of Edward F. Beale, 1857-1858.* Cambridge, 1929.

LITTLE, JAMES A., *Jacob Hamblin.* Salt Lake City, 1909.

LOWE, PERCIVAL G., *Five Years a Dragoon ('49-'54). And Other Adventures on the Great Plains.* Kansas City, Mo., 1906.

MAJORS, ALEXANDER, *Seventy Years on the Frontier.* New York, 1893.

MANYPENNY, GEORGE W., *Our Indian Wards.* Cincinnati, 1880.

MARCY, RANDOLPH B., *Adventure on Red River: Report on the Exploration of the Headwaters of the Red River by Captain Randolph B. Marcy and Captain G. B. McClellan* (Grant Foreman, ed.). Norman, Okla., 1937.

Thirty Years of Army Life on the Border. New York, 1866.

McCALL, GEORGE A., *Letters from the Frontiers Written during a Period of Thirty Years' Service in the Army of the United States.* Philadelphia, 1868.

McCONNELL, H. H., *Five Years a Cavalryman.* Jacksboro, Tex., 1889.

McCOY, JOSEPH G., *Historical Sketches of the Cattle Trade of the West and Southwest* (Ralph P. Bieber, ed.). Glendale, 1940.

McKAY, ROBERT H., *Little Pills.* Pittsburg, Kans., 1918.

MILLS, W. W., *Forty Years at El Paso, 1858-1898.* Chicago, 1901.

MOWRY, SYLVESTER, *Arizona and Sonora: The Geography, History, and Resources of the Silver Region of North America.* New York, 1864.

NEWMARK, HARRIS, *Sixty Years in Southern California, 1853-1913.* New York, 1916.

OLMSTED, FREDERICK LAW, *A Journey through Texas or a Saddle-trip on the Southwestern Frontier.* New York, 1857.

PARKER, WILLIAM B., *Notes Taken during the Expedition Commanded by Captain R. B. Marcy, U. S. A., Through Unexplored Texas in Summer and Fall of 1854.* Philadelphia, 1856.

PRICE, GEORGE FREDERIC, *Across the Continent with the Fifth Cavalry.* New York, 1883.

RANKIN, MELINDA, *Texas in 1850.* Boston, 1850.

"Reminiscences of Mendocino," *Hutchings' California Magazine,* III (San Francisco, 1859), 146-160, 177-181.

RITCH, WILLIAM G., *Illustrated New Mexico.* Santa Fe, 1883.

ROBINSON, FAYETTE, *California and Its Gold Regions with a Geographical and Topographical View of the Country, Its Minerals and Agricultural Resources.* New York, 1849.

RUSLING, JAMES FOWLER, *The Great West and the Pacific Coast.* New York, 1877.

SCHMITZ, JOSEPH (ed.), "Impressions of Texas in 1860," *Southwestern Historical Quarterly,* XLII (April, 1939), 334-350.

TILDEN, JR., BRYANT P., *Notes on the Upper Rio Grande.* Philadelphia, 1847.

TYSON, JAMES L., *Diary of a Physician in California.* New York, 1850.

VIELÉ, TERESA (Griffin), *Following the Drum: a Glimpse of Frontier Life.* New York, 1858.

WEBB, JAMES J., *Adventures in the Santa Fé Trade, 1844-1847* (Ralph P. Bieber, ed.). Glendale, 1931.

WHIPPLE, HENRY BENJAMIN, *Lights and Shadows of a Long Episcopate*. New York, 1899.

SECONDARY MATERIALS
BOOKS

ALBRIGHT, GEORGE LESLIE, *Official Explorations for Pacific Railroads*. Berkeley, Calif., 1921.

ALTER, J. CECIL, *James Bridger, Trapper, Frontiersman, Scout and Guide*; *a Historical Narrative*. Salt Lake City, 1925.

ANDERSON, NELS, *Desert Saints: the Mormon Frontier in Utah*. Chicago, 1942.

Armsmear: the Home, the Arm, and the Armory of Samuel Colt (Henry Barnard, ed.). New York, 1866.

BANCROFT, HUBERT HOWE, *History of Arizona and New Mexico*. San Francisco, 1889.

    History of California. 7 vols. San Francisco, 1884-90.

    History of North Mexican States and Texas. San Francisco, 1889.

    History of Oregon. 2 vols. San Francisco, 1886-88.

    History of Utah. San Francisco, 1889.

    The Native Races. 5 vols. San Francisco, 1882-83.

BARROWS, H. D., "Memorial Sketch of Col. J. J. Warner," Historical Society, Southern California, *Publications,* III. Los Angeles, 1895.

BEERS, HENRY PUTNEY, *The Western Military Frontier, 1815-1846*. Philadelphia, 1935.

BIEBER, RALPH P., "Fort Leavenworth," *Dictionary of American History,* III. New York, 1940.

BLEDSOE, A. J., *Indian Wars of the Northwest*. San Francisco, 1885.

BONSAL, STEPHEN, *Edward Fitzgerald Beale: a Pioneer in the Path of Empire. 1822-1903*. New York, 1912.

BRADLEY, GLENN D., *The Story of the Pony Express*. Chicago, 1913.

BROOKS, WILLIAM E., *Grant at Appomattox*. Indianapolis, 1942.

BROWN, JOHN HENRY, *History of Texas, 1685-1892*. 2 vols. St. Louis, 1893.

BUNNELL, LAFAYETTE H., *Discovery of the Yosemite and the Indian War of 1851*. New York, 1892.

CALLAHAN, EDWARD W., *List of Officers of the Navy of the United States and of the Marine Corps from 1775 to 1900*. New York, 1901.

CANNON, CARL L., "Jornada del Muerto," *Dictionary of American History,* III. New York, 1940.

CANNON, FRANK J., AND KNAPP, GEORGE L., *Brigham Young and his Mormon Empire*. New York, 1913.

CAUGHEY, JOHN WALTON, *California*. New York, 1940.

CLELAND, ROBERT GLASS, *History of California: The American Period*. New York, 1922.

CLUM, WOODWORTH, *Apache Agent: the Story of John P. Clum*. Boston, 1936.

COLLIER, JOHN, *The Indians of the Americas*. New York, 1947.

CONGER, A. L., *The Rise of U. S. Grant*. New York, 1931.

CREER, LELAND HARGRAVE, *Utah and the Nation*. Seattle, 1929.

CULLUM, GEORGE W., *Biographical Register of the Officers and Graduates of the U. S. Military Academy at West Point, N. Y. from Its Establishment in 1802 to 1890*. 5 vols. Boston, 1891, Cambridge, 1901, and Saginaw, Mich., 1910.

CURTIS, EDWARD S., *The North American Indian*. 16 vols. Cambridge, 1907-26.

DALE, EDWARD EVERETT, "The End of the Indian Problem," *The Quest for Political Unity in World History* (Stanley Pargellis, ed.): *Annual Report, American Historical Association, 1942*, III. Washington, 1944.

DELLENBAUGH, FREDERICK SAMUEL, *The Romance of the Colorado River*. New York, 1902.

DICK, EVERETT, *Vanguards of the Frontier*. New York, 1941.

Dictionary of American Biography. 20 vols. New York, 1928-37.

Dictionary of American History. 6 vols. New York, 1940.

DOBIE, J. FRANK, *A Vaquero of the Brush Country*. Dallas, 1929.

DUMAS, ALEXANDRE, *Un Gil-Blas en Californie*. Paris, 1861.

DUNN, JR., JACOB PLATT, *Massacres of the Mountains: a History of the Indian Wars of the Far West*. New York, 1886.

EDGAR, WILLIAM F., "Historical Notes of Old Land Marks in California," *Historical Society, Southern California, Publications*, III. Los Angeles, 1893.

ELLISON, JOSEPH, *California and the Nation, 1850-1869*. Berkeley, 1927.

ENGLEHARDT, FR. ZEPHYRIN, *The Missions and Missionaries of California*. 2 vols. San Francisco, 1908-12.

EXLEY, THOMAS M., *A Compendium of the Pay of the Army from 1785 to 1888*. Washington, 1888.

FARROW, EDWARD S., *A Dictionary of Military Terms*. New York, 1918.

FERGUSON, SAMUEL W., "With Albert Sidney Johnston's Expedition to Utah, 1857," *Kansas State Historical Society, Collections*, XII. Topeka, 1912.

FERGUSSON, HARVEY, *Rio Grande*. New York, 1933.

FOREMAN, GRANT, *Advancing the Frontier*. Norman, Okla., 1933.
A History of Oklahoma. Norman, 1942.

FREEMAN, DOUGLAS SOUTHALL, *R. E. Lee: a Biography*. 4 vols. New York, 1936.

FREEMAN, LEWIS R., *The Colorado River: Yesterday, Today, and Tomorrow*. New York, 1923.

FULLER, GEORGE W., *A History of the Pacific Northwest*. New York, 1931.

GANOE, WILLIAM A., *The History of the United States Army*. New York, 1942.

GARD, WAYNE, *Frontier Justice*. Norman, Okla., 1949.

GARRISON, GEORGE PIERCE, *Westward Extension, 1841-1850*. New York, 1906.

GIBBS, JOSIAH F., *The Mountain Meadows Massacre*. Salt Lake City, 1910.

GRINNELL, GEORGE BIRD, "Old Bent's Fort and Its Builders," *Kansas State Historical Society, Collections*, XV. Topeka, 1923.

HAFEN, LEROY R., *The Overland Mail, 1849-1869: Promoter of Settlement, Precursor of Railroads*. Cleveland, 1926.

HAFEN, LEROY, AND GHENT, W. J., *Broken Hand. The Story of Thomas Fitzpatrick, Chief of the Mountain Men*. Denver, 1931.

HAFEN, LEROY, AND YOUNG, FRANCIS MARION, *Fort Laramie and the Pageant of the West, 1834-1890*. Glendale, 1938.

HAMERSLY, THOMAS H. S., *Complete Regular Army Register of the United States for 100 Years, 1779-1879, with a Military History of the Department of War*. Washington, 1880.

HARMON, GEORGE DEWEY, *Sixty Years of Indian Affairs: Political, Economic, and Diplomatic, 1789-1850*. Chapel Hill, N.C., 1941.

HAZARD, LUCY LOCKWOOD, *The Frontier in American Literature*. New York, 1927.

HEITMAN, FRANCIS B., *Historical Register and Dictionary of the United States Army. 1789-1903*. 2 vols. Washington, 1903.

HEWITT, RANDALL H., *Across the Plains and over the Divide: a Mule-Train Journey from East to West in 1862 and Incidents Connected Therewith*. New York, 1906.

HILL, JOSEPH, J., *The History of Warner's Ranch and Its Environs*. Los Angeles, 1927.

HITTELL, JOHN S., *The Resources of California*. San Francisco, 1869.

HITTELL, THEODORE HENRY, *History of California*. 4 vols. San Francisco, 1897.

HODGE, FREDERICK WEBB, *Handbook of American Indians North of Mexico*. 2 vols. Washington, 1907-10.

HOLDEN, WILLIAM CURRY, "Frontier Defense, 1846-1860," *West Texas Historical Association Year Book*, VI. Abilene, Tex., 1930.

HOOPES, ALBAN, W., *Indian Affairs and Their Administration with Special Reference to the Far West, 1849-1860*. Philadelphia, 1932.

HOOVER, MILDRED BROOKE, *Historic Spots in California: Counties of the Coast Range*. Stanford University, Calif., 1937.

HOUGH, EMERSON, *The Passing of the Frontier*. New Haven, Conn., 1921.

HOWE, OCTAVIUS THORNDIKE, *Argonauts of '49. History and Adventures of the Emigrant Companies from Massachusetts. 1849-1850*. Cambridge, 1923.

HUNT, ELVID, *History of Fort Leavenworth, 1827-1927*. Fort Leavenworth, Kans., 1926.

HUNT, ROCKWELL D. AND SÁNCHEZ, NELLIE VAN DE GRIFT, *A Short History of California*. New York. 1929.

HUTCHINSON, WILLIAM, "Sketches of Pioneer Kansas Experience," *Kansas State Historical Society, Transactions*, VII. Topeka, 1902.

JAMES, GEORGE WHARTON, *Utah: the Land of Blossoming Valleys*. Boston, 1922.

JOHANNSEN, ALBERT, *The House of Beadle and Adams and Its Dime and Nickel Novels*. 2 vols. Norman, Okla., 1950.

JOHNSON, FRANCIS WHITE, *A History of Texas and Texans*. 5 vols. Chicago, 1914.

JOHNSTON, WILLIAM PRESTON, *Life of General Albert Sidney Johnston*. New York, 1879.

LADD, HORATIO O., *The Story of New Mexico*. Boston, 1891.

Lamb's Biographical Dictionary of the United States (J. H. Brown, ed.). 7 vols. Boston, 1900-03.

LEWIS, LLOYD, *Captain Sam Grant*. Boston, 1950.

LOCKWOOD, FRANK C., *Pioneer Days in Arizona. From Spanish Occupation to Statehood*. New York, 1932.

MACK, EFFIE MONA, *Nevada. A History of the State from Earliest Times through the Civil War*. Glendale, 1936.

MACLEOD, WILLIAM CHRISTIE, *The American Indian Frontier*. London, 1928.

MALIN, J. C., *Indian Policy and Westward Expansion, 1770-1854*, University of Kansas, "Humanistic Studies," II, No. 3. Lawrence, Kans., 1921.

MARSHALL, THOMAS MAITLAND, *A History of the Western Boundary of the Louisiana Purchase, 1819-1841*. Berkeley, 1914.

MOONEY, JAMES, "Calendar History of the Kiowa Indians," Bureau of American Ethnology, *Seventeenth Annual Report*, Part 1. Washington, 1898.

MOOREHEAD, WARREN K., *The American Indian in the United States, 1850-1914*. Andover, Mass., 1914.

MORRISON, WILLIAM B., *Military Posts and Camps in Oklahoma*. Oklahoma City, 1936.

NEVINS, ALLAN, *Frémont. The West's Greatest Adventurer*. 2 vols. New York, 1928.

New International Year Book for 1949. New York, 1950.

NEWTON, L. W., "Fort Brown," *Dictionary of American History*, I. New York, 1940.

NORTON, CHARLES B., *American Inventions and Improvements in Breech-Loading Small Arms*. Boston, 1882.

NYE, W. S., *Carbine and Lance*. Norman, 1937.

PAXSON, FREDERIC LOGAN, *The Last American Frontier*. New York, 1918.

PAZ, IRENEO, *Life and Adventures of the Celebrated Bandit Joaquín Murrieta: His Exploits in the State of California* (Frances P. Belle, tr.). Chicago, 1925.

PEARSON, EDMUND, *Dime Novels or Following an Old Trail in Popular Literature*. Boston, 1929.

PRICHARD, WALTER, "Red River Raft," *Dictionary of American History*, IV. New York, 1940.

RAMSDELL, CHARLES WILLIAM, "The Frontier and Secession," *Studies in Southern History and Politics*. New York, 1914.

REED, S. G., *A History of the Texas Railroads and of Transportation Conditions under Spain and Mexico and the Republic and the State*. Houston, 1941.

RENSCH, H. E. AND E. G., AND HOOVER, MILDRED BROOKE, *Historic Spots in California: Valley and Sierra Counties*. Stanford University, Calif., 1933.

RICHARDSON, RUPERT NORVAL, *The Comanche Barrier to South Plains Settlement: a Century and a Half of Savage Resistance to the Advancing White Frontier*. Glendale, 1933.

Texas, the Lone Star State. New York, 1943.

RICHARDSON, RUPERT NORVAL, AND RISTER, CARL COKE, *The Greater Southwest*. Glendale, Calif., 1934.

RISTER, CARL COKE, *Border Captives: the Traffic in Prisoners by Southern Plains Indians, 1835-1875*. Norman, 1940.

"Fort Worth," *Dictionary of American History*, II. New York, 1940.

Robert E. Lee in Texas. Norman, Okla., 1946.

The Southwestern Frontier, 1865-1881. Cleveland, 1928.

ROCK, J. L., AND SMITH, W. I., *Southern and Western Texas Guide, 1878.* St. Louis, 1878.

RODENBOUGH, THEOPHILUS F. (comp.), *From Everglade to Cañon with the Second Dragoons.* New York, 1875.

ROLFE, D. P., "Overland Freighting from Nebraska City," Nebraska State Historical Society, *Proceedings and Collections,* V. Series 2, Lincoln, Nebr., 1902.

ROOT, FRANK A., AND CONNELLEY, WILLIAM ELSEY, *The Overland Stage to California.* Topeka, Kans., 1901.

SCHMECKEBIER, LAURENCE F., *The Office of Indian Affairs: Its History, Activities, and Organization.* Baltimore, 1927.

SCOTT, H. L., *Military Dictionary.* New York, 1861.

SEMPLE, ELLEN CHURCHILL, *American History and Its Geographic Conditions.* Boston, 1903.

SEYMOUR, FLORA WARREN, *Indian Agents of the Old Frontier.* New York, 1941.

SHIPMAN, ALICE JACK ("Mrs. O. L."), *Taming the Big Bend.* Austin, 1926.

SMITH, JOHN RUSSELL, *North America.* New York, 1924.

STEGNER, WALLACE, *Mormon Country.* New York, 1942.

STENHOUSE, T. B. H., *The Rocky Mountain Saints.* Salt Lake City, 1904.

TAYLOR, GEORGE ROGERS (ed.), *The Turner Thesis Concerning the Role of the Frontier in American History:* II, *Problems in American Civilization* (Earl Latham, George Rogers Taylor, and George F. Whicher, eds.). Boston, 1949.

TAYLOR, THOMAS ULVAN, *Jesse Chisholm.* Bandera, Tex., 1939.

THIAN, RAPHAEL P., *Notes Illustrating the Military Geography of the United States, 1813-1880.* Washington, 1881.

THOBURN, JOSEPH B., "Indian Fight in Ford County, 1859," Kansas State Historical Society, *Collections,* XII. Topeka, 1912.

THRALL, HOMER S., *A Pictorial History of Texas.* St. Louis, 1879.

TRIPLETT, FRANK, *Conquering the Wilderness; or, New Pictorial History of the Life and Times of the Pioneer Heroes and Heroines of America.* New York, 1883.

TURNER, FREDERICK JACKSON, *The Frontier in American History.* New York, 1920.

TWITCHELL, RALPH EMERSON, *The Leading Facts of New Mexican History.* 2 vols. Cedar Rapids, Iowa, 1912.

UPTON, EMORY, *The Military Policy of the United States.* Washington, 1917.

WALTON, WILLIAM, *The Army and the Navy of the United States, 1776-1891.* 11 vols. Philadelphia, 1890.

WATKINS, ALBERT, "History of Fort Kearny," Nebraska State Historical Society, *Collections,* XVI. Lincoln, Nebr., 1911.

WEBB, WALTER PRESCOTT, *The Great Plains.* Boston, 1931.
    The Texas Rangers. Boston, 1935.

WELLMAN, PAUL I., *Death in the Desert.* New York, 1935.
    "Fort Cobb," *Dictionary of American History,* I. New York, 1940.

WHITNEY, ORSON F., *History of Utah.* 3 vols. Salt Lake City, 1892-1908.

WISSLER, CLARK, *Indians of the United States. Four Centuries of Their History and Culture.* New York, 1940.

WOOTEN, DUDLEY G., *A Comprehensive History of Texas, 1685-1897.* 2 vols. Dallas, 1898.

PERIODICALS AND NEWSPAPERS

"Aircraft Warning Drill" and ". . . Air Guard Warning Squadron," St. Louis *Post-Dispatch,* Jan. 22, March 1, 1951.

"Back to 1848 [Fort Bliss]," St. Louis *Post-Dispatch,* Nov. 21, 1948.

"Barracks Fades out as Military Post [Jefferson Barracks]," St. Louis *Post-Dispatch,* July 1, 1946.

BARROWS, WILLIAM, "The Great American Desert: There is None," *Magazine of Western History* (June, 1885), 113-132.

"Beale, a Pioneer of Pioneers," San Francisco *Call,* April 23, 1893.

BENDER, AVERAM B., "Frontier Defense in the Territory of New Mexico, 1846-1853," *New Mexico Historical Review,* IX (July, 1934), 249-272.

"Government Explorations in the Territory of New Mexico, 1846-1859," *New Mexico Historical Review,* IX, (Jan., 1934), 1-32.

"The Texas Frontier, 1848-1861," *Southwestern Historical Quarterly,* XXXVIII (Oct., 1934), 135-148.

"Bent's Fort" (Fort Wise and Fort Lyon), New York *Herald,* June 16, 1862.

BIEBER, RALPH P., "California Gold Mania," *Mississippi Valley Historical Review,* XXXV (June, 1948), 3-28.

"Buffalo 35 Years Ago, . . ., Now," St. Louis *Post-Dispatch,* Sept. 14, 1934.

CALDWELL, NORMAN W., "The Red River Raft," *Chronicles of Oklahoma,* XIX (Sept., 1941), 253-268.

"Careers of Beale and Henley," San Francisco *Daily Alta California,* May 4, 26, 1875, June 2, 1876.

COLGROVE, KENNETH W., "The Attitude of Congress toward the Pioneers of the West, 1820-1850," *Iowa Journal of History and Politics,* IX (April, 1911), 196-302.

"Comeback of the Indian," St. Louis *Post-Dispatch,* Dec. 20, 1939.

"Comeback of the Redskin," St. Louis *Post-Dispatch,* Dec. 22, 1940.

CRANE, R. C., "Some Aspects of the History of West and Northwest Texas since 1845," *Southwestern Historical Quarterly,* XXVI (July, 1922), 30-43.

CRIMMINS, M. L., "Fort Massachusetts, First United States Military Post in Colorado," *Colorado Magazine,* XIV (July, 1937), 128-135.

"Fort McKavett, Texas," *Southwestern Historical Quarterly,* XXXVIII (July, 1934), 28-39.

DERRICKSON, HOWARD, "Monumental Epic of Our West," St. Louis *Post-Dispatch,* July 10, 1949.

DRUMM, STELLA M., "Robert E. Lee and the Improvement of the Mississippi River," Missouri Historical Society, *Collections,* VI (Feb., 1929), 157-171.

EATON, W. CLEMENT, "Frontier Life in Southern Arizona, 1858-1861," *Southwestern Historical Quarterly,* XXXVI (Oct., 1932), 173-192.

ELLISON, WILLIAM H., "The Federal Indian Policy in California, 1846-1860," *Mississippi Valley Historical Review,* IX (June, 1922), 37-67.

ERATH, LUCY A., "Memoirs of George Bernard Erath," *Southwestern His-*

torical Quarterly, XXVI (Jan., 1923), 207-233, (April, 1923), 255-280, XXVII (July, 1923), 27-51, (Oct., 1923), 140-163.

FOREMAN, CAROLYN THOMAS, "Black Beaver," *Chronicles of Oklahoma*, XXIV (Autumn, 1946), 269-292.

"General Bennet Riley [1787-1853], Commandant at Fort Gibson and Governor of California," *Chronicles of Oklahoma*, XIX (Sept., 1941), 225-244.

FOREMAN, GRANT, "Early Trails through Oklahoma," *Chronicles of Oklahoma*, III (June, 1925), 99-119.

GALLAHER, RUTH A., "The Indian Agent in the United States before 1850," *Iowa Journal of History and Politics*, XIV (Jan., 1916), 3-55.

"The Indian Agent in the United States since 1850," *Iowa Journal of History and Politics*, XIV (April, 1916), 173-238.

GIBBS, JOSIAH F., "The Gunnison Massacre, 1853, Millard County, Utah; Indian Mareer's Version of the Tragedy, 1894," *Utah Historical Quarterly*, I (July, 1928), 67-75.

GIFFEN, HELEN S., "Fort Miller and Millerton," *Historical Society, Southern California Quarterly*, XXI (March, 1939), 5-15.

GREGG, KATE L., "Boonslickers in the Gold Rush to California," *Missouri Historical Review*, XLI (July, 1947), 345-360.

HARMON, GEORGE DEWEY, "The United States Indian Policy in Texas, 1845-1860," *Mississippi Valley Historical Review*, XVII (Dec., 1930), 377-403.

"Heintzelman's Career," Washington (D.C.) *Evening Star*, May 1, 1880.

HENSHALL, JOHN A., "A Bandit of the Golden Age," *Overland Monthly*, LIII (April, 1909), 313-319.

"In Honor of the First His-Honor" [William Carr Lane], St. Louis *Post-Dispatch*, July 30, 1943.

"Jefferson Barracks through Five Wars," *Missouri Historical Review*, XXXVI (April, 1942), 339-341.

"John Collier, Indians' Friend," St. Louis *Star-Times*, March 29, 1945.

JONES, CHARLES IRVING, "William Kronig, New Mexico Pioneer, from his Memories of 1849-1860," *New Mexico Historical Review*, XIX (July, 1944), 185-224, (Oct., 1944), 271-311.

KOCH, LENA CLARA, "The Federal Indian Policy in Texas, 1845-1860," *Southwestern Historical Quarterly*, XXVIII (Jan., 1925), 223-234, (April, 1925), 259-286, XXIX (July, 1925), 19-35, (Oct., 1925), 98-127.

McMURTRIE, DOUGLAS C., "The History of Early Printing in New Mexico," *New Mexico Historical Review*, IV (Oct., 1929), 372-410.

MORGAN, DALE L., "The Administration of Indian Affairs in Utah, 1851-1858," *Pacific Historical Review*, XVII (Nov., 1948), 383-409.

NANKIVELL, JOHN H., "Fort Garland, Colorado," *Colorado Magazine*, XVI (Jan., 1939), 13-28.

"Navajo School," St. Louis *Post-Dispatch*, March 18, 1951.

"Navajo Tribal Custom Respected . . . 1950 Agenda," St. Louis *Post-Dispatch*, Jan. 5, 1950.

"New Day for the Indian," St. Louis *Post-Dispatch*, May 12, 1940.

"New Deal Policy Offers Indians Self-Government . . .," St. Louis *Post-Dispatch*, Oct. 20, 1934.

"No Longer the Vanishing American," St. Louis *Post-Dispatch*, Sept. 25, 1943.

OGLE, RALPH H., "Federal Control of the Western Apaches, 1848-1886," *New Mexico Historical Review*, XIV (Oct., 1939), 309-365.

RAMSDELL, CHARLES W., "Internal Improvement Projects in Texas in the Fifties," Mississippi Valley Historical Association, *Proceedings*, IX (April, 1917), Pt. 1, pp. 99-109.

RASMUSSEN, LOUISE, "Artists of the Explorations Overland, 1840-1860," *Oregon Historical Quarterly*, XLIII (March, 1942), 56-62.

REEVE, FRANK D., "The Apache Indians in Texas," *Southwestern Historical Quarterly*, L (Oct., 1946), 189-219.

"The Government and the Navaho 1846-1858," *New Mexico Historical Review*, XIV (Jan., 1939), 82-114.

RIPPY, J. FRED, "Border Troubles along the Rio Grande, 1848-1860," *Southwestern Historical Quarterly*, XXIII (Oct., 1919), 91-111.

STODDARD, WALTER E., "William H. Warner, Soldier and Engineer," *Engineerogram* (Sacramento), Oct., 1939.

SYMONS, THOMAS W., "The Army and the Exploration of the West," *The Journal of the Military Service Institution of the United States*, IV (Sept., 1883), 205-249.

TERRY, DICK, "The American Indian and His Future," St. Louis *Post-Dispatch*, Oct. 7, 1945.

TUTTLE, E. D., "The River Colorado," *Arizona Historical Review*, I (July, 1928), 50-68.

MANUSCRIPTS

BARRETT, ARRIE, "Federal Military Outposts in Texas, 1846-1861," MS., M. A. thesis, University of Texas, 1927.

FORCE, EDWIN TRUESDELL, "The Use of the Colorado River in the United States, 1850-1933," MS., Ph.D. dissertation, University of California, 1937.

HOLDEN, WILLIAM CURRY, "Frontier Problems and Movements in West Texas, 1846-1900," MS., Ph.D. dissertation, University of Texas, 1928.

LEONARD, CHARLES BERDAN, "The Federal Indian Policy in the San Joaquin Valley: its Application and Results," MS., Ph.D. dissertation, University of California, 1928.

McPHERSON, HALLIE MAE, "William McKendree Gwin," MS., Ph.D. dissertation, University of California, 1932.

MARSHALL, THOMAS MAITLAND, "An Early Chapter in the Life of General Grant," MS., Ulysses S. Grant Papers, 1791-1932, M. H. S.

MITCHELL, RICHARD GERALD, "Joaquín Murieta," MS., M. A. thesis, University of California, 1927.

MOTT, MARGUERITE, "Activities in the Northwest, 1848-1861, under the Direction of the United State War Department," MS., M.A. thesis, Washington University, 1932.

NOËL, VIRGINIA PINK, "The United States Indian Reservations in Texas, 1854-1859," MS., M.A. thesis, University of Texas, 1924.

Outline Index of Military Forts and Stations, MSS., Adjutant General's Office, National Archives.

Sumpter, Jesse, "Life of Jesse Sumpter, the Oldest Citizen of Eagle Pass, Texas" (written by Harry Warren at dictation of Jesse Sumpter, 1902-1906), MS., Archives, University of Texas.

Syndergaard, Parley Rex, "The United States Military Expedition to Utah, 1857-1858," MS., M.A. thesis, Washington University, 1941.

Whittaker, Annie Eikel, "The Frontier Policy of the United States in the Mexican Cession, 1845-1860," MS., M. A. thesis, University of Texas, 1927.

Index

Abert, James, explores Rio Grande country, 96-97

Abert, John J., biographical note, 250; issues instructions to Stansbury, 58

Abiquiu, N. Mex., on "caravan route" to California, 61

Acoma, N. Mex., Sumner and Greiner conclude Indian treaties at, 155

Agua Caliente, Calif., Indians murder American citizens at, 196

Ake, William, marauding activities of, 170

Albuquerque, N. Mex., road from, to Tecolate, 70

Alexander, T. C., champion of Texas Rangers, 28

Algonquin Indians, in Texas, attitude toward white man and government, 9; see also Creeks and Southern Wichitas

Allen, Beverly S., special Indian commissioner in Oregon, 279

Alvarez, Manuel, learns of Apache depredations, 158

American River, Calif., Riley explores along, 104

Annuity goods, no solution of Indian problem, 17; Secretary of the Interior Smith's report, 19

Antelope Buttes, Okla., Marcy's first experience with Indians near, 56

Antonio, Juan, California Indian chief, metes out justice to tribesmen, 193-94

Apache Indians, character of, 10, 13; depredations of, attack Texas Santa Fe mail train, 141, New Mexican Apaches, 13; raid Texas settlements, 34; raid upper Rio Grande Valley, 151; ravage Mesilla Valley, 38-39; number of Texas Apache warriors, 10; opinion of military men, 10; see also Comanches, Kiowas, Northern Wichitas

Apacheria, range of New Mexican Apaches in, 13

Armijo, Navaho chief, begs for peace, 166

Army, "Army of the West," 52; bounties for western service, 258; champions of, in Congress, 110-11; clashes between civil and military authorities, 29-30; composition of, on eve of Civil War, 112; cost of transportation, 259-60; demands for increase in size of, 109-10; desertions in, 110, 126; doctors in, 261; double pay for western service, 110; "extra" pay in, 261; health in, 119-21; hospital facilities, 120; increase in size of, in 1850's, 110-12; ineffectiveness of infantry on frontier, 112-13, 141; military-geographical divisions, 243; number engaged in frontier duty, 112; op-position in Congress, 111; "our 'Skeleton Army,'" 110; pay of soldier, 121-23; paymaster, 122; peak strength at close of Mexican War, 109; peak strength of, in Utah, 183-84, 273; punishments in, 127-28; regulars versus volunteers, 28, 111-12; relation to frontier defense, 27, 108; size of, on eve of Civil War, 112; size of, prior to Mexican War, 109; size of, in West, 109; sutler, in frontier army, 122, 123; women camp followers in, 126; see also Camps, Frontier defense, Frontier soldier, Military posts, Volunteers

Artesian wells experiment, accomplishment of, 71-72; appropriations for, 71; in late 1850's and 1870's, 253; scarcity of water, 71

Austin, Tex., occupied by troops, 245

Babbitt's Falls, on Rio Grande, reached by Captain Love, 77

Bailey, Godard, recommendations concerning California Indians, 226; report on California reservations, 24, 226

Baldwin, Roger S., opinion of lands in Mexican Cession, 3

Bannock Indians, range and character of, 13

Barbour, George W., Indian commissioner in California, negotiates treaties, 195, 218-19

Barclay's Fort, Apaches raid on cattle herd near, 157; history of, 268

Barnards, Indian traders, influence on Indian relations, 136

Barnards' (Torreys') trading house, description of, 263

Barrow, Washington, subagent, New Mexico Territory, 149

Bartholow, Roberts, description of army ambulances, 120

Bartlett, John R., recommends Indian annihilation or removal, 152

Bateman, William, part in Mountain Meadows massacre, 185

Battle, Nicholas W., decries atacks on reserve Indians, 215

Baylor, John R., becomes enemy of Texas reservations, 213-14, 215; leads attack against reservation Indians, 215; resident agent, Comanche reserve, 209; see also Indian reservations

Beale, Edward F., biographical sketch, 63-64; California reservation program of, 220-22, 280; camel experiment of, 251; contemporary opinion of reservation policy, 221; expedition from Fort Defiance to eastern California, 64-66; expedition from Fort Smith to Colorado River, 66-67; ideal Indian official, 27; importance of surveys, 67; opens new route to California, 63-64; *see also* Explorations, Indian reservations, Trails to Far West

Beale's Crossing, Colorado River, emigrants attacked near, 201; Fort Mojave established at, 44

Beall, B. L., prohibits sale of liquor among troops, 125; sends Captain Davidson into Owens Lake country, 202-03

Bear Creek, Calif., Derby examines country along, 105-06; troops stationed on, 192

Bear River, Utah, Stansbury explores country along, 60

Beaubien, Charles, reports depredations of Apaches, 158

Beaver City, Utah, conviction of Mountain Meadows massacre participants at, 186

Beaver Lake, Calif., Mohave Indians attack Hoffman's camp at, 164-65

Bedell, Edward A., Indian agent, Utah, 174

Bell, David, defeated by New Mexican Apaches, 157-58

Bell, Peter H., dispatches Rangers to Rio Grande country, 138; favors reservation plan, 206

Benicia Barracks, Calif., condition of hospital equipment at, 120; history of, 246; troops stationed at, 41

Bent, Charles, murdered by New Mexican Indians, 149

Benton, Thomas Hart, pleads for frontier defense, 152; *see also* Frontier defense

Bent's Fort, Colo., history of, 251

Berçier, François, Warner's guide in California, 104

"Big Bend" sector, Tex., explorations in, 96; favorite resort for Indian attacks, 36

Big Sandy River, Utah, Mormons burn government supply trains on, 181

Big Wichita River, Tex., Marcy's exploration along, 95

Bigler, John, champions stronger defense policy, 45; enrolls volunteers, 28

Bishop, Samuel A., member of Beale's road party, clashes with Indians, 66

Black Beaver, Indian guide, Marcy's guide on Santa Fe expedition, 56

Black Cañon, Colorado River, Ives's expedition reaches mouth of, 85

"Black Waxy," Tex., 3

Blain, Samuel A., Indian agent, assists in removal of Texas reserve Indians, 216; *see also* Indian reservations

Blanco, Utah chief, defeated at Cochetopa Pass, 159

Boling, John, defeats Yosemite Indians, 196

Bonneville, Benjamin L. E., attempts to strengthen New Mexico defenses, 40; biographical note, 161, 269; commands Gila expedition, 40, 161-62

Boom towns, in western Utah, 187

Borland, Solon, recommends Marcy for Red River expedition, 79

Bosque Grande, N. Mex., description of, 98

Bosque Redondo, N. Mex., location of, 98

Bounties in the army, 258

Brandebury, Lemuel, clashes with Mormons, 178

Brazos agency, Tex., accomplishments of tribes at, 208, 210; *see also* Indian reservations

Brazos River, Tex., Marcy's exploration along, 95-96

Brent, J. Lancaster, report on California Indians in south, 199

Bridger, Jim, guides Stansbury on Great Salt Lake exploration, 58-59

Brocchus, Perry E., quarrels with Mormons, 178

Brooke, George M., launches a campaign against Texas tribes, 135

Brooke's Falls, on Rio Grande, reached by Love, 77

Brown, Orlando, criticizes Indian service, 21; recommends vigorous defense policy, 152; suggests reforms in Indian service, 21-22

Browne, J. Ross, description of Virginia City by, 187; reports on California reservations, 24, 225

Brownsville, Tex., terrorized by Cortinas, 266

Bryan, reconnaissance across central Texas, 94; *see also* Explorations

Buchanan, James, appoints new set of officials for Utah Territory, 179

"Bucking," abolished, 128, 262; description of, 128; *see also* Army

Buena Vista Lake, Calif., character of country, 106; Derby explores vicinity of, 106

Buffalo, extinction of, 130; increase in recent years, 262

Buffalo Hump, Comanche chief, member of Neighbors-Ford expedition, 256; sues for peace, 133

Burleson, E. N., reports on Texas reservation Indians, 214

Burnett, Peter H., opinion of Indians, 197

Burro Mountains, N. Mex., Gordon's expedition toward, 101-02

Butte Creek, Calif., Derby explores vicinity of, 105

Butterfield Stage Route, followed Marcy's southern trail, 57

Cache Creek, Okla., initial point of Marcy's Red River survey, 80

Cache Valley, Utah, reconnoitered by Stansbury, 59

Cajón Pass, Calif., Beale goes through, 64; troops stationed near, 41-42

Caldwell, Joseph P., criticizes use of infantry on frontier, 112

Calhoun, James S., biographical note, 149-50; ideal Indian agent, 27; negotiates treaties with Apaches, Navahos, and Utahs, 151, 154, 155; recommends "compulsory enlightenment," 151

California, agriculture, on eve of Civil War, 232, 282; prior to American conquest, 8; effect of gold discovery on labor and wages, 8, 102-03; land of contrasts, 7-8; lawlessness in, 103, 233; growth of manufacture in, 282; mineral wealth in, 282-83; missions in, at time of American occupation, 239; natural resources of, 8; population on eve of Civil War, 8, 231, prior to American conquest, 8; see also Explorations, Indian reservations, Indian wars, Military posts

Callahan, James H., defeats Indian raiders, 142; leads expedition into Mexico, 266

Camel experiment, 251; see also Beale, Edward F.

Campbell, Robert B., special Indian commissioner in Southwest, 274, 279

Camps, Camp Barranca, Tex., occupied by troops, 245; Camp Bragg, Calif., built, 44, 201; Camp Cass, Calif., occupied by troops, 247; Camp Cody, Calif., Carleton holds Indian council at, 204; Camp Colorado, Tex., built, 35, difficulty in obtaining drinking water, 244, liquor peddled among troops, 244; Camp Cooper, Tex., difficulty in obtaining drinking water, 244, established, 35; Camp Crittenden, Utah, brief history of, 246; Camp Edinburg, Tex., occupied by troops, 245; Camp Far West, Calif., location, 42, troops stationed at, 41-42; Camp Floyd, Utah, abandoned, 246, built, 41, 184, occupied, 41, 184, troops there engage in theatricals, 124; Camp Hudson, Tex., established, 245; Camp Johnston, Tex., Comanches encamped near, 207, occupied by troops, 245, 264; Camp Prentiss, Calif., occupied by troops, 247; Camp Radziminski, Okla., occupied by troops, 245, Van Dorn's base of operations, 143, 144; Camp

Rosario, Tex., occupied by troops, 245; Camp Scott, Wyo., Johnston's army in winter quarters, 41, 181; Camp Stanislaus, Calif., 192, troops stationed at, 192; Camp Verde, Tex., established, 245; Camp Wood, Tex., established, 36, 245; Camp Wright, Calif., location, 44; see also Forts, Military posts

Cañada, N. Mex., road from, to Abiquiu, 70

Canaje-Hexie, Wichita chief, warns Marcy about upper Red River country, 80

Canby, E. R. S., campaign against Navahos, 169

Cañon de Chelly, N. Mex., Calhoun's description of, 97; impregnability of, exploded, 97, 167; reputed stronghold of Navahos, 150; Simpson's exploration of, 97; Sumner's penetration of, 153; Walker's exploration of, 167

Cañon del Oro, Ariz., Steck distributes supplies among Apaches, 164

Cantonment Burgwin, N. Mex., established, 38

Capote, Apache chief, plans attack on Whiting-Smith camp, 92

Carabajal, José Maria Jesus, activities on lower Rio Grande, 266; see also Cortinas, Filibustering, White outlaws

"Caravan route," course of, 61

Carleton, James H., defeats Apaches in Raton Mountains, 158, 268; description of Gran Quivira, 99-100; holds Indian council at Camp Cody, 204; impressions of Mescalero Apaches, 99; impression of New Mexicans, 99; patrols New Mexico Territory, 153; reconnaissance of Rio Grande Valley, 99; see also Explorations, Indian wars

Carpenter, Helen M., comment on Indian treaties, 19

Carrington, Albert, assists Stansbury in survey, 60

Carroll, A. J., member of Ives's Colorado River survey, 84

Carson, Kit, feeds Utahs, 162; holds "talk" with Apache chiefs, 159; ideal Indian agent, 27

Carson River, Fort Churchill built on, 41, 188

Carson Valley, Nev., Indians take to warpath, 41; tribes in destitute condition, 187

Cart War, Tex., 266

Castroville, Tex., Lipan Indians massacred near, 133

"Cebolleteños," traffic in Indian children, 271

Cebolletita, N. Mex., Simpson recommends military post at, 97

Cedar City, Utah, report of Indian hostilities at, 64

Chacon, Apache chief, Calhoun makes treaty with, 154; defeated by Cooke, 158; defeated by Fauntleroy on upper Arkansas, 159

Chapitone, Navaho chief, accepts Washington's treaty, 150

Cherokee Indians, their visits to Texas, 134; see also Creeks, Seminoles

Chicken Creek, Utah, Chief Walker makes peace with Brigham Young, 176

Chihuahua, Mex., claims for Indian depredations, 245; part in Southwest overland trade, 88

Chisholm, Jesse, biographical note, 249-50; reports Mormon influence among Comanches, 142

Chorpenning Mail Company, portion of Simpson's route used by, 68

Chowchilla Indians, Calif., defeated by Kuykendall, 196

Cieneguilla, N. Mex., troops defeated by Indians near, 157-58

Claiborne, Thomas, reconnaissance of, 101

Clarke, N. S., arrives in California, 200-01; assumes command of Department of Pacific, 43; builds Camp Bragg and Fort Crook, 43-44, 201; defense policy in California, 43, 201

Clear Fork, Brazos River, Tex., Marcy locates Indian reservation on, 95-96

Clear Lake, Calif., Indians residing near, 191

Cochetopa Pass, Colo., Fauntleroy defeats Apaches and Utahs at, 159

Cocopa Indians, Calif., friendly toward Ives and his men, 85; won over by Derby, 83

Collier, John, influence on Indian policy, 236, 283

Collins, James L., biographical sketch, 269; report on Indian depredations, 160

"Colonel Stanton," steamer, brings troops to Texas, 132

Coloradas, Mangas, Apache chief, mistreatment of, by whites, 163; personality and influence of, 163-64; wreaks vengeance, 164

"Colorado," steamer, carries freight on lower Colorado River, 83; moves down to Matagorda, 76

Colorado Plateau, Ariz., character of, 86

Colorado River, Tex., opened to steam navigation, 75; survey of, 75

Colorado River, West, appropriation for survey of, 255; California legislature requests exploration of, 84; Coronado's ascent of, 82; Derby's survey of, 82-83; early interest in, 82; fertility of bottom lands of, 6; importance of Ives's survey of, 87; importance of, in recent period, 255-56; Ives's exploration of, 84-87; practical head of steamboat navigation of, 86, 255

Colt's revolver, character and effectiveness of, 260

Comanche Indians, attack U. S. public lands surveyors, 145; character and range of, 9-10; harry northern Mexican states, 138; Kennedy's characterization of, 9; Neighbors' estimate of number of, 10; plundering expeditions of, 132-33; raid Arkansas country, 34; reputation of, 9-10; traffic with white settlers, 132-33; Wild Cat's opinion of, 9; see also Apaches, Kiowas, Northern Wichitas

Comanche reservation, Tex., accomplishments of tribes on, 210-11; Leyendecker's influence on reserve Indians, 208-09; size and location of, 207-08; see also Indian reservations

Comanche Spring, Tex., Apaches threaten Whiting-Smith camp near, 92

Comanchéros, traffic in Indian plunder, 133

Comstock silver strike, effect on Indians, 187-88; effect on whites, 187-88

Conner's Station, Tex., temporary military camp, 245

Conrad, Charles M., orders movement of troops into Texas, 34, 137; questions need for additional military posts, 47; recommends constant display of military force, 44-45; see also Frontier defense, Military posts

Cooke, Philip St. George, career to Mexican War, 54; defeats New Mexican Apaches, 158; opens new wagon route to California, 54-55; see also Trails to Far West

Cooper, James F., influence of, on literature of frontier, 234

Cooper, Samuel, holds "talk" with Wild Cat at Eagle Pass, 137

Corpus Christi, Tex., new route opened by Michler from, 94

Cortinas, Juan Nepomuceno, marauding activities of, 266; see also Carabajal, Filibustering, White outlaws

Coshatee, Tom, member of Neighbors-Ford expedition, 256

Cradlebaugh, John, accuses whites of Mountain Meadows massacre, 186; Associate Justice, Utah Territory, 272

Creek Indians, distrust of Wild Cat, 134; visits to Texas, 134; see also Algonquins, Cherokees, Seminoles, Southern Wichitas

Crittenden, John J., calls halt to Indian expenditures, 23

Crook, George, defeats Pit River Indians, 201

Crump, J. R., opinion of Beale's route, 67

Cumming, Alfred, Governor of Utah Territory, 179, 272; relations with Johnston, 29; relations with Mormons, 183

Cutera, Apache chief, begs for help, 162

Daily Alta California, champions Indian reservations in early years, 218; defends General Wool, 200

Daily Missouri Republican, criticizes Washington's Navaho Expedition, 150-51

Dame, William H., participant in Mountain Meadows massacre, 274

Dana, Richard H., Jr., impressions of California, 8

Davidson, John W., expedition against Apache raiders, 163; expedition against Clear Lake tribes, 193; expedition into Owens Lake country, 203

Davis, Jefferson, analyzes causes for desertion, 127; criticizes General Wool, 200; plan of defense, 45

Davis, William Watts Hart, description of New Mexicans, 7; recommends vigorous Indian policy, 25

Davis's Landing, temporary military camp, 245

Day, Henry R., subagent at Parvan Indian agency, Utah, 173

Deas, George, favors the Hays trail, 91

Deer Creek, Calif., Indians attacked by whites on, 198

Delaware Indians, their migration to Texas, 133-34; *see also* Shawnees, Kickapoos

Denver, James W., accuses Brigham Young of stirring up Indians, 169; censures Brigham Young, 187

Derby, George H., describes California Indians, 105-07; marks out Indian reservation, 106; member of Riley's expedition to mining camps, 103; reconnaissances of, in California, 105-07; selects site for military post, 106; surveys Great Colorado River, 82-83; *see also* Explorations, Western rivers

Desertions, in regular army, 110, 122, 127

Devils' River, Tex., army paymaster attacked by Indians at, 140

Digger Indians, contemporary accounts of, 14; Simpson's description of, 68

Dime novels, spirit of frontier in, 234-35

Dodge, Augustus C., champions larger army, 111

Dodge, Frederick, plans for Washoe and Paiute tribes, 190; work among Utah tribes, 189-90

Dodge, Henry L., influence among Navahos, 159; murdered by Gila Apaches, 161

Dog Cañon, N. Mex., Lazelle's expedition into, 164

Domenech, Emmanuel Henri D., characterizes Texas frontiersmen, 232; describes military punishments, 127; describes Texas Rangers, 28

Doniphan, Alexander W., in charge at Santa Fe, 52

Dotson, Peter K., marshal in Utah territory, 272

Drummond, W. W., clashes with Mormons, 178

Eagle Pass, Tex., town on Rio Grande, 77, 95

Echols, William H., explores "Big Bend" sector, 96

Eckles, D. R., Chief Justice, Utah Territory, 272; indicts Brigham Young for high treason, 183

Egloffstein, F. W., member of Ives's Colorado River survey, 84

Ellis, Joe, member of Neighbors-Ford expedition, 256

El Paso, Mills's impressions of, 233; road from, to Fort Yuma, 69-70

Emigrants, to California, 8; effect of Comstock silver strike on, 187; effect of gold discoveries on, 8, 157, 169; to New Mexico, 157, 169; to Texas, 4-5; *see also* Gold discovery

Emory, William H., description of firearms at Fort Riley, 118; journal of, 53; military reconnaissance of, 53

Erath, George B., friend of reserve Indians, 215

Escopettes (*escopetas*), used by New Mexicans, 97

Explorations, Beale's expeditions along 35th parallel, 63-67; in California, 102-07, Derby's reconnaissance, 105-07, Mason's tour, 102-03, Riley's reconnaissance, 103-04, Warner's reconnaissance, 104-05; effect of, on frontier defense, 107; need for, 88; in New Mexico, 96-102, Abert and Peck explore Rio Grande country, 96-97, Carleton in Rio Grande Valley, 98-100, Claiborne's reconnaissance, 101, Gordon's expedition, 101-02, Jackson's survey, 101, Judd's explorations in Pecos Valley, 98, Lazelle's examination along Pecos, 101, Macomb's activities, 100-01, Simpson's explorations in Navaho country, 97-98, Sitgreaves' reconnaissance, 61-63, 98, Steen's reconnaissance, 101; in Texas, 88-96, in "Big Bend" sector, 96, Green's reconnaissance, 94, Hays's expedition, 89-91, Marcy's explorations along Brazos and Big Wichita rivers, 95-96, Michler's reconnaissances, 94, Neighbors-Ford expedition, 93-94, reconnaissances of M. L. Smith, Michler, and Bryan, 94, Persifor F. Smith's reconnaissance, 94-95, William F. Smith's explorations of Organ and Sacramento Mountains, 94, Whiting's reconnaissance, 94, Whiting-Smith trail, 91-92; in Utah Territory, 58-61, 67-69, Simpson explores Great Basin, 67-69, Stansbury explores Great Salt Lake, 58-61; see also Trails to Far West

"Explorer," steamer, reaches mouth of Black Cañon, 85; returns to Fort Yuma, 86; used by Ives in Colorado River survey, 84

"Explorer's Pass," in Colorado River country, named by Ives, 85

Factory System, 17

Fancher, Charles, leader of Mountain Meadows emigrant party, 185

"Fanny Major," boat, carries California tribes to Mendocino, 202

Far West, character of, on eve of Civil War, 229-30; its transformation, 229-232; see also Frontier

Faulkner, Charles J., recommends larger army, 110

Fauntleroy, Thomas T., commands Department of New Mexico, 146; defeats Apaches and Utahs at Cochetopa Pass, 159; defeats Apaches under Chacon, 159; dispatches troops into Pecos River country, 146; quarrels with civil authorities, 168; reorganization program of, 40-41; see also Forts, Indian wars, Military posts

Ferris, Benjamin G., Secretary of Utah Territory, 272

Filibustering, role of frontier army in, 119; Texans support Carabajal, 147, 266; see also Cortinas, White outlaws

Fitzpatrick, Thomas, negotiates treaty of Fort Atkinson, 138-39

Flogging, in army, abolished, 262; character and extent of, 128; see also Army

Floyd, John B., orders vigorous campaign against Navahos, 167-68; see also Indian wars

Ford, John S., assists in Spring Creek Indian treaty, 263-64; defeats Comanche under "Iron Jacket," 143; opens route across west Texas, 93-94; prophecy of, 138; reports on Brazos agency, 210; scouting expeditions of, 145; see also Explorations, Indian reservations, Indian wars

Forney, Jacob S., holds council with Bannock Indians, 187; recommends a "military thrashing," 25; reports on Carson Valley tribes, 187; Superintendent of Indian Affairs, 187; visits Goshoot Indians, 187

Forts, Fort Arbuckle, Okla., location, 35, 285, prevalence of drinking, 124, desertion from, 127; Fort Atkinson, Ia., occupied by troops prior to Mexican War, 242; Fort Belknap, Tex., abandoned, 245, condition of hospital equipment, 120, defense along Red River, 137, established, 35, 137, Indian agent Stem murdered near, 139, location, 35, 285, Neighbors killed at, 217; Fort Bliss, Tex., history of, 245, 285, importance of, 36; Fort Breckinridge, Ariz., history of, 40, 246; Fort Bridger, Wyo., history of, 41, 181, 285, Stansbury arrives at, 58; Fort Brown, Tex., abandoned, 245, established, 33, 285, importance of, 36, punishment for theft at, 127-28, reoccupied by troops, 36; Fort Buchanan, Ariz., condition of firearms at, 118, description of, 39-40, establishment, 39, 285, history of, 285; Fort Chadbourne, Tex., built, 35, location, 244, Southern Comanches visited by Neighbors near, 207; Fort Churchill, Nev., established, 41, 188, in Military Department of California, 246; Fort Clark, Tex., built, 35, importance of, 35, location, 285; Fort Cobb, Okla., effect on warlike tribes, 145, location, 35; Fort Conrad, N. Mex., established, 37; Fort Craig, N. Mex., history, 39, 285; Fort Crawford, Wis., Cooke stationed at, 54; Fort Croghan, Tex., location, 243; Fort Crook, Calif., established, 44, 201; Fort Davis, Tex., importance of, 36, history of, 285; Fort Defiance, Ariz., attacked by Navahos, 167, established, 38, location, 38, road from, to Colorado River, 70, scouting parties near, 102, site selected, 153, terminal for Beale's second expedition, 64-65; Fort Des Moines, Ia., 242; Fort Dodge, Ia., during winter months, 119; Fort Duncan, Tex., history of, 244, 285, importance of, 36; Fort Ewell, Tex., abandoned, 245, importance of, 36, location, 244-45; Fort Fillmore, N. Mex., established, 37, 285; Fort Garland, Colo., established, 40, 246, see Fort Massachusetts; Fort Gaston, Calif., location, 44; Fort Gates, Tex., location, 243; Fort Gibson, Okla., Cooke stationed at, 54, prior to Mexican War, 242; Fort Graham, Tex., abandoned, 245, description of, 34; Fort Hall, Ida., Stansbury explores new route to, 59; Fort Humboldt, Calif., established, 43, 285, Grant stationed at, 43; Fort Inge, Tex., importance of, 244, 245, location, 36, 285; Fort Jesup, La., prior to Mexican War,

242; Fort Jones, Calif., established, 43, 247; Fort Kearny, Nebr., history of, 32-33, 242, 285; Fort Lancaster, Tex., established, 36, 245; Fort Lane, Oreg., established, 43, 247, Indians murdered near, 198; Fort Laramie, Wyo., history of, 33, 285, troops from, desert for California, 126-27; Fort Leaton, trading post, Tex., established, 256, Whiting-Smith exploring party visit, 92; Fort Leavenworth, Kans., Cooke stationed at, 54, description of, at outbreak of Mexican War, 113, history of, 249, 285, Thespian society at, 124; Fort Lincoln, Tex., abandoned, 245, location, 245; Fort Mann, Kans., location, 32, repair depot, 242, temperance society at, 125; Fort Marcy, N. Mex., established, 33, 285, strengthened, 37; Fort Mason, Tex., abandoned, 245, built along inner line of defense, 137, history of, 243; Fort Massachusetts, Colo., history of, 38, 246, Heap's opinion of, 64, see also Fort Garland; Fort McIntosh, Tex., history of, 36, 244, 285, importance of, 36; Fort McKavett, Tex., abandoned, 245, built, 35, location, 244; Fort Merrill, Tex., importance of, 36, location, 244, malarial fever among troops, 119, reconnaissances from, to Forts Graham and Belknap, 94; Fort Miller, Calif., established, 43, 247, Indians seek protection at, 198; Fort Mojave, Ariz., established, 44, 247, 285; Fort Monroe, Va., troops dispatched from, to California, 199; Fort Phantom Hill, Tex., defense along Red River, 137, established, 35; Fort Polk, Tex., history of, 33, 243, importance of, 36; Fort Quitman, Tex., history of, 285, importance of, 36, shortage of timber at, 114; Fort Reading, Calif., abandoned, 119, established, 43, 247; Fort Ridgely, Minn., road from, to eastern California, 69; Fort Riley, Kans., condition of firearms at, 118, location, 285; Fort Scott, Kans., prior to Mexican War, 242; Fort Martin Scott, Tex., history of, 36, 245; Fort Smith, Ark., location, 242, 285, Marcy leads expedition from, 55; Fort Snelling, Minn., Cooke stationed at, 54, prior to Mexican War, 242; Fort Stanton, N. Mex., established, 39, 285; Fort Stockton, Tex., effect on warlike tribes, 145, history of, 285, importance of, 36; Fort Tejón, Calif., Beale secures provisions at, 65, brass band at, 124, established, 43, 285, importance of, 43; Fort Terrett, Tex., location, 245; Fort Terwaw, Calif., built, 44; Fort Thorn, N. Mex.,

history of, 39, 285, sickness among troops, 119; Fort Towson, Okla., prior to Mexican War, 242; Fort Umpqua, Oreg., established, 43, 247; Fort Union, N. Mex., description of, 38, 285, importance, of, 38, road from, to Santa Fe, 70; Fort Washita, Okla., location, 35, 242, temperance society at, 125; Fort Wayne, Ind., Cooke stationed at, 54; Fort Webster, N. Mex., history of, 38, 245-46, report of gold in vicinity of, 157; Fort Wilkins, Mich., prior to Mexican War, 242; Fort Worth, Tex., abandoned, 245, 285, importance of, 34, location, 34, 285; Fort Yuma, Calif., during summer months, 119, history of, 42; see also Camps, Military posts

Francis River, Calif., character of country, 106

Franklin, Mo., part in Southwest Overland trade, 88

Fredericksburg, Tex., warlike tribes trade with settlers at, 132

Freeman, Lewis R., opinion concerning head of navigation of Great Colorado, 255; see also Western rivers

Freeman, Thomas, explores Red River, 79; see also Western rivers

Freeman, W. G., his description of army uniforms, 116; see also Army, Frontier soldier

Frémont, John Charles, explorations of, 252

Fresno Indian farm, Calif., under Henley, 223; see also Indian reservations

Frontier, characteristics and influences of, 233-35; communication and travel in 1850's and 1860's, 232; lawlessness and administration of justice on, 232-33; overland freighting across, 232; southwestern, changes in mid-nineteenth century, 229-34; spirit of, in literature, 234-35; spirit of, in dime novels, 234-35; Turner thesis, 233, 283; see also Far West, Forts, Frontier defense, Frontier soldier, Indian treaties, Indian wars, Military posts, Southwest, White outlaws

Frontier defense, achievements of, on eve of Civil War, 236; Benton's plea for protection, 152; in California, 16, 191, citizens petition Governor McDougal for protection, 196, citizens petition General Hitchcock for arms, 196, Clarke's policy of, in, 43-44, Daily Alta California pleads for protection, 25, dual role of army in, 191, on eve of Civil War, 205, Los Angeles citizens prepare for defense, 196, military positions strengthened in, 33, military posts established, 197-98, number of troops,

44, petitions for protection, 43, 48-49, San Diego under martial law, 196, troops arrive in, 192, 197-98, 199, weaknesses of, 44; claims of Mexican government, 37; clashes between civil and military authorities, 28-29, 153-54, 155-56, 168, 200; effect of Gadsden Purchase on, 39, 139; evolution of policy of, 17-31; influence of, on military officers, 230-31; influence of, on Southwest, 231-32, 236; Indian danger exaggerated, 46-47, 199-200; influence of frontier press on, 47, 140-41, 156, 196-97, 201-02; influence of "special interests," 46-47, 200; influence of white outlaws, 147, 169-70, 266, 271, 275; knotty problem of, 10, 13, 16, 29-30; methods employed in dealing with, 17, 88; in New Mexico, complaints of settlers, 157, conditions on eve of Civil War, 170, forts along upper Rio Grande strengthened, 37, Indian danger, 37, petitions for protection, 37, 47, regular troops in Navaho country, 168, volunteer expeditions, 168-69; O'Reilly's "stockade-patrol" plan, 45; petitions and resolutions of frontiersmen, 35, 43, 46, 138, 140, 196, 202; Pope's analysis of and recommendations, 45-46, 49; in Texas, Secretary of War Conrad orders troops, 34-35, 137, criticism of government in action, 144, 145, dissatisfaction with policy in, 132, inauguration of vigorous defense, 131-32, legislature appropriates money for, 143, need for defense, 5, protection along Rio Grande, 133, Governor Runnels demands action, 143, Tarver condemns policy in, 45, volunteers and "minute men," 142; in Utah, Walker War, 176-77, influence of Mormons, 171-72; see also Forts, Indian depredations, Indian wars, Military posts, White outlaws

Frontier soldier, attractions for, 118; desertion of, 110, 122, 126-27; dress of, 116-17; drinking of, 124-26; duties of, 108, 118-19; firearms of, 117-18; food of, 115-16; gambling of, 123; health of, 119-21; living quarters of, 113-14; medical care of, 120-21; officers' pay, 121; pay of, 121-22; paymaster, 122; punishments of, 127-28; role of, 27, 100, 128-29 social life of, 123-26; theatricals of, 124; women camp followers, 126; see also Army, Frontier defense, Indian wars, Military posts

Fuller, C. A., work on Red River raft, 78

Gadsden Purchase, effect of, on frontier defense, 39, 139

Gaines, John P., special Indian commissioner in Oregon, 279

Galveston City Guards, organized, 142

Garland, Peter, enemy of Texas Indian reservations, 215

"General Jesup," steamer, on lower Colorado, 83

Gila expedition, 161-62; see Bonneville

Gila River, gold along tributaries of, 6

Gila tribes, attitude toward white man, 12; number of, 12

Gilbert, Charles C., tests steamboat navigation on lower Rio Grande, 76

Glisan, on drinking at Fort Arbuckle, 124

Goin, Patrick, member of Neighbors-Ford expedition, 256

Gold discovery, effect of, on California Indians, 191, on California labor supply and wages, 102, on California population, 102-03, on frontier army, 102, 126, on frontier defense, 16, on land routes, 51, on westward migration, 51; Mason's report of, 102-03; see also Emigrants

Goose Creek Mountains, Ida., Placerville Mail Stage attacked by Indians in, 201

Goose Lake, Calif., Warner murdered near, 42, 105

Gordon, W. H., expedition to Burro Mountains, 101-02; see Explorations

Gran Quivira, N. Mex., Carleton's description of, 99-100

Grand Cañon, Ariz., Ives reached mouth of, 86; see Western rivers

Grant, Ulysses S., service on western frontier, 230-31; stationed at Fort Humboldt, Calif., 43

Gravelly Ford, Ida., Placerville Mail Stage attacked by Indians near, 201

Graves, Edward A., criticizes New Mexican Indian policy, 157

Great American desert, delusion of, 230

Great Basin of Utah, object of mystery and interest, 67; route to California, 67; traders and trappers visit, 67

Great Father, Indian's respect for, 17

Green, Duff, reconnaissance of Rio Grande country, 94; see Explorations

Green River, Utah, Mormons burn government supply trains on, 181

Greiner, John, biographical note, 267; report on conditions in New Mexico, 153-54

Guaymas, Mex., Derby's description of, 82

Guerra, Antonio, ringleader of California Indian revolt, 196

Gull Island, discovered by Derby, 82-83

Gunnison, John W., assists Stansbury in exploration of Great Salt Lake, 58, 60-61; and company massacred by Indians, 175, 272; surveys Utah Lake, 60

Gunther's Island, Calif., natives massacred by whites on, 203; *see* Indian Island

Haight, Isaac C., part in Mountain Meadows massacre, 274

Halleck, Henry W., Secretary of California, 191

Haralson, Hugh A., recommends larger army, 110

Hardee, William Joseph, holds "talks" with Lipan and Comanche chiefs, 136-37

Hardie, James Allen, makes treaty with California chiefs, 275

Harney, William S., part in Utah Expedition, 179

Harris, B. D., clashes with Mormons, 178

Harte, Bret, influence of, on literature of frontier, 235; opinion of Indian Island massacre, 204

Hartnett, John, clashes with Mormons, 272

Hartz, E. L., explores "Big Bend" sector, 96

Hatch's Ranch, N. Mex., Claiborne and Mounted Rifles visit, 101; troops stationed at, 40

Hawkins, Thomas T., investigates Texas reservations, 214

Hayes, Benjamin, describes Pima Indians, 12

Hays, John C., biographical sketch, 89-90; defeats Indians in "Washoe War," 89, 204, 274; exploring expedition, 89-91; Indian subagent on Gila, 149; report on Tejón reservation, 224; *see also* Explorations

Hazen, William B., defeats Indians on headwaters of Nueces River, 145; expedition against Mescalero Apaches, 143; explores "Big Bend" sector, 96

Heap, Gwinn Harris, impression of Utah tribes, 173-74; opinion of Fort Massachusetts, 64

Heintzelman, Samuel Peter, biographical sketch, 255; champions steam navigation on upper Colorado, 83-84; defeats California tribes, 196; defeats Cortinas, 266; executes ringleaders of California Indian revolt, 196

Henley, Thomas J., administration of California Indian reservations, 223-26; appoints special Indian agents, 199; biographical sketch, 222

Heywood, Joseph L., clashes with Mormons, 178

Higbee, John M., part in Mountain Meadows massacre, 274

Highsmith, Samuel, member of Hays exploring expedition, 90

Hill, George W., part in Texas reservations, 208, 209; reports on Senaco's

Comanche band, 209; resident agent at Brazos agency, 209

Hill, Henry, paymaster, U. S. army, attacked by Indians, 140

Hitchcock, Ethan A., opinion of California Indian wars, 197; proclamation concerning deserters, 126; *see also* Army, Indian wars

Hoffman, William, biographical sketch, 270; established Fort Mojave, 44, 164-65; *see also* Indian wars

Holeman, Jacob H., in charge of Parowan Indian agency, Utah, 172-73; distributes gifts among Snake tribes, 173; recommendations for Utah tribes, 174; urges protection for emigrants, 173; *see also* Indian affairs in Utah

Holladay, Ben, overland freighting in 1860's, 232

Honey Lake, Calif., terminus of Pacific wagon road, 69; *see* Pacific wagon roads

Hoopa Valley, Calif., Fort Gaston built in, 44; tribes of, plan uprising, 44, 204

Horsehead Crossing, landmark in northwest Texas, 93

Houston, Sam, authorizes organization of "minute men," 146; champions cause of Indians, 23, 146; enrolls volunteers, 28; favors volunteers, 28, 111-12; opinion of infantry on frontier, 112-13; opinion of large, regular army, 111; orders Rangers into field, 146; tenders services of Texas volunteers, 146; *see also* Army, Texas Rangers, Volunteers

Howard, George T., part in Texas reservations, 208

Huero, Apache chief, defeated at Cochetopa Pass, 159

Humboldt, von, Baron Friedrich Heinrich Alexander, impression of California, 8

Hunter, Jack, Delaware Indian, guide on Whiting-Smith expedition, 92

Hunter, J. D., Indian agent, southern California district, 191

Hunter, R. M. T., opposes increase in soldier's pay, 123; *see* Frontier soldier

Hurt, Garland, establishes Indian farms, 189; Indian agent, Utah, 174; makes agreement with Shoshone chiefs, 177; *see also* Indian Affairs in Utah

Independence, Mo., attraction for frontier soldier, 123

Indian affairs, agents and subagents, 17-18; in California, influence of miners, 43, special agents in, 43, 218; during colonial period, 17; Commissioner of Indian Affairs, creation of, 18; Commissioners Brown and Lea, their criticism of, 21, reforms of, 21-22; Department of Indian Affairs, creation of, 18;

Department of War in control of, 17-18; evolution of administrative machinery, 17-18; expenditures for Indian service, 22-23, 217, 224; graft in Indian service, 23-24, 224-26; influence of speculators, 25, 46, 49; Mormon and non-Mormon agents, 174; reorganization of Indian service, 21-22; Spoils System in Indian service, 26-27, 223-24; Superintendent of, 17-18; *see also* Indian country, Indian depredations, Indian policy, Indian reservations, Indian wars

Indian agents, Calhoun's work, 153-55; distinction between agents and sub-agents, 18; duties of, 25-26, 135, 209-10; ideal agents, 27, 189-90, 267; influence of, 25-26; qualifications of ideal agent, 26; status of, in early years, 17-18; Whipple's impression of, 26-27; *see also* Indian affairs, Indian reservations, Indian wars

"Indian Country," administration of justice in, 29-30; complaint of Santa Fe *Weekly Gazette,* 16; creation of, 15; division of, 18; effect on frontier defense, 16; effect of gold discovery on, 16; influence of westward migration on, 20; interpretations of, 15-16; modification of, 15-16; spirituous liquor in, 18

Indian depredations, Benton's description of, 152; in California, attacks, 194-95, 199-200, emigrants reported murdered near Pima villages, 158; causes of, 138, 157, 160, 162-63, 205; Comanche raids, 131, 138-40, 145, 162-63; effects of, 141, 158; kidnaping women and children, 133, 151; in New Mexico, Apache raids, 39, 151, 157-58, 162-64, complaint of legislature, 160, Cooke defeats Apaches under Chacon, 158, federal troops defeated by Indians, 157-58, Kiowa raids, 151, loss of lives and property, 49-50, 157, 158, Navahos on warpath, 151, 167; in Texas, Apache raids, 34, 141, Callahan pursues raiders, 142, frontiersmen take matters into own hands, 142, Lewis's report, 133, loss of life and property, 133, Pease calls out Rangers, 142-43, Rangers and regulars battle Indians, 142-45, reports of press, 140-42, settlements in Comal and Webb counties abandoned, 145; in Utah, 173, 176, 188; *see also* Forts, Frontier defense, Military posts, Indian wars

Indian farms, in California, 221, 224; in New Mexico, 156, 279; in Utah, effects of Mormon war on, 189, extent of, 189,

279, work of Dodge and Wasson, 189-90; *see also* Indian reservations

Indian gifts, character of, 19-20; opinion of *Daily Alta California,* 20

Indian Intercourse Act of 1834, provisions of, 15, revision of, 15-16

Indian Island, Calif., natives massacred by whites on, 203, *see* Gunther's Island

Indian policy, annuities and presents, 17, 19-20; arms and ammunition furnished Indians, 20, 24-25, 30; brighter side of, 30-31, 236; in California, attitude of civil and military authorities, 197-98, attitude of press, 197, 201-02, government policy, 192; conflicting opinions concerning, 30; creation of "Indian country," 15; criticism of, 20-22, 25, 30; Department of the Interior in control of, 21; division of authority, 28-29, 157; expenditures for Indian service, 22-23, 217, 224; "experimentations on successive frontiers," 17; exponents of vigor, 152, 158, 169; Factory System, established, 17; Indian chieftains brought to Washington, 24; influence of F. D. Roosevelt and Collier, 236, 283; military campaigns, 17, 27; in New Mexico, Judge Davis's criticism of, 25, agent Graves's characterization of, 157, Meriwether's policy, 160-61; number of Indian officials, increase of, 240; opinion of *Cherokee Advocate,* 22; opinion in Congress, 22; partisan appointments, 26-27, 30, 223-24; Polk's recommendation, 149; territorial governors, superintendents, and agents, 21, 269; in Texas, attitude of settlers towards, 145; Medill's opinion, 20; treaties, 18, 22; weaknesses and inconsistencies of, 30; *see also* Indian affairs, Indian country, Indian depredations, Indian reservations, Indian wars

Indian reservations, in California, advocates of, 218, attempts of special agents, 218-19, Bailey's and Browne's reports, 24, 226, Beale's administration, 220-22, Beale's military reservation plan, 220-21, Beale's report, 222, breakdown of Beale's plan, 222, cost of program, 224, 281, failure of system, 228, Henley's administration, 222-26, Henley's Indian farms, 224, McDuffie's administration, 226-27, modified plan, 227, recommendation of legislature, 227, settlers memorialize Congress for, 220, significance of, 228; in Texas, appropriation for, 208, attempted attacks on, 215-16, attitude towards, of governors, 206, legislature, 207, press in early years, 206-07, secretaries of war, 206, tribes, 207; charges against reservation Indians,

213-14, cost of, 217, domestic difficulties on, 211, duties of agents, 209-10, effect of removal, 217, failure of, 217, Hawkins's investigation and report, 214, Indians as farmers, 210-11, life on, 208-11, location of, 207-08, Neighbors's achievement, 208-09, opposition towards, 212-16, problem of liquor, 211, removal to new home, 216-17

Indian's story, last chapter of, 236, 283

Indians, attitude of Congress toward, 205; in California, attitude of the law toward, 193, attitude of natives toward whites, 191, 192, 198, attitude of whites toward natives, 48, 193, 194, 195, character and number of, 15, complexity of problem, 191, Derby's descripion of, 105-06, 106-07, faith in white man's justice, 193-94, plight of tribes, 201, Spanish policy toward mission tribes, 191, white man's policy, 194, 198-205; crux of problem, 205; kidnapers and slavers, 133, 263; in New Mexico, number of, 13, Pueblo villagers, 11, semi-agricultural tribes, 11-12, tribesmen on warpath, 149-70, wild tribes, 12-13; people without a home, 20; policy of federal government toward, 20; slaves held by whites, 47-48, 248; in Texas, agricultural tribes, 9, 10, wild tribes, 9-10; in Utah, character of, 13-14, condition of tribes, 162, 187, contemporary accounts of western tribes, 14, Heap's impressions of 173, principal divisions of, 13-14, range of, 12, 14; white man's opinion of, 195, 197, 202

Indian traders, foment Indian wars, 19, 26, 46, 48, 132; influence of, on Indian treaties, 19; mar work of Indian agents, 26, 27, 136, 174; sell liquor to natives, 26, 46, 47, 174; traffic in Indian children, 47, 248; *See also Comancnéros*

Indian treaties, in California, commissioners make agreements with tribes, 218-19, hostility of legislature toward treaties, 220, Lalakas makes treaty, 201, United States Senate rejects treaties, 220, Vallejo's treaty, 275, Warner champions Indian treaties, 220; Fitzpatrick's Fort Atkinson treaty, 138-39; government policy, 17, 18, 22-23; increase in number of, 22-23; Indian's conception of, 18-19; influence of Indian traders on, 19; in New Mexico, Calhoun and Sumner negotiate treaty, 155, Collins and Bonneville negotiate treaty, 166, congressional appropriations for, 159, Meriwether's treaties, 160, Sumner and Greiner negotiate treaties, 155; one-

sidedness of, 47-48, 136; in Texas, Rogers negotiates treaty, 137, Rollins negotiates treaty, 136, Spring Creek Indian council, 263-64; white man's disregard of, 19

Indian wars, in California, 191-205, attacks on peaceful natives, 202, attitude of press, 196-97, 199-200, catching hostiles, 195-96, conspiracy of Hoopa Valley tribes, 204-05, Crook defeats Pit River tribe, 201, Davidson's expedition, 203, Hitchcock's opinion of, 197, Indian commissioners' opinion of, 197, Kern River war, 199-200, Kibbe's campaign, 202, Klamath tribes attacked by whites, 198, masacre on Indian Island, 203-04, northern tribes plan revenge, 201, one-sided contest, 205, Shoshones on warpath, 201, "Washoe War," 188, 204; causes of, 27, 130, 157, 160, 162, 173, 174, 176, 195, 196, 198, 205; influence of Indian traders, 19, 26, 46, 47, 132; in New Mexico, 149-70, Apaches and Utahs defeat federal troops, 157-58, Bonneville's Gila expedition, 161-62, Canby's campaign, 169, Fauntleroy defeats Apaches and Utahs, 159, defeats Chacon, 159, dispatches troops into Pecos River country, 146, influence of frontier press, 168-69, influence of legislature, 168, Miles's bloodless campaign, 159-60, Miles defeats Apaches, 161-62, Miles's Navaho expedition, 40, 165, Navaho war, criticism of, 166-67; in Texas, 130-48, influence of frontier press, 131-32, influence of Mormons, 142, proposed offensive against Comanches and Kiowas, 146, scouting activities, 145, Rangers and sporadic activities of regulars, 143, Van Dorn's expeditions, 144-45; in Utah, 173-77, influence of "white Indians," 188, Mormon influence, 177, Walker war, 64, 176; *see also* Forts, Indian depredations, Military posts

Ingalls, Rufus, reports on Mormon influence among Indians, 177

"Invincible," transport vessel, in Colorado River survey, 82

Ireteba, Mohave Indian guide, engaged by Ives, 85

Iron Jacket, Comanche chief, defeated by Ford, 143

Irving, Washington, influence of, on literature of frontier, 234

1s-sa-ki-ep (Wolf Shoulder), Comanche chief, pledges friendship, 56

Ives, Joseph C., explores Colorado Plateau, 86; fitness for Colorado River survey, 84; importance of surveys, 86-87; surveys Great Colorado River, 84-87; *see also* Western rivers

Jackson, W. H., exploration of, 101

Jarboe, W. S., campaign of, against California tribes, 202

Jefferson Barracks, Mo., Cooke stationed at, 54; history of, 243-44

Jesup, Thomas S., plan of defense, 45-49; recommends improvement of western rivers, 74

Johnson, George A., operations on upper Colorado River, 86; trip through Black Cañon, 86

Johnson, Henry, bill for survey of Red River, 78

Johnson, J. Neely, clashes with General Wool, 29, 200

Johnson, M. T., attacks Wichitas, 131; reports on Texas reservations, 210; urges peace policy, 215

Johnston, Adam, ideal Indian agent, 27; Indian subagent for Sacramento-San Joaquin tribes, 192; reports condition of Sacramento Valley tribes, 195

Johnston, Albert Sidney, biographical sketch, 272-73; commands Utah Expedition, 179; defense policy of, 49; disagrees with Governor Cumming, 29; paymaster in Texas, 122; service on western frontier, 230

Johnston, Joseph E., inspects Texas military posts, 94; recommends artesian wells in Texas, 71; service on western frontier, 230

Jones, James C., champions larger army, 111

Jones, Roger, recommends vigorous defense policy, 152; on size of military companies on frontier, 109-10

Jones, William Carey, special investigator, California tribes, 192

Jordan Valley, Utah, fertile soil, 7; explored by Stansbury, 60

Jornada del Muerto, N. Mex., description of, 253; Fort Craig near, 39; need of artesian wells in, 71

Joya, N. Mex., rumors of Indian depredations near, 97

Judd, Henry B., explores Pecos Valley, 98; *see* Explorations

Kane, Thomas L., peace-maker in Mormon war, 183; *see* Osborne, Dr.

Kaweah River, Calif., Indian depredations along, 194

Kearny, Stephen Watts, builds Fort Marcy, 33; career of, 51-52; expedition to California, 52-54; *see also* Trails to Far West

Kelley, Hall Jackson, interest in Oregon country, 51

Kennedy, William, opinion of Comanches, 9-10

Kern, R. H., member of Judd's expedition, 98

Kern River, Calif., Indian depredations along, 194

Kern River Farm, Calif., under Henley, 223

Kern River War, Calif., 199-200

Ketumse, Comanche chief, pleads for his people, 207

Keyes, E. D., reports on Nome Lackee Indian reservation, 224

Kibbe, William C., campaign against California tribes, 202

Kickapoo Indians, migrate to Texas, 133-34; murder Stem and Lepperman, 139; *see also* Delawares, Shawnees

King, John, protects Texas reservations, 215

King, Thomas Butler, special investigator for California tribes, 275

King's River farm, Calif., under Henley, 223

Kinney, John F., clashes with Mormons, 272

Kin-osh-a, Utah chief, surrenders Indians for trial, 175; *see* War-Kar

Kiowa Indians, character and range of, 10; on horse- and mule-stealing expedition, 56; raids of, 151; *see also* Apaches, Comanches, Northern Wichitas

Klamath reservation, Calif., under Henley, 223

Klamath River, Calif., whites attack peaceful tribes on, 198

Klingensmith, Philip, part in Mountain Meadows massacre, 274

Kuykendall, John J., defeats Chowchilla Indians, 196

Lalakas, Klamath Indian chief, makes treaty, 201

Lane, William Carr, administration of, 156; biographical sketch, 156

Largo, Sarcillo, Navaho chief, begs for peace, 166

Las Cruces, N. Mex., silver mines near, 6

Lassen's Rancho, Calif., Warner joined by military escort at, 104

Las Vegas, N. Mex., starting point of Judd's survey, 98

Lawlessness, extent of, in Southwest in 1850's, 232-33; methods of "Moderators," "Regulators," and "Vigilantes," 233; punishment of, 233; *see also* Filibustering, White outlaws

Lawson, Thomas, recommendations for

army medical service, 121, reports on, 121

Lazelle, Henry M., expedition against Apaches, 164; reconnaissance along Pecos, 101; *see also* Explorations, Indian wars

Lea, Luke, criticizes Indian service, 21; suggests reforms in Indian service, 22

Leavenworth, Henry, in Arikara campaign, 103

Lee, John Doyle, associates of, in Mountain Meadows massacre, 274; part in Mountain Meadows massacre, 185; trial and execution of, 186

Lee, Robert E., commands Department of Texas, 146; engineering work on Mississippi and Missouri rivers, 73; service on western frontier, 231

Leeper, Matthew, assists in removal of Texas reserve Indians, 216; resident agent, Comanche reserve, 209

Lemon, Dr., alias Captain Bill Snooks, marauding activities of, 169-70

Lepperman, E. [L?], murdered by Kickapoo tribesmen, 139

Lewis, G. K., report on Indian hostility, 133

Lewis, Joel, report on Mendocino reservation, 225

Leyendecker, influence on Comanche reserve Indians, 208-09

Lipan Indians, massacred by Texas Rangers, 133

Liquor, bootlegging, in Indian country, 26; consumption of, at military posts, 124-25; prohibition of, in Indian country, 18; sale of, among reservation Indians, 211

Little Colorado River, Ariz., Ives's march along, 86

Little Mountain, Kiowa chief, signs Fort Atkinson treaty, 264

Llano River, Tex., Rollins meets Wild Cat on, 134

Long, Stephen H., explores Red River, 79; *see* Western rivers

Loomis, Gustavus, establishes Camp (Fort) Belknap, 35

Loring, William L., conducts Mounted Riflemen to Oregon, 58; part in Gila Expedition, 161

Los Angeles, Calif., prepares for defense, 196

Love, John, biographical note, 254; surveys along Rio Grande, 76-77

Lovell, Charles S., campaign against Hoopa Valley tribes, 204-05

Lowe, Percival G., account of medical service in frontier army, 121

Lyon, Nathaniel, expedition against Pit River tribes, 193

McClellan, George B., explodes report of Indian danger, 47; member of Marcy's Red River survey, 79-80; service on western frontier, 230

McCloud River, Calif., prospectors attack Indians on, 198

McCulloch, Ben, peace commissioner, in Mormon war, 183

McCulloch's Station, Tex., temporary military camp, 245

McDougal, John, Governor of California, enrolls volunteers, 28; opinion of Indians, 197

McDuffie, James, administration of California Indian reservations, 226-27

McKee, Redick, Indian commissioner in California, negotiates treaties, 195, 218-19

McLane, George, attacks Navahos, 165

Macomb, John N., explorations in New Mexico, 100-01

Mail routes to Far West, character and schedules, 232, 283

"Major Babbitt," keel boat, Love ascends Rio Grande in, 76-77

"Major Brown," steamer, Tilden ascends Rio Grande in, 76

Manypenny, George W., on failure of California Indian reservations, 222

Manzano, N. Mex., Carleton's description of, 99

Marcy, Randolph B., biographical sketch of, 249; explores along Brazos and Big Wichita rivers, 95-96; locates and surveys Texas Indian reservations, 207-08; opens new trail to Santa Fe, 55-57; opinion of Wichitas, 9; part in Utah Expedition, 182; Red River survey of, 79-82; *see also* Explorations, Trails to Far West, Western rivers

Marcy, William L., orders Worth to Texas, 91

Maricopa Indians, assist emigrants, 12; character, and home of, 12; *see also* Papago Indians, Pima Indians

Mariposa Battalion, defeats California tribes, 196

Mariposa County, Calif., petition of, for men and arms, 196

Martinez, Mariano, Navaho chief, accepts treaty, 150

Mason, Richard B., issues instructions to Indian subagents, 191; military governor of California, 191; opinion of gold discovery, 102-03; prophecy concerning California's gold supply, 102; tours mining district, 102-03; *see also* Explorations, Gold discovery

Mattole Station, Calif., natives exterminated at, 202

Medill, William, Commissioner of Indian Affairs, opinion of federal Indian policy in Texas, 20-21

Mendocino reserve, Calif., under Henley, 223-25; under McDuffie, 226

Merced River, Calif., Indian depredations along, 194

Merchants' War, 147, 266; see Carabajal, Filibustering

Meriwether, David, Indian policy of, 157

Mescal Mountains, N. Mex., Reeve's expedition, 164

"Mesilla Guard," attacks peaceful Indians, 170, 271; see White outlaws

Messervy, William S., holds council with Navaho chiefs, 159

Michler, Nathaniel, explorations of, in Texas, 94

Mier, Mex., steamer "Major Brown" passes safely, 76

Milam Rifles, Tex., organized, 142

Miles, Dixon S., bloodless campaign against Apaches, 159-60; expedition against Navahos, 40, 165; part in Gila expedition, 161-62; see also Indian wars

Military administration, departments and divisions, at close of Mexican War, 243

Military posts, attacks on, by Indians, 49-50, 167-68; attitude towards numerous small posts, 44-45; in California, defenses strengthened, 33, dual role of posts, 41, line of posts built, 41-44; chain of posts prior to Mexican War, 242; drinking at, 124-25; effectiveness of, 32, 44-47, 49; examination of sites ordered, 33; extra pay at, 261; "fancy" women at, 126; Holeman urges erection of, 173; importance of, along Marcy's trail, 57-58; influence of frontier press on, 24-25, 35, 47, 140; influence of governors on, 45; influence of special interests on, 33, 45, 46-49; new line of defense, 32-33; in New Mexico, effect on wild tribes, 38-39, line of posts established, 37-40; number built in Southwest, 49; number prior to Mexican War, 32; Pope's criticism of, 45-46; Pope's recommendations, 49; principal posts in Southwest, 285; problem of supply, 115, 254; problem of water, 114; significance of, 50; social life at, 123-26; temperance societies at, 125-26; in Texas, abandoned, 36, 245, in "Big Bend" sector, 34, 36, 37, inner and outer chains of, 34-36, intermediate group of, 34, line of posts, 34-37, no solution, 37, problem of supply, 254; types of, 113-14; in Utah, defense during Mormon war, 41, defense prior to friction with Mormons, 41; see also Camps, Forts, Frontier defense, Indian depredations, Indian wars

Mills, W. W., characterization of El Paso in 1850's, 232-33

Mimbres River, N. Mex., copper found along sources of, 6

Minié gun, used by frontier army, 118

Mitchell, David D., proposes Indian treaty, 152

Mix, Charles E., Commissioner of Indian Affairs, 160; learns of Indian depredations in New Mexico, 160; receives report on California reservations, 226

Mohave Indians, attack Hoffman's camp at Beaver Lake, 164; character of, 12, 63; chiefs, description of, 165; friendly toward Ives's command, 85; range of, 12; sue for peace, 165

Mollhausen, H. B., member of Ives's Colorado River survey, 84

Monterey, Calif., population of, at close of Mexican War, 8

"Monterey," government transport vessel, carries Ives to mouth of Colorado, 84-85

Moore, Sewell, characterizatin of Indian agents, 214

Moqui Indians, character and home of, 11; see also Pueblo Indians, Zuñi Indians

Moqui villages, Ariz., scouting parties near, 102

Morgan, T. J., on complexity of Indian problem, 30

Mormon Battalion, Cooke's description of, 54

Mormon diggings, Calif., visited by Mason, 102

Mormons, "bad Indians" punished by, 173; influence on Indian wars, 142, 169, 177; part in Gunnison massacre, 175; part in Mountain Meadows massacre, 186; relations with Indians, 171-72, 174

Mormon war, 179-84; see Utah Expedition

Morning Courier and New-York Enquirer, champion of Indian reservations, 218

Mountain Meadows massacre, and Cradlebaugh's declaration, 186; description of, 185; effect on Indian relations, 184-85; Forney's version of, 186; Mormon version of, 186; participants in, 274; reports of non-Mormons, 186; Spoode's report of, 186; trials concerning, 186

Munroe, John, commander, Department of New Mexico, arrives, 151

Murieta, Joaquín, marauding activities of, 275

Murray, Edward, arrives at Howard's Point, 83

Murray, Walter, impressions of California, 7-8

"Mustangers," description of, 266

Navaho Indians, attack Fort Defiance, 167

attitude toward white man, 12; character of, 12; homes of, 12; Miles's expedition against, 40, 165-66; "Navajo War Song," 166; number of, 12; Washington's expedition against, 150-51

Neal, Alpheus D., member of Neighbors-Ford expedition, 256

Neches River, Tex., condition of, 75

Negro, Cuchillo, Apache chief, killed by Loring's men, 161

Neighbors, Robert S., assists in selection of Texas Indian reservations, 95-96, 207-08; biographical sketch of, 279; estimate of number of Comanches, 10; explores west Texas, 93-94; ideal agent, 27; killed at Fort Belknap, 217; negotiates Spring Creek Indian treaty, 263-64; prevents Indian outbreak, 130-31; work on Texas reservations, 208-17; see also Indian reservations, Indian wars

Neihardt, John G., and literature of frontier, 235

Nelson, Allison, attacks Texas reservations, 215

Newberry, John S., member of Ives's Colorado River survey, 84; member of Macomb's expedition, 100

Newby, Edward W. B., clashes with New Mexicans, 29

New Mexico, on verge of business boom, 154; character of country, 5-6; climate, 6; development of manufactures in, 232, 282; fertile areas, 5; governor and Superintendent of Indian Affairs in, 269; knowledge of the country, modified, 229-30; lawless elements in towns, 233; mineral deposits, 6; mining industry, 232; population, character of, 6, 96, 99, on eve of Civil War, 231; size and distribution of, 6-7; sheep trade with California, 5; standard of living in, 7; terra incognita, 6; see also Indians, Indian wars

Nim-ah-tio-cah, Shoshone chief, pledges peace, 177

Nome Cult reserve, Calif., under Henley, 223

Nome Cult Valley, Calif., natives slaughtered in, 202

Nome Lackee reserve, Calif., number of Indians on, 223; report of E. D. Keyes, 224

Norteños, character of, 256

Northern Wichita Indians, Marcy's opinion of, 9; see Apaches, Comanches, Kiowas

Oatman massacre, 153

Ogden River, Utah, Stansbury explores along, 58-59

Ogden Valley, Utah, fertile soil in, 7

Ogden's Hole, Utah, Stansbury's trail along, 58-59

Ojo Verde, Utah, reached by Macomb expedition, 100

"One Who Rides the Clouds," Southern Comanche chief, signs Fort Atkinson treaty, 264

O'Reilly, Henry, "stockade-patrol" plan of defense, 45; see Frontier defense

Organ Mountains, N. Mex., explored by William F. Smith, 94; report of silver mines near, 157

Ormsby, William M., expedition of, 188

Osborne, Dr., peace-maker in Mormon war, 183; see Kane, Thomas L.

Otter Creek, Okla., Wichita Indians visit Marcy near, 80

Overland freighting, character and importance of, 232; heyday of, 232

Overland mail, in 1850's, 232; Simpson's route used by, 69

Owens Lake, Calif., Davidson's expedition near, 203; Indian depredations along, 194

Pacific wagon roads, appropriations for, 65, 69; built, 69-70; influence of, 70-71; need for, 69; periodic demands for construction of, 69; Simpson's recommendation, 97; see also Roads

Paint Creek, Tex., explored by Marcy, 95

Paiute Indians, Gunnison party massacred by, 175; work of agents Dodge and Wasson among, 190

Papago Indians, attitude toward white man, 11; character of, 11-12; home of, 11; see also Pima Indians, Maricopa Indians

Papin, Pierre Melicourt, member of Judd's expedition, 98, 257

Parker, W. B., describes Preston, Tex., 95; member of Marcy's Brazos and Big Wichita expedition, 95

Parowan, Utah, Fancher party obtain supplies at, 185; report of Indian hostilities at, 64

Pattie, James, in California, 51; marvels at California's scenic wonders, 7

Pattie, Sylvester, in California, 51

Paymaster, U.S. army, duties on frontier, 122

Pease, Elisha M., calls out Rangers and "minute men," 141-42; enrolls volunteers, 28, 141; favors reservation plan, 206

Peck, William G., explores Rio Grande country, 96-97; see Explorations

Pecos Valley, N. Mex., explored by Judd, 98

Pelican Island, discovered by Derby, 83

Pfeiffer, Albert H., member, Macomb expedition, 100

Phelps, John S., urges vigorous Indian policy, 169

Piedras Negras, Mex., burned by Callahan and Texans, 266

Pierce, Franklin, offers governorship of Utah to Steptoe, 178

Pike, Zebulon M., explores Red River, 79; see Western rivers

Pilot Peak, Nev., vicinity explored by Stansbury, 60

Pima Indians, character of, 12; home of, 12; Judge Hayes's description of, 12; see also Maricopa Indians, Papago Indians

Pit River, Calif., Indians on, attacked by whites, 198

Pit River Indians, Warner murdered by, 105

Placerville and St. Joseph Telegraph Company, Simpson's route used by, 69

Placerville Mail Stage, attack by Shoshone Indians, 201

Polk, James K., Indian policy of, 149

Ponce's Ranch, Whiting-Smith party arrive at, 92-93

Pony Express, Indians destroy stations of, 188; Simpson's route used by, 69

Pope, John, conducts artesian wells experiment, 71-72; criticizes system of defense, 45-46; recommends system of defense, 49; service on western frontier, 230

Powell, L. W., peace commissioner in Mormon war, 183

Presidio del Norte, Mex., 256; see Norteños

Preston, Tex., Parker's description of, 95

Price, Sterling, clashes with New Mexicans, 29

Provo, Utah, Mountain Meadows massacre jury convened at, 186

Provo Valley, Utah, fertile soil in, 7

Pueblo Indians, character and number of, 11; need of protection, 11; see also Moqui Indians, Zuñi Indians

Pueblo Pintado, N. Mex., ruins of, examined by Simpson, 97

Pyramid Lake, Nev., suffering among tribes of, 189-90; Utah tribes defeated near, 188, 204

Rabbit Ear Creek, N. Mex., Jackson explores vicinity, 101

Ramsey, Alexander, criticizes Indian policy, 22

Rancho del Chino, Calif., occupied by troops, 43, 247

Rancho de Jurupa, Calif., occupied by troops, 43, 247

Raton Mountains, N. Mex., Apaches defeated in, 158, 268

Red River, La., congressional appropriation for removal of raft, 78; explorations of Freeman, Pike, and Long, 79; Fuller's work on raft, 78; influence of raft on transportation and settlement, 73-74; Johnson's bill for survey of, 78; Marcy's exploration of, 79-81; navigability of in latter nineteenth century, 78; relation to commerce and frontier defense, 78; revival of interest in, 78-79; Shreve's work on the raft, see also Western rivers

Redmond's Ranch, Tex., occupied by troops, 245

Reed, Lazarus H., clashes with Mormons, 272

Reeve, I. V. D., expedition against the Apaches, 164

Rencher, Abraham R., biographical note, 162, 269; enrolls volunteers, 28

Reynolds, J. W. B., criticizes use of infantry on frontier, 112

Riley, Bennet, biographical note, 103; examines San Joaquin and Sacramento valleys, 103-04; urges strict dealing with Indians, 192; see also Explorations, Indian wars

Ringgold Barracks, Tex., history of, 33, 243, 285; hospital equipment at, 120; importance of, 36

Rio Conejos, N. Mex., Indian tribes on, 162; report of gold discovery on, 154

Rio Grande, commercial importance of, 76; condition of, 77; examined by army officers in 1850's, 76-77; Love's survey, 77; military importance of, 76; Tilden's survey, 76

Rio Jemez, N. Mex., examined by Abert and Peck, 96-97

Rio Puerco, N. Mex., examined by Abert and Peck, 96

Rio San Jose, N. Mex., examined by Abert and Peck, 96

Roads, built in New Mexico Territory, 70; California builds her own roads, 70; condition of Texas roads in 1850's, 252; construction of, in Far Northwest, 70; see also Pacific wagon roads

Rock Creek, enemies of Texas reservations encamped near, 215

Rogers, John A., appointed special agent for Texas tribes, 135; negotiates treaty with Texas tribes, 137; see also Indian treaties, Indian wars

Rogers, William, expedition of, against California tribes, 194

Rollins, John H., appointed special agent for Texas tribes, 135; favors reservation experiment, 206; hears Wild Cat's grievances, 134; holds "talks" with Lipan and Comanche chiefs, 136-37; negotiates Spring Creek Indian treaty, 136; work of, among Texas tribes, 135-36; *see also* Indian reservations, Indian treaties, Indian wars

Rose, Stephen B., in charge of Uintah Indian agency, Utah, 173

Ross, Shapley P., assists in removal of Texas reserve Indians, 216; ideal Indian agent, 27; resident agent at Brazos agency, 209; *see also* Indian reservations

Ross's Station, Tex., temporary military camp, 245

Ruby Valley, Nev., Indian farm in, 189

Runnels, Hardin R., attempts solution of Texas reservation difficulties, 216; demands action against Indians, 143; reports Indian depredations, 142

Rush Springs, Okla., Van Dorn defeats Comanches near, 143-44

Rusk, Thomas J., favors larger regular army, 111

Russell, Majors, and Waddell, accused of profiteering in Mormon war, 184; operations in freighting, 184, 232

Sabine River, Tex., examination of, 75; improvement of navigation, 74; *see also* Western rivers

Sabino, N. Mex., population armed against Indians, 97

Sacramento Mountains, N. Mex., explored by William F. Smith, 94

Sacramento River, Calif., troops stationed at, 43

San Antonio, Tex., occupied by troops, 245

San Antonio River, Tex., survey of, 75

San Diego, Calif., population of, at close of Mexican War, 8; troops stationed at, 192; under martial law, 196

San Francisco, Calif., population of, at close of Mexican War, 8; *see* Yerba Buena

San Francisco Mountains, N. Mex., Sitgreaves explores along, 61

San Gabriel River, Calif., troops stationed on, 42

San Joaquin River, Calif., condition of Indian tribes along, 219

San Joaquin Valley, Calif., Indian depredations in, 194

San Joseph's Spring, N. Mex., on "caravan route" to Los Angeles, 61

San Juan Mountains, Colo., Steen explores vicinity of, 101

San Juan River, Calif., Indian experimental farm on, 221

San Luis Obispo, Calif., Derby explores along, 106

San Miguel, Calif., road from, 106

San Pedro Valley, N. Mex., fertility of, 5

San Pete Valley, Utah, Indian farm in, 189

San Sabá River, Tex., Rogers negotiates treaty on, 137

Santa Barbara, Calif., population of, at close of Mexican War, 8

Santa Fe, N. Mex., part in Southwest Overland trade, 88; road from, to Doña Ana, 70; veins of gold and silver reported found near, 6

Santa Fe trade, effect on settlement of Southwest, 20

Santa Fe *Weekly Gazette,* champion of frontier defense, 47

Satanta, Kiowa chief, signs Fort Atkinson treaty, 264

Scott, Winfield, declares O'Reilly's "stockade-patrol" plan impractical, 45; recommends increase in size of army, 109

Scott's Valley, Calif., tour of Indian commissioners in, 219

Sebastian, William K., recommends Marcy for Red River expedition, 79

Seminole Indians, distrust Wild Cat, 134; visits of, to Texas, 134

Senaco, Comanche chief, followers of, opposed to reservation life, 209; pleads for his people, 207

Sevier Lake, Utah, Gunnison and party massacred near, 175

Shall, David F., characterization of fortune-hunters by, 194

Sharps rifle, use of, 118

Shaved Head, principal Comanche chief, signs Fort Atkinson treaty, 264

Shaver, Leonidas, clashes with Mormons, 272

Shaw, Jim, member of Neighbors-Ford expedition, 256

Shawnee Indians, migrate to Texas, 133-34; *see also* Delawares, Kickapoos

Sherman, William T., in California, 102; service on western frontier, 230

Shields, James, urges increase in soldier's pay, 123; *see* Frontier soldier

Short Cut Pass, Utah, explored by Simpson, 68

Shoshone Indians, attack emigrants near Beale's Crossing, 201; attack Placerville Mail Stage, 201; range of, 13

Shreve, Henry Miller, work on Red River raft, 73-74

Shumard, George G., member of Marcy's Brazos and Big Wichita and Red River expeditions, 95, 254

Sibley, Henry H., threatened by Northern Comanches, 139

Sibley tent, character of, 113

Silver Lake, Utah, Mormons celebrate tenth anniversary on, 180

Simpson, James H., describes Marcy's northern trail, 57; explores Cañon de Chelly, 97, Great Basin of Utah, 67-69, Navaho country, 97-98; importance of his surveys in Great Basin of Utah, 68; recommends construction of wagon road, 97, military post at Cebolletita, 97; see also Explorations, Trails to Far West

Sinclair, Charles E., Associate Justice, Utah Territory, 272

Sitgreaves, Lorenzo, describes Zuñi and Colorado River country, 62; exploring expedition of, 61-63, 98; hardships of exploring party, 62-63; treats Indians fairly, 62-63; see also Explorations, Trails to Far West

Skinner, Alonzo, A., special Indian commissioner in Oregon, 279

Smith, Caleb B., report on Indian annuities, 19

Smith, Charles F., comment on "white Indians," 188

Smith, George A., commander in Walker Indian war, 176

Smith, Hugh N., proposal for defense, 152

Smith, Jedediah S., in California, 51; marvels at California's scenic wonders, 7

Smith, M. L., reconnaissance across central Texas, 94; see Explorations

Smith, Persifor F., disapproves use of volunteers, on frontier, 29; examines central and western Texas frontier, 94-95; inspects Texas military posts, 94; orders Mounted Riflemen to Rio Grande country, 138

Smith, Saul, proposes use of bloodhounds, 147

Smith, William F., assists in opening new trail across Texas, 91-92; explores Organ and Sacramento Mountains, 94; see also Explorations

Smuggling, extent of, in Mexico, by Texans, 266

Snooks, Bill, 169-70; see Lemon, Dr.

Sonoita Valley, N. Mex., attacked by Ake and desperadoes, 170; fertility of, 5

Sonoma, Calif., troops stationed at, 192

South Pass, Wyo., traversed by eastern Snake Indians, 13

Southwest, agricultural progress in, 282; amassing wealth in, 231-32; battleground between Indian and white man, 130; changes in mid-nineteenth century, 229-32; characteristics and influences of, in mid-nineteenth century, 233-34; effect of policy of frontier defense on, 229-32; on eve of Civil War, 231-34; frontier in late 1840's, 3-16;

frontier justice in, 233; growth of population and settlements in, 231; industrial progress in, 231-32, 282; lawlessness in, 232-33; a leader in nation, 236; lure of, 27; melting pot of classes, races, and cultures, 234; new counties in, 231; Overland trade in, 88; proposed offensive in, 146; see also Frontier, Frontier defense, Frontier soldier, Indian wars, White outlaws

Spoodes, Ute warrior, reports on Mountain Meadows massacre, 186

Spring Creek, Tex., Rollins negotiates Indian treaty near, 136

Stanislaus River, Calif., Indian depredations along, 194

Stansbury, Howard, explores Great Salt Lake, 58-61; explores new route from Great Salt Lake to Fort Hall, 59; gains Brigham Young's assistance in survey, 59; hardships experienced in exploring Great Salt Lake, 59-60; impression of Mormons, 59; see also Explorations, Trails to Far West

Steck, Michael, distributes supplies among Apaches, 164; humanitarian policy of, 156

Steen, Alexander E., explorations of, 101

Stem, Jesse, appointed special agent for Texas tribes, 135; holds "talks" with Lipan and Comanche chiefs, 136-39; murdered by Kickapoo tribesmen, 34, 139

Steptoe, Edward J., declines governorship of Utah, 178; investigates Gunnison massacre, 175

Stevens, Walter H., opens Colorado River, Tex., to steam navigation, 75

Stevenson, E. A., describes condition of California tribes, 199

Stewart, Joseph, defeats western Utah tribes, 204

Stiles, George P., clashes with Mormons, 178

Stockton, Calif., troops stationed at, 43

Strain, J. H., member of Marcy's Red River expedition, 254

Sullivan, D. C. ("Doc."), member of Neighbors-Ford expedition, 256

Sumner, Edwin V., clashes with New Mexicans, 29; clashes with Santa Fe Weekly Gazette, 156; commands Department of the West, 146; Indian policy of, in New Mexico, 153, 155-56; opposes use of volunteers on frontier, 29; penetrates Cañon de Chelly, 153

Sutler, in frontier army, 122, 123

Sutter, John A., Indian subagent in California, 191

Sutter's Fort, trading post, Calif., 192

Suydam, J. H., member of Marcy's Red River expedition, 254

Taché Lake, Calif., character of region, 106; see Ton Taché Lake

Taos, N. Mex., road from, to Santa Fe, 70; veins of gold and silver reported near, 6

Tarrant County, Tex., settlers of, organize "minute men," 142

Tarver, B. E., condemns frontier defense policy in Texas, 45

Taylor, Zachary, appoints special Indian agents for California, 195

Tejón Pass, Calif., Indian reservation at, 221

Tejón reserve, Calif., under Beale, 221; under Henley, 222-25; see also Indian reservations

Temperance societies, at military posts, 125-26

Temple, Oliver P., special Indian commissioner in Southwest, 264, 279

Ten Bears, Indian chief, signs Fort Atkinson treaty, 264

Texas, agriculture, on eve of Civil War, 232; attraction of settlers, 4, 5; "Black Waxy," 3; description of, by contemporary press, 4-5; development of manufacture, 232; inauguration of vigorous defense policy, 131-32; Indian attacks in, 4; knowledge about western portion, extended, 230; legislature appropriates money for defense, 143; Llano Estacado, description of, 4; the Panhandle, 4; population and settlements, on eve of Civil War, 231; productive areas, 3-4; roads, condition of, 252; settlers condemn government inaction, 144, 145; stock raising, 3-4, 232; timber, 4; tobacco, 3; see also Indians, Indian reservations, Indian wars

Texas Rangers, attack on Lipan tribe by, 133; Congress appropriates money for, 135; Father Domenech's description of, 28; Houston, champion of, 28; opinion of T. C. Alexander, 28; opinion of Dallas Herald, 28; Turner's description of, 28; see also Frontier defense, Indian wars

Texas State Gazette, berates federal government for inaction, 47; reports on Texas reservations, 208

Theatricals, in frontier army, 124

Thespian societies, popularity of, on frontier, 124

Tilden, Bryant P. Jr., surveys Rio Grande, 76

Todd, C. S., special Indian commissioner in Southwest, 264, 279

Ton Taché Lake, Calif., attitude of Indian tribes near, 106; character of region, 106

Trails to Far West, via Arkansas, 16; Beale's trail to California, 63-64; "caravan route," 61; Cherokee trail, 16; Cooke's trail, 54-55; interest of expansionists in land routes, 51; Kearny's trail along Gila, 52-53; Los Angeles-Salt Lake trail, Beale travels along, 64; Marcy's trail, opinion of frontier press, 57; Simpson's opinion of, 57; Missouri trails, 16; need of new routes, 51; see also Explorations

Trinity River, Calif., troops stationed at, 43

Trinity River, Tex., survey of, 75

Tulare Lake, Calif., Derby explores vicinity of, 106; Indians in vicinity of, 104

Tulare Valley, Calif., character of, 106; condition of Indians in, 219; explored by Derby, 106

Tule, character and extent of, in California, 106, 258

Tule River farm, Calif., under Henley, 223; see Indian reservations

Tuolumne River, Calif., Indian depredations along, 194; plight of Indian tribes, on, 201

Turner, Frederick Jackson, Turner thesis, 233, 283; see Frontier

Turner, P. D., description of Texas Rangers, 28

Twain, Mark, and literature of frontier, 235

Twiggs, David E., issues orders for expeditions against Comanches, 143, 144

Tyson, James L., describes mistreatment of California Indians, 48

"Uncle Sam," steamer, carries cargoes on lower Colorado River, 83

Underwood, Edmund, campaign against Hoopa Valley tribes, 205

United States officials, clash with Mormons, 177-78

Updegraff, Joseph, member of Marcy's Red River expedition, 254

Upper and Lower roads, Tex., importance of, 93-94

Utah, agriculture, growth of, 232; character of land, 7; Indian farms in, 189; manufacture, growth of, 232; mineral resources, development of, 7, 232; population and settlement, on eve of Civil War, 231; timber, 7; true character of country, established, 230

Utah Expedition, accomplishment of, 184; Army of Utah, difficulties of, 179-80; Buchanan's policy, 179; causes of, 177-79; end of conflict, 183; Mormons burn

322 INDEX

government supply trains, 181; Mormons prepare for defense, 181; Mormon strategy, 181; organization of, 179; peace commissioners, arrival of, 183; scorched earth policy, 180; unsavory phase of, 184; *see also* Mormon war
Utah Indians, principal divisions, 13; range of, 13-14
Ute Indians, character of, 12-13; range of, 12-13

Valdez, Noponiocino, interpreter, Macomb expedition, 100
Vallejo, Mariano G., Indian subagent in California, 191; makes treaty with California chiefs, 275
Van Dorn, expeditions against Comanches, 143-45
Van Vliet, Stewart, problem of supplying army of Utah, 180
Vasquez, Tiburcio, marauding activities of, 275
Vegas Wash, upper Colorado River, terminus of Ives's survey, 86
Vielé, Teresa, account of military punishments, 127
Virginia City, Nev., Browne's description of, 187
Visalia, Calif., settlers flee to, for safety, 199
Volunteers, attitude of army officers towards use of, 28-29; clash over relative merits of volunteers and regulars, 111-12; cost of, in California, 202; defeat western Utah tribes, 188, 204; Jarboe's campaign, 202; Kibbe's campaign, 202; operations of Kuykendall's company, 196; operations of Mariposa Battalion, 196; penetrate Navaho country, 168; punish California tribes, 194-95, 202; Texas towns organize companies of, 142; use of, in West, 28; Wright's operations, 196; *see also* Army, Frontier defense, Indian wars

Waco Indians, raid Texas settlements, 34
Waco Tanks, description of, 256
Wahm, Dr., member, Hays's expedition, 90
Walker (Walkara), Utah chief, description of, 176; at war with Mormons, 64, 176
Walker, J. G., advocates patience with Navahos, 167; explores Cañon de Chelly, 167
War-Kar, Utah chief, surrenders Indians for trial, 175; *see* Kin-osh-a
Warner, Jonathan Trumbull, biographical note, 246-47; champion of California Indians, 220; *see also* Warner's Ranch
Warner, William H., murdered by Pit

River Indians, 105, 192-93; surveys in California, 104-05
Warner Mountains, Calif., named after Captain Warner, 105
Warner's Ranch, Calif., description of, 246-47; occupied by troops, 42
Wasatch Mountains, Utah, attitude of Ute tribes east of, 14
Washington, John M., expedition against Navahos, 150; treaty with Navahos, 150
Washington Light Guards, organized, 142
Wasson, Warren, work among western Utahs, 190
"Water Moccasin," steamer, trips of, on Colorado River, Tex., 75-76
Weatherford, Tex., settlers of, condemn government peace policy, 145
Weaver, Pauline, guides Cooke's wagon road expedition, 54
Weber Valley, Utah, fertile soil, 7
Weed, Stephen H., defeats Indians near Pyramid Lake, 188
Weightman, Richard H., Indian agent, criticized, 153
Westport, Mo., Beale outfits expedition for California at, 64
Western rivers, engineering work of Robert E. Lee on, 73; importance of, 73-74; Quartermaster General Jesup, recommends improvements of, 74; surveys of, 73-87; surveys and improvements of Texas streams, 75-82; Texans demand improvements of, 75; Texas appropriations for improvements of, 75; *see also* Derby, Marcy, Ives
Whipple, A. W., survey for Pacific railroad route, 252
Whipple, Henry B., comment on Indian agents, 26
"Whiskey Point," on Missouri River, 125
White captives, held by Comanches, 263
White Eagle, Indian chief, signs Fort Atkinson treaty, 264
"White Indians," 188
"White Knives," 147
White outlaws, Ake, 170; Callahan Expedition, 147, 266; Cart War, 147, 266; Cortinas, 147, 266; effect on frontier defense, 147, 169-70, 174, 275; Holeman's report, 271; Lemon (Bill Snooks), 169-70, 271; Merchants' War, 147, 266; "Messilla Guard," 170, 271; Murieta, 275; in Utah Territory, 271; Vasquez, 275; *see also* Filibustering, Lawlessness
White scalpers, 266
Whitfield, John W., describes Indians' impressions of "Uncle Sam," 110
Whiting, William H. C., explores central Texas, 94; opens Colorado River, Tex.,

to steam navigation, 75; opens new trail across West Texas, 91-92; surveys lower Rio Grande, 76; see also Explorations, Western rivers

Wichita Indians, cruelty of, 131; Marcy's opinion of, 9; range of, 9; in Texas, 9

Wild Cat, Seminole chief, lays grievances before agent Rollins, 134; describes Comanches, 9; personality of, 134; plan of settling roving bands, 134; pleads for his people, 137; pursuit of, by Creek warriors, 134; reported on warpath, 139; see also Indians, Indian wars

Williamson, R. S., reports on Warner's expedition, 105

Wilson, Alexander, U. S. attorney, Utah Territory, 272

Wilson, Benjamin D., assists Beale at Tejón Indian reserve, 221, 280; ideal Indian agent, 27, 280

Wilson, John, biographical note, 250; Indian agent in California, 59, 172, 250; suggestions concerning Utah tribes, 172

Wind River, Wyo., range of eastern Snake Indians along, 13

Wingfield, Edward H., Indian agent, N. Mex., 153

Wood, Robert C., explores "Big Bend" sector, 96

Woodsville, Calif., settlers flee to, for safety, 199

Wool, John E., arrives in California, 198; clashes with Governor Johnson, 200; criticized by Secretary of War Davis, 200; criticized by Washington Union, 200; defended by Daily Alta California, 200; defends military policy in California, 200; reports on California Indians, 198; transferred to Atlantic seaboard, 200

Woolbridge, Sylvester, Jr., describes condition of Sierra Nevada tribes, 195

Wooley, Abraham R., Indian agent, N. Mex., 267

Worth, William J., opposed to numerous small military posts, 45; orders Whiting and Smith to reconnoiter Hays's trail, 91

Wozencraft, O. M., Indian commissioner in California, negotiates treaties, 195, 218-19

Wright, Ben, defeats Pit and Rogue River tribes, 196

Wyeth, Nathaniel J., interest in Oregon country, 51

Yavapai Indians, flee approach of Sitgreaves' party, 62-63

Yerba Buena, Calif., population of, at close of Mexican War, 8; see San Francisco

Yost, S. M., Indian agent, announces defeat of Navahos, 165-66; describes living quarters at Fort Defiance, 114

Young, Brigham, advises Indian agents, 171; gains friendship of chief Walker, 176; governor and Superintendent of Indian Affairs, 172; removed from governorship, 187; see also Mormon war

Young, Ewing, marvels at California's scenic wonders, 7; in California, 51

Yosemite Indians, Calif., defeated by Boling's men, 196

Yuma Indians, attack Sitgreaves' exploring party, 63; character of, 12; friendly toward Ives's expedition, 85; homes of, 12

Zuñi, N. Mex., starting point of Sitgreaves' survey, 61

Zuñi Indians, character of, 11; home of, 11; see also Moqui Indians, Pueblo Indians